Regents
Exams and
Answers

Chemistry

MICHAEL J. WALSH
Bronx High School of Science

STANLEY H. KAPLAN
Educational Counselor, New York City

Barron's Educational Series, Inc.
Woodbury, New York

CHEMISTRY

© 1965, 1966, 1967, 1968, 1969, 1970 BY BARRON'S EDUCATIONAL SERIES, INC.

All inquiries should be addressed to:
BARRON'S EDUCATIONAL SERIES, INC.
113 Crossways Park Drive
Woodbury, New York 11797

Library of Congress Catalog Card No. 57-58729

PRINTED IN THE UNITED STATES OF AMERICA

PREFACE

A Helpful Word to the Student:

This book is designed to strengthen your foundation in chemistry and to help you review for Regents and College Board examinations.

Special features include:

Regents examinations with step-by-step explanations of the answers. The examinations will help you discover and correct your weak points. Careful study of the answers will increase your skill in interpretation of the questions and in applying the facts learned during the school term. Each explanation also contains a wealth of information which can be useful for answering other questions on the same topic.

An index to the major categories of chemistry. You will find the index an invaluable tool in guiding you to questions and answers on all the basic topics such as atomic structure, ionization, organic chemistry, laboratory preparations, and chemical mathematics.

A detailed discussion of all the given choices in the multiple-choice type questions. How often have you asked yourself, "But why is this choice incorrect?" Explanations of the wrong choices will greatly enhance your understanding of the subject matter and alert you to the errors that are frequently made in multiple-choice questions.

Up-to-date explanations. The high school course in chemistry has undergone revolutionary changes in the past few years with present emphasis on the understanding of chemical principles rather than the rote memorization of chemical facts. The explanations to the older Regents have been completely revised to tie in the many new ideas that have been introduced into the classroom and to conform to the new Reference Tables introduced in 1964.

This book will be particularly valuable to you, *if used properly*. During the term the index will guide you to questions and answers on the topics you are studying. When reviewing for end-term examinations, the following approach will prove helpful:

First, take each examination under test conditions.

Second, do all questions even though a choice is allowed.

Third, mark the examination. Make notes on the topics which are trouble spots, and use the index to locate additional questions. Indicate in the book the questions you answered incorrectly, and do them again at some future time.

Fourth, read the explanations, even if you have chosen the correct answer. Remember, when you are studying, the correct answer is not enough; understanding is the key.

Years of experience working with high school students have proved to me that this book brings results — greater understanding, increased confidence, *and* higher test scores.

STANLEY H. KAPLAN
Editor, B.S., M.S. in Ed.

Periodic Table

KEY

Atomic Mass (Weight)	12.0115 +2 / +4 / +4
Symbol	**C**
Atomic Number	6 0.77
Electron Configuration	2 – 4

Common Oxidation States

Atomic Radius (Å)

Transition Elements

Period	IA	IIA	IIIB	IVB	VB	VIB	VIIB	VIII		
1	1.00797 +1 **H** 1 0.3 /									
2	6.939 +1 **Li** 3 1.25 2-1	9.0122 +2 **Be** 4 1.12 2-2								
3	22.98 +1 **Na** 11 1.86 2-8-1	24.312 +2 **Mg** 12 1.60 2-8-2								
4	39.102 +1 **K** 19 2.31 2-8-8-1	40.08 +2 **Ca** 20 1.97 2-8-8-2	44.95 +3 **Sc** 21 1.6 2-8-9-2	47.90 +2/+3/+4 **Ti** 22 1.46 2-8-10-2	50.94 +2/+3/+4/+5 **V** 23 1.31 2-8-11-2	51.996 +2/3/+6 **Cr** 24 1.25 2-8-13-1	54.938 +2/+3/+4/+7 **Mn** 25 1.29 2-8-13-2	55.847 +2/+3 **Fe** 26 1.26 2-8-14-2	58.93 +2/+3 **Co** 27 1.25 2-8-15-2	
5	85.47 +1 **Rb** 37 2.44 -8-18-8-1	87.62 +2 **Sr** 38 2.15 -8-18-8-2	88.9 +3 **Y** 39 1.8 -8-18-9-2	91.22 +4 **Zr** 40 1.57 -8-18-10-2	92.90 +3/+5 **Nb** 41 1.43 -8-18-12-1	95.94 +6/+3 **Mo** 42 1.36 -8-18-13-1	(99) +4/+6/+7 **Tc** 43 -8-18-14-1	101.07 +3 **Ru** 44 1.3 -8-18-15-1	102.9 +3 **Rh** 45 1.34 -8-18-16-1	
6	132.9 +1 **Cs** 55 2.62 -18-18-8-1	137.34 +2 **Ba** 56 2.17 -18-18-8-2	138.91 +3 **La** 57 1.87 -18-18-9-2	178.49 4 **Hf** 72 1.57 -18-32-10-2	180.94 +5 **Ta** 73 1.43 -18-32-11-2	183.85 +6 **W** 74 1.37 -18-32-12-2	186.2 +4/+6/+7 **Re** 75 1.37 -18-32-13-2	190.2 +3/+4 **Os** 76 1.34 -18-32-14-2	192.2 +3/+4 **Ir** 77 1.35 -18-32-15-2	
7	(223) +1 **Fr** 87 2.70 -32-18-8-1	(226) +2 **Ra** 88 2.20 -32-18-8-2	(227) +3 **Ac** 89 2.0 -32-18-9-2							

140.12 +3/+4 **Ce** 58 1.82	140.9 +3 **Pr** 59 1.82	144.24 +3 **Nd** 60 1.82	(147) +3 **Pm** 61	150.4 +2/+3 **Sm** 62	151.96 +2/+3 **Eu** 63 2.04

232.0 +4 **Th** 90 1.80	(231) +5/+4 **Pa** 91	238.03 +3/+4/+5/+6 **U** 92 1.4	(237) +3/+4/+5/+6 **Np** 93	(242) +3/+4/+5/+6 **Pu** 94	(243) +3/+4/+5/+6 **Am** 95

Numbers in parentheses are mass numbers of most stable or most common isotope.

Atomic weights conform to the 1961 values of the Commission on Atomic Weights.

of the Elements

			IIIA	IVA	VA	VIA	VII A	O
							1.00797 -1 **H** 1 0.3	4.0026 0 **He** 2 0.93
			10.811 +3 **B** 5 0.88 2-3	12.0115 +2 +4 -4 **C** 6 0.77 2-4	14.0067 +1 +2 +3 +5 -1 -2 -3 **N** 7 .7 2-5	15.9994 -2 **O** 8 0.66 2-6	18.9984 -1 **F** 9 0.64 2-7	20.183 0 **Ne** 10 1.12 2-8
	IB	IIB	26.981 +3 **Al** 13. 1.43 2-8-3	28.08 +2 +4 -4 **Si** 14 1.17 2-8-4	30.97 +3 +5 -3 **P** 15 1.10 2-8-5	32.064 +4 +6 -2 **S** 16 1.04 2-8-6	35.45 +1 +5 +7 -1 **Cl** 17 0.99 2-8-7	39.94 0 **Ar** 18 1.54 2-8-8
58.71 +2 +3 **Ni** 28 1.24 2-8-16-2	63.54 +1 +2 **Cu** 29 1.28 2-8-18-1	65.37 +2 **Zn** 30 1.33 2-8-18-2	69.72 +3 **Ga** 31 1.22 2-8-18-3	72.59 +2 +4 **Ge** 32 1.22 2-8-18-4	74.92 +3 +5 +3 **As** 33 1.21 2-8-18-5	78.96 +4 +6 -2 **Se** 34 1.17 2-8-18-6	79.9 +1 +5 -1 **Br** 35 1.14 2-8-18-7	83.8 0 **Kr** 36 1.69 2-8-18-8
106.4 +2 +4 **Pd** 46 1.38 -8-18-18	107.8 +1 **Ag** 47 1.44 -8-18-18-1	112.4 +2 **Cd** 48 1.49 -8-18-18-2	114.8 +3 **In** 49 1.62 -8-18-18-3	118.7 +2 +4 **Sn** 50 1.4 -8-18-18-4	121.8 +3 +5 +3 **Sb** 51 1.41 -8-18-18-5	127.6 +4 +6 +2 **Te** 52 1.37 -8-18-18-6	126.9 +1 +5 +7 -1 **I** 53 1.33 -8-18-18-7	131.30 0 **Xe** 54 1.90 -8-18-18-8
195.09 +2 +4 **Pt** 78 1.38 -18-32-17-1	196.96 +1 +3 **Au** 79 1.44 -18-32-18-1	200.5 +1 +2 **Hg** 80 1.55 -18-32-18-2	204.37 +1 +3 **Tl** 81 1.71 -18-32-18-4	207.2 +2 +4 **Pb** 82 1.75 -18-32-18-4	208.98 +2 +5 **Bi** 83 1.46 -18-32-18-5	(210) +2 +4 **Po** 84 1.65 -18-32-18-6	(210) **At** 85 1.40 -18-32-18-7	(222) 0 **Rn** 86 2.2 -18-32-18-8

157.25 **Gd** 64 1.79	158.9 +3 **Tb** 65 1.77	162.5 +3 **Dy** 66 1.77	164.93 +3 **Ho** 67 1.76	167.26 +3 **Er** 68 1.75	168.93 +3 **Tm** 69 1.74	173.04 +2 +3 **Yb** 70 1.93	174.97 +3 **Lu** 71 1.74	Lanthanide Series

(247) +3 **Cm** 96	(247) +3 **Bk** 97	(249) +3 **Cf** 98	(254) **Es** 99	(253) **Fm** 100	(256) **Md** 101	(254) **No** 102	(257) **Lw** 103	Actinide Series

THE UNIVERSITY OF THE STATE OF NEW YORK
THE STATE EDUCATION DEPARTMENT
BUREAU OF SECONDARY CURRICULUM DEVELOPMENT
ALBANY

Reference Tables for Chemistry

(A)

DENSITY AND SOLUBILITY OF SOME COMMON GASES

Name	Density grams/liter 0° C 760 mm.	Solubility*
air	1.29	———
ammonia	0.77	89.5
carbon dioxide	1.98	0.3346
carbon monoxide	1.25	0.0044
chlorine	3.21	0.9972†
nitrogen monoxide	1.34	0.0098
hydrogen	0.09	0.0002
hydrogen chloride	1.64	82.3
hydrogen sulfide	1.54	0.7066
nitrogen	1.25	0.0029
oxygen	1.43	0.0069
sulfur dioxide	2.93	22.83

*weight of gas in grams dissolved in 100 grams of water at 0°C and 760 mm. † at 10°C

(B)

SOLUBILITY CURVES

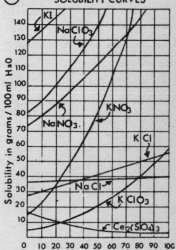

Temperature, °C

(C)

Charge on Some Ions

CH_3COO^-	ClO_4^-	$H_2PO_4^-$	NO_3^-
$CO_3^=$	$Cr_2O_7^=$	H_3O^+	OH^-
$C_2O_4^=$	HCO_3^-	Hg_2^{++}	$PO_3^\equiv$
ClO^-	$HPO_4^=$	MnO_4^-	$PO_4^\equiv$
ClO_2^-	HSO_3^-	NH_4^+	$SO_3^=$
ClO_3^-	HSO_4^-	NO_2^-	$SO_4^=$

(E)

SYMBOLS OF SOME PARTICLES

electron	$_{-1}^{0}e$	deuteron	$_{1}^{2}H$
neutron	$_{0}^{1}n$	triton	$_{1}^{3}H$
proton	$_{1}^{1}H$	alpha particle	$_{2}^{4}He$

(D)

TABLE OF SOLUBILITIES IN WATER

i-nearly insoluble ss-slightly soluble s-soluble d-decomposes n-not isolated	acetate	bromide	carbonate	chloride	hydroxide	iodide	nitrate	oxide	phosphate	sulfate	sulfide
aluminum	s	s	n	s	i	s	s	i	i	s	d
ammonium	s	s	s	s	s	s	s	n	s	s	s
barium	s	s	i	s	s	s	s	i	i	i	d
calcium	s	s	i	s	ss	s	s	ss	i	ss	d
copper II	s	s	i	s	i	d	s	i	i	s	i
iron II	s	s	i	s	i	s	s	i	i	s	i
iron III	s	s	n	s	i	s	s	i	i	ss	d
lead	s	ss	i	ss	i	ss	s	i	i	i	i
magnesium	s	s	i	s	i	s	s	i	i	s	d
mercury I	ss	i	i	i	n	i	s	i	i	ss	i
mercury II	s	ss	i	s	i	i	s	i	i	d	i
potassium	s	s	s	s	s	s	s	s	s	s	s
silver	ss	i	i	i	n	i	s	i	i	ss	i
sodium	s	s	s	s	s	s	s	d	s	s	s
zinc	s	s	i	s	i	s	s	i	i	s	i

(F)

HEAT AND FREE ENERGY OF FORMATION OF COMPOUNDS AT 25° C		
Compound	Heat of Formation kcal/mole(ΔH)*	Free Energy of Formation kcal/mole(ΔG)*
Aluminum oxide (s)	-399.09	-376.77
Ammonia (g)	-11.04	-3.98
Barium sulfate (s)	-350.2	-323.4
Calcium hydroxide (s)	-235.80	-214.33
Carbon dioxide (g)	-94.05	-94.26
Copper (II) sulfate (s)	-184.00	-158.2
Dinitrogen monoxide (g)	19.49	24.76
Ethyne (acetylene) (g)	54.19	50.00
Hydrogen fluoride (g)	-63.99	———
Hydrogen iodide (g)	5.93	———
Hydrogen oxide (ℓ)	-68.32	-56.69
Iron (II, III) oxide(s)	-267.0	-242.4
Lead monoxide (s)	-52.40	-45.25
Magnesium oxide (s)	-143.84	-136.13
Mercury (II) oxide (s)	-21.68	-13.99
Nitrogen monoxide (g)	21.60	20.72
Potassium chloride (s)	-104.18	-97.59
Sodium chloride (s)	-98.23	-91.79
Sulfur dioxide (g)	-70.96	-71.79
Zinc oxide (s)	-83.17	-76.05
(s) = solid (ℓ) = liquid (g) = gas		
*Minus sign indicates an exothermic reaction.		

(G)

HALF-LIVES OF SOME RADIOISOTOPES	
^{14}C	5,700 yrs.
^{45}Ca	152 days
^{36}Cl	4 x 10^5 yrs.
^{60}Co	5.3 yrs.
^{137}Cs	33 yrs.
^{131}I	8 days
^{42}K	12.4 hrs.
^{32}P	14.3 days
^{90}Sr	20 yrs.

(H)

ACID-BASE CHART	
Conjugate acid	Conjugate base
HCl	Cl$^-$
HNO$_3$	NO$_3^-$
H$_2$SO$_4$	HSO$_4^-$
H$_3$O$^+$	H$_2$O
HSO$_4^-$	SO$_4^=$
Al(H$_2$O)$_6^{+++}$	Al(H$_2$O)$_5$(OH)$^{++}$
NH$_4^+$	NH$_3$
H$_2$O	OH$^-$
NH$_3$	NH$_2^-$

(acid strength decreases ↓) (base strength decreases ↑)

(I)

HEATS OF REACTION	
t = 25°C p = 1 atm.	kcal/mole*
$H_2(g) + \frac{1}{2} O_2(g) = H_2O(g)$	-57.8
$H_2(g) + \frac{1}{2} O_2(g) = H_2O(\ell)$	-68.3
$S(s) + O_2(g) = SO_2(g)$	-71.0
$H_2(g) + S(s) + 2O_2(g) = H_2SO_4(\ell)$	-194.0
$\frac{1}{2} N_2(g) + \frac{1}{2} O_2(g) = NO(g)$	21.6
$\frac{1}{2} N_2(g) + O_2(g) = NO_2(g)$	8.1
$\frac{1}{2} N_2(g) + \frac{3}{2} H_2(g) = NH_3(g)$	-11.0
$C(s) + \frac{1}{2} O_2(g) = CO(g)$	-26.4
$C(s) + O_2(g) = CO_2(g)$	-94.1
$2C(s) + 3H_2(g) = C_2H_6(g)$	-20.2
*of the product formed (Minus sign indicates an exothermic reaction.)	

(J)

"REPRESENTATIVE" ELEMENTS

IA	IIA	IIIA	IVA	VA	VIA	VIIA
13.5 ← Ionization Energy*						
H				← Electronegativity**		
2.1						
5.4	9.3	8.3	11.2	14.5	13.6	17.3
Li	Be	B	C	N	O	F
1.0	1.5	2.0	2.5	3.0	3.5	4.0
5.1	7.6	6.0	8.1	10.9	10.3	13.0
Na	Mg	Al	Si	P	S	Cl
0.9	1.2	1.5	1.8	2.1	2.5	3.0
4.3	6.1	6.0	8.1	10.5	9.7	11.8
K	Ca	Ga	Ge	As	Se	Br
0.8	1.0	1.6	1.8	2.0	2.4	2.8
4.2	5.7	5.8	7.3	8.5	9.0	10.6
Rb	Sr	In	Sn	Sb	Te	I
0.8	1.0	1.7	1.8	1.9	2.1	2.5
3.9	5.2	6.1	7.4	8.0		
Cs	Ba	Tl	Pb	Bi	Po	At
0.7	0.9	1.8	1.8	1.9	2.0	2.2
	5.3		*1st. ionization energy in e.v.			
Fr	Ra					
0.7			**Arbitrary scale			

pH VALUES FOR EQUIVALENT (0.1N.) SOLUTIONS

hydrochloric acid	1.1	alum	3.2
sulfuric acid	1.2	boric acid	5.2
phosphoric acid	1.5	pure water	7.0
citric acid	2.2	sodium bicarbonate	8.4
acetic acid	2.9	borax	9.2

ammonium hydroxide	11.1
sodium carbonate	11.6
trisodium phosphate	12.0
sodium hydroxide	13.0
potassium hydroxide	13.0

STANDARD OXIDATION POTENTIALS

Ionic Concentrations 1 molar in water at 25°C

Half cell Reaction	$E°$(volts)
$Li = Li^+ + e^-$	3.02
$Rb = Rb^+ + e^-$	2.93
$K = K^+ + e^-$	2.92
$Cs = Cs^+ + e^-$	2.92
$Ba = Ba^{++} + 2e^-$	2.90
$Sr = Sr^{++} + 2e^-$	2.89
$Ca = Ca^{++} + 2e^-$	2.87
$Na = Na^+ + e^-$	2.71
$Mg = Mg^{++} + 2e^-$	2.37
$Be = Be^{++} + 2e^-$	1.70
$Al = Al^{+++} + 3e^-$	1.66
$Mn = Mn^{++} + 2e^-$	1.03
$H_2 + 2OH^- = 2H_2O + 2e^-$	0.83
$Zn = Zn^{++} + 2e^-$	0.76
$Cr = Cr^{++} + 3e^-$	0.74
$Fe = Fe^{++} + 2e^-$	0.44
$Cd = Cd^{++} + 2e^-$	0.40
$Co = Co^{++} + 2e^-$	0.28
$Ni = Ni^{++} + 2e^-$	0.23
$Sn = Sn^{++} + 2e^-$	0.14
$Pb = Pb^{++} + 2e^-$	0.13
$H_2 = 2H^+ + 2e^-$	0.00
$Sn^{++} = Sn^{++++} + 2e^-$	-0.14
$Cu^+ = Cu^{++} + e^-$	-0.16
$Cu = Cu^{++} + 2e^-$	-0.34
$2I^- = I_2 + 2e^-$	-0.54
$Fe^{++} = Fe^{+++} + e^-$	-0.77
$2Hg = Hg_2^{++} + 2e^-$	-0.80
$Ag = Ag^+ + e^-$	-0.80
$Hg_2^{++} = 2Hg^{++} + 2e^-$	-0.91
$NO + 2H_2O = NO_3^- + 4H^+ + 3e^-$	-0.96
$2Br^- = Br_2(\ell) + 2e^-$	-1.07
$2H_2O = O_2 + 4H^+ + 4e^-$	-1.23
$2 Cr^{+++} + 7H_2O = Cr_2O_7^{--} + 14H^+ + 6e^-$	-1.36
$2Cl^- = Cl_2 + 2e^-$	-1.36
$Au = Au^{+++} + 3e^-$	-1.42
$Mn^{+2} + 4H_2O = MnO_4^- + 8H^+ + 5e^-$	-1.52
$2F^- = F_2 + 2e^-$	-2.87

IONIZATION CONSTANTS OF ACIDS AND BASES AT 25°C

Acetic acid	1.8×10^{-5}
Boric acid	5.8×10^{-10}
Carbonic acid	4.3×10^{-7}
Hypochlorous acid	3.5×10^{-8}
Phosphoric acid	7.5×10^{-3}
Ammonium hydroxide	1.8×10^{-5}
Lead hydroxide	9.6×10^{-4}

Some acids and bases which are completely or nearly completely ionized in dilute solutions at 25°C:

Acids	Bases
hydrochloric	potassium hydroxide
nitric	sodium hydroxide
sulfuric	

SOME EQUILIBRIUM CONSTANTS AT 25°C

$Cu(s) + 2 Ag^+ (aq) = Cu^{+2} (aq) + 2 Ag(s)$	2×10^{15}
$CH_3COOH (aq) = H^+(aq) + CH_3COO^-(aq)$	1.8×10^{-5}
$AgCl (s) = Ag^+ (aq) + Cl^-(aq)$	1.7×10^{-10}

PRESSURE OF WATER VAPOR IN MILLIMETERS OF MERCURY

°C	mm.	°C	mm.	°C	mm.	°C	mm.
0.0	4.6	17.0	14.5	21.0	18.7	25.0	23.8
5.0	6.5	18.0	15.5	22.0	19.8	26.0	25.2
10.0	9.2	19.0	16.5	23.0	21.1	27.0	26.7
15.0	12.8	20.0	17.5	24.0	22.4	28.0	28.3

PHYSICAL CONSTANTS

Name	Symbol	Value
Speed of light	c	3.00×10^{10} cm/sec.
Avogadro's number	N_0	6.02×10^{23}
Universal gas constant	R	0.0821 liter-atm/mole-°K
Planck's constant	h	6.63×10^{-34} joule-sec.
Charge of electron	e	1.60×10^{-19} coul.
Mass of an electron	m_e	9.11×10^{-28} gm.
Mass of a proton	m_p	1.67×10^{-24} gm.
Mass of a neutron	m_n	1.67×10^{-24} gm.

Examination June, 1965   Chemistry (Experimental)

PART ONE   *Answer all questions in this part.*

DIRECTIONS (1-52): *For each statement or question, write in the space provided the* number *preceding the word or expression that, of those given, best completes the statement or answers the question.*   [52]

1. A solution of sugar in water is a   (1) homogeneous mixture   (2) heterogeneous mixture   (3) compound   (4) pure substance   1........

2. Any chemical change which absorbs heat energy as it progresses is   (1) isothermic   (2) exothermic   (3) nonthermic   (4) endothermic   2........

3. A sample of oxygen has a volume of 500 ml at a pressure of one atmosphere. If the temperature is kept constant, the volume of this gas sample at a pressure of two atmospheres is   (1) 125 ml   (2) 250 ml   (3) 500 ml   (4) 1000 ml   3........

4. Fifty ml of a gas are collected at 20°C. If the temperature is raised to 40°C., pressure remaining constant, the new volume will be

$$(1)\ 50 \times \frac{293}{313} \qquad\qquad (3)\ 50 \times \frac{20}{40}$$

$$(2)\ 50 \times \frac{313}{293} \qquad\qquad (4)\ 50 \times \frac{40}{20}$$

4........

5. The number of moles of any gas contained in an 11.2-liter volume at S.T.P. is   (1) 1.00   (2) 0.75   (3) 0.50   (4) 0.25   5........

6. The number of calories required to change the temperature of 250 grams of water from 22°C. to 25°C. is   (1) 83.3   (2) 250   (3) 375   (4) 750   6........

7. The maximum number of electrons that can occupy the 3s orbital is   (1) 1   (2) 2   (3) 3   (4) 6   7........

8. The sublevel of lowest energy is   (1) 2s   (2) 3s   (3) 2p   (4) 3d   8........

9. An atom containing 19 protons, 20 neutrons and 19 electrons has a mass number of   (1) 19   (2) 20   (3) 39   (4) 58   9........

10. Given the electron configuration $1s^2 2s^2 2p^6 3s^2$, the number of valence electrons is   (1) 1   (2) 2   (3) 3   (4) 6   10........

11. The electron configuration of an atom is $1s^2 2s^2 2p^6 3s^2 3p^3$. The atomic number of the atom is   (1) 15   (2) 6   (3) 3   (4) 5   11........

1

12. In a given horizontal row of the *Periodic Table*, the element having the lowest first ionization energy is in Group   (1) I A (2) II A   (3) O   (4) VII A

12.......

13. In the isotopes of a given element, the particle whose number varies is the   (1) ion   (2) electron   (3) neutron   (4) proton

13.......

14. In the reaction $^{238}_{92}U \rightarrow {}^{234}_{90}Th + X$, "X" represents   (1) a beta particle   (2) a neutron   (3) a positron   (4) an alpha particle

14.......

15. Element X, whose electron configuration is $1s^2 2s^2 2p^6 3s^1$, forms oxides of the type   (1) X_2O (2) XO (3) X_3O_2 (4) XO_2

15.......

16. In solid barium chloride, the ratio of barium ions to chloride ions is   (1) 1:1   (2) 1:2   (3) 2:1   (4) 2:3

16.......

17. Which pair of elements form a compound possessing the strongest ionic character?   (1) Na and F   (2) Rb and F (3) Li and I   (4) K and Cl

17.......

18. Which of the following is a reasonable representation of an ammonia molecule?

$$\text{(1)} \quad \overset{\displaystyle H}{H \cdot \overset{\displaystyle \cdot}{N} \cdot H}$$

$$\text{(3)} \quad H : \overset{\displaystyle \cdot\cdot}{\underset{\displaystyle H}{N}} : H$$

$$\text{(2)} \quad \overset{\displaystyle H}{\underset{\displaystyle H}{: \overset{\cdot\cdot}{N} \vdots H}}$$

$$\text{(4)} \quad H : \overset{\displaystyle \cdot\cdot}{\underset{\displaystyle H}{N}} : H$$

18.......

19. To break a chemical bond, energy is   (1) absorbed (2) released   (3) both absorbed and released   (4) not changed

19.......

20. The chemical name of FeO is   (1) iron (I) oxide (2) iron (II) oxide   (3) iron (III) oxide   (4) iron (IV) oxide

20.......

21. The calcium ion has the same electronic configuration as an (1) ion of Mg   (2) ion of Br   (3) atom of Ar   (4) atom of K

21.......

22. Which element has the smallest atomic radius?   (1) Na (2) Al   (3) P   (4) Cl

22.......

23. Nonmetallic atoms possess   (1) high ionization energies and low electronegativities   (2) high ionization energies and high electronegativities   (3) low ionization energies and low electronegativities   (4) low ionization energies and high electronegativities

23.......

24. The most active metal in Period 4 of the *Periodic Table* is (1) Fe (2) Sc (3) K (4) Ca

24........

25. The number of atoms of helium present in 2.0 grams of helium is (1) 1.50×10^{23} (2) 2.00×10^{23} (3) 3.01×10^{23} (4) 6.02×10^{23}

25........

26. A solution KNO_3, whose temperature is 50°C., contains 70 grams of KNO_3 in 100 ml of water. This solution is (1) unsaturated (2) saturated (3) supersaturated (4) dilute

26........

27. If the density of hydrogen is 9.0×10^{-2} grams per liter under standard conditions, 100 liters of hydrogen will weigh (1) 9 grams (2) 11.1 grams (3) 22.4 grams (4) 90 grams

27........

28. One-fourth mole of oxygen gas weighs (1) 32g. (2) 16 g. (3) 8 g. (4) 4 g.

28........

29. One liter of a sodium hydroxide solution contains 100. grams of NaOH. The molarity of the solution is (1) 1.0 M (2) 2.5 M (3) 0.25 M (4) 0.50 M

29........

30. In the reaction Zn (s) + 2HCl (aq) = H_2 (g) + Zn^{+2} (aq) + $2Cl^-$ (aq), the number of liters of hydrogen at S.T.P. liberated by reacting one-half mole of zinc with sufficient acid is (1) 5.6 (2) 11.2 (3) 22.4 (4) 33.6

30........

31. Crystals of NaCl, when added to a solution of this salt that is in equilibrium with excess sodium chloride, will (1) dissolve in the solution (2) form a supersaturated solution (3) cause additional sodium chloride crystals to separate from the solution (4) cause no change in the concentration of the solution

31........

32. The system $2SO_2$ (g) + O_2 (g) = $2SO_3$ (g) + 44 kcal is in equilibrium at 25°C. In order to increase the concentration of SO_3 one must (1) decrease the pressure on the system (2) increase the pressure on the system (3) decrease the concentration of O_2 (g) (4) increase the temperature of the system

32........

33. Increasing the temperature usually increases the rate of a chemical reaction. This is best explained by (1) a higher activation energy (2) a new reaction path (3) an increased number of effective collisions (4) an increased concentration of reactants

33........

34. For the general equilibrium system $A + B \rightleftarrows C$, which equilibrium constant most favors a high concentration of C? (1) 3×10^{-6} (2) 7×10^{-6} (3) 7×10^{-10} (4) 3×10^{-3}

34........

35. The weakest acid listed in *Table M* (*Ionization Constants of Acids and Bases*) is (1) acetic acid (2) boric acid (3) carbonic acid (4) phosphoric acid

35........

36. In the reaction $NH_3 + H_2O \rightleftarrows NH_4^+ + OH^-$, the water

molecule serves as (1) a proton donor (2) a proton acceptor (3) a weak base (4) an electron donor 36........

37. The hydrogen ion concentration of a solution is 1×10^{-6} M. The pH of this solution is (1) 10 (2) 8 (3) 6 (4) 4 37........

38. Which can behave as either an acid or a base? (1) NH_4^+ (2) NO_3^- (3) HSO_4^- (4) Cl^- 38........

39. A Brønsted conjugate acid base pair is related by the transfer of (1) an electron (2) a proton (3) an electron pair (4) a water molecule 39........

40. Which water solution will have the lowest freezing point? (1) 1 molal $BaCl_2$ (2) 1 molal $C_3H_5(OH)_3$ (3) 1 molal NaCl (4) 1 molal CH_3COOH 40........

41. One hundred ml of 2.0 M HCl is neutralized with 1.0 M NaOH. The volume of NaOH used is (1) 100 ml (2) 175 ml (3) 200 ml (4) 400 ml 41........

42. A reducing agent will always (1) lose electrons (2) decrease in oxidation number (3) be reduced (4) increase in mass 42........

43. In the electrolysis of fused (molten) calcium chloride, the product at the negative electrode is (1) Ca^{+2} (2) Cl^- (3) Cl_2 (4) Ca 43........

44. In the reaction represented by $MnO_2 + 4HCl \rightarrow MnCl_2 + 2H_2O + Cl_2$, the oxidation number of manganese has (1) decreased from 0 to -2 (2) decreased from $+4$ to $+2$ (3) increased from $+1$ to $+4$ (4) remained the same 44........

45. Chlorine gas is bubbled into a solution containing I^- (aq). Which equation best describes the reaction?
(1) I^- (aq) $+ Cl^-$ (aq) $= I$ (s) $+ Cl$ (g)
(2) I^- (aq) $+ \frac{1}{2}Cl_2$ (g) $= \frac{1}{2}I_2$ (s) $+ Cl^-$ (aq)
(3) $\frac{1}{2}I_2$ (s) $+ \frac{1}{2}Cl_2$ (g) $= I^-$ (aq) $+ Cl^-$ (aq)
(4) $2I^-$ (aq) $+ Cl_2$ (g) $= I_2$ (s) $+ Cl_2$ (g) 45........

46. At a constant temperature, a system tends to undergo a reaction so that in its final state, compared to its initial state, it has (1) lower energy and lower entropy (2) lower energy and higher entropy (3) higher energy and higher entropy (4) higher energy and lower entropy 46........

47. The oxidation number of chlorine in the compound $KClO_4$ is (1) -1 (2) $+1$ (3) $+5$ (4) $+7$ 47........

48. Copper reacts with dilute nitric acid according to the following equation:

$$3Cu + XHNO_3 \rightarrow 3Cu(NO_3)_2 + 2NO + 4H_2O$$

The coefficient represented by X is   (1) 8   (2) 6   (3) 5
(4) 4   48........

49. Which organic reaction is characteristic of unsaturated hydrocarbons?   (1) substitution   (2) addition   (3) saponification   (4) fermentation   49........

50. The functional group characteristic of organic acids is

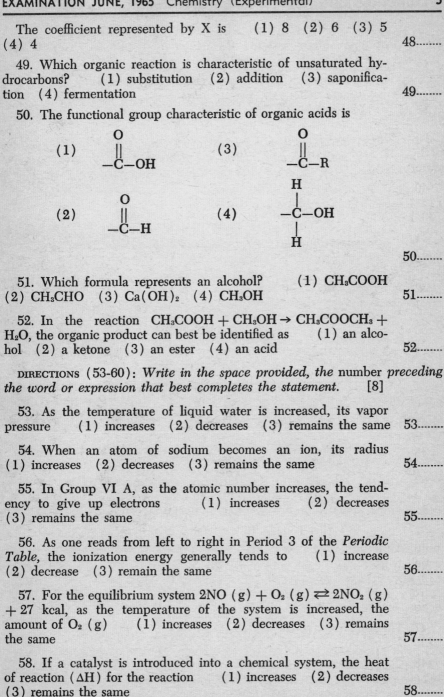

51. Which formula represents an alcohol?   (1) CH_3COOH
(2) CH_3CHO (3) $Ca(OH)_2$ (4) CH_3OH 51........

52. In the reaction $CH_3COOH + CH_3OH \rightarrow CH_3COOCH_3 + H_2O$, the organic product can best be identified as   (1) an alcohol   (2) a ketone   (3) an ester   (4) an acid   52........

DIRECTIONS (53-60): *Write in the space provided, the* number *preceding the word or expression that best completes the statement.*   [8]

53. As the temperature of liquid water is increased, its vapor pressure   (1) increases   (2) decreases   (3) remains the same   53........

54. When an atom of sodium becomes an ion, its radius
(1) increases   (2) decreases   (3) remains the same   54........

55. In Group VI A, as the atomic number increases, the tendency to give up electrons   (1) increases   (2) decreases
(3) remains the same   55........

56. As one reads from left to right in Period 3 of the *Periodic Table,* the ionization energy generally tends to   (1) increase
(2) decrease   (3) remain the same   56........

57. For the equilibrium system $2NO$ (g) $+ O_2$ (g) $\rightleftarrows 2NO_2$ (g) $+ 27$ kcal, as the temperature of the system is increased, the amount of O_2 (g)   (1) increases   (2) decreases   (3) remains the same   57........

58. If a catalyst is introduced into a chemical system, the heat of reaction (ΔH) for the reaction   (1) increases   (2) decreases
(3) remains the same   58........

59. As more solid $BaSO_4$ is added to a saturated $BaSO_4$ solution (temperature remaining constant), the magnitude of its K_{sp} (1) increases (2) decreases (3) remains the same   59........

60. When a catalyst is added to a system in equilibrium, the equilibrium concentration of the products (1) increases (2) decreases (3) remains the same   60........

PART TWO *This part consists of six groups. Choose four of these six groups. Be sure that you answer all questions in each group chosen. Write the answers to these questions in the space provided.*

GROUP 1

DIRECTIONS (61-65): *The diagram shows a change of phase curve in which the temperature (T) is plotted against time (m). Starting with a solid at a temperature below its melting point, there is a constant addition of heat. The pressure remains constant.*

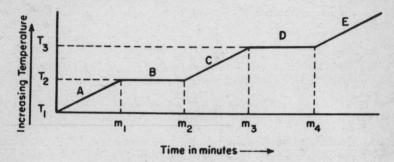

Write the number preceding the word or expression that best completes the statement or answers the question.   [5]

61. What is the phase of the substance in the portion of the curve labeled C?   (1) a solid (2) a liquid (3) a gas (4) It cannot be determined from the information given.   61........

62. The temperature labeled T_2 is the temperature at which the substance   (1) boils (2) melts (3) vaporizes (4) sublimes   62........

63. The substance begins to boil at the time labeled   (1) m_1 (2) m_2 (3) m_3 (4) m_4 63........

64. In which portion of the curve do the molecules have the highest average kinetic energy?   (1) A (2) B (3) E (4) D   64........

65. The portion of the curve labeled D represents the time during which the substance is   (1) being warmed as a solid (2) being warmed as a liquid (3) changing from solid to liquid at its melting temperature (4) changing from liquid to gas at its boiling temperature   65........

DIRECTIONS (66-70): *For* each *compound in 66 through 70, write the number of the structural formula,* chosen from the list below, *which best applies to that compound.*   [5]

Structural Formulas

(1) 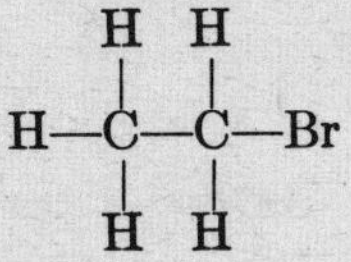
$$H-\underset{\underset{H}{|}}{\overset{\overset{H}{|}}{C}}-\underset{\underset{H}{|}}{\overset{\overset{H}{|}}{C}}-Br$$

(2) 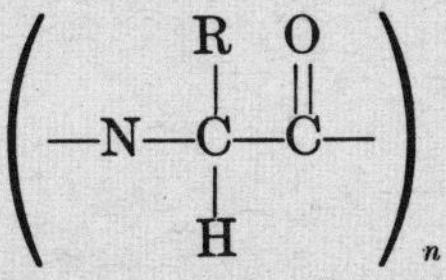
$$\left(-N-\underset{\underset{H}{|}}{\overset{\overset{R}{|}}{C}}-\overset{\overset{O}{\|}}{C}- \right)_n$$

CH₃OH

(3) 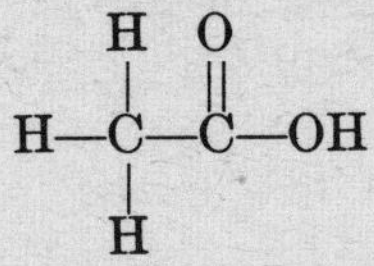
$$H-\underset{\underset{H}{|}}{\overset{\overset{H}{|}}{C}}-\overset{\overset{O}{\|}}{C}-OH$$

CH₃-O

(4) 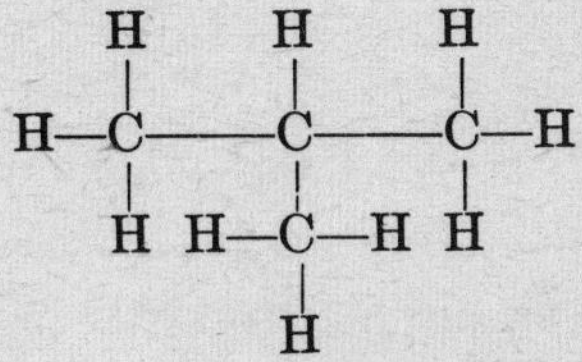
$$H-\underset{\underset{H}{|}}{\overset{\overset{H}{|}}{C}}-\underset{\underset{\underset{H}{|}}{\overset{|}{C}H-H}}{\overset{\overset{H}{|}}{C}}-\underset{\underset{H}{|}}{\overset{\overset{H}{|}}{C}}-H$$

(5) 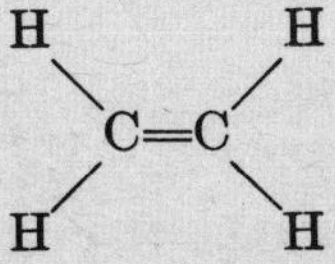
$$\underset{H}{\overset{H}{}}C=C\underset{H}{\overset{H}{}}$$

(6) 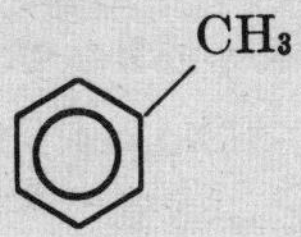
⬡—CH₃   *aromatic*

(7) 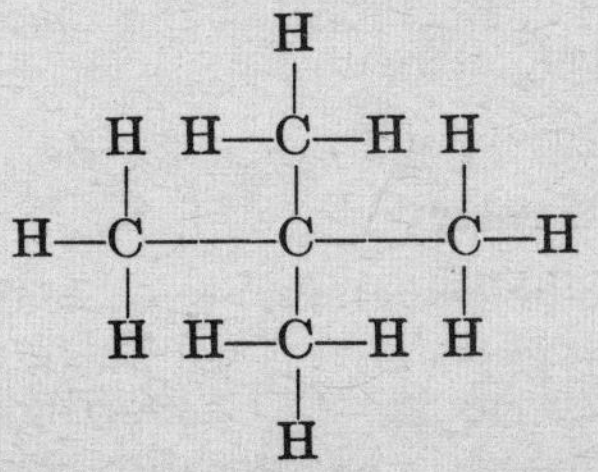
$$H-\underset{\underset{H}{|}}{\overset{\overset{H}{|}}{C}}-\underset{H-\underset{H}{\overset{|}{C}}-H}{\overset{H-\overset{\overset{H}{|}}{C}-H}{\overset{|}{C}}}-\underset{\underset{H}{|}}{\overset{\overset{H}{|}}{C}}-H$$

66. An isobutane   66.........

67. A compound which reacts with bromine by an addition reaction   67...5....

68. A halogen substitution product   68...1....

69. An aromatic compound   69...6....

70. A compound which reacts with CH_3OH to form an ester   70...3....

GROUP 2

DIRECTIONS (71-75): *The questions below pertain to the following electron configuration of a neutral atom:*

$$1s^2 \, 2s^2 \, 2p^6 \, 3s^2 \, 3p^2$$

Write the number preceding the word or expression that best completes the statement or answers the question.   [5]

71. The total number of protons in the nucleus of this element is   (1) 7   (2) 8   (3) 14   (4) 28   71........

72. The total number of electrons in the principal energy level M of this atom is   (1) 6   (2) 2   (3) 8   (4) 4   72........

73. This element is best described as being in Group   (1) VI *A* (2) II *A*   (3) II *B*   (4) IV *A*   73........

74. The total number of orbitals which contain at least one electron is   (1) 5   (2) 6   (3) 8   (4) 14   74........

75. The shifting of an electron from the 3s subshell to the 3p subshell of this atom   (1) occurs spontaneously   (2) requires the absorption of energy by the atom   (3) is impossible, because the 3p subshell is filled   (4) is impossible, because an electron can move only toward the nucleus   75........

DIRECTIONS (76-80): *For each phrase in questions 76 through 80, write the number of the bonds or binding forces, chosen from the list below, which is most closely associated with that phrase.*   [5]

Bonds or Binding Forces

(1) Ionic bonds   (5) Metallic bonds
(2) Network bonds   (6) Van der Waals forces
(3) Coordinate covalent bonds   (7) Covalent bonds
(4) Hydrogen bonds

76. Hold the iodine atoms together in the molecule I_2 76........

77. Hold the many molecules of I_2 together in a crystal of iodine   77........

78. Account for the relatively high boiling and freezing points of pure water   78........

79. Are illustrated by the compounds formed when fluorine
reacts with active metals   79........

80. Hold magnesium atoms in a crystal lattice   80........

GROUP 3

DIRECTIONS (81-85): *For each* phrase *in questions* 81 *through* 85, *write
the* number *of the formula, chosen from the list below,* which is most closely
associated with that phrase. [5]

Formulas

(1) HCl   (5) Cu
(2) Na   (6) Xe
(3) CH₄   (7) KBr
(4) SiO₂

81. Conducts an electric current in the molten state but not in
the solid state   81........

82. Conducts an electric current in aqueous solution but not in
the liquid phase   82........

83. Mobile electrons permit electrical conductivity in the solid
phase   83........

84. A nonpolar covalent compound   84........

85. An example of a network solid   85........

DIRECTIONS (86-90): *For each of questions* 86 *through* 90, *which are
based on the* Periodic Table of the Elements, *write the* number *preceding
the word or expression that best completes the statement or answers the
question.* [5]

86. The most metallic element in Group IV A is   (1) C
(2) Si   (3) Ge   (4) Sn   86........

87. Which is a transition element?   (1) Rb   (2) Sb   (3) Ag
(4) Xe   87........

88. In Group V A, the element with the smallest atomic radius
is   (1) Bi   (2) P   (3) As   (4) N   88........

89. The elements with the *least* chemical reactivity are in Group
(1) I A   (2) O   (3) III B   (4) VI A   89........

90. In the Period 3, the element with the *lowest* ionization
energy is   (1) Ar   (2) P   (3) Cl   (4) Na   90........

GROUP 4

DIRECTIONS (91-95): *Base your answers to questions* 91 *through* 95 *on
the information below. Write the* number *preceding the word or expression
that best completes the statement or answers the question.* [5]

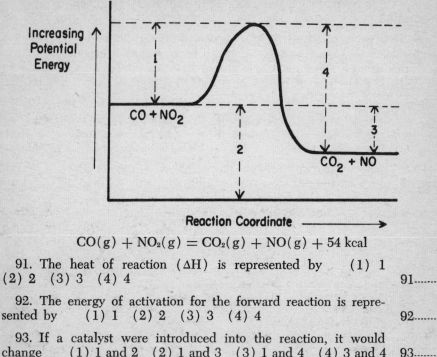

Increasing Potential Energy

CO + NO₂

CO₂ + NO

Reaction Coordinate ⟶

$$CO(g) + NO_2(g) = CO_2(g) + NO(g) + 54\ kcal$$

91. The heat of reaction (ΔH) is represented by   (1) 1
(2) 2   (3) 3   (4) 4   91........

92. The energy of activation for the forward reaction is represented by   (1) 1   (2) 2   (3) 3   (4) 4   92........

93. If a catalyst were introduced into the reaction, it would change   (1) 1 and 2   (2) 1 and 3   (3) 1 and 4   (4) 3 and 4   93........

94. The energy of activation for the reverse reaction is   (1) 1
(2) 2   (3) 3   (4) 4   94........

95. The energy liberated when two moles of NO_2 is consumed is approximately   (1) 13.5 kcal   (2) 27 kcal   (3) 54 kcal
(4) 108 kcal   95........

DIRECTIONS (96-100): *Base your answers to questions 96 through 100 on the information below. Write the* number *preceding the word or expression that best completes the statement or answers the question.*   [5]

Nitrogen, hydrogen and ammonia gases are placed in a closed system and allowed to reach equilibrium at a certain temperature according to the reaction $N_2 + 3H_2 \rightleftarrows 2NH_3 + 22$ kcal.

96. The temperature is increased and the pressure is kept constant. Compared to its original concentration, the new equilibrium concentration of   (1) NH_3 is less   (2) NH_3 is more   (3) N_2 is less   (4) H_2 is the same   96........

97. Some hydrogen is removed from the system while pressure and temperature are kept constant. Compared to the original concentration, the new equilibrium concentration of   (1) N_2 is

greater   (2) N_2 is unchanged   (3) NH_3 is greater   (4) NH_3 is unchanged   97........

98. A catalyst is added to the system while the pressure and temperature are kept constant. Compared to its original concentration, the new equilibrium concentration of   (1) NH_3 is more   (2) NH_3 is the same   (3) H_2 is more   (4) H_2 is less   98........

99. More nitrogen is added to the system while temperature and pressure are kept constant. Compared to the original concentration, the new equilibrium concentration of   (1) H_2 is greater   (2) NH_3 is greater   (3) NH_3 is less   (4) N_2 is unchanged   99........

100. The pressure on the system is increased while the temperature is kept constant. At the new equilibrium, the number of moles of   (1) NH_3 increases   (2) H_2 increases   (3) N_2 increases   (4) N_2 is unchanged   100........

GROUP 5

DIRECTIONS (101-105): *For each phrase in questions 101 through 105, write the number preceding the formula, chosen from the list below, which is most closely associated with that phrase.*   [5]

Formulas

(1) $(NH_4)_2 SO_4$ (5) HCl
(2) H_2O (6) Na_2CO_3
(3) NH_4Cl (7) H_3PO_4
(4) NH_2^-

101. The strongest base   101........

102. A salt whose aqueous solution has a pH greater than 7   102........

103. Can act as either an acid or a base   103........

104. Assuming 100 percent ionization, one gram-equivalent equals one-third mole   104........

105. The strongest acid   105........

DIRECTIONS (106-110): *Base your answers to questions 106 through 110 on Table L of the* Reference Tables for Chemistry. *Write the number preceding the word or expression that best completes the statement or answers the question.*   [5]

106. A new substance formed when copper is placed in a silver nitrate solution is   (1) Cu (2) Ag^+ (3) Ag (4) NO_3^- 106........

107. Which is the best reducing agent in Table L?   (1) Li (2) Li^+ (3) F^- (4) F_2 107........

108. Which element will reduce Pb^{+2} to Pb but *not* Mg^{+2} to Mg?   (1) Cu (2) Na (3) Ag (4) Zn 108........

109. Which reaction will *not* take place?   (1) $Mg + Cu^{++}$ → $Cu + Mg^{++}$ (2) $2Ag + 2H^+ → 2Ag^+ + H_2$ (3) $Cu + Br_2 →$ $Cu^{++} + 2Br^-$ (4) $Fe + Pb^{++} → Fe^{++} + Pb$ 109........

110. How many volts potential (E^0) for the overall reaction are given by combining the half reactions for the equation $2Al +$ $3Fe^{++} → 2Al^{+++} + 3Fe$?   (1) 1.22   (2) 2.10   (3) 2.44 (4) 3.66   110........

GROUP 6

DIRECTIONS (111-117): *Select the number preceding the word or expression that best completes the statement or answers the question.*

Base your answers to questions 111 *and* 112 *on the information below:*

204 grams of aluminum oxide are decomposed according to the following reaction:

$$2Al_2O_3 → 4Al + 3O_2$$

111. How many moles of Al_2O_3 are decomposed?   [1] (1) 1   (2) 2   (3) 3   (4) 4   111........

112. How many moles of aluminum are produced?   [1] (1) 1   (2) 2   (3) 3   (4) 4   112........

Base your answers to questions 113 *and* 114 *on the equation below:*

$$C_8H_{16} (g) + 12O_2 (g) → 8CO_2 (g) + 8H_2O (g)$$

113. When 10.00 liters of C_8H_{16} are burned, how many liters of water vapor are produced?   [1]   (1) 10.00   (2) 22.40 (3) 80.00   (4) 179.2   113........

114. How many liters of CO_2 are produced to burn completely 112 grams of C_8H_{16}?   [2]   (1) 10   (2) 22.4   (3) 80 (4) 179.2   114........

Base your answers to questions 115 *through* 117 *on the information below:*

A compound was found by analysis to consist of 85.3% carbon and 14.7% hydrogen. Its gas density at S.T.P. is 1.25 grams per liter.

115. What is the empirical formula of the compound?   [2] (1) CH   (2) CH_2 (3) CH_3 (4) C_3H_4 115........

116. What is the molecular mass (weight) of the compound? [2]   (1) 26   (2) 28   (3) 30   (4) 80   116........

117. What is the molecular formula of the compound?   [1] (1) C_6H_6 (2) C_2H_4 (3) C_3H_4 (4) C_2H_6 117........

Answers to Chemistry (Experimental)   June, 1965

1.   Ans.   **1**   A solution is a mixture. Any mixture is composed of two or more substances each of which keeps its own characteristic properties. A solution consists of a solute (sugar) and a solvent (water) each of which retains its properties in solution. In a solution, however, the particles of the solute are distributed *uniformly* throughout the solvent. Such a uniform mixture has similar properties throughout and is said to be a *homogeneous mixture*. Here the sugar molecules are uniformly dispersed throughout the aqueous medium.

2.   Ans.   **4**   As a chemical change, or reaction, progresses, heat energy may be absorbed or may be liberated. A reaction which absorbs heat energy is *endothermic*. Since the heat energy is absorbed from the surroundings, the temperature of the surroundings decreases.

3.   Ans.   **2**   *Boyle's Law* states that at a constant temperature, the volume of a confined gas varies inversely with the pressure applied to the gas. The *kinetic-molecular theory* helps to explain Boyle's Law. Since the temperature is constant, the average kinetic energy of the molecules is not changing. The pressure of a gas depends upon the number of bombardments of the molecules per unit surface area per unit time. If we wish to increase the number of bombardments, the walls of the container must be closer together so that the molecules which are moving at constant velocity hit the walls more often. In other words, the volume must decrease. Here the pressure is being doubled (from 1 atmosphere to 2 atmospheres). Since the volume varies inversely, the volume of the gas is halved, from 500 ml to 250 ml.

4.   Ans.   **2**   *Charles' Law* states that at a constant pressure, the volume of a confined gas varies directly with the Kelvin (Absolute) temperature. The *kinetic-molecular theory* helps to explain Charles' Law. Since the pressure is kept constant, the number of bombardments of the molecules per unit surface area per unit time remains the same. If the temperature is increased, the average kinetic energy and therefore the speed of the molecules is increased. If we wish the number of bombardments to remain the same (constant pressure), the walls of the container must be farther apart so that the molecules which are moving faster may hit the walls the same number of times. In other words, the volume must increase. Here the temperature is being increased from 20°C to 40°C. To change the Celsius (Centigrade) scale to the Kelvin (Absolute) scale, we must add 273° to each temperature. Thus the temperature is increased from $(20° + 273°)$ or 293°K to $(40° + 273°)$ or 313°K. Since the volume varies directly, the volume of the gas is increased from 50 ml to $50 \times \dfrac{313}{293}$ ml.

5. Ans. 3 At S.T.P. (0°C, 760 mm Hg), one mole of any gas occupies 22.4 liters. Therefore, 11.2 liters contains $\dfrac{11.2 \text{ l}}{22.4 \text{ l/mole}}$ or 0.500 mole, correct to 3 significant figures. Therefore among the choices given, we select choice (3), 0.50.

6. Ans. 4 Water has a specific heat of $1 \dfrac{\text{cal}}{\text{C°}}$. This means that 1 calorie of heat will raise the temperature of 1 gram of water 1 Celsius degree. This suggests the formula:

Heat energy = mass × specific heat × change in temperature
or   H = m × c × Δt
Here we have 250 grams which must rise (25°C − 22°C) or 3 C°.

$$H = 250 \text{ grams} \times 1 \frac{\text{cal}}{g\,C°} \times 3\ C°.$$

$$H = 750 \text{ cal.}$$

7. Ans. 2 An orbital is the region encompassing the probability distribution of a pair of electrons of an atom. It is often represented in diagrams as an "electron cloud."
An orbital refers to the probable average region covered by an electron. These orbitals differ in shape, size, and orientation in space. An orbital holds at most two electrons. No orbital can hold a second electron until all the orbitals in a sublevel are occupied by one electron. In the atom the sublevel s has 1 orbital with a maximum of two electrons. The sublevel p has 3 orbitals with a maximum of 6 electrons. The d sublevel has 5 orbitals with a maximum of 10 electrons. The f sublevel has 7 orbitals with a maximum of 14 electrons.
Here we are asked for the maximum number of electrons in the 3s orbital. Since any s sublevel of any principal level has only one orbital, the maximum number of electrons is two.

8. Ans. 1 The energy levels of an atom are classified as principal energy levels and secondary energy sublevels. The principal energy levels are designated by the principal quantum numbers n = 1, n = 2, n = 3 etc. The n = 1 or K energy level is the closest to the nucleus and therefore at lowest energy. Within the principal energy levels we have four secondary energy sublevels represented by s, p, d, f, in order of increasing energy. In the symbolism for electronic configuration the coefficient represents the principal quantum number. Thus 1s is the lowest possible energy level of an atom. In order of increasing energy we have 2s, 2p, 3s, 3p, 3d, etc. There are a few exceptions. Thus 4s is at a lower energy level than 3d and 6s is lower than 4f. Of the choices in the question, the sublevel of lowest energy is 2s since n = 2 is the lowest principal level and s is the lowest sublevel.

9. Ans. 3 The *mass number* of an atom is the sum of the number of protons and neutrons in the nucleus of an atom. In this case the atom has 19 protons and 20 neutrons. Its mass number is 19 + 20 or 39.

10. **Ans. 2** Valence electrons are the electrons found in the outermost principal energy level of an atom. Here, the last principal energy level is n = 3. It has one sublevel, 3s, with 2 electrons. Thus the number of valence electrons is 2.

11. **Ans. 1** The *atomic number* of an atom is shown by the number of protons in the nucleus. For the atom to be electrically neutral, the number of electrons in the principal energy levels must equal the number of protons in the nucleus, since protons have a $+1$ charge and electrons have a -1 charge. In the symbolism the coefficient is the quantum number of the principal energy level and the superscript the number of electrons in the designated sublevel. The electron configuration of this atom is $1s^2\ 2s^2\ 2p^6\ 3s^2\ 3p^3$. The total number of electrons is $2 + 2 + 6 + 2 + 3$ or 15. Thus there are also 15 protons.

12. **Ans. 1** The *first ionization energy* is the energy required to remove the outermost electron of an uncombined atom in the gaseous state. The ionization energy is affected by 2 factors: (1) the atomic radius and (2) the nuclear charge. When the atomic radius is large and the nuclear charge is small, for a given Period, the energy required to pull off the outermost electron is minimal, and therefore the first ionization energy is lowest. Since in any given Period, Group I A satisfies both factors (large atomic radius and smaller nuclear charge) an atom in Group I A has the lowest first ionization energy for a given Period, or horizontal row. Of the Groups given in the choices, the order of increasing ionization energy for any given horizontal row would be I A, II A, VII A, and 0 since atomic radius decreases and nuclear charge increases from left to right in any Period through Group VII A. These facts are confirmed in *Table J* which lists the ionization energies of the "Representative Elements."

13. **Ans. 3** *Isotopes* are atoms with the same atomic number (same element) but with different mass numbers. The mass number is the sum of the protons and neutrons in the atom. Since the atomic number or number of protons is the same for the same element, the difference in mass number must be due to a difference in the number of neutrons in the nucleus. Thus only the physical properties such as density and rate of diffusion are different among isotopes of the element. The chemical properties are the same. Examples of isotopes are ^1_1H, ^2_1H, and ^3_1H, with 0, 1 and 2 neutrons in the nucleus respectively.

14. **Ans. 4** The reaction $^{238}_{92}U \rightarrow\ ^{234}_{90}Th + X$ is a nuclear reaction showing the transmutation of $^{238}_{92}U$ to $^{234}_{90}Th$. In a nuclear equation, the superscript represents the mass number of the atom and the subscript the atomic number. The sum of the mass numbers on the left is equal to the sum of the mass numbers on the right. Since the total mass number on the left is 238, the mass number of X must be $238 - 234$ or 4 to give a total of 238 on the right. The sum of the atomic numbers on the left is equal to the sum of the atomic numbers on the right. Since the atomic number on the left is 92,

the atomic number of X must be $(92 - 90)$ or 2 so that the sum of the atomic numbers on the right is 92. Therefore X has a mass of 4 and an atomic number of 2. The symbol would be ^4_2X. Referring to Table E, we see that this particle is an alpha particle.

15. **Ans. 1** The formula of an oxide, as well as other compounds, is determined by the valences of the combining elements. Valence is the number of electrons lost or gained or shared by the atoms in making a bond. The valence electrons are those in the outer shell of the atom. Therefore element X, $1s^2\ 2s^2\ 2p^6\ 3s^1$, has 1 valence electron, the single electron in the 3rd or M energy level. Its oxidation state is therefore $+1$. The oxidation state of oxygen as shown in the Periodic Table is -2. Since any compound is electrically neutral, there must be 2 atoms of element X, oxidation state $+1$, to combine with one atom of O, oxidation state -2. The formula for the oxide is therefore X_2O.

Wrong Choices Explained:

(2) In the formula XO, the oxidation state of X would be $+2$, not $+1$.
(3) In the formula X_3O_2, 3 O's total a -6 oxidation state. Therefore each of the three X's would be $+2$, not $+1$.
(4) In the formula XO_2, 2 O's total a -4 oxidation state. Therefore, the oxidation state of X is $+4$.

16. **Ans. 2** Solid barium chloride is a salt, and therefore its crystals contain Ba^{+2} and Cl^- ions located at the lattice points of the crystal. For an electrically neutral compound, there must be twice as many Cl^- ions as Ba^{+2} ions. Therefore the ratio of barium to chloride ions is 1:2. This ratio is clearly seen when solid barium chloride is melted and the ions bound in the crystal lattice of the solid state dissociate to become free ions:

$$BaCl_2 \rightarrow 1Ba^{+2} + 2Cl^-$$

17. **Ans. 2** *Ionic compounds* are those in which there has been a *transfer* of electrons from atoms of metals to atoms of non-metals. This transfer has taken place because the metal, with a low electronegativity, shows little tendency to hold on to its valence electrons, and the nonmetal, with a high electronegativity, shows a great tendency to gain electrons. Thus, ionic compounds form when there is a great electronegativity difference between the elements. There is no exact point where we can say that a compound has become ionic. In general we can say that a compound has ionic bonds when the electronegativity difference is about 1.7 or more. A 1.7 difference would give the bond 50% ionic character. Let us determine the electronegativity difference for each of the pairs of elements listed:

(1) Na and F: Electronegativity difference $= 4.0 - 0.9 = 3.1$
(2) Rb and F: Electronegativity difference $= 4.0 - 0.8 = 3.2$
(3) Li and I: Electronegativity difference $= 2.5 - 1.0 = 1.5$
(4) K and Cl: Electronegativity difference $= 3.0 - 0.8 = 2.2$

From the above, we see that RbF, rubidium fluoride, is the compound with the strongest ionic character since it has the largest electronegativity difference of the pairs listed. The electronegativity difference of 3.2 indicates an ionic character of about 92%.

18. Ans. **3** Ammonia has the molecular formula NH_3. The hydrogen atom has a single electron in its electron configuration, H. The electron configuration of the nitrogen atom (see the *Periodic Table*) shows 5 electrons in

its valence shell, $\cdot \overset{\bullet}{\underset{\bullet\bullet}{N}} \cdot$. Thus it can bond with three electrons from three hy-

drogen atoms to form a stable octet.

Each hydrogen atom shares its single electron with an electron of the nitrogen atom. Since the electronegativity difference between N and H is $3.0 - 2.1$ or 0.9, the three bonds that can be formed are polar covalent with the shared pair under the control of the electronegative nitrogen atom most of the time. Note that each of the atoms now has a stable or complete valence shell since each H atom has two electrons and the N atom has 8 electrons. Note that one pair of electrons of the nitrogen atom is unshared. The displacement of the electrons toward the nitrogen atom gives the nitrogen end of the molecule a partial negative charge (δ^-) and the hydrogen end of the molecule a partial positive charge (δ^+). Thus the ammonia molecule is a dipole.

$$
\begin{array}{c}
\delta^- \\
\bullet\bullet \\
\delta^+ H \underset{\bullet\times}{\overset{\times}{\times}} N \overset{\times}{} H \delta^+ \\
H \\
\delta^+
\end{array}
$$

19. Ans. **1** When atoms combine to form molecules, bonds are formed between the atoms of the molecule. Each atom usually acquires a stable valence shell by transferring electrons to or from another atom or by sharing electrons with another atom. Since a stable energy state requires less energy, some energy is released in forming a bond. In order to break these chemical bonds between atoms or ions, energy must be absorbed to get the atoms of the molecule back to their original, higher energy level. In general, when chemical bonds are formed, energy is released; when chemical bonds are broken, energy is absorbed.

20. Ans. **2** When a metal has two or more oxidation states, the oxidation state assumed is indicated in the formula by means of a Roman numeral immediately following the symbol of the metal. When a compound is a *binary* compound (a compound consisting of only two elements), the nonmetal ends in the suffix *"ide."* Thus we have an oxide. The formula FeO has one oxygen atom with an oxidation state of -2. Since a compound is electrically neutral, the total positive charge is equal to the total negative charge. The oxidation number of iron is therefore $+2$. Thus the correct name for the binary compound is iron (II) oxide.

21. **Ans. 3** The *Periodic Table* tells us that the calcium atom has the electron configuration 2-8-8-2. The calcium atom loses its 2 electrons of the valence shell to become the calcium ion, with a configuration of 2-8-8. The *Periodic Table* shows that argon, an inert element, has the same electron configuration of 2-8-8.

22. **Ans. 4** Referring to the key on the *Periodic Table*, we note that the covalent atomic radius, expressed in Ångstrom units, (Å) is given directly below the symbol of the element. An Å unit is equal to 10^{-8} cm., an extremely small unit of length. The *Periodic Table* tells us that of the elements listed in the question, Cl has the smallest atomic radius, 0.99 Å. All the elements listed are in the 3rd horizontal row, or *Period 3*. Within a given Period, the atomic radius of an element decreases going from left to right because of the increasing nuclear charge. The increased positive charge tends to pull the outer shell of the atom closer to the nucleus, thus decreasing the atomic radius.

23. **Ans. 2** *Ionization energy* is the energy needed to remove the most loosely held electron from the outer shell of an atom in the gaseous phase. Since a nonmetal is defined as an element which gains electrons, it would not lose electrons easily, and thus a great deal of energy would be required to remove an electron. Thus, a nonmetal has a high ionization energy.

Electronegativity is defined as the attraction an atom has for a shared pair of electrons in forming a bond. Since nonmetals, as stated above, gain electrons, they must have a high electronegativity, or great attraction for electrons. These two facts are confirmed in *Table J, "Representative" Elements*, where fluorine, the most active nonmetal, has the highest ionization energy (17.3 e.v.) and the highest electronegativity (4.0).

24. **Ans. 3** A metal is an element that tends to lose its electrons. The more active the metal, the greater the tendency to lose electrons. The tendency to lose electrons is favored by a large atomic radius and a smaller nuclear charge, since both factors cause decreasing attraction for the electrons by the nucleus. Within Period 4, K is the element with the largest atomic radius (2.31 Å) and the smallest nuclear charge (+19). In general, within a given Period, the element farthest to the left is the most active metal, and the element farthest to the right is the most active nonmetal.

25. **Ans. 3** One mole or gram-molecular mass of an element or compound contains 6.02×10^{23} molecules. The *Periodic Table* tells us that the gram-molecular mass of helium (also called gram-atomic mass since helium is monatomic) is 4 grams. Here we have 2.0 grams of helium or $\dfrac{2.0 \text{ grams}}{4.0 \dfrac{\text{grams}}{\text{mole}}} =$ 0.50 mole of helium. Since 1 mole of helium has 6.02×10^{23} molecules of helium, 0.50 mole has 3.01×10^{23} molecules.

ALTERNATE METHOD:

Using proportions: $\dfrac{6.02 \times 10^{23} \text{ molecules}}{1 \text{ mole}} = \dfrac{x}{\frac{1}{2} \text{ mole}}$

$$x = 3.01 \times 10^{23} \text{ molecules}$$

NOTE: *Since 2.0 contains two significant figures, the answer correct to two significant figures is* 3.0×10^{23}.

26. Ans. **1** Referring to Table *B, Solubility Curves,* we see that at 50°C, it would require 85 grams to saturate the solution (a point *on* the curve indicates a point of saturation). Since there are only 70 grams present, the solution is unsaturated.

27. Ans. **1** Density is the ratio of the weight of a substance to its volume. It is usually measured in grams per liter. If the weight of 1 liter is 9.0×10^{-2} grams, then 100 liters will weigh $9.0 \times 10^{-2} \times 100$ or 900×10^{-2}. Since 10^{-2} is .01, $900 \times 10^{-2} = 900 \times .01 = 9$ grams.

NOTE: *Since the given value of* 100 *has only one significant figure, the answer must also contain one significant figure.*

28. Ans. **3** A mole contains a gram-molecular mass of a substance. The *Periodic Table* tells us that the gram-atomic mass or gram-atom of O is 16 grams. Since oxygen is diatomic, the gram-molecular mass of O_2 is 2×16 grams or 32 grams. Since one mole weighs 32 grams, one-fourth mole weighs $\frac{1}{4}$ of 32 or 8 grams.

ALTERNATE METHOD:

Using the equation: $\text{moles} = \dfrac{\text{grams}}{\text{gram molecular mass}}$

Substituting $\frac{1}{4}$ for the number of moles, and 32 grams/mole for the gram-molecular mass of O_2, we get

$$\tfrac{1}{4} \text{ mole} = \dfrac{x \text{ grams}}{32 \text{ g./mole}}$$

$$x = \tfrac{1}{4} \text{ mole} \times 32 \text{ grams/mole} = 8 \text{ grams}.$$

29. Ans. **2** The *molarity* of a solution measures the number of moles of solute dissolved in one (1.00) liter of *solution.* One mole of NaOH is one gram-formula mass:

$$\begin{array}{l} 1 \text{ Na} = 23 \\ 1 \text{ O } = 16 \\ \underline{1 \text{ H } = \ 1} \end{array}$$

g./form. mass of NaOH = 40. grams

Since one mole of NaOH is 40. grams, 100. grams would represent

$$\dfrac{100. \text{ grams}}{40. \dfrac{\text{grams}}{\text{mole}}} = 2.5 \text{ moles}.$$

Since 2.5 moles of NaOH are dissolved in 1 liter, the solution has a molarity of $2.5 \dfrac{\text{moles}}{\text{liter}}$ or 2.5 M.

NOTE: *The gram-formula mass of NaOH, 40. grams, has the least number of significant figures (two). The decimal point after the 40 indicates that both figures are significant. Thus, the answer (2.5 M) must also have two significant figures.*

30. Ans. **2** $Zn(s) + 2HCl \text{ (aq)} = H_2 \text{ (g)} + Zn^{+2} \text{ (aq)} + 2Cl^- \text{ (aq)}$. In a chemical equation, the ratio of the moles of the reactants and products is shown by the coefficients. According to the equation, 1 mole of Zn liberates 1 mole of H_2. Thus $\frac{1}{2}$ mole of Zn will liberate $\frac{1}{2}$ mole of H_2. At S.T.P., one mole of any gas occupies 22.4 liters. Therefore, $\frac{1}{2}$ mole of H_2 will occupy

$$\tfrac{1}{2} \; \cancel{\text{mole}} \times 22.4 \; \frac{\text{liters}}{\cancel{\text{mole}}} = 11.2 \text{ liters.}$$

31. Ans. **4** A solution of NaCl in equilibrium with excess (solid) sodium chloride is by definition a saturated solution. Equilibrium is a dynamic condition, not a static one. The rate at which the solute is dissolving equals the rate at which NaCl is crystallizing. If more solute is added, some may dissolve but an equal amount will crystallize out. Actually, then, no *additional* crystals of NaCl will dissolve. Thus, the concentration of the solution remains the same as more solute is added.

32. Ans. **2** *Le Chatelier's principle* states that if a system in equilibrium is subjected to a stress (such as increased pressure or temperature), the equilibrium will be displaced in the direction that relieves the stress. If an increased pressure is applied to the reaction, we should expect the reaction to go in the direction which creates a lower pressure. The pressure in a closed container is dependent upon the volume of the gas in that container. Volumes are proportional to the coefficients of the molecules as shown in the equation of the reaction. Here the equation is

$$2SO_2 \text{ (g)} + O_2 \text{ (g)} = 2SO_3 \text{ (g)} + 44 \text{ kcal.}$$

The gaseous reactants $2SO_2$ and O_2 occupy $2 + 1$ or 3 volumes. The product $2SO_3$ occupies 2 volumes. The relief of the pressure stress is on the right where there are fewer molecules and thus less volume. When pressure is applied to the system, the equilibrium point will be shifted toward the SO_3 at the right and so the concentration of SO_3 increases.

33. Ans. **3** Increasing the temperature increases the kinetic energy of the reacting particles, and thus increases the speed of the particles. As the speed of the particles increases, the number of collisions per unit time increases accordingly. With more collisions, the chance of a chemical reaction is increased. This is only part of the story, however. The increased kinetic energy of the particles also makes possible more effective collisions since there is available more energy to supply the activation energy needed for a chemical reaction.

34. **Ans. 4** The *equilibrium constant K* is the ratio of the product of the concentrations of the products formed to the product of the concentrations of the reactants. For the reaction

$$A + B = C, \qquad K = \frac{[C]}{[B][A]},$$

where the brackets indicate concentrations in moles per liter. Since C is in the numerator, a high concentration of C means the fraction will be relatively large and thus the equilibrium constant K will be large. Remember from algebra that as we go to the right on the real number line, the value of the numbers increases:

$$-2 \quad -1 \quad 0 \quad 1 \quad 2$$
$$\xrightarrow{\hspace{4cm}}$$
$$\text{larger}$$

Thus -3 is the largest exponent of the values listed and 3×10^{-3} represents the highest value of the equilibrium constant. Its decimal value is $3 \times .001$ or .003.

35. **Ans. 2** A *weak acid* is one which ionizes only slightly in water. The acids listed at the top of *Table M* are all weak acids since they have low ionization constants as shown by the negative exponents. As explained in the answer to question 34, a negative exponent with a large absolute value indicates a very small number, while a negative exponent with a small absolute value indicates a larger number. The ionization constants as given in *Table M* are

Acetic acid	1.8×10^{-5}
Boric acid	5.8×10^{-10}
Carbonic acid	4.3×10^{-7}
Phosphoric acid	7.5×10^{-3}

Of the above acids, boric acid has the smallest ionization constant and is therefore the weakest acid.

36. **Ans. 1** In the reaction

$$NH_3 + H_2O = NH_4^+ + OH^-$$

the water molecule is losing an H^+ ion or proton, and becoming an hydroxide (OH^-) ion.

$$H_2O \rightarrow H^+ + OH^-$$

Thus water is acting as an acid since it is, by the Brønsted-Lowry Theory, a proton donor. The water molecule, in losing a proton, is donating it to the NH_3 molecule, which becomes the ammonium ion, NH_4^+

$$NH_3 + H^+ \rightarrow NH_4^+$$

The ammonia is acting as a base since it is a proton acceptor.

37. **Ans. 3** The pH is defined as the logarithm of the reciprocal of the hydrogen ion concentration symbolized as $[H^+]$. Thus

$$pH = \log \frac{1}{[H^+]}$$

The concentration of the hydrogen is given as 1×10^{-6} moles per liter. Substituting 1×10^{-6} M for $[H^+]$,

$$pH = \log \frac{1}{(1 \times 10^{-6})}$$
$$pH = \log (1 \times 10^6)$$
$$pH = \log 10^6$$

Since the logarithm of a number is the exponent of the base 10,

$$pH = \log 10^6$$
$$pH = 6$$

38. **Ans. 3** A substance that behaves as an acid or base is amphiprotic (amphoteric). When acting as an acid, the substance is a proton donor. When acting as a base, the substance is a proton acceptor. The way an amphiprotic substance behaves depends upon the chemical environment. In an acid environment, the HSO_4^- ion can act as a base by accepting a proton or H^+ ion to form H_2SO_4:

$$HSO_4^- + H^+ \rightleftarrows H_2SO_4$$
$$\text{base}$$

In a basic environment, HSO_4^- can act as an acid, and lose an H^+ ion to form the SO_4^{-2} ion:

$$HSO_4^- + OH^- \rightleftarrows SO_4^{-2} + H_2O$$

39. **Ans. 2** According to the *Brønsted-Lowry Theory* an acid is a *proton donor*, and a base a *proton acceptor*. Any acid can lose a proton, leaving behind a negative ion. This negative ion can be identified as a base since it will accept a proton and become the acid once more. An acid-base pair that is related by the transfer of a proton is known as a *conjugate acid-base system*.

$$\text{Acid} \rightleftarrows \text{Base} + \text{Proton}$$

Table H, the *Acid-Base Chart*, lists some conjugate acid-base systems such as H_3O^+, H_2O; HSO_4^-, SO_4^{-2}; and NH_3, NH_2^-. In each case each specific pair is related by the transfer of an H^+ ion or proton.

40. **Ans. 1** In general, solutes lower the freezing point and raise the boiling point of the solvent in which the solutes are dissolved. The greater the number of particles present in a given weight of solvent, the greater will be the effect. These particles may be molecules or ions. A 1-molal solution contains 1 mole of solute in 1000 grams of water. Let us examine the number of moles of particles in each of the choices.

Choice (1) $BaCl_2 \rightarrow Ba^{+2} + 2Cl^-$ A mole of $BaCl_2$ dissociates to form 1 mole of Ba^{+2} and 2 moles of Cl^- for a total of 3 moles of particles, here ions.

Choice (2) $C_3H_5(OH)_3$, glycerol, an alcohol, does not dissociate or ionize since it is a nonpolar compound. Thus a 1-molal solution has 1 mole of $C_3H_5(OH)_3$ particles, here molecules.

Choice (3) $NaCl \rightarrow Na^+ + Cl^-$ One mole of $NaCl$ dissociates to form 1 mole of Na^+ and 1 mole of Cl^- ions or a total of 2 moles of particles, here ions.

Choice (4) $CH_3COOH \rightleftarrows H^+ + CH_3COO^-$ One mole of acetic acid will ionize very slightly and therefore contain slightly more than 1 mole of particles, here mostly molecules but some ions.

Thus 1 molal $BaCl_2$ with 3 moles of particles in solution, would have the lowest freezing point of the choices given.

41. Ans. **3** *Molarity* is a measure of concentration and is defined as moles of solute per liter of solution. Hydrochloric acid reacts with sodium hydroxide according to the following neutralization reaction:

$$HCl + NaOH \rightarrow NaCl + HOH$$

Note that one mole of HCl reacts with one mole of NaOH.

Since
$$molarity = \frac{moles}{liters},$$

Then
$$moles = molarity \times liters$$

Because the number of moles of HCl equals the number of moles of NaOH, we can say

$$(molarity \times liters)\ of\ HCl = (molarity \times liters)\ of\ NaOH$$
or
$$M_1 \times l_1 = M_2 \times l_2$$

or changing both sides to milliliters:
$$M_1 \times ml_1 = M_2 \times ml_2$$

Substituting
$$2.0\ M \times 100\ ml = 1.0\ M \times x$$
$$200\ ml = x$$

42. Ans. **1** A *reducing agent* is a particle in a reaction that loses electrons to a second particle. The gain of electrons by this second particle is known as reduction. Thus in the reaction of Cu and S to form CuS

$$Cu^0 + S^0 \rightarrow \overset{+2\ -2}{CuS}$$

the copper atom loses 2 electrons to become the copper (II) ion. We say the Cu^0 is the reducing agent. The S^0 has been reduced to S^{-2} by the gain of electrons.

43. Ans. **4** When calcium chloride, an ionic compound, is melted, it dissociates to give the Ca^{+2} ion and two Cl^- ions.

$$CaCl_2 \rightarrow Ca^{+2} + 2Cl^-$$

During the electrolysis of the fused or molten salt, the mobile ions are attracted to the electrode whose charge is opposite to that of the ion. The calcium ion, since it has a positive charge, is attracted to the negative electrode or cathode. It gains two electrons there and is reduced to form the free calcium atom, Ca^0. Thus the product at the negative cathode is calcium, Ca^0. The half reaction is shown as follows:

$$Ca^{+2} + 2e^- \rightarrow Ca^0$$

44. Ans. **2** First we find the oxidation number of Mn in MnO_2. Each oxygen atom has an oxidation state of -2, and thus 2 oxygen atoms have a

total oxidation state of -4. Since the compound as a whole is neutral, the oxidation state of Mn in MnO_2 is $+4$ $(-4 + 4 = 0)$. Now we find the oxidation number of Mn in $MnCl_2$. Each chlorine atom in $MnCl_2$ has an oxidation state of -1, and thus 2 chlorine atoms have a total oxidation state of -2. Since the compound as a whole is neutral, the oxidation state of Mn in $MnCl_2$ is $+2$ $(-2 + 2 = 0)$. The net equation for the reduction of manganese is

$$Mn^{+4} + 2e^- \rightarrow Mn^{+2}$$

By gaining 2 electrons the manganese has decreased its oxidation state from $+4$ to $+2$.

45. **Ans. 2** *Table L, Standard Oxidation Potentials*, lists the relative activity of certain metallic and nonmetallic particles in aqueous solution. Referring to *Table L*, we see that the position of the chloride ion, Cl^-, is below that of the bromide ion, Br^-. This means that Cl^- has a smaller tendency to lose electrons (be oxidized) than Br^-. This is the same as saying that the chlorine atom (Cl^0) has a greater tendency to gain electrons than the bromine atom (Br^0). In other words, the activity of the nonmetallic halogens *increases* as we go down *Table L* because they tend to gain electrons. This is in direct contrast to the activity of the metals which *decreases* as we go down the *Table* since metals lose electrons. Thus from *Table L* we learn that chlorine is more active than bromine. A chlorine atom will gain the extra electron that the bromide ion has obtained from a metal. Thus the Cl^0 is reduced to the Cl^- ion and the Br^- ion is oxidized back to the Br^0 atom. Since the halogen atoms exist as *diatomic* molecules in the free state, the equation for the reaction would be

$$\overbrace{I^- \text{ (aq)} + \tfrac{1}{2}Cl_2 \text{ (g)} \rightarrow \tfrac{1}{2}I_2 \text{ (s)} + Cl^- \text{ (aq)}}^{+1e^-}$$
$$\underbrace{\phantom{I^- \text{ (aq)} + \tfrac{1}{2}Cl_2 \text{ (g)} \rightarrow \tfrac{1}{2}I_2}}_{-1e^-}$$

46. **Ans. 2** The tendency for a system to undergo chemical change is dependent on 2 factors: (1) the change in energy of the system and (2) the change in entropy of the system. Factor 1: A system always tends to change from a higher energy state to a lower one, thereby releasing energy. This energy is represented mathematically as ΔH. Such a reaction is *exothermic*. For example, when two hydrogen atoms unite to form the hydrogen molecule, the formation of the covalent bond results in a release of energy—an exothermic reaction. Thus a system containing hydrogen atoms would react to form diatomic hydrogen molecules since nature favors a change toward a lower energy state. Factor 2: The other tendency in nature is to change to a system of more disorder and randomness. The degree of disorder is called *entropy*. For example, a solid crystal is more orderly or organized and thus has less entropy than the liquid phase. The tendency toward higher entropy favors the change from ice to water.

47. **Ans. 4** The oxidation number of the chlorine atom in $KClO_4$ is $+7$. Each oxygen atom has an oxidation state of -2; therefore four oxygen atoms

have a total oxidation state of -8; potassium has an oxidation state of $+1$. Since the compound as a whole is neutral, the oxidation state of Cl must be $+7$ $(-8 + 1 + 7 = 0)$.

48. **Ans. 1** $3Cu + XHNO_3 \rightarrow 3Cu(NO_3)_2 + 2NO + 4H_2O$ In the given reaction, the only coefficient needed to balance the equation is X. We can determine the X coefficient of HNO_3 by balancing the number of H's or the number of N's, or the number of O's on the two sides of the equation. In this case it is most convenient to balance the hydrogen atoms. Looking at the right side of the equation there are 2 atoms of hydrogen per molecule of water, and there are 4 molecules of water. Thus the total number of H atoms on the right is (4×2) or 8. Since the number of H atoms on the right side of the equation must equal the number of H atoms on the left side, there must be 8 H on the left side also. Since the only substance the hydrogen can come from on the left is the nitric acid and since each molecule of nitric acid contributes one hydrogen atom, there must be 8 molecules of nitric acid on the left. A check shows 24 atoms of oxygen on each side, and 8 atoms of nitrogen on each side.

49. **Ans. 2** An *unsaturated* hydrocarbon has double or triple bonds. One of these bonds can be broken by an electron-seeking reagent which then can form covalent bonds with the hydrocarbon. This addition of atoms to a compound by the breaking up of a double or triple bond is known as an *addition reaction*. An example of such a reaction is the addition of the electron-seeking (electronegative) halogen, iodine, to the unsaturated ethene molecule. Here a bond representing a pair of electrons breaks open. Each of the two atoms of the diatomic iodine molecule then forms a polar covalent bond with a carbon atom to form a saturated iodine substitution compound of ethane:

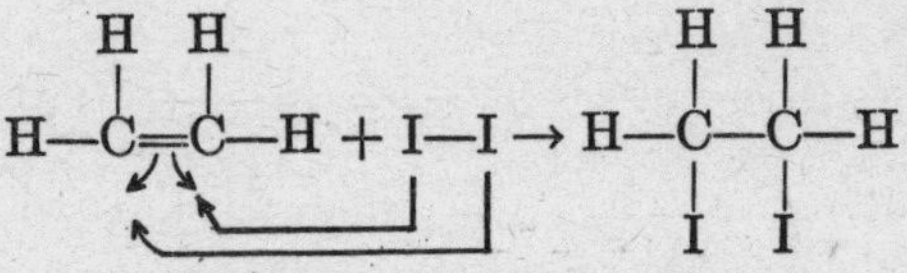

50. **Ans. 1** The organic acids are characterized by the $-COOH$ or carboxyl group. The simplest organic acid is formic acid, $HCOOH$. Two other acids are acetic acid, CH_3COOH and propanoic acid, CH_3CH_2COOH. The carboxyl group can be represented structurally as

51. **Ans. 4** An alcohol is characterized by a hydroxyl group, $-OH$, attached to a hydrocarbon radical, R. Thus the alcohols have the general formula ROH. The only choice satisfying this requirement is CH_3OH, methanol.

52. Ans. **3** When acetic acid reacts with methyl alcohol, the *ester* methyl acetate and water are formed. The process is known as *esterification*. Esters have the general structural formula

$$R—C—O—R$$
$$\underset{O}{\overset{\|}{}}$$

The esterification reaction can be shown structurally as follows:

acetic acid   methyl alcohol   methyl acetate   water

The concentrated sulfuric acid is a dehydrating agent and removes the water as it is formed. Thus, in accordance with Le Chatelier's principle, the reaction proceeds to the right to fill the "void" and relieve the stress of the removal of water.

53. Ans. **1** Temperature is a measure of the average kinetic energy of the molecules of a substance. Thus as the temperature of liquid water increases, so does the average kinetic energy of the water molecules. Those molecules that have a high enough kinetic energy and are near the surface of the liquid escape into the air into the gaseous phase, giving the water a vapor pressure in a closed system. If the temperature is increased, the kinetic energy of the molecules increases. More vapor molecules escape from the water, increasing the vapor pressure. For example at 10.0°C, the equilibrium pressure of the water vapor is 9.2 mm of Hg. At 100.0°C the equilibrium vapor pressure has risen to 760.0 mm of Hg.

54. Ans. **2** Referring to the *Periodic Table* in the *Reference Tables* we see that sodium has three energy levels and the electron configuration 2-8-1. In becoming the Na^+ ion, sodium loses its one valence electron and now has two energy levels with the configuration 2-8. Since the number of occupied energy levels has decreased by one, the atomic radius of the particle has decreased.

55. Ans. **1** As the atomic number increases in any Group, the number of energy levels increases. Therefore the atomic radius is greater, and the pull of the nucleus on the outer valence electrons decreases. Thus the tendency of the atom to lose electrons increases. This tendency is seen in *Table J*. As we go down Group VI *A*, the energy needed to remove the first electron from the valence shell (ionization energy) decreases since the electrons are held more loosely.

56. Ans. **1** Ionization energy is the energy required to remove the most loosely-held electron from the outer shell of an atom in the gaseous phase. The value of the ionization energy increases as we go to the right in *any* Period. This increase is due to the increasing positive charge (more protons)

as we go to the right in the direction of increasing atomic number. A greater positive charge of the nucleus exerts a stronger pull on the valence shell. Thus more energy (ionization energy) must be supplied to remove an electron from the atom.

57. Ans. **1** *Le Chatelier's Principle* states that if a system in equilibrium is subjected to a stress (such as increased temperature or pressure), the equilibrium will be displaced in the direction that relieves the stress. Here the stress is the addition of heat which results in an increase in temperature. We are given an *exothermic* reaction, a reaction that releases heat.

$$2NO\ (g) + O_2\ (g) = 2NO_2\ (g) + 27\ kcal$$

As the reaction proceeds to the right, heat is being given off and the temperature of the system is rising. The addition of more heat will therefore drive the reaction to the left. Such a reversal of this reaction results in the breakup of NO_2 to form O_2 and NO and the absorption of an equivalent amount of heat energy. This endothermic reaction produces a temperature drop, thus relieving the high temperature stress. Since the NO_2 is decomposing as the reaction proceeds to the left, the yield of O_2 increases.

58. Ans. **3** The *heat of reaction* (ΔH) is the heat energy released or absorbed in a chemical reaction. It is indicated by arrow 4 in the potential energy diagram below. The heat of reaction is equal to the difference between the potential energy of the final products as shown by arrow 5 and the potential energy of the initial reactants as shown by arrow 1. *Activation energy* is the energy needed to change the reactants into the activated complex so that a chemical reaction may take place. These complexes are at the top of the curves at A and A'. From here the reaction can "roll downhill" and go forward to form the products, or fall back in a reverse direction to re-form the reactants. A *catalyst* is a substance that changes the activation energy of the reaction by changing the *mechanism* of the reaction and thus the type of complex formed, but it does *not* change the overall reaction itself. *Without a catalyst* the curves of the reaction follow along the line RAP. The activation energy is indicated by arrow 2. *With a catalyst,* less activation energy is needed as shown by arrow 3 or curve RA'P. However the curves start at the same point R (repre-

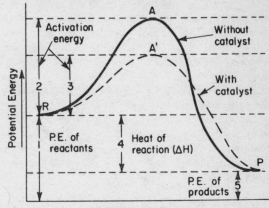

senting the potential energy of the reactants) and end at the same point P (representing the potential energy of the products). There is no change in the heat of reaction (ΔH) with the use of a catalyst. Arrow 4 applies to both curves.

59. Ans. **3** The solubility product constant (K_{sp}) is a measure of the solubility of an ionic solid. In any saturated solution the ions of the solute are in equilibrium with the excess solid phase. Thus an equation for an equilibrium constant can be formulated. For example, in the ionic solid A_2B_3, the dissociation equation is

$$A_2B_3 \rightarrow 2A^{+3} + 3B^{-2}$$

At equilibrium at a definite temperature we have

$$K_{eq} = \frac{[A^{+3}]^2[B^{-2}]^3}{[A_2B_3]}$$

Since $[A_2B_3]$ is also a constant in a saturated solution at a definite temperature, we can combine the K_{eq} and $[A_2B_3]$ to get a new constant called the K_{sp}:

$$K_{sp} = [A^{+3}]^2[B^{-2}]^3$$

This equation tells us that in a saturated solution at constant temperature, the K_{sp} depends only upon the concentration of the ions in solution. As more *solid* $BaSO_4$ is added to a *saturated* solution, no additional $BaSO_4$ can dissolve. If some $BaSO_4$ does dissolve to form the mobile ions, an equal number of mobile ions will precipitate out as solid $BaSO_4$. Thus the concentration of the ions and therefore the K_{sp} remains the same.

60. Ans. **3** A catalyst lowers (or raises) the activation energy of a reaction (see answer to question 58) and thus increases (or decreases) equally the rate of reaction in both the forward and reverse directions. Since the rate of reaction is increased (or decreased) equally in both directions, there is no net change in the equilibrium concentration of either the reactants or the products.

PART TWO

GROUP 1

61. Ans. **2** A phase curve shows the changes in phase of a substance from solid to liquid to gas as the system *absorbs* energy. As heat is applied to a system, *the temperature rises as long as the substance is in the same phase* for the heat increases the average kinetic energy of the molecules. However,

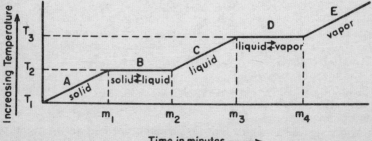

there are two definite points on the temperature scale at which the phase changes—the melting point and the boiling point. At these two temperatures the heat absorbed weakens the bonds between the particles (molecules or ions) and increases the potential energy of the system. *The temperature does not change while the phase of the system is changing.*

Now let us identify the various portions of the curve. We start with a solid at a temperature below its melting point as stated in the question. In section A, the temperature of the solid rises from T_1 to the melting point T_2 in the time interval from 0 to m_1. Then the temperature T_2 remains constant in section B as the solid melts to form the liquid phase from time m_1 to time m_2. Section C is the liquid phase. The temperature rises from T_2 to the boiling point T_3 at time m_3. Section D represents the period during which the liquid is changing to a gas with the temperature remaining at T_3. At time m_4 all the liquid has changed to a gas. Any heat that is added to the gas can result only in an increase in its temperature as shown in section E.

From the discussion above we see that the phase of the portion of the curve labeled C is the liquid phase, since the temperature rises from the melting point T_2 to the boiling point T_3.

62. Ans. 2 From the discussion in answer to question 61, we see that temperature T_2 is the melting point. On the graph, T_2 intersects the curve at section B from time m_1 to time m_2. This temperature remains constant until all the solid has melted. The heat being absorbed by the system increases its potential energy by breaking the bonds that hold the molecules of the solid in a rigid pattern.

63. Ans. 3 A substance normally begins to boil when the equilibrium vapor pressure of the substance equals the atmospheric pressure. At this point, heat energy is absorbed by the particles in the liquid phase to break away from the liquid and escape into the gaseous phase. The temperature will not rise since the added heat is being used to overcome the attractive forces between particles in the liquid phase and thus increase the potential energy of the system. On the given phase diagram, D is the portion of the curve where the liquid phase C is being changed to the gaseous phase E. The beginning of portion D is where the liquid first begins to boil. Reading down the dotted line from this point, we see the boiling commences at time m_3.

64. Ans. 3 The kinetic energy possessed by a substance is the energy of the molecules due to their motion. Not all the molecules of the substance have the same kinetic energy, but the *average* kinetic energy is proportional to the absolute (Kelvin) temperature of the substance. On the phase diagram, the temperature increases as we go up the curve. The portion of the curve at the *highest* temperature is therefore portion E, where all the molecules are in the gaseous phase. Since, in portion E, the temperature is the highest, the molecules must have the highest average kinetic energy.

65. Ans. 4 When a substance is changing from liquid to gas at its boiling temperature, heat energy is absorbed to break intermolecular forces. As

a result the temperature does not rise with addition of heat energy until all the liquid has been changed into a gas. On the diagram section D comes right after section C, the liquid phase. Since during section D the temperature remains constant, this portion must be the time during which the liquid is changing to gas at the boiling point.

66. Ans. 4 Isobutane is an isomer of n-butane. Butane is a hydrocarbon of the alkane series which has the general formula C_nH_{2n+2}. Since butane has 4 carbons, its formula is C_4H_{10}. An *isomer* is a compound with the same molecular formula but different structural formula because of different arrangement of the atoms in the molecule.

The compound n-butane or normal butane is a straight-chain hydrocarbon having the structural formula

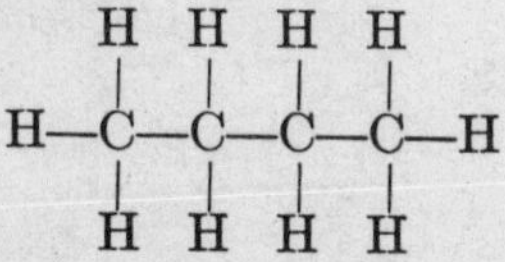

or $CH_3CH_2CH_2CH_3$

Isobutane is a branched chain hydrocarbon with one carbon atom bonded to the center carbon atom of a chain of 3 carbon atoms. Its structural formula can be written as

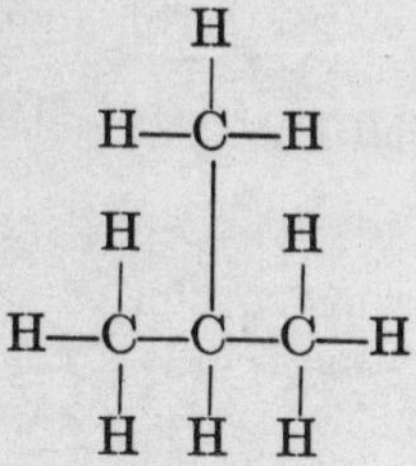

or

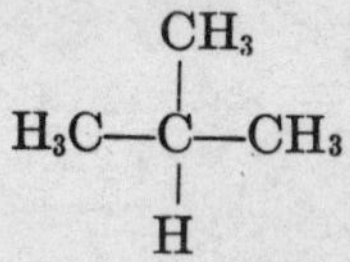

67. Ans. 5 The addition of atoms to a compound by the breaking up of a double or triple bond is known as an *addition reaction*. Ethene (ethylene) C_2H_4, is an unsaturated hydrocarbon with a double bond. The extra bond can break and form covalent bonds with two additional monovalent atoms such as Br or Cl to form a saturated halogen substitution compound.

$$C_2H_4 + Br_2 \rightarrow C_2H_4Br_2$$

The reaction can be written structurally to show the mechanism involved:

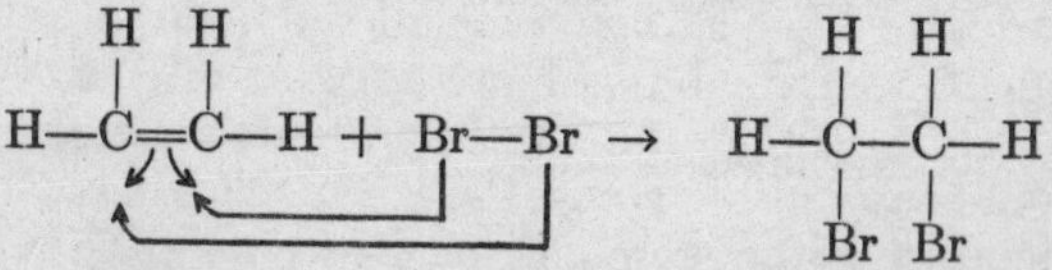

Ethene   Bromine   1,2-dibromoethane
(Ethylene)

68. Ans. 1 C_2H_6 is a *saturated* hydrocarbon, known as ethane, since it satisfies the general formula for members of the alkane series, C_nH_{2n+2}.

A saturated hydrocarbon has only single bonds. Each carbon atom has four other atoms attached to it. The only means by which another atom can enter the compound is to replace one of the atoms already bonded with the carbon. Such a reaction is known as a *substitution reaction*. Thus when bromine reacts with a saturated hydrocarbon such as ethane (C_2H_6) a halogen-substituted compound may be formed containing one bromine atom in place of the hydrogen atom:

$$H-\underset{\underset{H}{|}}{\overset{\overset{H}{|}}{C}}-\underset{\underset{H}{|}}{\overset{\overset{H}{|}}{C}}-\boxed{H + Br}-Br \rightarrow H-\underset{\underset{H}{|}}{\overset{\overset{H}{|}}{C}}-\underset{\underset{H}{|}}{\overset{\overset{H}{|}}{C}}-Br + H-Br$$

    ethane   bromine   bromoethane   hydrogen bromide

69. **Ans.** **6** There are 5 principal groups of hydrocarbons—the alkane, alkene, alkadiene, alkyne and benzene series. The first four groups have the carbon atoms arranged usually in either straight or branched chains. These straight or branched chain hydrocarbons are sometimes referred to as *aliphatic hydrocarbons*. The fifth group is a group known as the *aromatic* hydrocarbons. These are, in general, hydrocarbons arranged in 6-member carbon rings in which all the carbon-carbon bonds are equivalent, having properties intermediate between single and double bonds. The first member in the aromatic series of hydrocarbons is benzene. Its formula is C_6H_6. Its structural formula can be written as follows:

Choice 6 is toluene, a substituted benzene ring, where a methyl ($-CH_3$) group has replaced a hydrogen. Its molecular formula is $C_6H_5CH_3$.

70. **Ans.** **3** An *ester* is a compound formed by the reaction between an organic acid and an alcohol. In this question, CH_3OH, methyl alcohol, is the given reactant. To form an ester, an acid is required to react with this alcohol. Choice 3 is acetic acid. It is an organic acid because of the characteristic carboxyl ($-COOH$) group, which written structurally is

$$-\overset{\overset{\textstyle O}{\|}}{C}\diagdown_{OH}.$$

The equation for the esterification reaction is

$$H-\underset{\underset{H}{|}}{\overset{\overset{H}{|}}{C}}-O\boxed{H + H-O}-\underset{\underset{H}{|}}{\overset{\overset{O}{\|}}{C}}-\overset{\overset{H}{|}}{C}-H \rightarrow H-\underset{\underset{H}{|}}{\overset{\overset{H}{|}}{C}}-O-\underset{\underset{H}{|}}{\overset{\overset{O}{\|}}{C}}-\overset{\overset{H}{|}}{C}-H + H-OH$$

  methanol   acetic acid   methyl acetate   water

GROUP 2

71. Ans. 3 The electron configuration of the neutral atom is given as $1s^2\ 2s^2\ 2p^6\ 3s^2\ 3p^2$. In the symbolism of the electron configuration, the coefficient of the sublevel is the *principal quantum number* and the superscript the number of electrons in that sublevel. We can find the total number of electrons by adding up the number of electrons in all the subshells. The total is $(2 + 2 + 6 + 2 + 2)$ or 14 electrons. Since the atom is neutral, the charge of the nucleus must be equal and opposite to the charge of the electrons. Therefore the nucleus must have a charge of $+14$, or contain 14 protons.

72. Ans. 4 The principal energy levels of an atom can be denoted either by letters (K, L, M, N, O, P, Q) or by number (1, 2, 3, 4, 5, 6, 7). The principal energy level M therefore can be denoted energy level $n = 3$. Referring to the given atom, we see that the 3rd energy level has electrons in the s subshell and p subshell. The coefficient of the subshell indicates the principal energy level of which the subshell is a part. The number of electrons is indicated by the superscript above each subshell. We see that there are 2 electrons in the 3s subshell and 2 electrons in the 3p subshell. Altogether there are $2 + 2$ or 4 electrons in the 3rd energy level or principal energy level M.

73. Ans. 4 The Groups of elements of the *Periodic Table* are its vertical columns. The elements of a Group exhibit similar or related properties because each member of the Group has the same number of electrons in the valence shell or outer energy level. Groups are numbered by Roman numerals to indicate the number of valence electrons. For example, all the elements in Group II A have 2 valence electrons in the outer shell. In the given atom, the outer shell $(3s^2\ 3p^2)$ has $2 + 2$ or 4 electrons. Thus this element would be placed in Group IV A.

74. Ans. 3 An orbital is the region encompassing the probability distribution of an electron of an atom. It is often represented in diagrams as an "electron cloud." Four quantum numbers are needed to describe the most probable location and energy of an electron. The *principal quantum number* or principal energy level ($n = 1, 2, 3$, etc.) gives the average distance of the electron from the nucleus. The *secondary quantum number* or sublevel gives the shapes of the orbital and is designated by the letters s, p, d and f. The *magnetic quantum number* gives the spacial orientation of the various shapes indicated by s, p, d and f. There is one spacial orientation for sublevel s, 3 for sublevel p, 5 for d and 7 for f. Finally we have the *spin quantum number* which gives the direction of the spin of the electron, clockwise or counterclockwise. These quantum numbers can be used to identify any electron of an atom since no two electrons have the same four quantum numbers. Most important is the fact that an orbital can have 0, 1 or 2 electrons; but if there are 2, they must have opposite spins. Although an orbital may hold up to 2 electrons, each orbital in a sublevel must be occupied by one electron with parallel spins before a second electron can be added to complete a pair. A convenient system of orbital notation is the following:

☐ unoccupied orbital ☐↑ orbital with one electron

☐↑↓ orbital with two electrons (opposite spins)

The p sublevel with 3 orbitals would fill up in the following order:

2p⁰ ☐☐☐   2p⁴ ↑↓ ↑ ↑

2p¹ ↑☐☐   2p⁵ ↑↓ ↑↓ ↑

2p² ↑ ↑ ☐   2p⁶ ↑↓ ↑↓ ↑↓

2p³ ↑ ↑ ↑

Let us represent by orbital notation the neutral atom whose given electron configuration is $1s^2\ 2s^2\ 2p^6\ 3s^2\ 3p^2$

Electron configuration: $1s^2$ $2s^2$ $2p^6$ $3s^2$ $3p^2$

↑↓   ↑↓   ↑↓ ↑↓ ↑↓   ↑↓   ↑ ↑ ☐

number of occupied orbitals: 1   1   3   1   2

$1s^2$	1 occupied orbital
$2s^2$	1 occupied orbital
$2p^6$	3 occupied orbitals
$3s^2$	1 occupied orbital
$3p^2$	2 occupied orbitals
Total	8 occupied orbitals

Note that in $3p^2$, only 2 of the three orbitals are occupied and that 2 electrons cannot occupy one orbital in the 3p sublevel until each has at least one electron. Thus the total number of orbitals containing at least 1 electron (the occupied orbitals) is 8.

75. **Ans. 2** Electrons in orbitals nearer the nucleus are at lower energy levels than those in orbitals farther from the nucleus. Thus the 3s subshell, which is closer to the nucleus than the 3p subshell, is at a lower energy level than the 3p. In order for an electron in the 3s subshell to shift to the higher 3p energy level, the atom must absorb energy. When electrons have absorbed energy and have shifted to a higher energy level the atom is said to be in an "excited state."

76. **Ans. 7** A *covalent bond* is the bond formed when two atoms share electrons. When the electrons are shared by 2 atoms of the same element, they are shared equally since the electronegativity difference is zero. The resulting bond is *nonpolar covalent*. When the electrons are shared between atoms of different elements and therefore different electronegativities, they are shared unequally and the resulting bond is *polar coxalent*. In the molecule I_2, the two iodine atoms obviously have the same electronegativity, and therefore they share the electrons equally. The bond between the two iodine atoms is nonpolar covalent. The center of positive and negative charge is midway between the nuclei of the atoms.

77. Ans. **6** *Van der Waals forces* are weak forces of attraction between nonpolar molecules. Van der Waals forces depend on the number of electrons in the molecules and the distance between the molecules. It is believed that these forces are created by the chance distribution of electrons that produce temporary dipole attractions. The greater the number of electrons, the greater will be the attractive forces between molecules. Thus the higher the molecular mass (more protons and therefore more electrons) of a nonpolar molecule, the stronger the van der Waals forces. It is these van der Waals forces between the I_2 molecules that keep the iodine molecules in a rigid crystal pattern of the solid phase. Van der Waals forces between the molecules help to explain why Cl_2 is a gas, Br_2 is a liquid and I_2 is a solid. Going down Group VII *A*, the atomic number increases. Consequently the number of protons increases with an accompanying increase in the number of electrons. As stated above, van der Waals forces increase with an increase in the number of electrons in the molecule. Thus F_2 is a gas of low density. Cl_2 is a "thicker" gas of greater density since the greater van der Waals forces pull the molecules closer together. In the case of Br_2 the van der Waals forces are strong enough to bring the molecules so close that bonds are created to form the liquid phase, bromine. Finally the molecules of the heaviest of the four common halogens, iodine, is held together at the lattice points of the crystal *solid* by the very strong van der Waals forces.

78. Ans. **4** *Hydrogen bonds* are formed between molecules in which hydrogen is covalently bonded to an atom of small atomic radius and high electronegativity such as oxygen and fluorine. The hydrogen atom has a very small share of the electron pair. Acting almost as a bare proton, it is attracted to the electronegative atom of an adjacent molecule. This intermolecular attraction accounts for the abnormally high boiling and freezing (melting) points of pure water. A higher temperature (more heat energy) is needed to overcome the intermolecular attraction created by strong hydrogen bonds. H_2S has weaker hydrogen bonding between molecules because of the decreased electronegativity of the S atom *(Table J)*. This explains why H_2S is a gas at room temperature since the hydrogen bonds are not strong enough to bring the molecules close enough to form the liquid phase. The following table comparing the melting point and boiling point of H_2O (l) and H_2S (g) will clearly show the effect of hydrogen bonding:

	H_2S	H_2O
Melting point (Freezing point):	−85.5°C	0°C
Boiling point:	−60.3°C	100°C

79. Ans. **1** An *ionic bond* is formed by the *transfer* of one or more electrons from an atom of low electronegativity to an atom of high electronegativity. For such a transfer to take place, the electronegativity difference must be 1.7 or more. Active metals such as sodium, lithium and potassium have low electronegativities while active nonmetals such as fluorine have very high electronegativities. Thus sodium fluoride has an electronegativity difference (see *Table J*) of (4.0 − 0.9) or 3.1. This extremely high electronegativity difference indicates a compound possessing a strong ionic bond. The degree of ionic character is about 72%.

80. Ans. 5 *Metallic bonds* occur between atoms that have low ionization energies and therefore readily lose their valence electrons. As a consequence metallic crystals are composed of positive ions in fixed positions of a lattice structure in a sea of freely-moving electrons. These valence electrons have been donated by the metallic atoms and can be said to belong to the crystal as a whole. The delocalization and mobility of the electrons explains the unique electrical conductivity by metals in the solid phase and distinguish the metallic bond from an ionic or covalent bond.

GROUP 3

81. Ans. 7 A substance is a conductor of electricity if it contains freely-moving charged particles. These charged particles may be (1) freely-moving ions found in molten ionic compounds or in solutions of soluble ionic compounds and (2) freely-moving electrons found in most metallic crystals such as those of copper and silver. Potassium bromide is an ionic compound (electronegativity difference 2.8 − 0.8 or 2.0) and in the solid state it has crystals which are composed of positive and negative ions in rigid patterns at the lattice points of the crystal. These ions may vibrate around fixed positions but they are not freely moving because of the electrostatic forces of attraction between the oppositely charged ions. Thus *solid* potassium bromide crystals, even though ionic, do not conduct the electric current. If these solid crystals of KBr are melted, the bonds between the ions are weakened and thus the ions in the molten stage become freely-moving charged particles.

82. Ans. 1 As stated in the answer to problem 81, a conductor of electricity must contain mobile, charged particles. These can be electrons in a metallic crystal or freely-moving ions obtained either by dissolving electrolytes in a polar solvent or by melting an ionic compound. Hydrogen chloride is a polar covalent compound. The valence electrons are shared and thus the compound exists in molecular form rather than ionic. When HCl gas is cooled to −85°C, it condenses to form liquid HCl. The units are still molecules. Since no ions are present, there are no charge carriers in liquid HCl to conduct electricity. An aqueous (water) solution of HCl is known as hydrochloric acid. The polar molecules of HCl react with the polar water molecules to form hydronium ions and chloride ions:

$$HCl + H_2O \rightarrow H_3O^+ + Cl^-$$

The mobile hydronium and chloride ions present in an aqueous solution of HCl act as charge carriers and conduct electricity.

83. Ans. 5 The atoms in metallic crystals such as copper are held together by *metallic bonding*. Metallic bonding occurs between atoms which have low ionization energies and vacant valence orbitals. A low ionization energy indicates a ready tendency for an atom to lose electrons. A metal consists of an arrangement of positive ions, located at the crystal lattice points immersed in a "sea" of mobile electrons, given off by the valence shell of each metal atom. These mobile electrons can be considered as belonging to the

crystal as a whole rather than to individual atoms. The mobility of the electrons distinguishes the metallic bond from an ionic or covalent bond, and accounts for the electrical conductivity of metals in the solid or liquid (mercury) phase.

84.   Ans.   3   Methane has the structural formula

$$\begin{array}{c} \quad\;\; H \\ \quad\;\; | \\ H-C-H \\ \quad\;\; | \\ \quad\;\; H \end{array}$$

The electronegativity difference between C and H is 2.5 − 2.1 or 0.4. Thus each of the four bonds are weakly polar covalent. However the hydrogen atoms are arranged symmetrically about the carbon atom. The center of positive charge coincides with the center of negative charge. Even though the bonds are polar covalent the molecule as a whole is nonpolar covalent.

85.   Ans.   4   Network bonds are covalent bonds that link the atoms into a network which extends throughout the substance. There is an absence of the simple discrete particles such as molecules or ions. The result is a *network solid* or *macromolecule*. Network solids are usually hard, have extremely high melting points, and are poor conductors of heat and electricity. SiO_2, silicon dioxide, consists of silicon atoms covalently bonded to oxygen atoms which are in turn bonded to other silicon atoms, forming a network solid

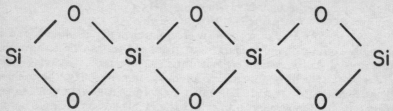

86.   Ans.   4   A metallic element is an element whose atoms tend to lose electrons. Atoms with a larger atomic radius will lose electrons more easily, since the nuclear attraction decreases with increasing distance. Looking at the *Periodic Table* we see that Sn, tin, has the largest atomic radius within Group IV A because it has the greatest number of energy levels of the given choices. Since Sn has the largest atomic radius, it loses electrons the most readily and thus is the most metallic element of all the choices. The metallic nature of Sn is shown by the fact that it possesses a luster, conducts heat and electricity, and forms basic solutions.

87.   Ans.   3   *Transition elements* are elements whose inner subshells are partially filled or those elements whose 2 outermost shells may be involved in chemical reactions. Transition elements are found in the *B* Groups of the *Periodic Table*. Ag, silver, is in Group I *B* and is therefore a transition element. Silver, like copper and gold, has one electron in its valence shell and

thus has one oxidation state of +1. Although the next to the outermost energy level is complete with 18 electrons, the d electrons of this shell have about the same energy level as the outer s shell. Thus one or two electrons can be removed from the next to the outermost level of 18 electrons giving additional oxidation states of +2 and +3. A silver oxidation state of +2 has been accomplished but only with extremely powerful oxidizing agents. Since an inner shell is involved in a chemical reaction, however, silver is a transition element along with its other two Group I B members, gold and copper.

88. Ans. 4 Referring to the key ou the *Periodic Table*, we note that the covalent atomic radius, expressed in *Ångstrom* units, (Å) is given directly below the symbol of the element. An Ångstrom unit is equal to 10^{-8} cm., an extremely small unit of length. The *Periodic Table* tells us that of all the elements in Group V *A*, nitrogen, N, has the smallest atomic radius, 0.70 Å. The reason is obvious. Of the elements listed, nitrogen has the least number of electron shells. It is in Period 2 with two energy levels. The smaller number of shells means that the atom has smaller atomic radius.

89. Ans. 2 Elements in Group O are the monatomic noble gases. Having a complete outer shell, the electron configurations are stable and thus these elements are relatively inert, having the least chemical reactivity of all the elements. Some of the noble gases do experience some chemical activity since krypton, xenon and radon react under certain conditions with fluorine and oxygen to form compounds.

90. Ans. 4 Ionization energy is the energy measured in electron volts needed to remove the most loosely held electron from an atom of an element in the gaseous phase. *Table J* tells us that the ionization energy decreases as we go to the left and down. Cs and Fr have the lowest ionization energies of all the elements, with a value of 3.9 e.v. for Cs and perhaps a little less for Fr. These lower ionization energies can be explained by the greater distance of the valence shell from the nucleus because of the many energy levels and because in Group I *A*, Cs and Fr have the least positive nuclear charge of any of the elements in their respective Periods. Of the elements listed, Na has the smallest ionization energy, having a value of 0.9 e.v. Its position in Group I *A* gives it the fewest number of protons in the nucleus of all the elements in Period 3. This smaller nuclear charge means a weaker hold on the valence electrons of sodium.

GROUP 4

91. Ans. 3 The heat of reaction (ΔH) is the heat energy released or absorbed in a chemical reaction. ΔH represents the difference between the heat content (H) of the products and the heat content of the reactants. Thus we get the formula

$$\Delta H = H_{products} - H_{reactants}$$

The heat content of a substance measures the internal energy that is stored during the formation of the substance. Thus the heat content is a form of potential energy. On the graph shown, the heat content of the products is

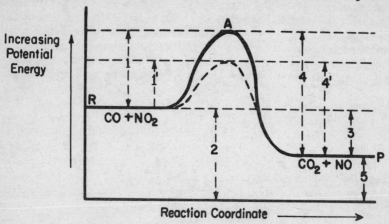

$$CO \text{ (g)} + NO_2 \text{ (g)} = CO_2 \text{ (g)} + NO \text{ (g)} + 54 \text{ kcal}$$

shown by arrow 5 and the heat content of the reactants is shown by arrow 2. The heat of reaction is $H_P - H_R$ as shown by the arrow marked 3. Note that the energy content of the products at P is less than the energy content of the reactants at R. In other words the system has released or lost energy. This indicates that the reaction shown by the graph is an *exothermic* one. In the formula $\Delta H = H_P - H_R$, ΔH is negative for an exothermic reaction since H_P has a smaller value than H_R. Chemists have arbitrarily established the formula so that a *negative* ΔH indicates an exothermic reaction since an exothermic reaction releases energy and *decreases* the internal energy of the system. Since the energy of the system is less than it was originally, the sign of ΔH is negative.

NOTE: *If the heat content of the products (H_P) were greater than the heat content of the reactants (H_R), then ΔH would be positive and the reaction an endothermic one.*

92. Ans. **1** A chemical reaction takes place if there is an effective collision between two species, for example two molecules. To be effective the colliding molecules must be able to supply enough energy to break the bonds between the atoms of the molecules so that the atoms can become reactive and form new bonds and new molecular compounds. The energy that supplies the initial boost to raise the energy content of the reactants (R) to a point (A) where a reaction can take place is termed *activation energy*. On the graph the activation energy is shown by arrow 1 which extends a vertical distance from R to A. When the colliding molecules possess this activation energy, an intermediate structure results called the *activated complex*. This is located at the top of the curve at A. The activated complex has the maximum heat content of the system. The life of the activated complex is an extremely short one. It is during this brief interval that both molecules have pene-

trated each other's electron clouds. With old bonds breaking and new bonds forming, the molecular complex shows partial bonding of reactants and products simultaneously. The short-lived activated complex immediately breaks apart, either continuing on to form the products or going back to form the initial reactants. This property of an activated complex can be shown in the reaction between molecules of AB and CD:

$$AB + CD = \begin{array}{c} A-B \\ \times \\ C-D \end{array} = AD + CB$$

$$\text{reactants} = \text{activated} = \text{products}$$
$$\text{complex}$$

93. Ans. 3 When an accelerator catalyst is added to a reaction, it changes the pathway of the reaction and lowers the activation energy. The activated complex that is formed at the top of the new curve has a lower potential energy content. With a lower energy requirement at the peak the activation energy required in the forward reaction from R to P is lowered from the larger value without the catalyst shown by arrow 1 to a smaller value with the catalyst shown by arrow 1'. In the reverse reaction from P to R, the activation energy required is lowered from the larger value without the catalyst shown by arrow 4 to the smaller value with the catalyst shown by arrow 4'. Thus the introduction of a catalyst changes the forward and reverse activation energies shown by arrows 1 and 4.

94. Ans. 4 The activation energy for a reverse reaction is the minimum energy needed by the products CO_2 and NO to start reacting to form the initial reactants, CO and NO_2. On the diagram, the activation energy of the reverse reaction is the energy needed to get CO_2 and NO up to the top of the curve where the activated complex is formed. As stated above in the answer to question 93, this is arrow 4.

95. Ans. 4 Because the products, CO_2 and NO, are at a lower potential energy level than the initial reactants, CO and NO_2, energy is liberated, and the reaction is exothermic. In the given reaction,

$$CO \ (g) + NO_2 \ (g) = CO_2 \ (g) + NO \ (g) + 54 \ kcal$$

1 mole of CO and 1 mole of NO_2 react to form the products and 54 kcal of heat energy. This means that 54 kcal of energy are liberated when one mole of NO_2 is consumed. Since two moles of NO_2 are being consumed, (2×54) or 108 kcal of heat energy are liberated.

96. Ans. 1 Le Chatelier's principle states that if a system in equilibrium is subjected to a stress (such as increased temperature or pressure), the equilibrium will be displaced in the direction that relieves the stress. Here the stress is an increase in temperature. We are given an exothermic reaction, a reaction that releases 22 kcal of heat.

$$N_2 + 3H_2 = 2NH_3 + 22 \ kcal.$$

As the reaction proceeds to the right, heat is being given off and the temperature of the system is rising. The addition of more heat will therefore drive the reaction to the left. Such a reversal of this reaction results in the breakup of NH_3 into H_2 and N_2 accompanied by the absorption of an equivalent amount of heat energy. This endothermic reaction produces a temperature drop, thus relieving the high temperature stress. Since the NH_3 is decomposing as the reaction proceeds to the left, the concentration of NH_3 at the new equilibrium is less than its orignal concentration.

Note: It should be pointed out that the rates of all reactions, both endothermic and exothermic, are increased by an increase in temperature, since the kinetic energy of the molecules and thus the number of effective collisions increase. However, the rates of the opposing reactions are increased unequally, resulting in a shift in the equilibrium and in changed concentrations of products and reactants.

97. Ans. 1 In accordance with Le Chatelier's principle, if the concentration stress is changed, the reaction will go in the direction which results in a relief of the stress. In the reaction

$$N_2 + 3H_2 = 2NH_3$$

we are told that the concentration of the hydrogen is being reduced. This means that the ratio of the concentration of the product NH_3 as compared to the reduced concentrations of the reactants has increased. Thus the removal of H_2 drives the reaction to the left which lowers the concentration of NH_3 and increases the concentration of H_2 and N_2. A new equilibrium is reached with a greater percentage of N_2 and a smaller percentage of NH_3 in the new equilibrium.

The same answer can be reasoned through by using the kinetic molecular theory. If hydrogen is removed, the frequency of effective collisions between H_2 and N_2 decreases, and thus the forward rate of reaction is decreased. However, the reverse rate still continues as before, and the concentrations of H_2 and N_2 are thus increased.

98. Ans. 2 In a system at equilibrium, a catalyst increases the rate of *both the forward and reverse reactions equally*, and thus produces no net change in the equilibrium concentrations. Thus the equilibrium concentrations of H_2, N_2 and NH_3 remain the same. A catalyst may cause equilibrium to be reached more quickly, but it does not affect the point at which equilibrium is reached. According to chemical kinetics, an accelerator catalyst lowers the *activation energy*, the minimum energy needed to get the reacting particles to react by establishing an activated complex. By lowering the activation energy, the energy barrier is lowered an equal amount for both the forward and reverse reaction.

99. Ans. 2 Le Chatelier's principle states that if a system in equilibrium is subjected to a stress, the equilibrium will be displaced in the direction that relieves the stress. Here the stress is the addition of nitrogen, which means that the N_2 concentration is increased. In order to relieve the stress of increased concentration, the equilibrium must shift to the right. The amount

of N_2 is thereby reduced, and the stress is relieved. Since the reaction is displaced in the forward direction, more NH_3 will be produced, and thus the new equilibrium concentration of NH_3 is more than its original concentration.

According to chemical kinetics, adding N_2 will increase the number of effective collisions between N_2 and H_2 molecules, since the N_2 concentration has been increased. The number of NH_3 molecules is thereby increased as a result. Thus, the new equilibrium concentration of NH_3 is more than its original concentration.

100. Ans. 1 Using Le Chatelier's principle we can expect that a stress of increased pressure will displace the equilibrium in the direction that decreases the pressure. The pressure in a closed system is dependent upon the volume of the gases in the container. Volumes are proportional to the coefficients of the molecules as shown in the equation of the reaction. Here the equation is

$$N_2 + 3H_2 = 2NH_3 + 22 \text{ kcal}$$

The reactants N_2 and $3H_2$ in the container have $1 + 3$ or 4 volumes. The product $2NH_3$ has 2 volumes. Thus the relief of the pressure stress is on the right where there are fewer molecules. When pressure is applied to the system, the equilibrium point will be shifted toward the NH_3 at the right. Thus the number of moles of NH_3 increases.

According to the kinetic molecular theory, an increased pressure in effect increases the concentration of the molecules per unit volume. The result is more effective collisions in the reaction going in the direction that decreases the molecular concentration.

GROUP 5

101. Ans. 4 A Brønsted-Lowry base is a proton (H^+ ion) acceptor. Thus the strongest base would be the substance that most readily accepts protons. Referring to *Table H, Acid-Base Chart*, we see that in the right column (conjugate base) the base strength decreases as we read up the column. The strongest base is NH_2^- at the bottom of the column. The amine ion accepts a proton to form ammonia, NH_3:

$$NH_2^- + H^+ \rightleftarrows NH_3$$

The longer arrow to the right indicates that the forward reaction is favored.

102. Ans. 6 The pH of a solution measures the concentration of H^+ ions in a solution. The lower the pH, the higher the H^+ concentration. An aqueous solution that is acidic has a high H^+ concentration and thus a low pH (below 7). A neutral aqueous solution has an equal number of H^+ and OH^- ions and has a pH of 7. A basic solution has a low H^+ concentration (high OH^- concentration) and thus a pH above 7.

Sodium carbonate is a salt produced by the action of weakly-ionized carbonic acid and highly-dissociated sodium hydroxide, a strong base, as shown by *Table M, Ionization Constants of Acids and Bases.* Salts produced from either weak acids or weak bases will hydrolyze when placed in water. In the solution of sodium carbonate there are Na^+ ions, CO_3^{-2} ions and H_2O molecules. According to the Brønsted-Lowry Theory, the carbonate ion is a strong base since it shows a very great tendency to gain protons. Here the carbonate ion gains a proton from the water molecule to form the bicarbonate ion and the hydroxide ion:

$$CO_3^{-2} + H_2O = HCO_3^- + OH^-$$

The hydroxide ions remain in solution since sodium hydroxide remains completely dissociated. Since the CO_3^{-2} ion accepts an H^+ ion, the H^+ concentration decreases. Now that there are more OH^- ions than H^+ ions, the solution is basic and the pH is greater than 7

103. Ans. 2 A substance that acts as either an acid or a base depending on its chemical environment is called an *amphoteric* (*amphiprotic*) substance. It acts as a weak base in the presence of a strong acid. According to the Brønsted-Lowry Theory, an acid is a proton donor and a base is a proton acceptor. Thus a species (molecule or ion) that can gain a proton and also lose a proton is amphoteric.

Water can donate a proton, thus acting as an acid, leaving the hydroxide ion, OH^-. Water can accept a proton, thus acting as a base, forming the hydronium ion, H_3O^+.

$$H_2O + H_2O \quad = \quad H_3O^+ + OH^-$$

as a base

$+H^+$

as an acid

$-H^+$

104. Ans. 7 The gram-equivalent mass of an acid or base is equal to the mass of that substance that is equivalent to (will react with or replace) 1 mole of H^+ ions.

Assuming 100% ionization, 1 molecule of H_3PO_4 produces 3 H^+ ions:

$$H_3PO_4 \rightarrow 3H^+ + PO_4^{-3}$$

Thus 1 mole of H_3PO_4 produces 3 moles of H^+ ions. Therefore only $\frac{1}{3}$ of a mole of H_3PO_4 is needed to produce 1 mole of H^+ ions. Since the gram-equivalent is the mass that is equivalent to 1 mole of H^+ ions, the gram-equivalent of H_3PO_4 is equal to $\frac{1}{3}$ of a mole of H_3PO_4.

ALTERNATE METHOD:

We can determine a gram-equivalent mass by use of the formula

$$\text{gram-equivalent mass} = \frac{\text{gram-molecular mass}}{\text{total positive or negative valence}}$$

Since the total positive valence of H_3PO_4 is $+3$, we have

$$\text{gram-equivalent mass} = \frac{\text{gram-molecular mass}}{3} \quad \text{or}$$

$\frac{1}{3}$ gram-molecular mass or $\frac{1}{3}$ mole

105. Ans. 5 A Brønsted-Lowry acid is a proton donor. The strongest acid is the substance that most readily donates protons. Referring to *Table H*,

Acid-Base Chart in the *Reference Tables*, we see under the column to the left entitled "Conjugate Acid" that acid strength decreases going from top to bottom. The strongest acid, HCl, is at the top of the column. The action of the HCl as a Brønsted acid is shown by the equation:

$$HCl + H_2O \longrightarrow H_3O^+ + Cl^-$$

$$\llcorner \qquad -H^+ \qquad \lrcorner$$

as an acid

106. **Ans. 3** *Table L (Standard Oxidation Potentials)* gives a list of the more common metals and their tendency to lose electrons (be oxidized). The most active metals have the greatest tendency to lose electrons and are at the top of the chart. They possess the highest oxidizing potentials. An active metal will replace a less active one from a solution of its salt. *Table L* tells us that Cu loses electrons more readily than Ag. Copper thus will lose electrons to the silver and replace it. This can be shown in the following redox equation:

$$Cu^0 (s) + 2Ag^+ (aq) \rightarrow 2Ag^0 (s) + Cu^{+2} (aq)$$

107. **Ans. 1** A reducing agent loses electrons and is therefore itself oxidized. The strongest reducing agent must therefore have the highest oxidation potential on *Table L*. Referring to *Table L*, we see that lithium (Li) is at the top of the Table and therefore is the best reducing agent. The E^0 for the reaction, $Li = Li + e^-$, is +3.02 volts.

108. **Ans. 4** The element that reduces Pb^{+2} to Pb must be above Pb on *Table L*. However, the element must be below Mg since the question states that the element cannot reduce Mg^{+2} to Mg. Zn is the only choice that lies between Pb and Mg on *Table L*. Zinc will reduce Pb^{+2} to Pb according to the following equation:

$$Zn + Pb^{+2} \rightarrow Zn^{+2} + Pb$$

109. **Ans. 2** Oxidation potentials on *Table L* can be used to determine whether a specific redox reaction will take place *spontaneously*. In the reaction

$$2Ag + 2H^+ \rightarrow 2Ag^+ + H_2$$

silver is below hydrogen in *Table L* and cannot replace the H^+ ion from solution. Silver shows less of a tendency to lose electrons than hydrogen:

For hydrogen: $E^0 = 0.00$ for the reaction $H_2 = 2H^+ + 2e^-$
For silver: $E^0 = -0.80$ for the reaction $Ag = Ag^+ + e^-$

Thus hydrogen will remain in its oxidized H^+ form.

110. **Ans. 1** We are given the reaction

$$2Al + 3Fe^{+2} \rightarrow 2Al^{+3} + 3Fe$$

This is an oxidation-reduction reaction in which the Al^0 atom is oxidized to the Al^{+3} ion and the Fe^{+2} ion is reduced to the Fe^0 atom. The potential (E^0) of the overall reaction can be found by combining the E^0 of the oxidation half-reaction and the E^0 of the reduction half-reaction.

From *Table L* we find that

(1) Oxidation: $Al^0 = Al^{+3} + 3e^-$; $E^0 = 1.66$ volts
(2) Oxidation: $Fe^0 = Fe^{+2} + 2e^-$; $E^0 = 0.44$ volts

Equation (2) can be reversed and made the desired reduction half-reaction. In doing so, the E^0 must change its sign since reduction is the opposite of oxidation. Thus equation 2 becomes:

(3) Reduction: $Fe^{+2} + 2e^- = Fe^0$; $E^0 = -0.44$ volts

In any oxidation-reduction reaction the electrons gained must equal the electrons lost. Thus we multiply equation

(1) by 2 and equation (3) by 3, so that 6 electrons are lost in equation (1) and gained in equation (3). It is most important to note that the E^0 *is constant* and does not depend on the number of ions or atoms oxidized or reduced. The balanced equations are

(4) Oxidation: $2Al = 2Al^{+3} + 6e^-$; $E^0 = 1.66$ volts
(5) Reduction: $3Fe^{+2} + 6e^- = 3Fe^0$; $E^0 = -0.44$ volts

We add the two equations. Note the electrons lost and gained are equal and cancel out. The equation for the overall reaction is

$$2Al^0 + 3Fe^{+2} \rightarrow 2Al^{+3} + 3Fe^0; E^0 = 1.66 - 0.44 = 1.22 \text{ volts}$$

GROUP 6

111. Ans. 2 A mole is a gram-molecular mass of a substance. We can find the number of moles a substance contains by dividing the mass of the substance by the mass of 1 mole.

$$\text{Moles} = \frac{\text{grams}}{\text{g. mol. mass}}$$

Therefore, moles of $Al_2O_3 = \dfrac{\text{grams of } Al_2O,}{\text{g. mol. mass of } Al_2O_3}$

In order to find the g. molecular mass of Al_2O_3 we add up the atomic masses of the atoms in the compound:

$$\text{Molecular mass of } Al_2O_3$$

$$2 \text{ Al} = 2 \times 27 = 54$$
$$\underline{3 \text{ O} = 3 \times 16 = 48}$$
$$\text{g. mol. mass of } Al_2O_3 = 102 \text{ grams}$$

$$\text{moles of } Al_2O_3 = \frac{204 \text{ grams}}{102 \dfrac{\text{grams}}{\text{mole}}}$$

$$= 2.0 \text{ moles of } Al_2O_3$$

The answer expressed to 2 significant figures is 2.0 moles. Note that the number of moles depends on the mass of Al_2O_3. The equation has no bearing on the calculation.

112. Ans. 4 The equation tells us that when two moles of Al_2O_3 react they form 4 moles of Al atoms. In the answer to question 111 we found that

there were actually 2.0 moles of Al_2O_3 that decomposed. Thus the number of moles of aluminum produced is 4.0 moles.

113. Ans. 3 The *volumes* of *gases* that react or are formed in a chemical reaction at constant temperature and pressure are proportional to the number of *moles* as shown by the numerical coefficients in the equation of that reaction. The reaction is given as

$$C_8H_{16} \text{ (g)} + 12 \text{ } O_2 \text{ (g)} \rightarrow 8CO_2 \text{ (g)} + 8H_2O \text{ (g)}$$

We are concerned with two substances, C_8H_{16} and H_2O.

Actual volumes:　　　　10 liters　　　　　　x
　　　　　　　　　　　C_8H_{16}　　$\rightarrow$　　　$8H_2O$
Equation volumes:　1 molar volume　8 molar volumes

Note that according to the equation, 1 molar volume of C_8H_{16} reacts to form 8 molar volumes of H_2O. Thus 10 liters of C_8H_{16} react to form 8×10 or 80 liters of H_2O.

114. Ans. 4 In any reaction the actual number of moles of any reactants or products is proportional to the equation number of moles of these reactants or products. The equation of the reaction is given as:

$$C_8H_{16} + 12 \text{ } O_2 \rightarrow 8CO_2 + 8H_2O$$

We are concerned with two substances only, C_8H_{16} and CO_2. We are given the mass of C_8H_{16} and asked to find the volume of CO_2. The equation states that 1 mole of C_8H_{16} reacts to from 8 moles of CO_2. The other reactants and products are not involved in this problem. We must first find the gram-molecular mass of C_8H_{16}:

Molecular mass of C_8H_{16}:
$$8 \text{ C} = 8 \times 12 = 96$$
$$\underline{16 \text{ H} = 16 \times 1 = 16}$$
g. mol. mass of $C_8H_{16} = 112$ grams

Thus we see that the given mass of 112 grams is exactly 1.00 mole of C_8H_{16}. The number of moles of CO_2 produced is 8×1.00 or 8.00 moles of CO_2. Since one mole or gram-molecular mass of any gas occupies 22.4 liters, 8.00 moles of CO_2 would have a mass of 8.00×22.4 or 179.2 liters or 179 liters correct to 3 significant figures.

115. Ans. 2 An *empirical formula* represents the simplest ratio in which atoms combine to form a compound. It is sometimes referred to as the simplest formula. In order to find the empirical formula, assign an arbitrary value, say 100 grams, for the mass of the compound.
Step 1: Multiply the mass by the given percents to find the mass of each element in the compound.

Mass of carbon $= .853 \times 100$ grams $= 85.3$ grams of carbon
Mass of hydrogen $= .147 \times 100$ grams $= 14.7$ grams of hydrogen

Step 2: Divide each gram mass by the gram-atomic mass of the corresponding element to find the number of gram-atoms of each element.

(A gram-atom of an element contains a mole or 6.02×10^{23} atoms of the element.)

G. atoms of C = 85.3 grams $\div$ 12 grams/g. atom = 7.1 g. atoms

G. atoms of H = 14.7 grams $\div$ 1 gram/g. atom = 14.7 g. atoms

The ratio of number of atoms of C to the number of atoms of H in the compound is 7.1 g. atoms:14.7 gram atoms or 7.1:14.7.

Step 3: Reduce the ratio 7.1:14.7 by dividing both sides of the ratio by 7.1:

$$7.1 \div 7.1 = 1; \ 14.7 \div 7.1 = 2.07 = 2$$

The reduced ratio of 1:2 represents the simplest ratio of the number of C and H atoms in the formula. Thus the required empirical formula is CH_2.

116.   Ans. **2**   A mole or a gram-molecular mass of a gas occupies 22.4 liters at S.T.P. To determine the gram-molecular mass of the compound, we must find the mass of 22.4 liters of the compound. We are given that the density of the gas is 1.25 grams per liter. That means that one liter of the gas has a mass of 1.25 grams. Therefore 22.4 liters of the gas would have a mass of 22.4×1.25 or 28.0 grams. Thus the molecular mass of the compound is 28 grams.

ALTERNATE METHOD:

The molecular mass of a compound can be determined from the gas density at S.T.P. Since density is mass per unit volume, we can write

$$\text{density} = \frac{\text{g. mol. mass}}{\text{mole volume}}$$

$$1.25 \ \frac{\text{g.}}{\text{l.}} = \frac{\text{g. mol. mass}}{22.4 \ \text{l./mole}}$$

Cross-multiplying, we get

$$\text{g. mol. mass} = 28 \ \frac{\text{g.}}{\text{mole}}$$

117.   Ans. **2**   The molecular formula of a compound shows the actual number of atoms of each element in the compound. The empirical or simplest formula may or may not be the molecular formula. We know from the answer to question 115 that the empirical formula of the hydrocarbon is CH_2. But any multiple of CH_2 such as C_2H_4, C_3H_6 or C_4H_{12} would still contain the same ratio of C atoms to H atoms. In other words the true molecular formula is (empirical formula)$_x$: or in this case $(CH_2)_x$; where x is the correct multiple we are seeking.

We can find x if we know the empirical-formula mass and molecular mass of the compound.

Empirical formula mass of $CH_2 = 1 \times 12 + 2 \times 1 = 14$

Molecular mass of $(CH_2)_x = 28.0$ (see answer to question 116)

Since (empirical formula mass)$_x$ = molecular mass, we have

$$(14)x = 28.0$$
$$x = 2.0$$

Since the multiple is 2, $(CH_2)_x$ becomes $(CH_2)_2$ or C_2H_4.

Examination June, 1966 Chemistry (Experimental)

PART ONE

DIRECTIONS (1–60): *For each statement or question, write in the space provided the* number *preceding the word or expression that, of those given, best completes the statement or answers the question.* [60]

1. The pressure on 10 liters of a gas at S.T.P. is changed to 2 atmospheres, temperature remaining constant. The new volume is   (1) 5 liters (2) 10 liters (3) 15 liters (4) 20 liters   1........

2. What is the number of molecules in 16.0 grams of oxygen gas?   (1) 6.02×10^{23} (2) $\dfrac{6.02 \times 10^{23}}{2}$ (3) $2(6.02 \times 10^{23})$ (4) $\dfrac{6.02 \times 10^{23}}{4}$ 2........

3. At what temperature is the vapor pressure of a liquid equal to the prevailing atmospheric pressure?   (1) freezing point (2) boiling point (3) melting point (4) sublimation point   3........

4. When 20 grams of water cools from 30°C. to 20°C., the amount of heat given off is   (1) 600 cal.   (2) 500 cal. (3) 400 cal. (4) 200 cal.   4........

5. What is the number of orbitals that make up any p sublevel? (1) 1 (2) 2 (3) 3 (4) 5   5........

6. Which particle has a mass of approximately 1 mass unit and a unit positive charge?   (1) neutron (2) proton (3) electron (4) alpha particle   6........

7. When a radioactive nucleus emits a beta particle, the atom's (1) mass number is increased by 1   (2) mass number is decreased by 1 (3) atomic number is increased by 1 (4) atomic number is decreased by 1   7........

8. Given the electron configuration $1s^2\ 2s^2\ 2p^6\ 3s^2\ 3p^4$, what is the number of valence electrons?   (1) 1   (2) 2   (3) 6   (4) 4   8........

9. The maximum number of electrons in the 3d sublevel is (1) 6 (2) 2 (3) 8 (4) 10   9........

10. Which two particles have the same electronic configuration? (1) Cl^+ and F^- (2) Cl^- and S^{-2} (3) Cl^- and Ne   (4) Cl^- and K   10........

11. Which furnishes evidence that electrons in atoms are in

definite energy levels?   (1) atomic radii   (2) mass defects
(3) electronegativities   (4) spectral lines   11.........

12. Which molecule is *not* a dipole?   (1) HBr (2) H_2O
(3) NH_3 (4) CCl_4 12.........

13. Hydrogen bonds are formed between molecules in which
hydrogen is covalently bonded to an element whose atomic radius
and electronegativity, respectively, are   (1) large and low
(2) large and high (3) small and high (4) small and low   13.........

14. When two hydrogen atoms combine to form a hydrogen
molecule, energy is   (1) absorbed (2) released (3) both
absorbed and released (4) neither absorbed nor released   14.........

15. Which electron-dot formula is a reasonable representation
for the water molecule?

(1) $H \!:\! \overset{..}{\underset{..}{O}} \!:\! H$ (3) $H \overset{..}{\underset{O}{:}} H$

(2) $\overset{..}{\underset{..}{O}}$ with H ... H (4) $H \!:\! H \!:\! \overset{..}{\underset{..}{O}} \!:\!$

15.........

16. In which is there coordinate covalent bonding?   (1) CO_2
(2) NH_4 (3) H_2O (4) HCl   16.........

17. Which compound has the greatest ionic character?
(1) LiI (2) NaCl (3) KBr (4) RbF   17.........

18. The attraction that *nonpolar* molecules have for each other
is primarily caused by   (1) hydrogen bonding (2) electronegativity differences (3) high ionization energy (4) van der
Waals forces   18.........

19. Which halogen can have only a *negative* oxidation state in
compounds?   (1) fluorine   (2) chlorine   (3) bromine
(4) iodine   19.........

20. Which Group in the *Periodic Table* contains an element
whose hydroxide is amphiprotic (amphoteric)?   (1) III A
(2) O (3) VII A (4) VI A   20.........

21. If X represents an element of Group III A, what is the general formula for its oxide?   (1) X_3O_4 (2) X_3O_2 (3) X_5O_2
(4) X_2O_3 21.........

22. The atomic number of a transition element in Period 4 is
(1) 19 (2) 22 (3) 33 (4) 35   22.........

23. In Period 3, as the atomic numbers increase, the pattern
according to which the properties of the elements change is

(1) metal → metalloid → nonmetal → noble gas (2) metal → nonmetal → noble gas → metalloid (3) nonmetal → metalloid → metal → noble gas (4) nonmetal → metal → noble gas → metalloid   23........

24. Which represents a mole?   (1) 16 grams of sulfur (2) 16 grams of oxygen gas (3) 6.02×10^{23} molecules of helium (4) 22.4 liters of sodium   24........

25. A compound contains carbon and hydrogen in the mole ratio 1:2. The molecular mass of this compound could be   (1) 42 (2) 21 (3) 15 (4) 12   25........

26. When 20.0 grams of NaOH is dissolved in 500. ml. of solution, the concentration of this solution is   (1) 1.0 M (2) 0.50 M (3) 20 M (4) 4.0 M   26........

27. How many liters of oxygen will combine with 3.0 liters of hydrogen to produce water according to the equation below?

$$2H_2(g) + O_2(g) = 2H_2O(g)$$

(1) 11.2 (2) 6.0 (3) 3.0 (4) 1.5   27........

28. In the reaction $Cu(s) + 2Ag^+(aq) = Cu^{+2}(aq) + 2Ag(s)$, how many moles of copper are consumed when 0.02 mole of silver is formed?   (1) 0.01 (2) 0.02 (3) 0.04 (4) 0.20   28........

29. One hundred ml. of H_2O is saturated with KNO_3 at 10°C. What is the approximate number of additional grams of KNO_3 required to saturate this solution at 50°C.?   (1) 10 (2) 40 (3) 60 (4) 83   29........

30. A catalyst can increase the rate of a chemical reaction by (1) increasing the value of the equilibrium constant (2) increasing the energy of the products (3) decreasing the energy of the products (4) decreasing the required activation energy   30........

31. For a chemical system at equilibrium, a rise in temperature will (1) favor the endothermic reaction (2) favor the exothermic reaction (3) decrease the rates of the reactions (4) have no effect upon the equilibrium   31........

32. The equilibrium constant for a given system changes when (1) the temperature of the system is changed (2) the pressure of the system is changed (3) the concentration of one or more of the reactants is changed (4) a catalyst is added   32........

33. An increase in the rate of *all* chemical reactions results from (1) an increase in pressure (2) a decrease in pressure (3) an increase in temperature (4) a decrease in temperature   33........

34. When solid ammonium chloride is dissolved in a beaker of water, the temperature of the mixture decreases. The reaction

occurring in the beaker is   (1) exothermic and spontaneous
(2) exothermic and not spontaneous   (3) endothermic and spontaneous   (4) endothermic and not spontaneous   34........

35. In the general reaction $A + B = AB$, which equilibrium constant most favors the production of AB?   (1) 9.1×10^{-10}
(2) 4.3×10^{-7} (3) 4.7×10^{-12} (4) 3.5×10^{-3} 35........

36. If 50. ml. of a 0.20 N solution of NaOH are required to
titrate 10. ml. of an acid solution, what is the concentration of the
acid solution?   (1) 1.0 N   (2) 2.5 N   (3) 0.10 N   (4) 0.50 N   36........

37. What is the pH of a solution that has a hydronium, H_3O^+
(aq), concentration of 0.001 mole per liter?   (1) 1   (2) 2
(3) 3   (4) 11   37........

38. In the reaction $NH_3 + HCl \rightarrow NH_4Cl$, the NH_3 is   (1) an
electron acceptor   (2) a proton acceptor   (3) a proton donor
(4) a reducing agent   38........

39. The conjugate base of the HSO_4^- ion is   (1) H_2SO_4
(2) SO_4^{-2} (3) H_2O (4) OH^- 39........

40. The solution with the highest boiling point is 1 molal
(1) KCl   (2) C_2H_5OH (3) Na_2SO_4 (4) $C_6H_{12}O_6$ 40........

41. A solution of sodium acetate (CH_3COONa) in water is likely
to have a pH of   (1) 9   (2) 2   (3) 7   (4) 5   41........

42. In the reaction $S^{-2} + H_2O = HS^- + OH^-$, the two acids are
(1) S^{-2} and H_2O (2) H_2O and OH^- (3) S^{-2} and HS^- (4) H_2O
and HS^- 42........

43. Oxygen has an oxidation number of zero in   (1) H_2O_2
(2) OF_2 (3) H_2O (4) O_2 43........

44. In the reaction represented by the balanced equation

$$16HCl + 2KMnO_4 \rightarrow 8H_2O + 2KCl + 2MnCl_2 + 5Cl_2,$$

the oxidation state of manganese changes from +7 to   (1) -7
(2) +2   (3) 0   (4) +4   44........

45. In the reaction $Cu(s) + 2Ag^+(aq) = Cu^{+2}(aq) + 2Ag(s)$,
(1) Cu is the oxidizing agent   (2) Cu is reduced   (3) Ag^+ is the
oxidizing agent   (4) Ag^+ is oxidized   45........

46. During the electrolysis of fused $CaCl_2$, which occurs?
(1) Calcium ions are reduced.   (2) Calcium atoms are reduced.
(3) Chloride ions are reduced.   (4) Chlorine atoms are reduced.   46........

47. Which metal can reduce the chromium (III) ion?   (1) Al
(2) Fe   (3) Ni   (4) Pb   47........

48. On the basis of the data in *Table L* (*Standard Oxidation*

Potentials), which reaction occurs spontaneously?   (1) $Cu + 2H^+$
(2) $2Br^- + Cl_2$ (3) $Fe + Cr^{+3}$ (4) $2Br^- + I_2$ 48........

49. The compounds C_2H_5OH and CH_3OCH_3 are examples of
(1) hydrocarbons   (2) alcohols   (3) isomers   (4) esters   49........

50. The structure of an alkene contains   (1) only single
bonds   (2) a double bond   (3) two double bonds   (4) a triple
bond   50........

51. Which compound is an organic acid?

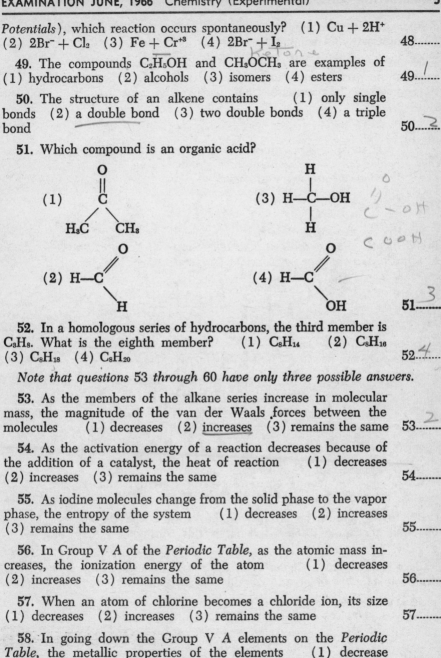

52. In a homologous series of hydrocarbons, the third member is
C_3H_8. What is the eighth member?   (1) C_8H_{14} (2) C_8H_{16}
(3) C_8H_{18} (4) C_8H_{20} 52........

Note that questions 53 through 60 have only three possible answers.

53. As the members of the alkane series increase in molecular
mass, the magnitude of the van der Waals forces between the
molecules   (1) decreases   (2) increases   (3) remains the same   53........

54. As the activation energy of a reaction decreases because of
the addition of a catalyst, the heat of reaction   (1) decreases
(2) increases   (3) remains the same   54........

55. As iodine molecules change from the solid phase to the vapor
phase, the entropy of the system   (1) decreases   (2) increases
(3) remains the same   55........

56. In Group V A of the *Periodic Table*, as the atomic mass increases, the ionization energy of the atom   (1) decreases
(2) increases   (3) remains the same   56........

57. When an atom of chlorine becomes a chloride ion, its size
(1) decreases   (2) increases   (3) remains the same   57........

58. In going down the Group V A elements on the *Periodic
Table*, the metallic properties of the elements   (1) decrease
(2) increase   (3) remain the same   58........

59. As one goes from lithium to fluorine in Period 2 of the

Periodic Table, the atomic radius of the elements   (1) decreases
(2) increases   (3) remains the same   59........

60. In the reaction $N_2(g) + O_2(g) + 43.2$ kcal. $= 2\ NO(g)$, as
pressure decreases, the number of moles of $NO(g)$ produced
(1) decreases   (2) increases   (3) remains the same   60........

PART TWO

*This part consists of six groups. Choose four of these six groups. Be sure
that you answer all questions in each group chosen. Write the answers to
these questions in the space provided.*

GROUP 1

DIRECTIONS (61–62): *Base your answers to questions 61 and 62 on the
graph below, which represents the relationship of the pressure and volume
of a given mass of a gas at constant temperature.*

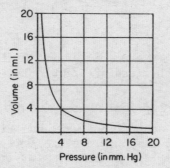

Pressure (in mm. Hg)

Write the number *preceding the word or expression that best completes
the statement or answers the question.*   [2]

61. When the pressure equals 8 mm of mercury, what is the
volume in milliliters?   (1) 1   (2) 2   (3) 8   (4) 16   61........

62. In this graph the product of the pressure and the volume
equals a constant. $[PV = K.]$ What is this constant?   (1) 16
(2) 12   (3) 8   (4) 4   62........

*Base your answers to questions 63 through 65 on the data below, which
represent an experiment to determine the heat of combustion of a solid.*

Mass of empty container	200. g.
Mass of container with water	375. g.
Temperature of water before reaction	24.0° C.
Temperature of water after reaction	30.0° C.
Mass of solid burned	2.00 g.

Write the number that, when inserted in the blank, best completes each
statement.   [3]

63. Compute the temperature change of the water in degrees centigrade. [1] 63.........

64. Compute the number of calories absorbed by the water. [1] 64.........

65. Compute the heat of combustion of the solid in calories per gram. [1] 65.........

DIRECTIONS (66–70): *For each type of reaction in questions 66 through 70, write the number preceding the equation, chosen from the list below, which best represents that type of reaction.* [5]

(1) $C_2H_6 + Cl_2 \rightarrow C_2H_5Cl + HCl$
(2) $C_6H_{12}O_6 \rightarrow 2C_2H_5OH + 2CO_2$
(3) $CH_3COOH + CH_3OH \rightarrow CH_3COOCH_3 + H_2O$
(4) $n\ C_2H_4 \rightarrow (C_2H_4)n$
(5) $C_3H_5(C_{17}H_{35}COO)_3 + 3NaOH \rightarrow C_3H_5(OH)_3 + 3C_{17}H_{35}COONa$
(6) $C_2H_5Cl + KOH \rightarrow C_2H_5OH + KCl$
(7) $C_2H_2 + 2Br_2 \rightarrow C_2H_2Br_4$

66. Halogen addition 66.........

67. Halogen substitution 67.........

68. Esterification 68.........

69. Fermentation 69.........

70. Polymerization 70.........

GROUP 2

DIRECTIONS (71–75): *Write the number preceding the word or expression that, of those given, best completes the statement or answers the question.* [5]

Base your answers on the following electron configuration of a neutral atom:

$$1s^2\ 2s^2\ 2p^6\ 3s^2\ 3p^4$$

71. This element is best classified as a   (1) metal   (2) non-metal   (3) metalloid   (4) transition element 71.........

72. In this element, the energy level which contains the most electrons has the principal quantum number   (1) 1   (2) 2   (3) 3   (4) 4 72.........

73. Which sublevel contains 3 electron pairs?   (1) $1s$ (2) $2p$ (3) $3s$ (4) $3p$ 73.........

74. What is the total number of protons in the nucleus of this atom?   (1) 5   (2) 11   (3) 16   (4) 27 74.........

75. What is the number of valence electrons in this atom?
(1) 6   (2) 2   (3) 8   (4) 4   75........

DIRECTIONS (76–80). *The chart below represents the elements in Period
2 of the* Periodic Table. *For each statement in question 76 through 80, write
the number of the symbol, chosen from the chart below, which is most
closely associated with that statement.*   [5]

Li	Be	B	C	N	O	F	Ne
(1)	(2)	(3)	(4)	(5)	(6)	(7)	(8)

76. This element usually forms four covalent bonds in compounds.   76........

77. This element forms an ionic compound with chlorine in a
1:1 ratio.   77........

78. This element exhibits the largest variety of oxidation states. 78........

79. This element does *not* form compounds with other elements. 79........

80. This element forms a polar covalent molecule with hydrogen
in a 1:2 ratio.   80........

GROUP 3

DIRECTIONS (81–85): *For each of statements 81 through 85, write the
number preceding the bond or binding forces, chosen from the list below,
which is most closely associated with that statement.*

Bonds or Binding Forces

(1) Ionic bonds
(2) Network bonds
(3) Coordinate covalent bonds
(4) Hydrogen bonds
(5) Metallic bonds
(6) Van der Waals forces
(7) Triple covalent bonds

81. Account for the unusually high boiling point of H_2O 81........

82. The "sea" of mobile electrons results in electrical conductivity in the solid state.   82........

83. Diamond has an extremely high melting point (above
3,500°C.)   83........

84. Helium and hydrogen can exist in the liquid and/or solid
phases under conditions of low temperature and high pressure.   84........

85. The hydronium ion is a hydrated proton.   85........

DIRECTIONS (86–90): *The graphs below show the relationship between
a particular physical or chemical property as the y-axis and increasing atomic
number as the x-axis.*

For *each* of questions 86 through 90, write the *number* of the graph which best shows the relationship between increasing atomic number and the physical or chemical property for the group or period given.   [5]

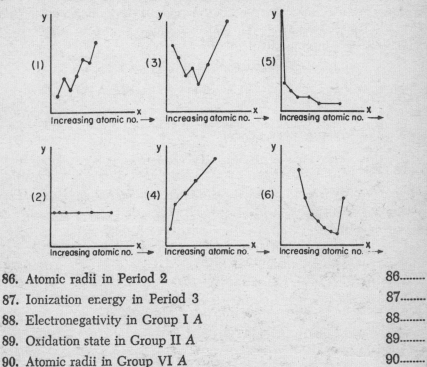

86. Atomic radii in Period 2   86........
87. Ionization energy in Period 3   87........
88. Electronegativity in Group I *A*   88........
89. Oxidation state in Group II *A*   89........
90. Atomic radii in Group VI *A*   90........

GROUP 4

DIRECTIONS (91–100): *Write the* number *preceding the word or expression that best completes the statement or answers the question.*   [10]

Base your answers to questions 91 through 94 on the information below:

    49 grams of pure H_2SO_4 are added to enough water to make 1,000 ml. of solution.

91. What is the molarity of the solution?   (1) 1.0 M
(2) 0.50 M   (3) 0.25 M   (4) 0.10 M   91........

92. Assuming complete ionization, the concentration of $H^+(aq)$ ion in the final solution is   (1) 1.0 M   (2) 0.50 M   (3) 0.25 M
(4) 0.10 M   92........

93. The normality of the solution is   (1) 1.0 N   (2) 0.50 N
(3) 0.25 N   (4) 0.10 N   93........

94. If an additional liter of H_2O is added to the solution, the molarity of the new solution is　　(1) 1.0 M　　(2) 0.50 M (3) 0.25 M　(4) 0.10 M　　　　　　　　　　　　　94........

Base your answers to questions 95 through 97 on the information below:

16.0 grams of copper react with concentrated nitric acid according to the following equation:

$$Cu + 4HNO_3 \rightarrow Cu(NO_3)_2 + 2H_2O + 2NO_2 \uparrow$$

95. How many moles of $Cu(NO_3)_2$ are produced?　　(1) 1.00 (2) 0.25　(3) 0.50　(4) 4.00　　　　　　　　　　　　95........

96. How many grams of water are produced?　　　(1) 9.00 (2) 2.00　(3) 36.0　(4) 4.00　　　　　　　　　　　　96........

97. How many liters of the gas NO_2 (measured at S.T.P.) are produced?　　　(1) 5.6　(2) 11.2　(3) 22.4　(4) 33.6　　　97........

Base your answers to questions 98 through 100 on the information below:

A gaseous compound is found by analysis to consist of 80.0% carbon and 20.0% hydrogen by mass. The density of the gas at S.T.P. is 1.34 grams per liter.

98. The empirical formula of the compound is　　　(1) CH (2) C_2H_3　(3) CH_3　(4) CH_4　　　　　　　　　　　98........

99. The mass of one mole of this compound is　　(1) 16.0 g. (2) 26.0 g.　(3) 27.0 g.　(4) 30.0 g.　　　　　　　　　99........

100. The molecular formula of the compound is　　(1) CH_4 (2) C_2H_2　(3) C_2H_3　(4) C_2H_6　　　　　　　　　100........

GROUP 5

DIRECTIONS (101-110): *Write the* number *preceding the word or expression that best completes the statement or answers the question.*　　[10]

Base your answers to questions 101 through 105 on the information below:

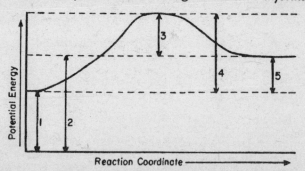

$$\tfrac{1}{2}N_2(g) + O_2(g) = NO_2(g) \qquad \triangle H = +8.10 \text{ kcal./mole}$$

101. The heat of reaction is represented by number (1) 5
(2) 2 (3) 3 (4) 4   101.........

102. The potential energy of the reactants is indicated by
number   (1) 1   (2) 2   (3) 5   (4) 4   102.........

103. The position of the activated complex is indicated by the
top of the arrow numbered   (1) 1   (2) 2   (3) 3   (4) 5   103.........

104. The activation energy of the exothermic reaction (reverse)
is indicated by number   (1) 1   (2) 2   (3) 3   (4) 4   104.........

105. When 2.00 moles of NO_2 are produced, the energy ab-
sorbed in kcal. is   (1) 32.4   (2) 16.2   (3) 8.10   (4) 4.05   105.........

Base your answers to questions 106 through 110 on the information below:

Sulfur dioxide, oxygen and sulfur trioxide are placed in a closed system
and allowed to reach equilibrium at a certain temperature according to
the reaction

$$2SO_2(g) + O_2(g) = 2SO_3(g) + 45.0\,kcal.$$

106. The equilibrium constant expression for this reaction in
the forward direction is

(1) $K = \dfrac{[SO_2]^2[O_2]}{[SO_3]^2}$ (2) $K = \dfrac{[SO_2][O_2]}{[SO_3]}$ (3) $K = \dfrac{[SO_3]^2}{[SO_2]^2[O_2]}$

(4) $K = [SO_3]^2[SO_2]^2[O_2]$ 106.........

107. The $\triangle H$ for the formation of 1 mole of SO_3 is
(1) −22.5 kcal.   (2) +22.5 kcal.   (3) −45.0 kcal.
(4) +45.0 kcal.   107.........

Note that questions 108 through 110 have only three possible answers.

108. The pressure is increased and the temperature is kept constant. Compared to the original number of moles of SO_2, the
number of moles of SO_2 present after the new equilibrium is
reached is   (1) greater   (2) less   (3) unchanged   108.........

109. The temperature is decreased and the pressure is kept
constant. Compared to the original number of moles of O_2, the
number of moles of O_2 present after the new equilibrium is
reached is   (1) greater   (2) less   (3) unchanged   109.........

110. Additional SO_2 is added to the system, and the pressure
and temperature are kept constant. Compared to the original
number of moles of SO_3, the number of moles of SO_3 present after
the new equilibrium is reached is   (1) greater   (2) less
(3) unchanged   110.........

GROUP 6

DIRECTIONS (111–120): *Write the* number *preceding the word or expression that best completes the statement or answers the question.* [10]

111. Which is the strongest acid?   (1) HCl   (2) H_2O
(3) NH_3 (4) NH_4^+ 111........

112. Which base is weaker than water?   (1) NH_3
(2) OH^- (3) SO_4^{-2} (4) HSO_4^- 112........

Question 113 refers to the following reaction:

$$CO_3^{-2}(aq) + H_2O(l) = HCO_3^-(aq) + OH^-(aq)$$

113. Which represents an acid-base conjugate pair?
(1) CO_3^{-2} and H_2O (2) H_2O and OH^- (3) H_2O and HCO_3^-
(4) HCO_3^- and OH^- 113........

114. The concentration of $H^+(aq)$ in a solution is 1×10^{-2} M. What is the concentration of OH^- (aq) in the solution? $[K_w = [H^+][OH^-] = 1 \times 10^{-14}]$ (1) 1×10^{-1} M
(2) 1×10^{-7} M   (3) 1×10^{-10} M   (4) 1×10^{-12} M   114........

115. Which species is *not* amphiprotic (amphoteric)?
(1) H_2O (2) NO_3^- (3) NH_3 (4) HSO_4^- 115........

116. When the following redox reaction is completely balanced, what is the coefficient in front of Fe^{+2}?

$$\_\_Fe^{+2} + MnO_4^- + 8H^+ \rightarrow \_\_\_\_\_Fe^{+3} + Mn^{+2} + 4H_2O$$

(1) 5   (2) 2   (3) 3   (4) 4   116........

117. Of the following, which is the best reducing agent in Table L?   (1) Sn^{+2} (2) Ca^0 (3) Fe^{+2} (4) Ni^0 117........

118. Which element will reduce Ag^+ to Ag but will *not* reduce Zn^{+2} to Zn?   (1) Cu   (2) Au   (3) Al   (4) Mg   118........

119. How many volts potential (E^0) for the overall reaction are found by combining the half reactions for the equation below:

$$2Cr + 3Pb^{+2} = 2Cr^{+3} + 3Pb$$

(1) 0.61   (2) 0.87   (3) 1.22   (4) 1.86   119........

120. Of the nonmetals listed in Table L, which is the *least* active oxidizing agent?   (1) F_2 (2) Cl_2 (3) Br_2 (4) I_2 120........

Answers to Chemistry (Experimental) June, 1966

PART ONE

1. Ans. **1** *Boyle's Law* states that at a constant temperature, the volume of a confined gas varies inversely with the pressure applied to the gas. The *kinetic molecular theory* helps to explain Boyle's Law. Since the temperature is constant, the average kinetic energy of the molecules is not changing. The pressure of a gas depends upon the number of bombardments of the molecules per unit surface area per unit time. If we wish to increase the number of bombardments, the walls of the container must be closer together so that the molecules which are moving at constant speed may hit the walls more often. In other words, the volume must decrease. Here the pressure is being doubled (from 1 atmosphere to 2 atmospheres). Since the volume varies inversely, the volume of the gas is halved.

2. Ans. **2** A *mole* (gram-molecular mass) of any gas contains approximately 6.02×10^{23} molecules and has a mass equal to the molecular mass of the gas in grams. Thus, every 32 grams of oxygen gas (molecular weight $= 32$) contains 6.02×10^{23} molecules. We can use the proportion:

$$\frac{32 \text{ grams}}{6.02 \times 10^{23} \text{ molecules}} = \frac{16 \text{ grams}}{x}$$

Divide 16 into each numerator and cancel out the grams units.

$$\frac{2}{6.02 \times 10^{23} \text{ molecules}} = \frac{1}{x}$$

$$x = \frac{6.02 \times 10^{23}}{2} \text{ molecules}$$

3. Ans. **2** The *vapor pressure* of a liquid is the pressure exerted in a confined space by the molecules that leave the liquid phase and enter the gaseous or vapor phase. Molecules are always escaping from the liquid, and thus the liquid always exerts a vapor pressure. At any specific temperature an equilibrium is set up between the molecules leaving the liquid and the molecules re-entering it. As the temperature increases, the kinetic energy of the molecules increases. More molecules leave the liquid and so the equilibrium vapor pressure increases. When the vapor pressure of a liquid is large enough to equal the atmospheric pressure exerted upon the liquid, a vapor bubble will form within the liquid. At first the bubbles form only at the bottom of the liquid where the temperature is hottest. These bubbles decrease in size and gradually disappear as they rise to cooler layers. The equilibrium vapor pressure of the liquid diminishes and the bubbles are crushed by the pressure of the atmosphere. If, however, the temperature reaches a point where the equilibrium vapor pressure at the surface of the liquid is equal to the air pressure, the

bubbles will maintain themselves throughout the liquid. We now say the liquid is boiling. Thus the boiling point is that temperature at which the equilibrium vapor pressure of a liquid is equal to the atmospheric pressure.

4. **Ans. 4** The specific heat of water is $1 \frac{cal.}{g.C°}$. Thus, when 1 gram of water rises 1 C° in temperature, it gains 1 calorie, and when 1 gram of water cools 1 C°, it loses 1 calorie. Here we have 20 grams of water that cool from 30°C to 20°C for a drop of 10 C°.

Calories lost = Specific Heat × mass of water × change in temperature

Calories lost = $1 \frac{cal.}{g.C°} \times 20 \, g. \times 10 \, C° = 200$ calories

Thus 200 calories are given off. Note that in the above calculation, the units g. and C° cancel, giving us our answer in calories.

5. **Ans. 3** An *orbital* is the region encompassing the probability distribution of an electron of an atom. It is often represented in diagrams as an *electron cloud*. In the orbital model of the atom, the orbits or shells of the atom are called *principal energy levels*. The principal quantum number (n) represents the principal energy level and indicates the average distance of an orbital from the nucleus of an atom. These levels are, in order of increasing distance from the nucleus, K(n = 1), L(n = 2), M(n = 3), N(n = 4), etc.
Each principal energy level has one or more filled or partially filled sublevels of energy, up to a maximum of four sublevels, sublevels *s*, *p*, *d* and *f*.
When n = 1, there is only one sublevel called 1*s*.
When n = 2, there are two sublevels called 2*s* and 2*p*.
When n = 3, there are three sublevels called 3*s*, 3*p* and 3*d*.
When n = 4, there are four sublevels called 4*s*, 4*p*, 4*d* and 4*f*.
For higher principal energy levels, there are still a maximum of only four occupied sublevels. Each sublevel consists of one or more *orbitals*. These orbitals differ in shape, size and orientation in space and each can hold no more than two electrons. In the atom, any *s* sublevel has 1 orbital with a maximum of two electrons. Any *p* sublevel has 3 orbitals with a maximum of 6 electrons. Any *d* sublevel has 5 orbitals with a maximum of 10 electrons. Any *f* sublevel has 7 orbitals with a maximum of 14 electrons. Here we are asked for the number of *orbitals* in any *p* sublevel. That number is 3.

6. **Ans. 2** The atom consists of three types of basic particles. The particles in the nucleus, are the proton and the neutron. The *proton* has a mass of approximately one mass unit and a unit positive charge. This is shown by *Table E* of the *Reference Tables*. The symbol for the proton is given as ^1_1H.

7. **Ans. 3** A *beta particle* is an electron emitted by the nucleus. One may wonder how a nucleus can emit an electron if the nucleus contains only protons and neutrons. The answer lies in the fact that the neutron sometimes

decomposes into an electron and a proton. The electron is given off as a beta particle, and the proton that is formed remains in the nucleus, increasing the atomic number by one.

8. **Ans. 3** Valence electrons are the electrons in the outer principal energy level of the atom. The rest of the atom, excluding the valence shell, is called the *kernel*. Here, the electron configuration is given as $1s^2 \, 2s^2 \, 2p^6 \, 3s^2 \, 3p^4$. In the symbolism for electron configuration the coefficient indicates the principal energy level, and the superscript indicates the number of electrons in the sublevel of the principal energy level.

In the K shell (n = 1) we have $1s^2$ for a complete shell of two electrons.

In the L shell (n = 2) we have $2s^2 \, 2p^6$ for a complete shell of 2 + 6 or 8 electrons.

In the M shell (n = 3) we have $3s^2 \, 3p^4$ for an incomplete shell of 2 + 4 or 6 electrons. Since this shell is the outermost shell, these are the valence electrons.

9. **Ans. 4** As explained in the answer to question 5, the d sublevel contains 5 orbitals. Since each orbital has a maximum of 2 electrons, the 3d sublevel (d sublevel of principal energy level n = 3) has a maximum of 5×2 or 10 electrons.

10. **Ans. 2** The *Periodic Table of the Elements* tells us that the electronic structure of the element chlorine in Group VII *A* is 2-8-7 and that of sulfur in Group VI *A* is 2-8-6. Both chlorine and sulfur gain electrons in being reduced to their ions. The chlorine atom gains one electron to become the Cl^- ion with the electron structure 2-8-8. Sulfur gains 2 electrons to become the S^{-2} ion with the electron structure 2-8-8. Thus Cl^- and S^{-2} have identical electron configuration of 2-8-8.

11. **Ans. 4** The line spectrum of an atom, as seen through a spectroscope, is produced when the vapor of the substance is subjected to an electronic discharge, or other high-energy source. The spectrum consists of visible bright lines of characteristic colors as well as lines in the ultraviolet and infrared regions. Some of the electrons in the atoms absorb the energy and move to higher energy levels. The atoms are now called *excited atoms* because of the higher energy state of the electrons. The excited, or higher energy position, is not a stable one. Thus, there is a tendency for the electrons to fall back to lower energy levels (ground state) and liberate the energy they had absorbed. In the meanwhile, other electrons have moved to higher energy levels. An equilibrium is set up with electrons moving in both directions as long as the high energy source is present. The electrons in different atoms of the same element do not all liberate the same amount of energy as they move back toward the nucleus. To produce the visible hydrogen spectrum, the single electron in a hydrogen atom, for example, might fall back from n = 3 to n = 2, or from n = 4 to n = 2, or from n = 5 to n = 2, or from n = 6 to n = 2, where n is the number of the energy level. The amount of return jump determines the energy of the light emitted, and therefore its wavelength and color.

The four return jumps to n = 2 produces the visible spectrum of hydrogen, as shown below. When the excited electrons fall back to the n = 1 energy level from higher energy levels, X-ray wavelengths are given off rather than visible light.

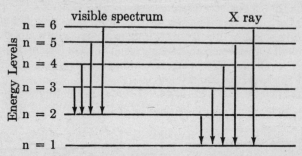

The fact that there are definite spectral lines shows that there are only a few discrete amounts of energy that electrons can absorb or release. The fact that electrons can take on only certain energy values is evidence that the electrons in atoms are in definite energy levels.

12. Ans. 4 A dipole is a molecule with assymmetrically arranged polar covalent bonds. Since the centers of positive and negative charge do not coincide because of the lack of symmetry, the molecule as a whole has a positive and a negative region. In a molecule with symmetrical distribution of electrical charge, the centers of positive and negative charge do coincide and the molecule is not a dipole. The molecule of CCl_4 is tetrahedrally shaped, with the carbon situated in the center of the tetrahedron and the Cl atoms at each corner. The electronegativity of C is 2.5 and that of Cl is 3.0. Thus the chlorine atoms draw the shared electrons away from the carbon atom, leaving the central carbon with a δ^+ or partial positive charge. The net negative charge is obtained from the sum of the partial negative charges of the four chlorine atoms. We might expect CCl_4 to be a polar compound. However, the chlorine atoms are distributed symmetrically about the central carbon atom. As a result, the center of negative charge of the chlorine atoms is also located in the center of the tetrahedron. Thus the centers of positive and negative charges coincide, and the molecule is not a dipole. The electron dot formula of CCl_4 can be represented as

$$Cl$$
$$\overset{\cdot\times}{Cl \times C \times Cl}$$
$$\underset{Cl}{\times\cdot}$$

13. Ans. 3 *Hydrogen bonds* are weak chemical bonds formed between molecules in which a hydrogen atom is covalently bonded to a second element of small atomic radius and high electronegativity, usually fluorine, oxygen or nitrogen. The small atomic radius and high electronegativity of this element

give it almost complete control of the pair of electrons shared with the hydrogen. The hydrogen atom for all practical purposes is a bare proton which can be readily attracted to the highly electronegative element of an *adjacent* molecule. For example, hydrogen fluoride exhibits hydrogen bonding since fluorine, in the upper right hand corner of the *Periodic Table*, has a small atomic radius and high electronegativity. The positively charged hydrogen of one molecule forms a hydrogen bond with the negatively-charged fluoride of another molecule (Fig. 1).

Fig 1.   Fig 2.

$$H \overset{\times}{\underset{\cdot\cdot}{\cdot}}\overset{\cdot\cdot}{\underset{\cdot\cdot}{F}}\colon \cdots\cdots H \overset{\times}{\underset{\cdot\cdot}{\cdot}}\overset{\cdot\cdot}{\underset{\cdot\cdot}{F}}\colon \quad or \quad H{-}O\cdots\cdots H{-}O$$

Hydrogen bonding accounts for the different complex molecules of hydrogen fluoride such as H_2F_2, H_3F_3, etc. A hydrogen bond also occurs in water between the hydrogen atom of one water molecule and oxygen atom of another (Fig 2).

14. **Ans. 2** When two hydrogen atoms combine to form a hydrogen molecule, a nonpolar bond is formed between the two hydrogen atoms. Each atom has acquired a stable valence shell of two electrons shared by both atoms. Since a stable energy state requires less energy, some energy is released. In general when bonds are formed, energy is released; when bonds are broken, energy is absorbed. The formation of the hydrogen molecule can be shown by the following:

$$H\cdot + {}_\times H \rightarrow H \overset{\times}{\cdot} H + \text{energy}$$

15. **Ans. 2** The bond between the hydrogen and oxygen atoms in the water molecule is polar covalent. The oxygen, having a much greater positive charge in the nucleus, has a greater electronegativity and therefore a stronger attraction for the shared pair of electrons. In the electron-dot formula, it is most important to realize that the atoms in the water molecule are not linear (arranged along a straight line). If the arrangement of the atoms were linear, the water molecule would be symmetrical and, although the individual bonds would be polar, the molecule as a whole would be nonpolar. We know that water is a polar molecule and studies of the crystalline structure of ice show that the polar bonds are at approximate right angles to each other, rather than being in a straight line. The size of the angle between the bonds in the water molecule is about 105°. The increase in size from 90° is due to the repulsion of the hydrogen atoms each of which has a partial positive charge.

16. **Ans. 2** The nitrogen atom has 5 electrons in its valence shell, $\left(\cdot\overset{\cdot\cdot}{N}\cdot\right)$

It can form 3 polar covalent bonds with 3 hydrogen atoms since each hydrogen

has an electron available for sharing, H $\overset{..}{\underset{\times}{N}}$ H Note that the nitrogen atom
$$\overset{\cdot\times}{H}$$

still has an unshared pair of electrons. A bond can be formed between a hydrogen ion and the nitrogen at this point since the H$^+$ ion has been stripped of its electron and is a bare proton,

$$\left[\begin{array}{c} H \\ \overset{..}{H \times N \times H} \\ \overset{\times \cdot}{H} \end{array}\right]^+$$

Such a bond in which the shared pair of electrons are *both* donated by only one of the atoms (in this case, the nitrogen atom) is called a *coordinate covalent bond*. The ammonium ion is now positively-charged because of the addition of the positively-charged proton:

$$NH_3 + H^+ \rightarrow NH_4^+$$

Note that once the NH_4^+ ion is formed, it is impossible to tell which hydrogen atom was the free proton. The whole ion obtains a net positive charge, with the center of positive charge at the center of the molecule, not at any one hydrogen atom.

17.   Ans.   4   *Ionic* compounds are those in which there has been a *transfer* of electrons from atoms of metals to atoms of nonmetals. This transfer has taken place because the metal, with a low electronegativity, shows little tendency to hold on to its valence electrons, and the nonmetal, with a high electronegativity, shows a great tendency to gain electrons. Thus, ionic compounds form when there is a great *electronegativity difference* between the elements. There is no exact point where we can say a bond has become ionic. In general we can say that a compound has ionic bonds when the electronegativity difference is about 1.7 or more. A 1.7 electronegativity difference would give the bond about 50% ionic character. In this question, the greatest electronegativity difference is between rubidium (electronegativity of 0.8) and fluorine (electronegativity of 4.0). The difference is (4.0 − 0.8) or 3.2. The bond is strongly ionic.

18.   Ans.   4   *Van der Waals forces* are weak forces of attraction between nonpolar molecules. Van der Waals forces depend on the number of electrons in the molecules, and the distance between the molecules. It is believed that these forces are created by the chance distribution of electrons that produce temporary dipole attractions. The greater the number of electrons, the greater will be the attractive forces between molecules. Thus the higher the molecular weight of a nonpolar molecule, the stronger the van der Waals forces. Van der Waals forces also increase when the molecules are closer to each other as a result of low temperature and high pressure. Van der Waals forces make it possible for nonpolar molecules such as hydrogen, oxygen and helium to exist in liquid phase when at low temperature and high pressure.

19. Ans. **1** When two atoms combine to form a compound, the atom with the higher electronegativity assumes a negative oxidation state, and the atom with the lower electronegativity assumes a positive oxidation state. In order to find an element that can assume only a negative oxidation state, we must find the element with the highest electronegativity, since it is impossible for the most electronegative element to bond with a more electronegative element. Referring to *Table J*, *"Representative" Elements*, we see that the element fluorine has the highest electronegativity, an electronegativity of 4.0. Fluorine will always assume a negative oxidation state, even when combining with very electronegative elements such as oxygen (to form $\overset{+2\ -1}{OF_2}$) or chlorine (to form $\overset{+1\ -1}{ClF}$). Fluorine is so electronegative, in fact, that it will even combine with some noble gases (Group 0) to form compounds such as KrF_2 and XeF_6.

20. Ans. **1** Certain hydroxides may have either acid or basic properties, depending upon their chemical environment. Such hydroxides are called *amphiprotic* (amphoteric). They act as weak bases (small tendency to gain protons) in the presence of a strong acid and as weak acids (small tendency to lose protons) in the presence of a strong base.

The hydroxides of zinc, aluminum, tin and antimony are examples of amphiprotic substances. These substances are found in Groups II B, III A, IV A, and V A, respectively. Of these Groups, the only one listed in the answers is Group III A.

21. Ans. **4** Referring to the *Periodic Table of the Elements*, we find that the only oxidation state for the elements in Group III A is +3. (It is true that Thallium can have an oxidation state of +1, but it also has a state of +3, and we are asked for the general formula.) Since oxygen has an oxidation state of −2, the formula for the oxide of X would be X_2O_3.

22. Ans. **2** *Transition elements* belong to the *B* Groups and Group VIII as shown on the *Periodic Table* between Group II *A* and III *A*. These elements contain inner sublevels that are only partially filled. Referring to the *Periodic Table*, we see that the atomic numbers of the transition elements in Period 4 range from 21 (Sc) through 30 (Zn). Element number 22 (Ti) is a transition element.

23. Ans. **1** *Metals* tend to lose electrons and *nonmetals* tend to gain electrons. *Metalloids* have characteristics of both metals and nonmetals. The *noble gases* have complete outer rings and therefore no oxidation state. As we move to the right in the *Periodic Table* in the direction of increasing atomic number, the electronegativity and ionization energy both increase. This means a gradual change from metallic to nonmetallic characteristics for the elements, as it becomes more difficult to lose electrons and easier to gain them. Thus in Period 3, Na, Mg and Al are active metals; silicon is a metalloid; P, S and Cl are relatively active nonmetals; Ar is a noble gas and is almost completely unreactive because of its complete outer shell of 8 electrons.

24. Ans. **3** A *mole* (gram-molecular mass) of any gas contains approxi-

mately 6.02×10^{23} molecules and occupies 22.4 liters at S.T.P. Thus 6.02×10^{23} molecules of helium would represent a mole of helium.

25. Ans. 1 If a compound contains carbon and hydrogen in the mole ratio of 1:2, it means that 1 mole of carbon atoms will combine with 2 moles of hydrogen atoms to produce one mole of the compound. The simplest formula for a compound of this composition is CH_2. The general formula for such a compound is $(CH_2)_x$, where x is any positive integer. Since the atomic mass of carbon is 12 and that of hydrogen is 1, the formula mass of CH_2 is $12 + 2(1)$ or 14. The molecular mass of $(CH_2)_x$ must be a multiple of 14. Of the choices given, the only multiple of 14 is 3×14 or 42. The actual formula of the compound $(CH_2)_x$ is $(CH_2)_3$ or C_3H_6. The molecular mass is 42.

26. Ans. 1 A *molar* solution contains one mole of solute dissolved in one liter (1000 ml.) of *solution*. In order to find out the molarity of a solution, we must determine the number of moles of solute present in one liter of solution. $\left(\text{Recall that molarity is expressed in } \dfrac{\text{moles}}{\text{liter}}.\right)$

The number of grams in one mole of sodium hydroxide, NaOH, is equal to its gram-formula mass. We find the gram-formula mass by adding up the atomic masses:

$$1\ Na = 1 \times 23 = 23$$
$$1\ O\ \ = 1 \times 16 = 16$$
$$\underline{1\ H\ \ = 1 \times\ \ 1 = \ \ 1}$$
$$\text{Gram formula mass} = 40 \text{ grams}$$

Here we have 20.0 grams of NaOH dissolved in 500 ml. ($\frac{1}{2}$ liter) of solvent. Therefore, one liter would contain 2×20.0 or 40.0 grams of NaOH. Since we found above that 40 grams is exactly one mole, we have 1.0 mole of NaOH dissolved in 1 liter of solution. The solution has a concentration of 1.0 mole per liter or 1.0 molar or 1.0 M.

ALTERNATE METHOD

$$\text{Number of moles of solute} = \frac{\text{mass of solute}}{\text{mole mass}}$$
$$= \frac{20.0 \text{ grams}}{40 \text{ g/mole}}$$
$$= 0.50 \text{ mole}$$

$$\text{Molarity} = \frac{\text{moles of solute}}{\text{liters of solution}}$$
$$= \frac{0.50 \text{ mole}}{0.50 \text{ liter}}$$
$$= \frac{1.0 \text{ mole}}{\text{liter}} \quad \text{or} \quad 1.0 \text{ M}$$

The gram-formula mass of NaOH (40 g.) contains only two significant figures. Thus the quotient must contain only 2 significant figures.

27.   Ans.   4   The *volumes* of *gases* that react or are formed in a chemical reaction at constant temperature and pressure are proportional to the number of *moles* as shown by the numerical coefficients in the equation of that reaction. The reaction is given as

$$2H_2(g) + O_2(g) = 2H_2O(g)$$

The coefficients of this equation tell us that the volume of oxygen is one-half the volume of the hydrogen with which it combines. Thus 3.0 liters of hydrogen will combine with $\frac{1}{2}$ of 3.0 liters or 1.5 liters of oxygen.

28.   Ans.   1   In any reaction, the number of moles of reactants consumed and the number of moles of products formed are proportional to the numerical coefficients of the substances in the equation.

The reaction is given as

$$Cu(s) + 2Ag^+(aq) = Cu^{+2}(aq) + 2Ag(s)$$

The coefficients of the equation tell us that 1 mole of $Cu(s)$ is consumed when 2 moles of $Ag(s)$ are produced. In other words, the moles of copper consumed is one-half that of the silver formed. Since 0.02 mole of silver is formed, one-half of 0.02 or 0.01 mole of copper is consumed.

29.   Ans.   3   We refer to the Solubility Curves of Table *B* of the Periodic Table. At 10°C., we read up to the KNO_3 curve (where the solution is saturated) and then to the left. We find that a saturated solution at this temperature requires approximately 23 grams of KNO_3 in 100 ml. of H_2O. At 50°C., we find that the amount of KNO_3 needed to saturate 100 ml. of water is 83 grams. The additional number of grams needed is (83 − 23) or 60 grams.

30.   Ans.   4   In order to initiate a chemical reaction, energy is required to break the bonds of the reacting species. The minimum energy required is known as the *activation energy*. Most catalysts are accelerators and have the effect of changing the mechanism of the chemical reaction in such a way that the activation energy needed is decreased. The potential energy of the reactants can reach the "peak" in less time and so the rate of reaction is increased. In certain cases the catalyst changes the mechanism of the reaction in such a way that the required activation energy is increased. Thus the time required to reach the "peak" is increased and the reaction is slowed down.

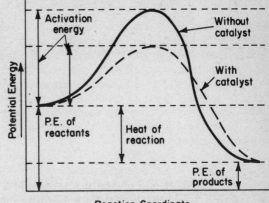

Reaction Coordinate

31. Ans. 1 *Le Chatelier's Principle* states that if a system in equilibrium is subject to a stress (such as increased pressure or temperature), the equilibrium will be displaced in the direction that relieves the stress. In other words, a rise in temperature will drive the reaction to the "cool" or endothermic side where heat is being absorbed. Thus in the equation

$$N_2 + 3H_2 = 2NH_3 + 22 \text{ kcal.}$$

an increase of temperature in the system will drive the reaction to the left since NH_3 absorbs heat as it decomposes to form N_2 and H_2.

32. Ans. 1 The equilibrium constant represents the ratio of the product of the concentrations of the products (on the right) to the ratio of the product of the concentrations of the reactants (on the left). Thus in the reversible reaction $A + B \rightleftarrows C + D$,

$$K = \frac{[C][D]}{[A][B]}$$

When a temperature change occurs, the speed of the forward and reverse reactions are both changed, but they are changed *unequally*. Thus the rate at which C and D are formed (forward reaction) may increase faster than the rate at which C and D react (reverse reaction). The result will be a change in the value of K.

33. Ans. 3 The rate of chemical reaction depends on four factors. They are (1) *nature* of the reactants, (2) *concentration* of the reactants, (3) *temperature* and (4) *catalyst* present. Of these, the only factor that will increase the rate of *all* chemical reactions is an increase in temperature. An increase in temperature provides greater collision frequency and collision efficiency. The collision frequency is increased because the molecules are moving at a greater speed and therefore will collide more often. The collision efficiency is increased since the more energetic molecules have the necessary activation energy for combination. Thus the rate at which the chemical reaction occurs is increased.

34. Ans. 3 A *spontaneous reaction* is one that takes place without the addition of energy from an outside source. The energy of activation comes solely from the reactants. An endothermic reaction is one that absorbs heat from the surroundings. We are told that the solid ammonium chloride dissolves in a beaker of water and that the temperature of the mixture decreases. Since we are not told that additional heat is added, the reaction occurs without additional activation energy and is therefore spontaneous. Since the temperature of the mixture decreases, the reaction must be absorbing heat. It is therefore endothermic.

35. Ans. 4 The magnitude of the equilibrium constant can be used to predict the extent of a chemical reaction. The equilibrium constant is defined as the ratio of the product of the concentrations of the products to the product

of the concentrations of the reactants. Thus in the equation $A + B = AB$, the equilibrium constant is

$$K = \frac{[AB]}{[A][B]}$$

Note the AB is in the numerator of the fraction. Thus if we wish to increase the production of AB, we choose the equilibrium constant of highest value since a large numerator increases the value of the fraction, here K. Remember from algebra that as we go to the right on the real number line, the value of the numbers increases:

$$\xrightarrow{ -4 \;\; -3 \;\; -2 \;\; -1 \;\; 0 \;\; 1 \;\; 2 }$$
larger

Thus -3 is the largest exponent of the choices given, and the equilibrium constant we are looking for is 3.5×10^{-3}.

36. **Ans. 1** When titrating two solutions to the equivalence point, the *number of equivalents added* must be equal to the *number of equivalents in the solution being titrated*. In order to find the number of equivalents in a solution, we multiply the normality $\left(\dfrac{\text{equivalents}}{\text{liter}} \right)$ by the volume (liters). Since the number of equivalents are equal, we arrive at the following equation:

$$\text{Normality}_1 \times \text{Liters}_1 = \text{Normality}_2 \times \text{Liters}_2$$

or dividing by 1000:

$$\text{Normality}_1 \times \text{Milliliters}_1 = \text{Normality}_2 \times \text{Milliliters}_2$$

$$.20 \, \frac{\text{equiv.}}{\text{liter}} \times 50. \, \cancel{ml.} = x \times 10. \, \cancel{ml}$$

$$10. \, \frac{\text{equiv.}}{\text{liter}} = 10.x$$

$$x = 1.0 \, \frac{\text{equiv.}}{\text{liter}} \text{ or } 1.0 \text{ N}$$

Note that since each number in the question has 2 significant figures, the answer must contain two significant figures.

37. **Ans. 3** The pH of a solution indicates the concentration of hydronium ions in a solution. A pH of less than 7 is acidic, a pH of 7 is neutral, and a pH of more than 7 is basic. The concentration of the hydronium ion is given as 0.001 moles per liter. Expressed in standard (scientific or exponential) notation the concentration of the hydronium ion is 1×10^{-3} moles per liter or $[H_3O^+] = 1 \times 10^{-3}$ where [   ] is the symbol indicating concentration in moles per liter. The pH is defined as the logarithm of the reciprocal of the hydronium ion concentration,

$$pH = \log \frac{1}{[H_3O^+]}; \quad pH = \log \frac{1}{1 \times 10^{-3}} \quad \text{or} \quad \log \frac{1}{10^{-3}}$$

$$\text{Since } \frac{1}{10^{-3}} = 10^3; \quad pH = \log 10^3$$

The logarithm of a number is the exponent to the base 10 which will give that number. Therefore

$$pH = 3$$

The pH of the solution is 3.

38. Ans. 2 In the reaction

$$NH_3 + HCl \rightarrow NH_4Cl$$

the NH_3 molecule attracts a proton from the HCl to form a coordinate covalent bond with the unshared pair of electrons from the nitrogen. The NH_3 molecule is therefore a *proton acceptor*.

39. Ans. 2 According to the *Brønsted-Lowry Theory* an acid is a *proton donor* and a base is a *proton acceptor*. Any acid can lose a proton and become a base. This base can regain the proton to become an acid. The acid and base are related by the transfer of a proton and together are called a conjugate acid-base pair. In order to find the conjugate base of a given acid, we simply remove a proton. To find the conjugate base of HSO_4^- we remove a proton and obtain SO_4^{-2}:

$$\underset{\text{acid}}{HSO_4^-} - H^+ = \underset{\text{conjugate base}}{SO_4^{-2}}$$

The conjugate base of HSO_4^- is SO_4^{-2}.

The list of conjugate acid-base pairs may be found in *Table H*. HSO_4^- is listed in the left-hand column as a moderately strong acid. Its conjugate base listed in the column to the right is SO_4^{-2}.

40. Ans. 3 When a substance is dissolved in water, the boiling point of the solution is higher than that of the pure solvent. The greater the number of solute particles, the greater is the elevation of the boiling point. The elevation in boiling point is proportional to the moles of particles per kilogram of solvent. A 1 molal solution contains 1 mole of solute in 1000 grams of water. Let us examine the number of moles of particles (molecules or ions) in each of the choices.

Choice (1) $KCl \rightarrow K^+ + Cl^-$; a mole of KCl dissociates to form 1 mole of K^+ and 1 mole of Cl^- ions or a total of 2 moles of particles, here ions.

Choice (2) C_2H_5OH, ethyl alcohol, does not dissociate or ionize since it is a nonpolar compound. Thus a 1 molal solution has 1 mole of C_2H_5OH particles, here molecules.

Choice (3) $Na_2SO_4 \rightarrow 2Na^+ + SO_4^{-2}$; one mole of Na_2SO_4 dissociates to form 2 moles of Na^+ ions and 1 mole of SO_4^{-2} ions forming a total of 3 moles of particles, here ions.

Choice (4) $C_6H_2O_6$, the carbohydrate glucose, is a nonpolar compound and therefore does not ionize. Thus 1 mole of $C_6H_2O_6$ in solution has 1 mole of particles, here molecules. Therefore Na_2SO_4 with 3 moles of particles in a 1 molal solution has the greatest effect on the elevation of the boiling point of the solution.

41. Ans. 1 Sodium acetate is a salt produced by the action of weakly-ionized acetic acid and highly-dissociated sodium hydroxide, a strong base, as shown by *Table M, Ionization Constants of Acids and Bases.* Salts produced from either weak acids or weak bases will hydrolyze when placed in water. In the solution of sodium acetate there are Na^+ ions, CH_3COO^- ions and H_2O molecules. According to the *Brnøsted Theory* the acetate ion is a strong base since it shows a great tendency to gain protons. Here the acetate ion gains a proton from the water molecule to form a molecule of acetic acid and the hydroxide ion:

$$CH_3COO^- + H_2O = CH_3COOH + OH^-$$

The hydroxide ions remain in solution since sodium hydroxide remains completely dissociated. Since the hydroxide ions are in excess, the solution is basic, and the pH must be above 7. Of the choices given, the only one above 7 is choice (1).

42. Ans. 4 According to the Brønsted-Lowry Theory, an acid is a proton donor. In the equation

$$S^{-2} + H_2O \rightarrow HS^- + OH^-$$

the H_2O donates a proton to the S^{-2}, becoming OH^-. Thus the H_2O acts as an acid. In the reverse reaction, the HS^- ion is a Brønsted acid since it donates a proton to the OH^- and becomes the S^{-2} ion. The two acids are H_2O and HS^-.

43. Ans. 4 An atom has an oxidation state of zero if it exists by itself or if it is bonded to a like atom to form a diatomic molecule. An atom can achieve an oxidation state only if electrons are lost or gained to form ionic bonds or if electrons are shared unequally to form polar bonds. It is the unequal distribution of charge that gives the atom an oxidation state. Here the diatomic oxygen molecule, O_2, has an oxidation number of zero since the electronegativity difference between two like molecules (here oxygen) is zero. The valence electrons are equally shared and so the charge distribution in the oxygen molecule is uniform.

44. Ans. 2 We are told that in the formula $KMnO_4$, Mn has an oxidation state of $+7$. We must now determine the oxidation state of Mn in $MnCl_2$. The molecule $MnCl_2$ as a whole is neutral. The two chloride ions contribute a total of 2×-1 or -2. Therefore the Mn must have an oxidation state of $+2$ to yield a neutral molecule. Thus the oxidation state of Mn changes from $+7$ to $+2$.

45. Ans. 3 *Oxidation* is the loss of electrons; *reduction* is the gain of electrons. An *oxidizing agent* oxidizes another substance; therefore an oxidizing agent is itself reduced through the gain of electrons. A *reducing agent* reduces another substance; therefore a reducing agent is itself oxidized by the loss of electrons. In the reaction

$$Cu(s) + 2Ag^+(aq) \rightarrow Cu^{+2}(aq) + 2Ag(s)$$

the following oxidation and reduction reactions occur:

Oxidation: $Cu - 2e^- \rightarrow Cu^{+2}$
Reduction: $2Ag^+ + 2e^- \rightarrow 2Ag$

Since the silver ion (Ag^+) is being reduced to the silver atom, it must be acting as an oxidizing agent because it is gaining electrons from the copper.

46. Ans. 1   As explained in the answer to question 45, reduction is the gain of electrons and oxidation is the loss of electrons. In the electrolysis of $CaCl_2$, the salt is first fused (melted) to break the lattice bonds of the solid state and produce free, mobile ions.

$$CaCl_2 \rightarrow Ca^{+2} + 2Cl^-$$

The ions are then electrolyzed to atoms and molecules. The following are the two half-reactions of the electrolysis:

$$Ca^{+2} + 2e^- \rightarrow Ca^0$$
$$2Cl^- - 2e^- \rightarrow Cl_2{}^0$$

Thus the calcium ion gains 2 electrons and is reduced to the calcium atom.

47. Ans. 1   In the reduction of the chromium (III) ion, the chromium ion gains 3 electrons to become the chromium atom.

$$Cr^{+3} + 3e^- \rightarrow Cr^0$$

Reduction will occur if a more active metal than chromium, a metal that has a greater tendency to lose electrons than chromium, is present. In this case, the chromium (III) ion will be compelled to accept electrons from the more active metal. These more active metals can be found above chromium in the *Table of Oxidation Potentials* (*Table L*). As its name implies, this table measures the relative tendency of metals (and some nonmetals) to lose electrons. In *Table L* zinc and metals above zinc will reduce the chromium ion. Of the choices given, only aluminum is above zinc in *Table L*.

48. Ans. 2   In a replacement reaction, a more active element replaces a less active element from a compound. In the reaction

$$Cl_2 + 2Br^- \rightarrow 2Cl^- + Br_2,$$

the chlorine atom replaces the bromide ion from its compound. The positive ion of the compound is omitted since it is a spectator ion. The chlorine atom is reduced to the chloride ion, gaining an electron from the bromide ion and oxidizing the bromide ion to the bromine atom. We see from *Table L, Standard Oxidation Potentials*, that the chloride ion is below the bromide ion, and thus has a greater tendency to gain electrons (smaller tendency to lose electrons).

Thus a reaction between the bromide ion and the chlorine atom will occur spontaneously.

49. Ans. 3 *Isomers* are compounds that have the same molecular formula but different structural formulas and therefore different chemical properties. The molecular formula of a compound tells us the elements in the compound and the number of atoms of each element. The structural formula of a compound gives in addition the atom arrangement and valence bonds of the atoms in the molecules. Thus the molecular formula for methyl alcohol is

CH_3OH or CH_4O. The structural formula is

$$H-\overset{\overset{\displaystyle H}{|}}{\underset{\underset{\displaystyle H}{|}}{C}}-O-H.$$

All compounds have one molecular formula and most have one structural formula that represents the compound. Organic compounds, however, may have different structural formulas for the same molecular formula. Such compounds are called *isomers*. The two compounds given are ethyl alcohol and dimethyl ether. Although both C_2H_5OH and CH_3OCH_3 can be written as C_2H_6O and thus have the same number and types of atoms, they have different structural formulas:

$$H-\overset{\overset{\displaystyle H}{|}}{\underset{\underset{\displaystyle H}{|}}{C}}-\overset{\overset{\displaystyle H}{|}}{\underset{\underset{\displaystyle H}{|}}{C}}-OH \qquad H-\overset{\overset{\displaystyle H}{|}}{\underset{\underset{\displaystyle H}{|}}{C}}-O-\overset{\overset{\displaystyle H}{|}}{\underset{\underset{\displaystyle H}{|}}{C}}-H$$

ethyl alcohol C_2H_5OH \qquad dimethyl ether CH_3OCH_3

Thus C_2H_5OH and CH_3OCH_3 are isomers.

50. Ans. 2 Hydrocarbons are classified according to the type of bond present in the molecule. Each class of hydrocarbons forms a series of compounds known as a *homologous series*. When the members of a series are arranged in order, we find that the molecules increase in size by a CH_2 or methylene group and that the series obeys a definite algebraic formula. Each hydrocarbon in the alkene series has one double bond and conforms to the homologous formula C_nH_{2n}. A member of this series, for example, is propene,

C_3H_6, which has the structural formula $H-C=\overset{\overset{\displaystyle }{}}{\underset{\underset{\displaystyle H}{|}}{C}}-\overset{\overset{\displaystyle H}{|}}{\underset{\underset{\displaystyle H}{|}}{C}}-H.$

51. Ans. 4 The structural formula $H-\overset{\overset{\displaystyle O}{\|}}{C}-OH$ or $HCOOH$ is formic acid and is recognized as an organic acid because of the characteristic carboxyl group. The carboxyl group is written as —COOH or

$$-\overset{\overset{\displaystyle O}{\parallel}}{C}-OH.$$

The carboxyl group will donate an H^+ ion or proton and in doing so acts as an acid.

$$HCOOH \rightleftharpoons H^+ + HCOO^-$$

52. Ans. 3 C_3H_8 or $C_3H_{2(3)+2}$ is the third member of the *alkane series*, with the homologous formula C_nH_{2n+2}. The eighth member of this series would have the formula $C_8H_{2(8)+2}$ or C_8H_{18}. The alkane hydrocarbons have single bonds only and are known as saturated hydrocarbons.

53. Ans. 2 *Van der Waals forces* are weak attractive forces that exist between nonpolar molecules. They are caused by chance distribution of electrons resulting in very shortlived dipole attractions. Therefore the greater the number of electrons, the greater are the van der Waals forces. The increase of molecular mass of the alkane hydrocarbons is due to the greater number of atoms in the molecule. More atoms mean more electrons and therefore greater van der Waals forces. Van der Waals forces help to explain the high boiling point of alkane hydrocarbons of higher molecular mass. A higher temperature is needed to break the stronger intermolecular forces of attraction that exist in alkane hydrocarbons of higher molecular mass.

54. Ans. 3 The *heat of reaction* (ΔH) is the heat energy released or absorbed in a chemical reaction. It is indicated by arrow 4 in the potential energy diagram shown. The heat of reaction is equal to the difference between the potential energy of the final products at P as shown by arrow 5 and the potential energy of the initial reactants at R as shown by arrow.

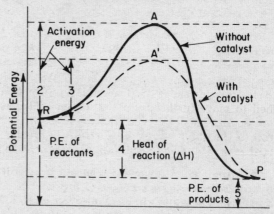

Reaction Coordinate

1. . Activation energy is the energy needed to change the reactants into activated complex so that a chemical reaction may take place. These complexes are at the top of the curves at A and A'. From here the reaction can "roll downhill" and go forward to form the products or fall back in a reverse direction to reform the reactants.

Without a catalyst the curve of the reaction is the line RAP. The activation energy is indicated by arrow 2. With a catalyst, less activation energy is needed as shown by arrow 3 on curve RA'P. However, the curves start at the same point R and end at the same point P. There is no change in the heat of reaction (ΔH) with the use of a catalyst.

55. **Ans. 2** *Entropy* is the property of a substance that describes the amount of disorder or lack of organization of a system. The more disordered the system, the higher the entropy. Solids are systems that are organized in definite crystalline patterns. Liquids have lost this crystal pattern. The molecules or ions have become less organized. The gaseous phase has the most randomness or disorder. Thus the three phases of matter in order of increasing entropy are solid, liquid and gas. In general, at constant temperature, systems tend to undergo changes that increase the entropy. When iodine sublimes, it changes from a highly organized molecules in a crystalline solid to disorganized, random molecules in iodine vapor. The entropy of the system has greatly increased.

56. **Ans. 1** The *ionization energy* is the energy in electron volts needed to remove the most loosely held electron from an atom in the gaseous phase. *Table J* of the *Reference Tables* gives us the ionization energy of the *"Representative"* *Elements*. As we go down Group V A in the direction of increasing atomic mass, we see that the values for the ionization energy are 14.5, 10.9, 10.5, 8.5 and 8.0 e.v. So we see that the ionization energy decreases as the atomic mass of the Group V A elements increases. More energy levels are present, the atomic radius increases and the smaller nuclear pull on the valence electrons results in lower ionization energy requirements.

57. **Ans. 2** The neutral chlorine atom contains 17 protons and 17 electrons. When the chlorine atom (electron configuration 2-8-7) becomes a chloride ion (2-8-8), it gains an electron for a net total of 18 electrons. Since the nucleus remains the same, we have the same positive charge of +17 attracting 18 electrons instead of 17. There is less pull on each electron causing the valence shell to move further from the nucleus. The result is an increase in atomic radius. Also recall that like charges repel each other. The addition of an electron to the outer energy level creates a greater tendency of the electrons to repel each other. The result is again an increase in atomic radius.

58. **Ans. 2** An element is more metallic if it shows a greater tendency to *lose electrons*. As we go down Group V A of the *Periodic Table*, the number of electron energy levels increases. Since the valence electrons are a greater distance from the nucleus, the pull of the nucleus on these electrons is not as great. Therefore the atoms show a greater tendency to lose their electrons and the metallic character increases. The greater tendency to lose electrons is confirmed by consulting *Table J*. As we go down Group V A the electronegativity and ionization energy decreases, an indication of an increase in the metallic character of the elements.

59. **Ans. 1** The atomic radius indicates the size of the atom. As we move to the right in Period 2 of the *Periodic Table* from lithium to fluorine, we see that the atomic radius decreases from 1.52 Å to 0.64 Å. The increase in nuclear

charge due to the increasing number of protons pulls the electrons more tightly around the nucleus.

60. Ans. **3** *Le Chatelier's Principle* states that if a system in equilibrium is subject to a stress (such as increased pressure or temperature), the equilibrium will be displaced in the direction that relieves the stress. Here a decreased pressure is being applied to the following reaction:

$$N_2(g) + O_2(g) + 43.2 \text{ kcal} \rightarrow 2NO(g)$$

Therefore, we would expect the reaction to go in that direction which creates a higher pressure. The pressure in a closed container is dependent upon the volume of the gas in that container. Volumes are proportional to the number of moles shown by the coefficients of the equation written above. Thus the reactants N_2 and O_2 in the container have $1 + 1$ or 2 volumes. The product $2NO$ also has 2 volumes. As the reaction takes place, there is no change in the volume. With no change in volume, a pressure change will not shift the equilibrium. Therefore, as the pressure in the system is decreased, the amount of NO produced remains the same.

PART TWO

GROUP 1

61. Ans. **2** In order to find the volume at any given pressure, we locate the given pressure value along the horizontal axis, read up to the curve and then read to the left to the vertical axis. Since the pressure is 8 mm., we read up the 8 mm. line until we reach the graph curve. Reading to the left we see that the volume at this point is approximately 2 ml.

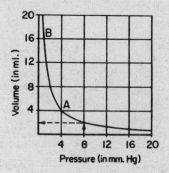

62. Ans. **1** The value of the constant (K) is equal to the product of the pressure and volume at any point on the curve $(PV = K)$. At point A, the pressure is 4 mm. and the volume is 4 ml. The product of the pressure and the volume is (4 mm. $\times$ 4 ml.) or 16 mm.-ml. Taking another point, point B, we see the values of the volume and pressure are 16 ml. and 1 mm. respectively. The product is 16 ml. $\times$ 1 mm. or again 16 mm.-ml. The value of the constant is 16.

63. Ans. **6.0C°** Since the change in the temperature (ΔT) is equal to the final temperature (T_f) minus the initial temperature (T_i), we have

$$\Delta T = T_f - T_i$$
$$= 30.0°C - 24.0°C$$
$$= 6.0 \ C°$$

64. Ans. **1,050 cal.** The specific heat of water is $1 \ \dfrac{\text{cal.}}{\text{g.C°}}$. This means that it requires 1 calorie of heat to raise the temperature of 1 gram of water 1 C°. In order to find the total number of calories absorbed by the water, we multiply the specific heat by the number of grams, by the number of centigrade degrees the temperature has increased:

Number of calories = specific heat × mass of water × temperature change

The mass of water is found by subtracting the mass of the empty container from the mass of the container with the water.

Mass of water = 375. g. − 200. g. = 175. g.

Number of cal. = $1 \ \dfrac{\text{cal.}}{\cancel{\text{g}}.\cancel{\text{C}}°} \times 175. \cancel{\text{g}}. \times 6 \ \cancel{C}° = 1{,}050$ cal.

65. Ans. **525** The heat of combustion as measured in calories per gram is the number of calories released by a substance when burned divided by the number of grams of substance burned. Therefore, heat of combustion = 1,050 cal. ÷ 2 grams = $525 \ \dfrac{\text{cal.}}{\text{g.}}$.

66. Ans. **7** *Addition* is the adding of one or more atoms at the double or triple bond of an unsaturated hydrocarbon. This results in partial or complete saturation of the bond. Choice (7) shows the addition of bromine to acetylene (ethyne). Ethyne has a triple bond. If one of the extra bonds breaks open, each of the two single electrons that are now unshared can form a bond with each of two monovalent bromine atoms. If both extra bonds break open, each of the four electrons that are made available can bond with each of 4 bromine atoms. The given equation illustrates the latter. Written structurally the equation is:

$$\text{H—C} \equiv \text{C—H} + 2\text{Br—Br} \rightarrow \text{H—}\overset{\displaystyle \text{Br} \ \ \text{Br}}{\underset{\displaystyle \text{Br} \ \ \text{Br}}{\text{C}—\text{C}}}\text{—H}$$

67. Ans. **1** Substitution means replacement of one kind of atom or group by another kind of atom or group. For saturated hydrocarbons, reactions (except for combustion and decomposition) necessarily involve replacement of one or more hydrogen atoms. In equation (1), a chlorine atom replaces a hydrogen atom in the saturated hydrocarbon ethane. The product is the alkyl

halogenide chloroethane. The substitution can be best shown by a structural equation:

$$\underset{\begin{array}{c}H\\|\\H\end{array}}{H-C}\!-\!\underset{\begin{array}{c}H\\|\\H\end{array}}{C}\!\boxed{H + Cl}\!-\!Cl \rightarrow \underset{\begin{array}{c}H\\|\\H\end{array}}{H-C}\!-\!\underset{\begin{array}{c}H\\|\\H\end{array}}{C}\!-\!Cl + H\!-\!Cl$$

68. **Ans. 3** *Esterification* is the reaction of an acid with an alcohol to give an ester and water.

$$\underset{\text{acid}}{R-\overset{\overset{\textstyle O}{\|}}{C}-\boxed{OH}} + \underset{\text{alcohol}}{R'-O-\boxed{H}} \xrightarrow{H_2SO_4} \underset{\text{ester}}{R-\overset{\overset{\textstyle O}{\|}}{C}-O-R'} + \underset{\text{water}}{H-OH}$$

The sulfuric acid serves as a dehydrating agent to remove the water as it is formed. As a result the reaction shifts to the right and the yield of the ester increases.

Choice (3) shows the esterification of acetic acid and methanol to form methyl acetate and water.

$$\underset{\text{acetic acid}}{\underset{\begin{array}{c}|\\H\end{array}}{\overset{\begin{array}{c}H\\|\end{array}}{H-C}}-\overset{\overset{\textstyle O}{\|}}{C}-OH} + \underset{\text{methanol}}{\underset{\begin{array}{c}|\\H\end{array}}{\overset{\begin{array}{c}H\\|\end{array}}{H-C}}-O-H} \rightarrow \underset{\text{methyl acetate}}{\underset{\begin{array}{c}|\\H\end{array}}{\overset{\begin{array}{c}H\\|\end{array}}{H-C}}-\overset{\overset{\textstyle O}{\|}}{C}-O-\underset{\begin{array}{c}|\\H\end{array}}{\overset{\begin{array}{c}H\\|\end{array}}{C}}-H} + \underset{\text{water}}{H-OH}$$

69. **Ans. 2** *Fermentation* is a process by which enzymes secreted by living organisms act as catalysts for the breakdown of organic molecules. The most common products of fermentation are alcohols and acids. Equation (2) shows the fermentation of the sugar glucose to form ethyl alcohol (ethanol) and carbon dioxide. The catalyst or enzyme is zymase, secreted by the yeast plant.

70. **Ans. 4** *Polymerization* is the linking of small molecules of similar structure to form large chain molecules. Equation (4) shows the polymerization of n molecules of ethene (C_2H_4) to form a single chain molecule $(C_2H_4)_n$. Polymerization is used to make such products as synthetic rubber, polyethylene and other large chain molecules. In nature, proteins and starches are produced by polymerization.

GROUP 2

71. **Ans. 2** The electron configuration of the neutral atom is given as $1s^2\,2s^2\,2p^6\,3s^2\,3p^4$. This atom has three principal energy levels. The third level $(n = 3)$ has 2 sublevels, $3s^2$ and $3p^4$. Since the superscript gives the number

of electrons in the subshells, we have $2 + 4$ or 6 electrons in the $n = 3$ level. Elements with 6 electrons in their outer shell are in Group VI A and are best classified as nonmetals, since most members of this Group show a strong tendency to gain two electrons and complete their valence shell. The element can be identified by adding up the number of electrons in all the subshells. The total is $(2 + 2 + 6 + 2 + 4)$ or 16 electrons. This means the atom has 16 protons and an atomic number of 16. The element with atomic number 16 is sulfur, an active nonmetal.

72. **Ans. 2** In the symbolism of the electron configuration, the coefficient of the sublevel is the principal quantum number and the superscript the number of electrons in that sublevel. In the given atom, the $n = 1$ level has 2 electrons, the $n = 2$ level has $2 + 6$ or 8 electrons, and the $n = 3$ has $2 + 4$ or 6 electrons. The energy level with the most electrons is the 2nd level with a principal quantum number of 2.

73. **Ans. 2** The sublevel that contains three electron pairs (3 orbitals) would have a total of 6 electrons. Looking at the given configuration, we see that the only sublevel with 6 electrons is the $2p$ sublevel.

74. **Ans. 3** As stated in 71 above, the total number of electrons in the atom is 16. Since the atom is neutral, the charge of the nucleus must be equal and opposite to the charge of the electrons. Therefore the nucleus must have a charge of $+16$, or contain 16 protons.

75. **Ans. 1** The valence electrons are the electrons in the outermost principal energy level of the atom. The atom in this question has 3 energy levels. The outermost $(n = 3)$ level contains all the valence electrons. The $n = 3$ level contains the sublevels $3s^2$ and $3p^4$. Thus the total number of valence electrons in the outer shell is $2 + 4$ or 6.

76. **Ans. 4** The element in Period 2 that forms 4 covalent bonds would have 4 electrons in its outer shell and thus an oxidation state of $+4$. The element with this oxidation state would be located in Group IV A of the *Periodic Table*. That element is carbon. Carbon forms covalent bonds because its electronegativity of 2.5 is about midway in the scale ranging from 0.7 to 4.0. The electronegativity difference with either metals or nonmetals would usually be less than 1.7 and therefore the bonds would be polar covalent.

77. **Ans. 1** Chlorine has an oxidation state of -1 in binary ionic compounds, when the chlorine exists as the negative chloride ion. In order for an element to combine with chlorine in the ratio of $1:1$, that element must have an oxidation state of $+1$. The only element in Period 2 with an oxidation state of $+1$ is lithium, the element in Group I A.

78. **Ans. 5** Referring to the *Periodic Table of the Elements*, we see that the element in Period 2 with the greatest number of oxidation states is nitrogen,

with 8 different states ranging from -3 to $+5$. The only other element in Period 2 with more than one listed oxidation state is carbon, with 3 different states.

79. Ans. 8 The only elements that do not form compounds with other elements are some of the noble gases. These elements already have a stable outer shell of 8 electrons, and do not have to combine with other elements to become more stable. In the *Periodic Table* they are found in Group *O*. In Period 2 the noble gas is neon. In recent years, scientists have been able to combine some of the noble gases with the most active halogen, fluorine, to form such compounds as XeF_6 and KrF_2. Scientists have not been able to combine neon with other elements to form a compound.

80. Ans. 6 From the *Periodic Table* we see that hydrogen has an oxidation state of $+1$ or -1. In order for hydrogen to form a compound with another element in the ratio of 2 parts hydrogen to one part of the other element, the element must have an oxidation state of either $+2$ or -2. In Period 2, beryllium has an oxidation state of $+2$ and oxygen has an oxidation state of -2. Thus hydrogen might combine with either Be or O to form BeH_2 or H_2O. Beryllium hydride, BeH_2, however, is a nonpolar covalent molecule, since the atoms are in a linear arrangement. We say that the center of positive charge coincides with the center of negative charge so that there is no resultant charge. Structurally the BeH_2 molecule can be shown as follows:

$$\overset{\delta^-}{H}-\overset{\delta^+}{Be}-\overset{\delta^-}{H}$$

Water (H_2O) however, is a polar molecule because the atoms form an angle of 105°. The center of positive charge is in the region of the two hydrogen atoms and the center of the negative charge is in the region of the oxygen atoms. Since the charges do not coincide, the molecule is a dipole. Structurally the H_2O molecule is shown as follows:

$$\overset{\delta^-}{O}$$
$$\delta^+H \quad 105° \quad H\delta^+$$

Thus in Period 2 the element that forms the polar covalent compound with hydrogen is oxygen of Group VI *A*.

GROUP 3

81. Ans. 4 A hydrogen bond is formed between the hydrogen atom of one molecule and a very active nonmetallic atom of another molecule. A chain of molecules is the result. Hydrogen bonds can be formed between hydrogen and flourine and hydrogen and oxygen, for example:

$$\overset{\delta^+}{H}-\overset{\delta^-}{F}\cdots\overset{\delta^+}{H}-\overset{\delta^-}{F} \qquad \overset{\delta^+}{H}-\overset{\delta^-}{O}\cdots\overset{\delta^+}{H}-\overset{\delta^-}{O}$$

$$\underset{H^{\delta^+}}{\diagdown} \qquad \underset{H^{\delta^+}}{\diagdown}$$

A very active element such as fluorine or oxygen has a high electronegativity and a small atomic radius. When a hydrogen atom is bonded to a highly electronegative atom, the hydrogen atom has a very small share of the electron pair. Acting almost like a bare proton, it can be attracted to the electronegative atom of an adjacent molecule.

When a liquid boils, the forces of attraction between the molecules are broken and throughout the liquid molecules boil off as independent molecules of the vapor phase. The strong hydrogen bonds between the molecules of water are quite difficult to break, even with heat. Thus, H_2O has a high boiling point. The compound H_2S has a much lower boiling point because of the weak hydrogen bond between the hydrogen atom of one molecule and the less electronegative sulfur atom of another molecule.

82. Ans. **5** *Metallic bonding* occurs between atoms with low ionization energies and vacant valence orbitals. A low ionization energy indicates a ready tendency for an atom to lose electrons. A metal consists of an arrangement of positive ions, located at the crystal lattice points immersed in a "sea" of mobile electrons, given off by the valence shell of each metal atom. These mobile electrons can be considered as belonging to the crystal as a whole rather than to individual atoms. The mobility of the electrons distinguishes the metallic bond from a ionic or covalent bond, and accounts for the electrical conductivity of metals in the solid or liquid phase.

83. Ans. **2** *Network bonds* are covalent bonds. They link the atoms in a network which extends throughout the substance with an absence of the simple discrete species such as molecules and ions. The result is a network solid or a macromolecule. Network solids are usually very hard, have extremely high melting points, and are poor conductors of heat and electricity. A diamond is an excellent example of a network solid. The strong bonds between carbon atoms keep them in a rigid tetrahedral pattern. Very high temperatures are needed to melt the diamond by breaking these bonds. Note: The diamond crystal is very hard because the strong bonds prevent the scraping off of surface molecules. The rigid pattern of the carbon atoms makes the diamond a poor conductor of heat and the lack of mobile electrons and ions makes the diamond a poor conductor of electricity.

84. Ans. **6** As stated in the answer to question 18, *van der Waals forces* are weak attractive forces that exist between nonpolar molecules. These forces are the result of a momentary imbalance of electron charge distribution that causes a very brief polarization of the molecule. Van der Waals forces make it possible for small nonpolar molecules such as hydrogen, helium and oxygen to

exist in the liquid and solid phases under conditions of low temperature and high pressure. At low temperature and high pressure, the molecules are closer to each other and thus the van der Waals forces are greater, strong enough to change gaseous hydrogen and helium to the liquid and even to the solid phases.

85. Ans. 3 A *coordinate covalent bond* is one in which both electrons forming the bond are donated by the same single atom. In the case of the hydronium ion, a proton forms a coordinate covalent bond with the oxygen of the water molecule, using one of the two unshared pairs of electrons from the oxygen. The result is a *hydrated proton* or *hydronium ion*. The hydration of the proton can be shown by the following equation:

$$
H^+ + H^\times \,{}^{\bullet}H \rightarrow \left[\begin{array}{c} H \\[-2pt] \vdots O_\times \\ H^\times \;\; {}^{\bullet}H \end{array} \right]^+
$$

Note that once the H_3O^+ ion is formed, it is impossible to tell which hydrogen atom was the original free proton.

86. Ans. 6 From the *Periodic Table* we see that as the atomic number of the element increases across Period 2, the atomic radius of the element decreases. The greater number of protons in the nucleus exerts a greater pull on the electrons of the atom. The values of the atomic radii in Period 2 are 1.52, 1.12, 0.88, 0.77, 0.70, 0.66, 0.64 and 1.12 Å. Note that when we reach Group 0, the size of the atom increases, apparently because of the creation of a stable valence shell. On the graph each dot stands for an element in the Period. The graph that declines steadily for seven elements and then increases for the eighth element (Group O) is graph (6).

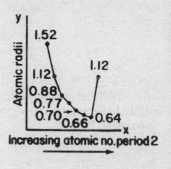

87. Ans. 1 As we go to the right in Period 3, of Table J, the ionization energies do not follow a set pattern, sometimes increasing and sometimes decreasing, but showing an overall increase. The energies are 5.1, 7.6, 6.0, 6.0, 8.1, 10.9, 10.3, and 13.0 e.v. The graph that shows this relation for the seven elements listed in the period is Graph (1).

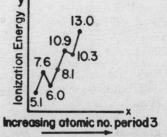

88. **Ans.** **5** Going down Group I A, in *Table J*, we find that the values for the electronegativity are 2.1, 1.0, 0.9, 0.8, 0.8, 0.7 and 0.7. The graph that shows this relationship is Graph (5).

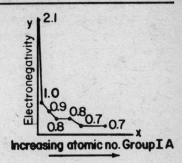

89. **Ans.** **2** Looking at the *Periodic Table*, we see that the oxidation state of all the elements in Group II A have the same value of $+2$. This relationship is shown by graph (2), since all points have the same value.

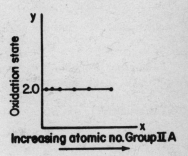

90. **Ans.** **4** Looking at the *Periodic Table*, we see that the values for the atomic radii as we go down Group VI A are 0.66, 1.04, 1.17, 1.37 and 1.65. Thus the atomic radii increases consistently as we go down Group VI A. The additional energy level in each Period as we go down the Periodic Table accounts for this increase. The graph that shows this relation is graph (4).

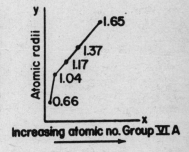

GROUP 4

91. **Ans.** **2** A *molar* solution contains one mole of solute dissolved in one liter (1000 ml.) of *solution*. In order to find out the molarity of a solution, we determine the number of moles of solute that are dissolved in one liter of solution.

The number of grams in one mole of sulfuric acid, H_2SO_4, is equal to its gram-molecular mass. We find the gram-molecular mass by adding up the atomic masses:

$$2\text{ H} = 2 \times 1 = 2$$
$$1\text{ S} = 1 \times 32 = 32$$
$$4\text{ O} = 4 \times 16 = 64$$
$$\text{Gram-molecular mass} = 98 \text{ grams}$$

Since 98 grams is one mole, 49 grams is $\dfrac{49\text{ g}}{98\text{ g}}$ or 0.50 mole of H_2SO_4. Since the volume of the solution is 1 liter, the morality of the solution is 0.50 molar.

NOTE: *The answer should contain as many significant figures as are present in the least accurate number in the division computation. Since the given 49 grams contains two significant figures, the answer, 0.50 M, has two significant figures.*

92. **Ans. 1** Sulfuric acid dissociates in water according to the equation:

$$H_2SO_4(aq) \rightarrow 2H^+(aq) + SO_4^{-2}(aq)$$

The number of moles of each substance is shown by its coefficient. One mole of sulfuric acid supplies two moles of hydronium ions and one mole of sulfate ions. Since the concentration of the sulfuric acid was found to be 0.50 M (see answer to question 91), the concentration of H^+ ions is 2 × 0.50 or 1.0 molar.

93. **Ans. 1** A *normal* solution contains a *gram-equivalent mass* of solute dissolved in a liter of solution. The gram-equivalent mass of an acid such as H_2SO_4 is equal to the gram-molecular mass divided by the number of *available protons* (or hydrogen ions). In this case there are 2 hydrogen ions. The gram-molecular weight of H_2SO_4 is 98 grams. The gram-equivalent weight is therefore 98 ÷ 2 or 49 grams. Since we added 49 grams of H_2SO_4 to make one liter of solution, the solution is 1.0 N.

94. **Ans. 3** If an additional liter of water is added to the solution, it will still contain 0.50 moles of H_2SO_4, but the new volume will be two liters. The molarity in moles per liter will become 0.50 mole ÷ 2.0 liters or 0.25 M.

95. **Ans. 2** Since one mole of copper atoms weighs 64 grams (see *Periodic Table*), 16.0 grams of copper would be $\dfrac{16.0 \text{ g.}}{64 \dfrac{\text{g.}}{\text{mole}}}$ or 0.25 mole of Cu.

In the reaction

$$Cu + 4HNO_3 \rightarrow Cu(NO_3)_2 + 2H_2O + 2NO_2 \uparrow,$$

the coefficients of the equation tell us the number of moles of each substance in the reaction. For each mole of the reactant Cu, one mole of the product $Cu(NO_3)_2$ is formed. Thus the number of moles of $Cu(NO_3)_2$ produced is 0.25 mole.

96. **Ans. 1** From the equation we see that 1 mole of copper produces 2 moles of water. Since we have 0.25 mole of copper, the number of moles

of water produced is 2×0.25 or 0.50 mole of water. Since one mole of water has a mass of $(2 + 16)$ or 18 grams, 0.50 mole of water has a mass of 0.50×18 or 9.0 grams.

97. **Ans. 2** Here we are concerned with the *volume* of NO_2 produced.
STEP 1: Determine the number of moles of the substance whose volume we are asked to find.

$$\text{Moles of } NO_2 \text{ formed} = \frac{\text{Equation moles of } NO_2}{\text{Equation moles of Cu}} \times \text{moles of Cu consumed}$$

$$= \frac{2 \text{ moles of } NO_2}{1 \text{ mole of Cu}} \times 0.25 \text{ mole of Cu}$$

$$= 0.50 \text{ mole of } NO_2 \text{ formed}$$

STEP 2: Find the number of liters of NO_2 by multiplying the number of moles of NO_2 by the gram-molecular volume of gases, 22.4 liters/mole at S.T.P.

$$\text{Volume of } NO_2 \text{ formed} = 0.50 \text{ mole } NO_2 \times 22.4 \text{ liters/mole of } NO_2$$
$$= 11.2 \text{ liters } NO_2 \text{ formed}$$

NOTE: *If significant figures are considered, the correct answer is 11 liters. Here the closest answer is given in choice (2), 11.2.*

98. **Ans. 3** An *empirical formula* is a chemical formula which names the elements in the substance and the simplest ratio of the atoms of these elements. It is sometimes referred to as the simplest formula. In order to find the emprical formula, assign an arbitrary value, say 100 grams, for the mass of the compound.
STEP 1: Multiply the mass by the given percents to find the mass of each element in the compound.

$$\text{Mass of carbon} = .80 \times 100 \text{ grams} = 80 \text{ grams of carbon}$$
$$\text{Mass of hydrogen} = .20 \times 100 \text{ grams} = 20 \text{ grams of hydrogen}$$

STEP 2: Divide each mass by the atomic mass of the corresponding element to find the number of gram-atoms of each element. (A gram-atom of an element contains a mole or 6.02×10^{23} atoms of the element.)

$$\text{G. atoms of } C^2 = 80 \text{ grams} \div 12 \text{ grams/g atom} = 6\tfrac{2}{3} \text{ g. atoms}$$
$$\text{G. atoms of H} = 20 \text{ grams} \div 1 \text{ gram/g atom} = 20 \text{ g. atoms}$$

The ratio of the number of atoms of C to the number of atoms of H in the compound is $6\tfrac{2}{3}$ g. atoms:20 g. atoms or $6\tfrac{2}{3}$:20.
STEP 3: Reduce the ratio $6\tfrac{2}{3}$:20 by dividing both terms of the ratio by $6\tfrac{2}{3}$.

$$6\tfrac{2}{3} \div 6\tfrac{2}{3} = 1; \quad 20 \div 6\tfrac{2}{3} = 3$$

The reduced ratio of 1:3 represents the ratio of the number of C and H atoms in the formula. Thus the required empirical formula is CH_3.

99. **Ans. 4** One mole of any gas occupies 22.4 liters at S.T.P. We are given the density of the gas and asked for the mass of one mole. To find the

mass of 22.4 liters, we multiply the density (or mass of one liter) by the volume (number of liters).

$$\text{Mass of 1 mole} = 1.34 \frac{\text{grams}}{\text{liter}} \times 22.4 \text{ liters}$$

$$= 30.0 \text{ grams}$$

100. Ans. 4 The *molecular formula* is the true formula of the compound. The *empirical formula* is the simplest formula (see answer to question 98). The empirical or simplest formula may or may not be the molecular formula. We know from the answer to question 98 that the empirical formula of the hydrocarbon is CH_3. But any multiple of CH_3 such as C_2H_6, C_3H_9 or C_4H_{12} would still contain the same ratio of C atoms to H atoms. In other words the true molecular formula is (Empirical formula)$_x$ or in this case $(CH_3)_x$ where x is the correct multiple we are seeking.

We can find x if we know the empirical-formula mass and gram-molecular mass of the compound.

$$\text{Empirical-formula mass of } CH_3 = 1 \times 12 + 3 \times 1 = 15$$
$$\text{Molecular mass of } (CH_3)_x = 30.0 \text{ (see answer to question 99)}$$

Since (empirical formula mass)$_x$ = molecular mass, we have

$$(15)x = 30.0$$
$$x = 2.0$$

Since the multiple is 2, $(CH_3)_x$ becomes $(CH_3)_2$ or C_2H_6.

GROUP 5

101. Ans. 1 The *heat of reaction* (ΔH) is the heat energy released or absorbed in a chemical reaction. ΔH represents the difference between the heat content (H) of the products and the heat content of the reactants. Thus we get the formula

$$\Delta H = H_{products} - H_{reactants}$$

The heat content of a substance measures the *internal energy* that is stored during the formation of the substance; thus the heat content is a form of *potential energy*. On the graph shown below, the heat content of the products at P is shown by arrow 2, and the heat content of the reactants at R is shown by arrow 1. The heat of reaction (ΔH) is $H_P - H_R$ as shown by the arrow marked 5. Note that the difference in length of arrows 2 and 1 is equal to the length of arrow 5. Note also that the energy content of the products at P is greater than the energy content of the re-

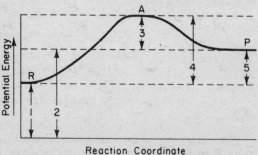

actants at R. In other words the system has *absorbed* or gained energy. This indicates that the reaction shown by the graph is an *endothermic* one. In the formula $\Delta H = H_P - H_R$, ΔH *is positive for an endothermic reaction* since H_P has a larger value than H_R. Chemists have arbitrarily established the formula so that a *positive* ΔH indicates an endothermic reaction because an endothermic reaction absorbs energy and *increases* the internal energy of the system. The value of ΔH in the question is given as $+8.10$ kcal./mole. The positive ΔH confirms what the graph tells us, that the reaction is an endothermic one.

NOTE: If the reaction is *reversed*, the reaction is an *exothermic* one since the final heat content of the products at R is less than the original heat content of the reactants at P. This *loss of heat* by the system would be indicated by a *negative* value for ΔH.

102. Ans. **1** The system contains 100% reactants at the beginning of the curve (R) where the reaction coordinate is zero because the reaction has not yet started. The potential energy or heat content of the reactants is represented by the height of the curve at R and is indicated by the arrow numbered 1.

103. Ans. **3** A chemical reaction takes place if there is an effective collision between two species, for example two molecules. To be effective the colliding molecules must be able to supply enough energy to break the bonds between the atoms of the molecules so that the atoms can become reactive and form new bonds and new molecular compounds. The energy that supplies the initial boost to raise the energy content of the reactants (R) to a point (A) where a reaction can take place is termed *activation energy*. On the graph the activation energy is shown by number 4 on the line that extends a vertical distance from R to A. When the colliding molecules possess this activation energy, an intermediate transitional structure results called the *activated complex*. This is located at the top of the curve above the arrow numbered 3. The activated complex has the maximum heat content of the system. The life of the activated complex is an extremely short one. It is during this brief interval that both molecules have penetrated each other's electron clouds. With old bonds breaking and new bonds forming, the molecular complex shows partial bonding of reactants and products simultaneously. The short-lived activated complex immediately breaks apart, either continuing on to form the products or going back to form the initial reactants. This property of an activated complex can be shown in the reaction between molecules AB and CD:

$$AB + CD = \quad A{\diagdown\!\!\!\!\diagup}B \quad = AD + CB$$
$$\text{reactants} \quad C\!\!-\!\!D \quad \text{products}$$
$$\text{activated}$$
$$\text{complex}$$

The lines in the activated complex represent the transitional bonding that exists.

104. Ans. **3** Here we are concerned with the *reverse reaction* proceeding from P to R with the reactants at P and the products at R. This reaction as mentioned in the answer to question 101 is exothermic since the final products

at R have *less* heat content than the original reactants at P. The activation energy is the energy absorbed by the reactants to form the activated complex at A. This rise in energy level is indicated by arrow 3, the vertical distance between P and A.

105. **Ans. 2** The equation of the reaction is

$$\tfrac{1}{2}N_2(g) + O_2(g) = 1NO_2(g).$$

The heat of reaction (ΔH) is given as $+8.10$ kcal./mole. The positive sign indicates an endothermic reaction which results in an *absorption* of heat and an increase in heat content. When one mole of NO_2 is produced, 8.10 kcal. of heat is absorbed. Thus, if 2.00 moles of NO_2 are produced, 2×8.10 or 16.2 kcal of heat are absorbed.

106. **Ans. 3** When a reversible reaction reaches equilibrium at a given temperature—that is when the rate of the formation of the products is equal to the rate of formation of the reactant in the opposite direction—an equilibrium constant can be derived. This constant is equal to the product of the molar concentration of the products (on the right) divided by the molar concentration of the reactants (on the left) with each concentration raised to the power equal to the number of moles of that substance appearing in the equation. In expressing the constant mathematically brackets are used to indicate concentrations measured in moles per liter. For the given equation:

$$2SO_2(g) + O_2(g) = 2SO_3(g)$$

SO_3, the substance on the right, is in the numerator raised to the second power (there are two moles of SO_3) and the SO_2 and O_2, substances on the left, are in the denominator with the SO_2 also raised to the second power. The equilibrium constant would be:

$$K = \frac{[SO_3]^2}{[SO_2]^2[O_2]}$$

107. **Ans. 1** In the given equation of the reaction, the coefficient of SO_3 is 2. This means that the formation of *two* moles of SO_3 produces 45.0 kcal. Thus in forming *one* mole of SO_3, 22.5 kcal are released. Since the energy content of the system is *less* because of this loss of heat, the value of the heat of reaction, ΔH, is negative. Thus the value of ΔH is -22.5 kcal.

108. **Ans. 2** *Le Chatelier's principle* states that if a system in equilibrium is subjected to a stress (such as increased temperature or pressure), the equilibrium will be shifted in the direction that relieves the effects of stress. Here the stress is an increase in pressure. Therefore we expect the reaction to go in the direction which creates a lower pressure. The pressure in a closed container is dependent upon the volume of the gas in that container. Volumes of gases are proportional to the number of moles as shown by the coefficients of the molecules in the equation of the reaction. Here the equation is

$$2SO_2 + O_2 = 2SO_3 + 45.0 \text{ kcal.}$$

The reactants $2SO_2$ and O_2, in the container occupy $2 + 1$ or 3 molar volumes. The product $2SO_3$ occupies 2 molar volumes. Thus the relief of the pressure stress is on the right where there is less volume (fewer molecules). When pressure is applied to the system, the equilibrium point will be shifted toward the SO_3 on the right, and away from the SO_2 on the left. Thus the number of moles of SO_2 present will be less than the original number of moles present.

109. Ans. **2** Again using Le Chatelier's principle, an increase in the temperature of a system in equilibrium will displace the equilibrium in a manner that results in the absorption of heat. Conversely, a decrease in temperature will displace the equilibrium in the direction that results in the release of heat. We are given an *exothermic* reaction, a reaction that releases heat.

$$2SO_2 + O_2 = 2SO_3 + 45.0 \text{ kcal.}$$

As the reaction proceeds to the right, heat is being given off and the temperature of the system is rising. The removal of heat (decease in temperature) will therefore favor the forward reaction, and the amount of O_2 present will decrease.

110. Ans. **1** Here the stress is the stress of increased concentration of SO_2. In accordance with Le Chatelier's principle, increasing the concentration of SO_2 will force the reaction to the right to consume the added SO_2 and thus relieve the stress of the increased concentration. Since the reaction will go to the right, the number of moles of SO_3 present after the new equilibrium is reached will be greater than the original number of moles.

111. Ans. **1** According to the *Brønsted-Lowry Theory*, an acid is a *proton donor* and a base a *proton acceptor*. The strength of an acid is measured by its tendency to lose the proton and become a base. *Table H* of the Reference Tables lists conjugate acid-base systems. The acids are listed at the left, with the strongest acid at the top. The strongest acid listed is hydrochloric acid, HCl.

112. Ans. **4** Bases are listed on the right side of *Table H*, with the weakest bases at the *top*. Note that a strong acid has a weak conjugate base. Since the acid shows a strong tendency to lose its proton, the negative ion that is produced will show little tendency to regain it. Any base above water on the right side of *Table H* is a weaker base than water. Of the choices given, only HSO_4^- is above water, and, therefore, a weaker base than water.

113. Ans. **2** A *conjugate acid-base pair* consists of an acid and the negative ion created by the removal of a proton from that acid. Examples of conjugate pairs as given in *Table H* are HCl, Cl^-; H_2SO_4, HSO_4^-; H_3O^+, H_2O; and NH_3, NH_2^-. Note that each conjugate acid-base pair is related by the transfer of a proton.

$$\text{Acid} - H^+ \rightarrow \text{Base} \quad \text{or} \quad \text{Base} + H^- \rightarrow \text{Acid}$$

In the reaction given,

$$CO_3^{-2} + H_2O = HCO_3^- + OH^-$$

the H_2O acts as an acid in the forward reaction, donating a proton to the CO_3^{-2} ion. The H_2O without its proton is now a base, an OH^- ion. At the same time the CO_3^{-2} ion acts as a base and gains a proton to become an acid, the HCO_3^- ion. Thus the reaction contains two conjugate acid-base pairs—(H_2O, OH^-) and (HCO_3^-, CO_3^{-2}). Each conjugate pair is related by the transfer of a proton.

114. **Ans. 4** The product of the concentrations of the H^+ ion and the OH^- ion in water is a constant represented as K_w. Its value is 1×10^{-14}

$$K_w = [H^+][OH^-] = 1 \times 10^{-14}$$

The brackets indicate that the concentrations are expressed in moles per liter. If we are given one concentration and asked for the other, all we need do is substitute in the above equation. In this case we are given that the concentration of the H^+ ion is 1×10^{-2} M. (M stands for molar or moles per liter)

$$[H^+][OH^-] = 1 \times 10^{-14}$$
$$(1 \times 10^{-2})[OH^-] = 1 \times 10^{-14}$$
$$[OH^-] = \frac{1 \times 10^{-14}}{1 \times 10^{-2}}$$
$$[OH^-] = 1 \times 10^{-12} \, M$$

115. **Ans. 2** An *amphiprotic (amphoteric)* substance is a substance that acts as an acid or a base depending on its chemical environment. It acts as a weak base in the presence of an acid and as an acid in the presence of a strong base. According to the Brønsted-Lowry Theory, an acid is a proton donor and a base is a proton acceptor. Thus a species (molecule or ion) that can gain a proton and also lose a proton is amphiprotic. The NO_3^- ion cannot act as an acid since it cannot lose a proton it does not have. It can act only as a base by accepting a proton to form the acid HNO_3:

$$NO_3^- + H^+ \rightleftarrows HNO_3$$

One can recognize amphiprotic species by referring to *Table H*. If the same species appears in both columns, it is amphiprotic since it is both an acid and a base.

116. **Ans. 1** In a balanced redox reaction, the number of electrons lost by one species must equal the number of electrons gained by the other. Using the ion-electron method, we can break down the given redox reaction into two half-reactions:

Oxidation:

$$(1) \quad Fe^{+2} - 1e^- \rightarrow Fe^{+3}$$

One electron must be lost to raise the oxidation state of Fe from $+2$ to $+3$.

Reduction:

$$MnO_4^- + 8H^+ + ? \rightarrow Mn^{+2} + 4H_2O$$

The net charge on the left is (-1 and $+8$) or $+7$. The net charge on the right is $+2$. To change from $+7$ to $+2$, five electrons must be gained. Thus the reduction half-reaction becomes

$$(2) \quad MnO_4^- + 8H^+ + 5e^- \rightarrow Mn^{+2} + 4H_2O$$

In order for the number of electrons lost to equal the number of electrons gained, we must multiply the first equation by 5 and then add the resulting equation to the second:

$$5Fe^{+2} - 5e^- \rightarrow 5Fe^{+3}$$
$$\underline{8H^+ + MnO_4^- + 5e^- \rightarrow Mn^{+2} + 4H_2O}$$

Adding we get,

$$5Fe^{+2} + MnO_4^- + 8H^+ \rightarrow 5Fe^{+3} + Mn^{+2} + 4H_2O.$$

Note that the electrons cancel out ($+5e^-$ and $-5e^-$) leaving no free electrons.

117. Ans. **2** *Table L, Standard Oxidation Potentials*, lists some metals and a few nonmetals in the order of decreasing tendency to lose electrons. Recall that the loss of electrons is termed oxidation, and that the best reducing agents are the ones most easily oxidized. Since a reducing agent loses electrons, the strongest reducing agent has the highest oxidation potential and is at the top of the table. Of the choices given, Ca^0 is the closest to the top of the list.

118. Ans. **1** Any metal above Ag on *Table L* will reduce the Ag^+ ion to the Ag^0 atom. Any metal below zinc on *Table L* will not reduce the Zn^{+2} ion to the zinc atom. Of the choices given, only copper is above silver but below zinc on *Table L*.

119. Ans. **1** The equation $2Cr + 3Pb^{+2} = 2Cr^{+3} + 3Pb$ actually consists of two half-reactions. The Cr^0 atom is oxidized to the Cr^{+3} ion and the Pb^{+2} ion is reduced to the Pb atom. Referring to *Table L* we can write the two oxidation half-reactions with their standard oxidation potentials (E_0).

$$(1) \quad Cr = Cr^{+3} + 3e^-; \quad E^0 = 0.74$$
$$(2) \quad Pb = Pb^{+2} + 2e^-; \quad E^0 = 0.13$$

We must rewrite equation (2) as a reduction half-reaction since Pb^{+2} is being reduced to Pb and not vice versa. We can change an oxidation half-reaction to a reduction half-reaction by reversing the equation and changing the sign of E^0. Thus $Pb = Pb^{+2} + 2e^-$; $E^0 = 0.13$ becomes

$$(3) \quad Pb^{+2} + 2e^- = Pb; \quad E^0 = -0.13$$

We get the balanced half-reactions (electrons gained = electrons lost) by multiplying equation (1) by 2 and equation (3) by 3.

$$(4) \quad 2Cr = 2Cr^{+3} + 6e^- \quad E^0 = 0.74$$
$$(5) \quad 3Pb^{+2} + 6e^- = 3Pb \quad E^0 = -0.13$$

Note that the E^0 is a constant and does not depend on the moles of the ions or atoms in the half-reactions. Adding the two half-reactions and their standard oxidation potentials we get the equation of the overall reaction together with its E^0.

$$2Cr + 3Pb^{+2} = 2Cr^{+3} + 3Pb; \quad E^0 = (0.74) + (-0.13) = 0.61$$

120. **Ans. 4** As mentioned in the answer to question 117, *Table L* lists half-reactions primarily for metals, in the order of decreasing tendency to lose electrons. Since reducing agents lose electrons, the strongest reducing agent is at the top of the Table and the strongest oxidizing agent is at the bottom of the Table. Here we are asked for the nonmetal that is the *least* active oxidizing agent (most active reducing agent). This would be the nonmetal that is highest on *Table L*. This nonmetal is I_2 with a E^0 of -0.54.

7

Examination June, 1967　Chemistry (Experimental)

PART ONE　*Answer all questions in this part.*

DIRECTIONS (1–60): *For each statement or question, write in the space provided, the* number *preceding the word or expression that, of those given, best completes the statement or answers the question.* [60]

1. Gases deviate from the ideal gas behavior because molecules (1) are colorless (2) attract each other (3) contain covalent bonds (4) show Brownian motion　　　　　　　　　　1........

2. Which set of conditions represents the easiest way to liquefy a gas? (1) low temperature and high pressure (2) low temperature and low pressure (3) high temperature and low pressure (4) high temperature and high pressure　　　2........

3. Forty ml. of a gas is collected at 25°C. If the temperature is raised to 50°C. and the pressure remains constant, the new volume of the gas, expressed in milliliters, is equal to

(1) $40 \times \frac{323}{298}$ (2) $40 \times \frac{298}{323}$ (3) $40 \times \frac{25}{50}$ (4) $40 \times \frac{50}{25}$　　3........

4. A sample of water is boiling in an open vessel. The vapor pressure of the water, expressed in millimeters of mercury, is approximately (1) 100 (2) 273 (3) 0 (4) 760　　4........

5. If 150 grams of water is heated from 20° C. to 30° C., the number of calories of heat energy absorbed is approximately (1) 10 (2) 150 (3) 1,500 (4) 15,000　　5........

6. The number of orbitals in the $2p$ subshell is (1) 1 (2) 2 (3) 3 (4) 6　　6........

7. The element whose electron configuration is $1s^2 2s^2 2p^6 3s^2$ is a (1) metalloid (2) metal (3) noble gas (4) non-metal　　7........

8. If the atomic number of element X is 7, the best electron dot symbol for the element is

(1) X· (2) Ẍ (3) ·Ẍ: (4) ·Ẍ:　　8........

9. When a radioactive nucleus emits an alpha particle, the mass number of the atom (1) increases, and its atomic number decreases (2) decreases, and its atomic number decreases (3) decreases, and its atomic number remains the same (4) remains the same, and its atomic number decreases　　9........

1

10. Which electron configuration represents an atom in an excited state? (1) $1s^2 2s^2 2p^6 4s^1$ (2) $1s^2 2s^2$ (3) $1s^2 2s^2 2p^6$ (4) $1s^2 2s^2 2p^6 3s^2 3p^1$ 10........

11. Neutral atoms of ^{23}Na and ^{24}Na *differ* with respect to (1) atomic volume (2) number of electrons (3) number of neutrons (4) number of protons 11........

12. An element has the electron configuration $1s^2 2s^2 2p^6 3s^2 3p^2$. The number of valence electrons is (1) 6 (2) 2 (3) 3 (4) 4 12........

13. Which is the electron configuration for a neutral atom with an atomic number of 18? (1) $1s^2 2s^2 2p^6 3s^1 3p^7$ (2) $1s^2 2s^2 2p^6 3s^7 3p^1$ (3) $1s^2 2s^2 2p^6 3s^2 3p^6$ (4) $1s^2 2s^2 2p^8 3s^2 3p^4$ 13........

14. When sodium and chlorine unite chemically, energy is (1) released, and ionic bonds are formed (2) released, and covalent bonds are formed (3) absorbed, and ionic bonds are formed (4) absorbed, and covalent bonds are formed 14........

15. Oxygen has an oxidation state of +2 in the compound (1) H_2O_2 (2) CO_2 (3) H_2O (4) OF_2 15......

16. Experiment shows that H_2O is a dipole while CO_2 is not a dipole. The two structures which best illustrate this fact are

(1) O=C=O,   O   (3) C ,   H—H—O
              / \   // \\
             H   H   O   O

(2) O=C=O , H—O—H (4) O   ,   H
                              ‖ |
                              C=O   O—H   16........

17. Multiple covalent bonds exist in a molecule of (1) F_2 (2) H_2 (3) N_2 (4) Cl_2 17........

18. Which bond has the *least* ionic character? (1) P—Cl (2) H—Cl (3) Br—Cl (4) O—Cl 18........

19. Which is likely to have the highest melting point? (1) He (2) CsF (3) NH_3 (4) $CHCl_3$ 19........

20. In which noble gas are the Van der Waals forces the greatest? (1) Ne (2) Ar (3) Kr (4) Xe 20........

21. Elements which generally exhibit multiple oxidation states and whose ions are usually colored are (1) metalloids (2) transition elements (3) nonmetals (4) gases 21........

22. Which group in the *Periodic Table* contains both metals and nonmetals? (1) I B (2) II A (3) O (4) IV A 22........

23. Which group in the *Periodic Table* contains the *least* reactive elements? (1) I A (2) VI B (3) III A (4) O 23........

24. As one reads from left to right in Period 2, ionization energy generally (1) decreases, and atomic size decreases (2) decreases, and atomic size increases (3) increases, and atomic size increases (4) increases, and atomic size decreases 24........

25. What volume will 1.5×10^{23} molecules of oxygen occupy at S.T.P.? (1) 1.48 liters (2) 3.8 liters (3) 5.6 liters (4) 89.6 liters 25........

26. In the reaction $Zn(s) + 2H^+(aq) = Zn^{+2}(aq) + H_2(g)$, how many liters of hydrogen gas measured at S.T.P. are produced when 6.54 grams of Zn is reacted with sufficient acid? (1) 1.12 (2) 2.24 (3) 11.2 (4) 22.4 26........

27. The empirical formula of a compound is CH_2. One mole of this compound has a mass of 42 grams. Its molecular formula is (1) CH_2 (2) C_2H_2 (3) C_3H_6 (4) C_3H_8 27........

28. In the reaction $2HCl + Ca(OH)_2 \rightarrow CaCl_2 + 2H_2O$, how many moles of water are produced when 0.4 mole of $Ca(OH)_2$ is consumed? (1) 0.1 (2) 0.2 (3) 0.8 (4) 0.4 28........

29. The number of moles of KCl in 1,000 ml. of 3-molar solution is (1) 1 (2) 2 (3) 3 (4) 1.5 29........

30. Which water solution will have the lowest freezing point? (1) 1 molal $CaCl_2$ (2) 1 molal NaCl (3) 1 molal $C_{12}H_{22}O_{11}$ (4) 1 molal CH_3COOH 30........

31. In the reaction $2C_2H_6(g) + 7O_2(g) \rightarrow 4CO_2(g) + 6H_2O(g)$, how many liters of oxygen is required for the complete combustion of 14 liters of ethane? (1) 7.0 (2) 2.0 (3) 49 (4) 98 31........

32. Which conditions most favor a spontaneous chemical reaction? (1) decreasing energy content and decreasing entropy (2) decreasing energy content and increasing entropy (3) increasing energy content and increasing entropy (4) increasing energy content and decreasing entropy 32........

33. Which carbonate is *least* soluble in water?

Formula	K_{sp}
(1) $BaCO_3$	5×10^{-9}
(2) $CaCO_3$	4.8×10^{-9}
(3) $FeCO_3$	2×10^{-11}
(4) $PbCO_3$	1×10^{-13}

33........

34. For the system $2A(g) + B(g) = 3C(g)$, the expression for the equilibrium constant K is   (1) $\dfrac{[2A] \ [B]}{[3C]}$ (2) $\dfrac{[A]^2 \ [B]}{[C]^3}$

(3) $\dfrac{[3C]}{[2A] \ [B]}$ (4) $\dfrac{[C]^3}{[A]^2 \ [B]}$ 34........

35. Given $H_2(g) + \frac{1}{2}O_2(g) = H_2O(g) + 57.8$ kcal., the reaction is   (1) exothermic, and the $\triangle H$ is negative (2) endothermic, and the $\triangle H$ is negative (3) exothermic, and the $\triangle H$ is positive (4) endothermic, and the $\triangle H$ is positive   35........

36. What is the most logical value of the equilibrium constant K for a reaction in which the original reactants are largely converted to products?   (1) 1.0 (2) 0 (3) 10. (4) 1.0×10^{-4} 36........

37. The system $2SO_2(g) + O_2(g) = 2SO_3(g) + 44$ kcal. is in equilibrium at 25° C. Which change in conditions would result in the largest increase in concentration of SO_3?   (1) increased pressure, increased temperature   (2) increased pressure, decreased temperature (3) decreased pressure, decreased temperature (4) decreased pressure, increased temperature   37........

38. The effect of a catalyst in a chemical reaction is to change the   (1) activation energy   (2) equilibrium concentration (3) heat of reaction (4) final products   38........

39. When the pH of a solution is 2, the hydrogen ion concentration in moles per liter is   (1) 1×10^{-14} (2) 1×10^{-2} (3) 1×10^{-7} (4) 1×10^{-12} 39........

40. Which Brönsted acid is strongest?   (1) NH_3 (2) H_2O (3) NH_4^+ (4) HSO_4^- 40........

41. The best conductor of electricity is a 1.0 M solution of (1) boric acid (2) acetic acid (3) sulfuric acid (4) phosphoric acid   41........

42. Given that $K_w = [H^+] \ [OH^-] = 1 \times 10^{-14}$. What is the concentration of the $H^+(aq)$ in the solution if the concentration of $OH^-(aq)$ in the solution is 1×10^{-6} molar?   (1) 1×10^{-7} M (2) 1×10^{-14} M (3) 1×10^{-8} M (4) 1×10^{-2} M   42........

43. An acid-base conjugate pair for the reaction $H_3BO_3(s) + H_2O(l) = H_3O^+(aq) + H_2BO_3^-(aq)$ is (1) H_3BO_3 and H_3O^+ (2) H_2O and $H_2BO_3^-$ (3) H_3BO_3 and $H_2BO_3^-$ (4) H_3O^+ and OH^- 43........

44. If one mole of sulfuric acid reacts with an excess of sodium hydroxide, how many moles of water are formed?   (1) 1 (2) 2   (3) 3   (4) 4   44........

45. The oxidation number of sulfur in K_2SO_3 is   (1) +6 (2) −2   (3) +3   (4) +4   45........

46. During the electrolysis of fused NaCl, which reaction occurs at the positive electrode?   (1) Chloride ions are oxidized. (2) Chloride ions are reduced.   (3) Sodium ions are oxidized. (4) Sodium ions are reduced.   46........

47. When the equation for the following redox reaction is completely balanced, what is the coefficient in front of the Cl^{-1}? $Cr_2O_7^{-2} + 14H^+ + \ldots Cl^{-1} \rightarrow 2Cr^{+3} + \ldots Cl_2 + 7H_2O$ (1) 6 (2) 2   (3) 3   (4) 4   47........

48. Four colorless salt solutions are placed in separate test tubes and a strip of copper is placed in each solution. Which solution finally turns blue?   (1) $Pb(NO_3)_2$ (2) $Zn(NO_3)_2$ (3) $AgNO_3$ (4) $Cd(NO_3)_2$ 48........

49. Which reaction occurs spontaneously? (1) $Zn + Pb^{+2} = Zn^{+2} + Pb$ (2) $3Pb + 2Cr^{+3} = 3Pb^{+2} + 2Cr$ (3) $Br_2 + 2Cl^- = Cl_2 + 2Br^-$ (4) $Au + 3Ag^+ = Au^{+3} + 3Ag$ 49........

50. Which is the strongest oxidizing agent?   (1) F_2 (2) I_2 (3) Au^{+3} (4) Ag^+ 50........

51. The E^0 value for the reduction of $Cu^{+2}(aq)$ to $Cu(s)$ by metallic nickel is   (1) +0.11 V.   (2) +0.23 V. (3) +0.34 V.   (4) +0.57 V.   51........

52. What is the name of the compound below?

$$\begin{array}{ccccc} & H & H & H & H \\ & | & | & | & | \\ H- & C- & C- & C- & C-H \\ & | & | & | & | \\ & H & H & Cl & H \end{array}$$

(1) 1—chlorobutane   (2) 2—chlorobutane   (3) 3—chlorobutane   (4) 4—chlorobutane   52........

53. Which two compounds are isomers of each other? (1) CH_3OCH_3 and CH_3CH_2OH (2) CH_3CH_2Cl and C_6H_5Cl (3) CH_3COCH_3 and CH_3OCH_3 (4) $CH_3(CH_2)_2CH_3$ and $CH_3(CH)_2CH_3$ 53........

54. Which compound is an organic acid?   (1) CH_3COOH (2) CH_3COOCH_3 (3) C_3H_5OH (4) $CH_3CHOHCH_3$ 54........

55. The reaction

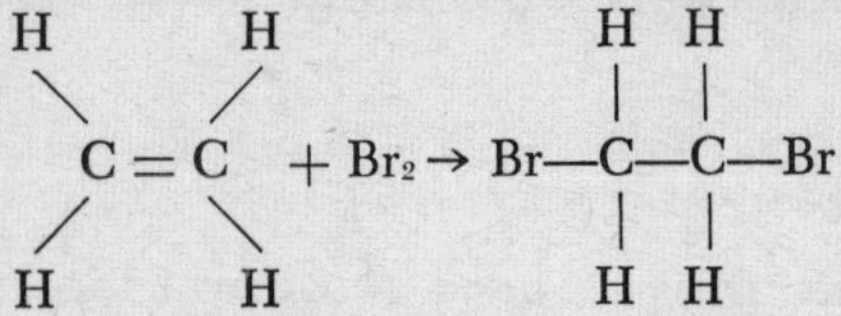

$$
\begin{array}{c}
H \quad\quad H \quad\quad\quad\quad H\ H \\
\backslash \quad\ / \quad\quad\quad\quad\quad |\ \ | \\
C = C \ + Br_2 \rightarrow Br—C—C—Br \\
/ \quad\ \backslash \quad\quad\quad\quad\quad |\ \ | \\
H \quad\quad H \quad\quad\quad\quad H\ H
\end{array}
$$

is an example of   (1) substitution   (2) hydrogenation
(3) polymerization   (4) addition   55........

56. The general formula for the alkane series is   (1) C_nH_{2n}
(2) C_nH_{2n-2} (3) C_nH_{2n+2} (4) C_nH_{2n-6} 56........

Note that questions 57 through 60 have only three choices.

57. As the volume occupied by one mole of CO_2 increases, temperature remaining constant, the pressure exerted by the gas
(1) decreases   (2) increases   (3) remains the same   57........

58. As two atoms of hydrogen combine to form a molecule of hydrogen, the total energy of the two atoms   (1) decreases
(2) increases   (3) remains the same   58........

59. When a magnesium ion is changed to an atom, its radius
(1) decreases   (2) increases   (3) remains the same   59........

60. Given the equilibrium system $H_2(g) + I_2(g) = 2HI(g)$.
As pressure increases, temperature remaining constant, the number of moles of HI   (1) decreases   (2) increases   (3) remains the same   60........

PART TWO   *This part consists of six groups. Choose four of these six groups. Be sure that you answer all questions in each group chosen. Write the answers to these questions in the space provided.*

GROUP 1

DIRECTIONS (61–65): *Base your answers to questions 61 through 65 on the graph below, which represents the uniform heating of a sample of a substance, starting with the solid below its melting point.*

Write the number of the word or expression that best completes each statement or answers each question.   [5]

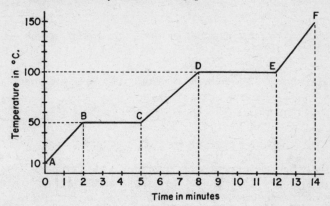

A steady source of heat delivers 100 calories per minute.

61. The sample undergoes a phase change between points
(1) A and B   (2) C and D   (3) D and E   (4) E and F   61........

62. The melting point temperature of the substance in ° C. is
(1) 10   (2) 50   (3) 100   (4) 150   62........

63. The number of calories required to heat the sample to its melting point is   (1) 50   (2) 200   (3) 300   (4) 400   63........

64. The number of calories required to melt the sample at its melting temperature is   (1) 100   (2) 200   (3) 300
(4) 500   64........

65. The sample is at its highest average kinetic energy at point
(1) A   (2) E   (3) C   (4) F   65........

DIRECTIONS (66–70): *For each substance in questions 66 through 70, write the number of the organic reaction, chosen from the list below, which will produce this substance.*   [5]

Organic Reactions

(1) Esterification   (4) Fermentation
(2) Saponification   (5) Substitution
(3) Polymerization   (6) Halogen addition

66. Ethanol   66........

67. Glycerol   67........

68. Methyl acetate   68........

69. Polyethylene   69........

70. Dichloromethane   70........

GROUP 2

DIRECTIONS (71–75): *Given below are electron configurations for some neutral atoms. Write the* number *of the configuration which best answers each* question.　　[5]

Key: ⊞ represents a pair of electrons with opposite spins.

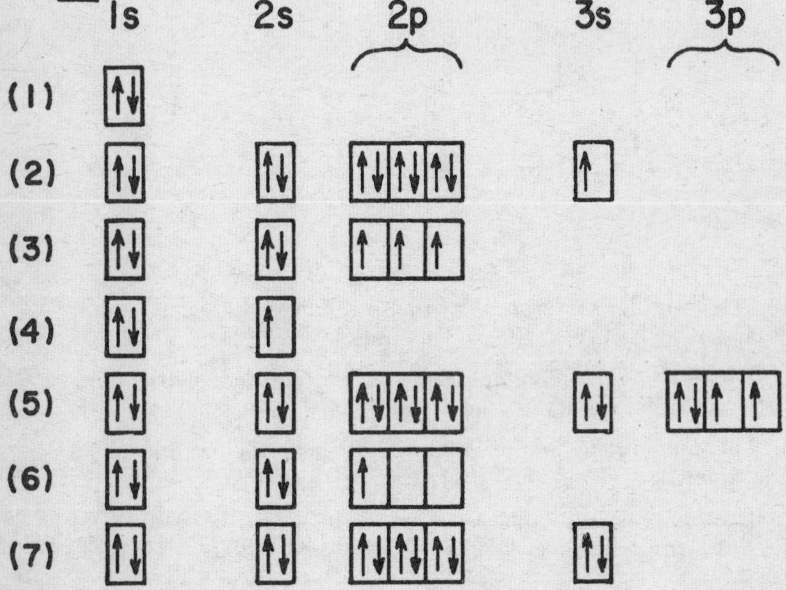

	1s	2s	2p	3s	3p
(1)	↑↓				
(2)	↑↓	↑↓	↑↓ ↑↓ ↑↓	↑	
(3)	↑↓	↑↓	↑ ↑ ↑		
(4)	↑↓	↑			
(5)	↑↓	↑↓	↑↓ ↑↓ ↑↓	↑↓	↑↓ ↑ ↑
(6)	↑↓	↑↓	↑		
(7)	↑↓	↑↓	↑↓ ↑↓ ↑↓	↑↓	

71. Which configuration is correct for nitrogen?　　71........

72. Which is the configuration with the lowest first ionization energy?　　72........

73. Which is the configuration of the element with six valence electrons?　　73........

74. Which configuration is correct for a noble gas?　　74........

75. Which configuration belongs to a Group II A element?　　75........

DIRECTIONS (76–80): *For each description in questions 76 through 80, write the* number *of the diagram which best illustrates that description.* [5]

(1) 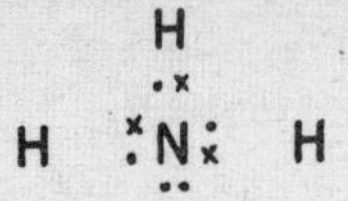 H   :N: H
     H
    .x

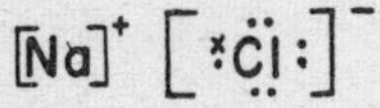

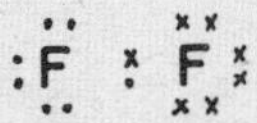

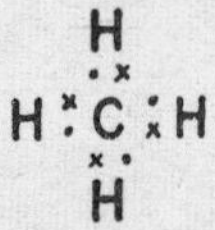

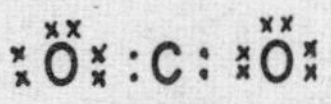

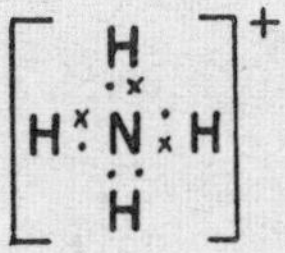

76. A nonpolar, covalent bond   76........

(2) [Na]⁺ [:Cl:]⁻

77. A polar, covalent molecule   77........

(3) :F : F:

78. An ionic compound   78........

(4) H:C:H
    H
    H

79. A compound whose molecules have a linear structure   79........

(5) :O::C::O:

(6) [H:N:H]⁺
      H
      H

80. A coordinate covalent bond   80........

GROUP 3

DIRECTIONS (81–85): *For each of statements 81 through 85, write the* number *preceding the bond or binding forces,* chosen from the list below, *which is most closely associated with that statement.*   [5]

Bonds or Binding Forces

(1) Ionic bonds
(2) Network bonds
(3) Coordinate covalent bonds
(4) Hydrogen bonds

(5) Metallic bonds
(6) Van der Waals forces
(7) Triple covalent bonds

81. A proton combines with water to form a hydronium ion.   81........

82. Mobility of valence electrons results in good electrical conductivity in the solid phase.   82........

83. Nonconductors in the solid phase become electrical conductors in the liquid phase.   83........

84. Solid iodine sublimes readily upon heating.   84........

85. The boiling point of hydrogen fluoride is much higher than that of hydrogen chloride, hydrogen bromide, or hydrogen iodide.   85........

DIRECTIONS (86–90): *For each statement in questions 86 through 90, write the symbol of the element in Period 3 of the* Periodic Table of the Elements *which is most closely associated with that statement.* [5]

86. This element combines to form a strong binary acid. 86........

87. This element has the largest atomic radius. 87........

88. This element assumes only a +3 oxidation state in chemical combination. 88........

89. This element is best described as a metalloid. 89........

90. This element is the *least* reactive of the elements in Period 3. 90........

GROUP 4

DIRECTIONS (91–100): *For each of questions 91 through 100, write the number of the word or expression that best completes the statement or answers the question.* [10]

91. What is the percent by mass of sulfur in sulfur dioxide?
(1) 16% (2) 33% (3) 50% (4) 67% 91........

92. How many moles of H_2SO_4 are present in 250 ml. of a 2.00 M solution? (1) 0.50 (2) 1.25 (3) 2.00 (4) 8.00 92........

93. If 500 ml. of 1.0 M H_2SO_4 is diluted with H_2O to a new volume of 1,000 ml., the molarity of the new solution is
(1) 1.0 (2) 2.0 (3) 0.25 (4) 0.50 93........

Base your answers to questions 94 and 95 on the following information: 192 grams of CuS is oxidized completely according to the reaction $2CuS + 3O_2 \rightarrow 2\,CuO + 2SO_2$.

94. How many moles of CuO are produced? (1) 1 (2) 2
(3) 3 (4) 4 94........

95. How many liters of O_2, measured at S.T.P., are consumed?
(1) 11.2 (2) 22.4 (3) 44.8 (4) 67.2 95........

Questions 96 through 100 refer to the gas nitrogen (II) *oxide (molecular formula* NO).

96. What is the mass of two moles of this gas? (1) 15 grams
(2) 30 grams (3) 60 grams (4) 22 grams 96........

97. The gas occupies a volume of 33.6 liters at S.T.P. The number of moles of gas present is (1) 1.00 (2) 1.50
(3) 3.00 (4) 4.50 97........

98. How many molecules of NO are contained in two moles?

(1) $\dfrac{6.02 \times 10^{23}}{2}$ (3) $2(6.02 \times 10^{23})$

(2) 6.02×10^{23} (4) 2×22.4 98........

99. If two moles of this gas react completely with oxygen according to the equation $2NO + O_2 \rightarrow 2NO_2$, how many moles of O_2 will be consumed?   (1) 1   (2) 2   (3) $\frac{1}{2}$ (4) 4   99........

100. What is the density of the gas at S.T.P.?
(1) 1.25 g./l.   (2) 1.34 g./l.   (3) 1.43 g./l.   (4) 1.64 g./l.   100........

GROUP 5

DIRECTIONS (101–110): *For each of questions 101 through 110, write the number of the word or expression that best completes the statement or answers the question.* [10]

Base your answers to questions 101 through 105 on the graph below, which illustrates a potential energy diagram for the reaction $Br + H_2 =$ $HBr + H$, *an intermediate step in the reaction between bromine and hydrogen.*

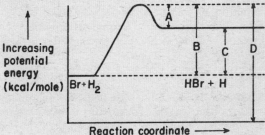

101. Which interval on the graph corresponds to the heat of reaction for this reaction?   (1) A   (2) B   (3) C   (4) D   101........

102. Which interval on the graph corresponds to the energy of activation for the forward reaction?   (1) A   (2) B (3) C   (4) D   102........

103. On the graph, the activation energy for the reverse reaction ($HBr + H \rightarrow Br + H_2$) is given by interval   (1) A (2) B   (3) C   (4) D   103........

104. If a catalyst were introduced into the reaction, which interval would *not* be changed?   (1) A   (2) B   (3) C (4) D   104........

105. The effect on the *rate* of the reaction of raising the temperature of the system would be to
(1) decrease only the rate of the reaction $Br + H_2 \rightarrow HBr + H$
(2) decrease only the rate of the reaction $HBr + H \rightarrow Br + H_2$
(3) increase only the rate of the reaction $Br + H_2 \rightarrow HBr + H$
(4) increase the rate of both forward and reverse reactions 105........

Base your answers to questions 106 *through* 110 *on the information below:*

Ammonium chloride, NH_4Cl, is dissolved in a flask containing water. After several days, solid NH_4Cl still remains on the bottom of the stoppered flask.

106. If more solid NH_4Cl is added to the system and the temperature remains unchanged, the concentration of the solution will (1) increase, and the amount of solid on the bottom will remain the same (2) remain the same, and the amount of solid on the bottom will increase (3) decrease, and the vapor pressure will increase (4) decrease, and the amount of solid on the bottom will increase. 106........

107. If the stopper is left off the flask for several weeks, what can be observed? (1) The amounts of liquid and solid will remain unchanged. (2) The level of the liquid will remain the same, and the amount of solid NH_4Cl will increase. (3) The level of the liquid will fall, and the amount of solid NH_4Cl will remain the same. (4) The level of the liquid will fall, and the amount of solid NH_4Cl will increase. 107........

Note that questions 108 *through* 110 *have only* three *choices.*

108. If the flask and its contents are cooled, the amount of solid NH_4Cl in the bottom of the flask will (1) decrease (2) increase (3) remain the same 108........

109. If more water is added and the temperature is kept constant, the mass of solid NH_4Cl in the bottom of the flask will (1) decrease (2) increase (3) remain the same 109........

110. If a soluble salt yielding Cl^- ions is stirred into the system, the concentration of the $NH_4^+(aq)$ ions will (1) decrease (2) increase (3) remain the same 110........

GROUP 6

DIRECTIONS (111–120): *Write the* number *preceding the word or expression that best completes* each *statement or answers* each *question.* [10]

111. Given a 0.1 M solution of each of the following, which solution will contain the largest concentration of hydronium ions? (1) $NaHSO_4$ (2) NH_4Cl (3) HCl (4) NH_3 111........

112. Which is the conjugate base of the hydrated aluminum ion? (1) OH^- (2) Al^{+3} (3) $Al(H_2O)_6^{+3}$ (4) $Al(H_2O)_5(OH)^{+2}$

112........

113. Which of these is the weakest acid? (1) hypochlorous acid (2) nitric acid (3) hydrochloric acid (4) acetic acid

113........

114. The addition of solid sodium carbonate to pure water causes (1) an increase in the hydronium ion concentration (2) an increase in pH (3) no change in pH (4) a decrease in hydroxide ion concentration

114........

115. In the reaction $NH_3 + H_2O = NH_4^+(aq) + OH^-(aq)$, which are the two Brönsted bases? (1) NH_4^+ and H_2O (2) NH_4^+ and OH^- (3) NH_3 and H_2O (4) NH_3 and OH^-

115........

Base your answers to questions 116 through 120 on the diagram below.

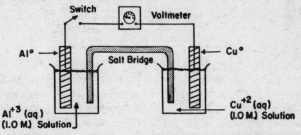

$$2Al(s) + 3Cu^{+2}(aq) = 2Al^{+3}(aq) + 3Cu(s)$$

116. If 2 moles of Al reacts according to the equation above, the number of moles of *electrons* transferred will be (1) 1 (2) 2 (3) 3 (4) 6

116........

117. In this reaction, the oxidizing agent is the (1) Al (2) Al^{+3} (3) Cu^{+2} (4) Cu

117........

118. When the switch is closed, what will be the maximum voltage reading? (1) 0.00 (2) 2.00 (3) 1.32 (4) 0.72

118........

119. Electrons flow from the (1) Al to the Cu (2) Al^{+3} to the Al (3) Cu^{+2} to the Cu (4) Cu to the Al

119........

120. When chemical equilibrium is attained by this cell, the voltage will be (1) 0.00 volts (2) 2.00 volts (3) −1.32 volt (4) −1.44 volt

120........

Answers to Chemistry (Experimental)　June, 1967

PART ONE

1. Ans. **2** The ideal gas laws make four assumptions about the behavior of gases. (1) The individual particles of a gas are in a continuous, straight line, random motion; (2) there may be a transfer of energy between the particles through collisions, but the energy of the system as a whole remains the same; (3) the volume of the particles of the gas are negligible as compared to the volume of the space they occupy and (4) the particles of gas have no attraction for one another. In reality the particles of gas have some volume and exert some attraction for one another. The attraction between the molecules of gases is due to van der Waals forces. For example according to Boyle's Law, the volume varies inversely with the pressure applied. Doubling the pressure should compress the gas to exactly half the volume. However, the attraction between the molecules is increased at high pressure and so the volume is decreased more than the amount it would decrease if it behaved ideally.

2. Ans. **1** A gas liquefies when its molecules are crowded together to such an extent that the attractive forces between the molecules cause them to condense to a liquid form. As explained in the answer to question 1, gases have weak forces of attraction between them. The increased pressure forces the molecules closer together since the same number of molecules occupy a smaller space. Low temperature means low kinetic energy, so that the molecules of the gas are moving more slowly. This decrease in speed means that the molecules will not have sufficient kinetic energy to overcome the van der Waals forces between the molecules. These forces are strong enough to produce a liquid.

3. Ans. **1** *Charles' Law* states that at a constant pressure, the volume of a confined gas varies directly with the Kelvin (Absolute) temperature. The *kinetic molecular theory* helps to explain Charles' Law. Since the pressure is kept constant, the number of bombardments of the molecules per unit surface area per unit time remains the same. If the temperature is increased, the average kinetic energy and therefore the speed of the molecules is increased. If we wish the number of bombardments to remain the same (constant pressure), the walls of the container must be farther apart so that the molecules which are moving faster may hit the walls with the same frequency. In other words, the volume must increase. Here the temperature is being increased from 25°C to 50°C. To change the Celsius (centigrade) scale to Kelvin (Absolute) scale, we must add 273° to each temperature. Thus the temperature is increased from $(25° + 273°)$ or 298°K to $(50° + 273°)$ or 323°K. Since the volume varies directly with the absolute temperature, we multiply the given

volume of 40 ml. by a ratio of absolute temperatures which will result in a larger volume. Here we multiply by $\dfrac{323°C}{298°C}$. Thus the new volume is

$$40 \text{ ml.} \times \frac{323°C}{298°C} \quad \text{or} \quad 40 \times \frac{323}{298} \text{ ml.}$$

4. Ans. **4** The *vapor pressure* of a liquid is the pressure exerted in a confined space by the molecules that leave the liquid phase and enter the gaseous or vapor phase. Molecules are always escaping from the liquid, and thus the liquid always exerts a vapor pressure. At any specific temperature an equilibrium is set up between the molecules leaving the liquid and the molecules re-entering it. As the temperature increases, the kinetic energy of the molecules increases. More molecules leave the liquid and so the equilibrium vapor pressure increases. When the vapor pressure of a liquid is large enough to equal the atmospheric pressure exerted upon the liquid, a vapor bubble will form within the liquid. At first the bubbles form only at the bottom of the liquid where the temperature is the highest. These bubbles decrease in size and gradually disappear as they rise to cooler layers. The equilibrium vapor pressure of liquid diminishes and the bubbles are crushed by the pressure of the atmosphere. If, however, the temperature reaches a point where the equilibrium vapor pressure at the surface of the liquid is equal to the air pressure, the bubbles will maintain themselves throughout the liquid. We now say the liquid is boiling. Thus the boiling point is that temperature at which the equilibrium vapor pressure is equal to the atmospheric pressure. Standard atmospheric pressure is 760 millimeters of mercury. Thus when the water boils in an open container, its vapor pressure must be 760 millimeters of mercury.

5. Ans. **3** The specific heat of water is $1 \dfrac{\text{cal.}}{\text{g.C}°}$. Thus, when 1 gram of water rises 1 C° in temperature, it gains 1 calorie, and when 1 gram of water cools 1 C°, it loses 1 calorie. Here we have 150 grams of water that are heated from 20°C. to 30°C. for an increase of 10C°.

Calories lost = specific Heat × mass of water × change in temperature

Calories lost = $1 \dfrac{\text{cal.}}{\text{g.C}°} \times 150 \text{ g.} \times 10 \text{ C}° = 1{,}500$ calories

Thus 1,500 calories are given off. Note that in the above calculation, the units g. and C° cancel, giving us our answer in calories.

6. Ans. **3** In the orbital model of the atom, the energy levels of the electrons are represented by quantum numbers. The principal quantum number (n) represents the principal energy level and indicates the average distance of an orbital from the nucleus of an atom. (An orbital is the highly probable location in which electrons may be found.) These levels are, in order of increasing distance from the nucleus, K($n = 1$), L($n = 2$), M($n = 3$)

$N (n = 4)$, etc. Each principal energy level has one or more filled or partially filled sublevels of energy, up to a maximum of four sublevels, sublevels s, p, d and f.

When $n = 1$, there is only one sublevel called $1s$
When $n = 2$, there are two sublevels called $2s$ and $2p$
When $n = 3$, there are three sublevels called $3s$, $3p$, and $3d$
When $n = 4$, there are four sublevels called $4s$, $4p$, $4d$ and $4f$

For higher principal energy levels, there are even more sublevels. Each sublevel consists of one or more orbitals. These orbitals differ in shape, size and orientation in space and each can hold no more than two electrons. In the atom any s sublevel has 1 orbital with a maximum of two electrons. Any p sublevel has 3 orbitals with a maximum of 6 electrons. Any d sublevel has 5 orbitals with a maximum of 10 electrons. Any f sublevel has 7 orbitals with a maximum of 14 electrons. Therefore the number of orbitals in the $2p$ subshell is 3.

7. Ans. **2** The electron configuration of the neutral atom is given as $1s^2\, 2s^2\, 2p^6\, 3s^2$. The atom has 3 principal energy levels. The third level $(n = 3)$ uses 1 sublevel, $3s^2$. Since the superscript gives the number of electrons in the subshells, we have 2 electrons in the $n = 3$ level. Elements with 2 electrons in their outer shell are in Group IIA provided that they have complete inner shells. Here the given element has complete inner shells of 2 and 8 respectively. Elements in Group IIA are best classified as metals since they show a great tendency to lose their valence electrons.

8. Ans. **3** Referring to the Periodic Table, we see that the element having atomic number 7 is nitrogen, N. Nitrogen has an electronic configuration of 2–5. An electron dot symbol for an element just shows the element with the valence electrons. The nucleus and inner shells, collectively called the kernel, is not represented in the electron dot diagram. Since the valence shell, or outermost energy level, of nitrogen has 5 electrons the correct electron dot

symbol is $\cdot \overset{\cdot}{N} \colon$ Using X to replace N, we get choice (3).

9. Ans. **2** When a radioactive nucleus emits an *alpha particle*, the process is called nuclear disintegration or transmutation. An alpha particle is a helium nucleus, and is represented as ^4_2He (see *Table E*). Its atomic number is 2 and its mass number is 4. When the radioactive nucleus emits an alpha particle, the mass number is decreased (by 4) and the atomic number is decreased (by 2).

10. Ans. **1** When the vapor of a substance is subjected to an electronic discharge or other high-energy source, some of the electrons in the atoms absorb energy and move to higher energy levels. The atoms are now called excited atoms because of the higher energy state of the electrons. Choice (1) gives an atom with an electron configuration of $1s^2\, 2s^2\, 2p^6\, 4s^1$. The electron in the $4s$ subshell has been promoted from its *ground state* position in the $3s$

subshell of the third principal energy level to the higher energy position of the $4s$ subshell in the fourth principal energy level. The equation for this reaction is

$$1s^2 2s^2 2p^6 3s^1 + \text{energy} = 1s^2 2s^2 2p^6 4s^1$$

11. **Ans.** **3** Neutral atoms of ^{23}Na and ^{24}Na are *isotopes*. They have the same atomic number but different mass numbers. Referring to the *Periodic Table* we see that the atomic number is 11. Thus, the nucleus has 11 protons. The number of neutrons equals the mass number minus the atomic number. ^{23}Na has $(23 - 11)$ or 12 neutrons. ^{24}Na has $(24 - 11)$ or 13 neutrons.

Wrong Choices Explained:

(1) The atomic volume depends on the atomic radius of the atom. The larger the atomic radius, the larger the atomic volume. Since atomic radius only changes with the number of electron shells or with the amount of positive nuclear charge (protons), the atomic radius for isotopes of the same element is constant. Thus, the atomic volumes of isotopes of sodium are the same.

(2) As stated above, ^{23}Na and ^{24}Na have the same atomic number, 11. Thus each nucleus has 11 protons, and since the atoms are electrically neutral, each atom must have 11 electrons in its energy levels.

(4) Since ^{23}Na and ^{24}Na are same element (sodium), they have the same atomic number (11). Since the atomic number equals the number of protons in an atom, both isotopes have the same number of protons (11).

12. **Ans.** **4** The valence electrons are the electrons in the outermost principal energy level of the atom. The atom in this question has 3 energy levels. The outermost $(n = 3)$ level contains all the valence electrons. The $n = 3$ level contains the sublevels $3s^2$ and $3p^2$. Thus the total number of valence electrons in the outer shell is $2 + 2$ or 4.

13. **Ans.** **3** The atomic number of an element is the number of protons in the nucleus of an atom of that element. We are told that the atomic number of this neutral atom is 18, that is, the nucleus of the atom contains 18 protons. Since the atom is neutral there must be an equal number of electrons outside the nucleus as protons in the nucleus. Thus the atom must contain 18 electrons. The K shell, with only one orbital, the $1s$ orbital, can hold two electrons. This is designated by $1s^2$. The L shell has two subshells, $2s$ and $2p$, with 2 electrons in the $2s$ and 6 electrons in the $2p$. The M shell has 3 subshells, $3s$, $3p$ and $3d$. Two electrons go in the $3s$ and 6 in the $3p$. We now have the electron configuration $1s^2 2s^2 2p^6 3s^2 3p^6$, with a total of 18 electrons. This is the required electron configuration.

Wrong Choices Explained:

(1) The $3p$ subshell is shown with 7 electrons. This is impossible since any p subshell has a maximum of 3 orbitals or 6 electrons.

(2) The $3s$ subshell is shown with 7 electrons. This is impossible since any

s subshell can have but one orbital. Thus the maximum number of electrons an *s* subshell can hold is 2.

(4) The $2p$ subshell can hold a maximum of 6 electrons, not 8.

14. Ans. 1 When atoms of sodium and chlorine unite, the one electron in sodium's valence shell is transferred to the chlorine atom, forming an ionic bond. This can be confirmed by finding the electronegativity difference between sodium and chlorine. The electronegativity of chlorine (see *Table J*) is 3.0 and that of sodium is 0.9. The difference is 2.1, indicating a strong ionic bond. Each atom has acquired a stable valence shell of 8 electrons by the transfer of 1 electron. Since a stable energy state requires less energy, some energy is released. In general, when bonds are formed, energy is released; when bonds are broken, energy is absorbed. The formation of the sodium chloride can be shown by the following:

$$\text{Na} \times + \ \cdot \ddot{\text{Cl}} : \ \rightarrow \left[\text{Na} \right]^{+} \left[\overset{\times}{\underset{\cdot\cdot}{\cdot}} \ddot{\text{Cl}} : \right]^{-} + \text{energy}$$

15. Ans. 4 Oxygen is a nonmetal, and thus it usually exhibits a negative oxidation state, since nonmetals gain electrons when combining chemically. The only case in which oxygen can have a positive oxidation state is if it loses electrons rather than gains. In other words, oxygen must combine with an element that can attract electrons more strongly than oxygen. Referring to *Table J*, we see that fluorine, electronegativity = 4.0, is the only element that is more electronegative than oxygen (3.5). Fluorine has an oxidation state of -1. Since there are two fluorine atoms, the total negative charge in the compound OF_2 is -2. Since the compound as a whole must be electrically neutral, the total positive charge must equal the total negative charge or $(+2 -2) = 0$. Thus oxygen has an oxidation state of $+2$ in OF_2.

Wrong Choices Explained:

Choices (1), (2) and (3): As stated above, oxygen has a positive oxidation state only when it combines with an element whose electronegativity is greater than that of oxygen. In such a case the other more electronegative atom would attract the electrons from the oxygen atom giving the oxygen a positive charge. Only fluorine has a higher electronegativity than oxygen. Thus oxygen will exhibit a negative oxidation state when combining with H or C.

16. Ans. 1 The bonds between the hydrogen and oxygen in the water molecule and the carbon and oxygen in the carbon dioxide molecule are polar covalent. The oxygen, having a much greater positive charge in the nucleus, has a greater electronegativity than carbon or hydrogen and therefore a stronger attraction for the shared pairs of electrons. Thus each bond in both molecules is polar. We are told that CO_2 is nonpolar. This means that the carbon dioxide molecule must be a symmetrical molecule with a linear (straight line) arrangement of the molecules. Thus the two oxygen atoms and the central carbon atom are arranged in the structure $\overset{\delta^-}{\text{O}}\!=\!\overset{\delta^+}{\text{C}}\!=\!\overset{\delta^-}{\text{O}}$. The centers of positive and negative charges coincide.

Water, however, is a polar molecule. That means the molecule is asymmetrical. Studies of the crystalline structure of ice show that the polar bonds in the water molecule are at approximate right angles to each other, rather than being in a straight line. The size of the angle between the bond in the water molecule is approximately 105°. The increase in size from 90° is due to the repulsion of the hydrogen atoms each of which has a partial positive charge. The structure of the water molecule is usually represented as

17. **Ans. 3** A covalent bond is one formed by the sharing of a pair of electrons. A multiple covalent bond is formed when more than one pair of electrons are shared between adjacent atoms. The nitrogen atom has 5 electrons in its outer valence shell. It must therefore share 3 electrons with another nitrogen atom to form a stable octet. As a result 3 covalent bonds are present in the diatomic nitrogen molecule. These multiple covalent bonds can be shown by a graphic formula $N\equiv N$ or by the electron-dot formula $: N \overset{x}{\underset{x}{:}} \overset{x}{\underset{x}{N}} \overset{x}{}$.

Wrong Choices Explained

(1) The fluorine atom has 7 electrons in its outer shell. To achieve a stable shell of 8 electrons, two fluorine atoms must share a pair of electrons to form a diatomic molecule F_2 with one covalent bond. Structurally the fluorine molecule can be shown as F—F or $: \overset{..}{\underset{..}{F}} \overset{xx}{\underset{xx}{:}} \overset{xx}{F} \overset{x}{}$

(2) The hydrogen atom has only one electron. Two hydrogen atoms bond covalently to form the hydrogen molecule H_2 with a single covalent bond. The electrons are shared to form a stable K shell of 2 electrons. Structurally, the hydrogen molecule can be represented as H—H or $H \overset{x}{.} H$.

(4) Like fluorine in choice (1), chlorine has 7 electrons in its outer ring and so a single covalent bond is again formed.

18. **Ans. 3** The percent ionic character in a bond is determined by the electronegativity difference of the two elements forming the bond. The electronegativity of an atom is the attraction the atom has for a shared pair of electrons in a bond. Thus, when 2 atoms of nearly equal electronegativities form a bond they compete nearly equally for the shared pair of electrons in the bond. In such a case the electrons are shared nearly equally. As the difference in electronegativities increases, the sharing becomes more unequal. The more electronegative atom attracts the electron pair more strongly than does the less electronegative atom. The bond tends to become ionic in character. The larger the electronegativity difference, the greater the ionic character of the bond. The electronegativity of Br is 2.8 and that of Cl is 3.0. Therefore, the electronegativity difference is 3.0 − 2.8 or 0.2. Since this is the smallest electronegativity difference of the given choices the bond between Br and Cl has the least ionic character.

Wrong Choices Explained:

(1) The electronegativity of P is 2.1 and that of Cl is 3.0. Hence, the difference is $3.0 - 2.1$ or 0.9.

(2) The electronegativity of H is 2.1 and that of Cl is 3.0. Therefore the electronegativity difference is $3.0 - 2.1$ or 0.9.

(4) The electronegativity of O is 3.5 and that of Cl is 3.0. Thus, the electronegativity difference is $3.5 - 3.0$ or 0.5.

19. Ans. **2** When a substance melts, the forces of attraction holding the particles in the rigid, solid state are weakened. The particles, ions or molecules, can move more freely and we say that the substance has melted. When the forces of attraction are very great in the solid state, more heat energy is needed to weaken the attractive forces between the particles. In general, ionic compounds have the strongest forces of attraction between particles because of the electrostatic force between ions. As the bond becomes less ionic and thus more nonpolar, the particles exist as molecules rather than ions. Here only the weaker dipole and van der Waals forces between molecules exist. As a result the melting point is lower for nonpolar and polar compounds than for ionic compounds. The only exceptions to this rule are compounds having network bonding, such as diamond or quartz (SiO_2), which have attractive forces stronger than those of ionic compounds, and thus have the highest melting points. Cesium fluoride, CeF, is an ionic compound since the electronegativity difference is greater than 1.7 (Ce = 0.7, F = 4.0; electronegativity difference equals $4.0 - 0.7 = 3.3$). Crystals of CeF contain Ce^+ ions and F^- ions at the lattice points. They are held in place by the strong electrostatic attraction of positive and negative charges. Because of the strong attractive forces in ionic compounds such as cesium fluoride, a very high temperature is needed to break these forces.

Wrong Choices Explained:

(1) and (3): He, helium, is an inert monatomic gas. NH_3, ammonia, is also a gas at room temperature with weakly polar molecules. In general, the forces between the molecules of a gas are very weak van der Waals forces and thus gases have very low melting points, always below room temperature.

(4) $CHCl_3$, chloroform, is an organic compound called a halogen substitution product. In general, all organic compounds are nonpolar or weakly polar, and thus have weak attractive forces and low melting points.

20. Ans. **4** *Van der Waals forces* are the weak attractive forces between nonpolar molecules in the absence of dipole attraction. Van der Waals forces appear to be due to chance distribution of electrons resulting in momentary dipole attraction. It is thought now that they may result from the attraction of the positive nucleus of one molecule for the electrons in a neighboring molecule. In general, van der Waals forces increase with an increasing number of electrons (hence with increasing molecular size and molecular mass) and with decreasing distance between molecules. All the given choices are monatomic molecules. In xenon, Xe, which has the largest atomic number and thus the

most electrons, the van der Waals forces are the greatest. As we go up Group O, the group of the noble gases, the van der Waals forces decrease with the decreasing number of electrons. The forces decrease in the order Kr, Ar, Ne and He.

21. Ans. **2** Transition elements have partially filled inner shells. These elements are located in the *"B"* groups and Group VIII of the *Periodic Table*. Transition elements usually exhibit multiple oxidation states and their ions are usually colored in solution. For example, Cu, a transition element in Group II *B* in the *Periodic Table*, has oxidation states of $+1$ and $+2$. In aqueous solution, the Cu^{+2} ion gives the solution a blue color.

Wrong Choices Explained:

(1) Metalloids are those elements having some properties of metals and other properties of nonmetals. Examples of metalloids are boron, silicon, arsenic and tellurium.

(3) Nonmetals are those elements which tend to gain electrons in chemical reactions. They are found in Groups V, VI, VII and thus have 5, 6, or 7 electrons in the outer shell. They may have multiple oxidation states, but they do not have colored ions.

(4) A gas is just a phase of an element or compound. Gaseous elements can have multiple oxidation states, such as chlorine, but do not form colored ions.

22. Ans. **4** Atoms of metals have low ionization energies and low electronegativities and thus they tend to lose electrons when combining with other elements. Metals usually exhibit physical properties such as luster, high thermal and electrical conductivity, malleability and ductility. Atoms of nonmetals have high ionization energies and high electronegativities and thus they tend to gain electrons when combining with metals, or share electrons when combining with other elements. Nonmetals tend to be gases or solids (except for liquid bromine) and the solid phase nonmetals have low thermal and electrical conductivities and no metallic luster. Group IV *A* contains both metals and nonmetals. Carbon is a nonmetal, silicon and germanium are metalloids, tin and lead are metals.

Wrong Choices Explained:

(1) Group I *B* contains the transition elements, copper, silver and gold, all of which are metals.

(2) Group II *A* contains the alkaline earth elements all of which are metals.

(3) Group O contains the inert gases, which are not classified as metals or nonmetals.

23. Ans. **4** The elements in Group O are known as the "inert gases," "rare gases" or "noble gases." The reason these elements are so unreactive is that their outermost shell is complete, which results in an electron configuration that is stable. However experiments in recent years have shown that these gases are not truly inert, since it is now possible to form compounds of xenon,

radon and krypton with fluorine and oxygen. An example is XeF_4, xenon tetrafluoride.

Wrong Choices Explained:

(1) The elements in Group I A are called the alkali metals, and are very reactive. Because the atoms of these elements have such low ionization energies, they readily lose their valence electrons in reacting to form compounds.

(2) The elements in Group VI A have 6 electrons in their outer shells and thus don't have their outer shells complete. They achieve a more stable configuration by reacting in chemical reactions by either gaining or losing electrons to make the outer shells complete.

(3) Group III A contains elements with 3 electrons in the valence shell. These elements are reactive because in a chemical reaction they can lose their 3 electrons from the valence shell, leaving a complete outer shell.

24. Ans. 4   The *ionization energy* is the energy required to remove one electron from the valence shell of an atom in the gaseous phase. There are two main factors affecting the ionization energy. First is atomic radius. As the atomic radius decreases, the ionization energy increases. The valence shell electrons are harder to pull off because the attractive force of the positive nucleus is greater when the distance between the negative electrons and positive nucleus decreases. The second factor is the nuclear charge (number of protons). As the nuclear charge increases, the ionization energy increases because the nucleus exerts a greater attractive force on the valence electrons. Referring to the *Periodic Table* we see that in *Period* 2, in going from left to right, the atomic radius decreases from 1.52 for Li to 0.64 for F. Since the atomic radius or size of the atom is decreasing, the ionization energy must be increasing as stated above. Checking on *Table J* in the *Reference Tables* we find that indeed the ionization energy increases from left to right. Li has an ionization energy of 5.4 electron volts (ev) while F has an ionization energy of 17.3 electron volts.

25. Ans. 3   One mole of any gas at S.T.P. (standard temperature and pressure, 0°C. 760 mm-Hg) will occupy 22.4 liters. A mole of a substance known as the gram molecular mass contains an Avogadro number or 6.02×10^{23} molecules. Thus a mole of oxygen gas at S.T.P. contains 6.02×10^{23} molecules which occupy 22.4 liters. Then 1.5×10^{23} molecules of oxygen gas, which is about $\frac{1}{4}$ of 6.02×10^{23} molecules, will occupy one fourth of 22.4 liters at S.T.P. or $(\frac{1}{4} \times 22.4) = 5.6$ liters.

26. Ans. 2   In any reaction the actual number of moles of any reactants or products is proportional to the equation number of moles of these reactants or products. The equation of the reaction is given as:

$$Zn(s) + 2H^+(aq) = Zn^{+2} + H_2(g)$$

We are concerned with two substances only, Zn and H_2. We are given the mass of Zn and asked to find the volume of H_2. The equation states that one mole of Zn reacts to form one mole of H_2. The other reactants and products are not involved in this problem.

We must first find the gram-molecular mass of Zn. Looking on the *Periodic Table* we find the gram-molecular mass of Zn is 65.4 grams. The given weight of zinc in the reaction is 6.54 g. Therefore $\frac{1}{10}$ of a mole of zinc is involved in the reaction and therefore $\frac{1}{10}$ of a mole of H_2 gas is formed. Since 1 mole of a gas occupies 22.4 liters, $\frac{1}{10}$ of a mole of gas occupies 2.24 liters.

27.   Ans.   **3**   The *empirical formula* or formula unit of a compound gives the simplest ratio of the atoms in a compound. To find the molecular formula, or actual formula, of the compound we must find how many formula units there are in the molecular formula. First, we must find the mass of the given empirical formula, CH_2

$$
\begin{aligned}
&\text{Formula mass of } CH_2 \\
&1\,C = 1 \times 12 = 12 \\
&\underline{2\,H = 2 \times\ 1 = 2} \\
&\text{Formula mass} = 14 \text{ grams} \\
&\qquad\qquad\qquad\quad \text{per formula unit}
\end{aligned}
$$

Next, we divide the molecular mass (42 g.) by the formula unit mass to find how many formula units fit into the molecule. Thus:

$$42 \text{ g./mole} \div 14 \text{ g./formula unit} = 3 \text{ formula unit/mole.}$$

Since there are 3 formula units per mole, the molecular formula is $(CH_2)_3$ or C_3H_6.

28.   Ans.   **3**   In any reaction, the number of moles of reactants consumed and the number of moles of products formed are proportional to the numerical coefficients of the substances in the equation.

The reaction is given as:

$$2HCl + Ca(OH)_2 \rightarrow CaCl_2 + 2H_2O$$

The coefficients of the equation tell us that 2 moles of H_2O are produced when 1 mole of $Ca(OH)_2$ is consumed. In other words, the moles of water produced is twice the moles of calcium hydroxide consumed. Since 0.4 moles of calcium hydroxide are consumed, twice 0.4 or 0.8 moles of H_2O are formed.

ALTERNATE METHOD:

We are concerned with two substances, calcium hydroxide and water.

Actual number of moles: 0.4   x

$$\boxed{Ca(OH)_2} + 2HCl \rightarrow CaCl_2 + \boxed{2H_2O}$$

Equation number of moles: 1   2

This gives us the proportion:

$$\frac{x}{2 \text{ moles}} = \frac{0.4}{1 \text{ mole}}$$

$$x = 2 \times 0.4 = 0.8 \text{ moles}$$

29. **Ans. 3** A *molar* or 1-molar of KCl solution contains one mole of the solute KCl dissolved in 1000 ml. (1 liter) of *solution*. Then a 3-molar solution has three times as much KCl or 3 moles of KCl dissolved in 1000 ml. of water.

30. **Ans. 1** In any solution the presence of dissolved solute particles affect some properties of the solvent, such as the freezing point, the boiling point, and the vapor pressure of the solvent. These properties are called *colligative properties* since the properties depend on the *number* of particles and not on the nature of the particles. The presence of a solute lowers the freezing point of the solvent. The greater the number of solute particles per liter of solution, the more the freezing point is lowered. Since all the given solution are 1 molal concentrations (1 mole of solute per kilogram of water), we must find which substance yields the greatest number of particles. Calcium chloride is a salt which dissociates in water according to the following equation:

$$CaCl_2 \xrightarrow{H_2O} Ca^{+2} + 2Cl^-$$

Thus one mole of $CaCl_2$ yields one mole of Ca^{+2} ions and 2 moles of Cl^- ions, or a total of 3 moles of particles. NaCl, sodium chloride, is a salt which dissociates in water as follows:

$$NaCl \xrightarrow{H_2O} Na^+ + Cl^-$$

Thus one mole of NaCl produces one mole of Na^+ ions and one mole of Cl^- ions or a total of 2 moles of particles. $C_{12}H_{22}O_{11}$, a sugar, dissolves in water but does not dissociate since sugars are organic compounds with practically non-polar molecules. Thus in a 1 molal solution of $C_{12}H_{22}O_{11}$, there is only one mole of particles.

CH_3COOH, acetic acid, is a weak organic acid which ionizes very slightly in water:

$$CH_3COOH + H_2O \rightleftharpoons H_3O^+ + CH_3COO^-$$

Thus one mole of acetic acid produces less than 2 moles of particles because ionization is incomplete. Thus, of all the given solutions, 1 molal $CaCl_2$ produces the largest number of particles and lowers the freezing point the most. The order of solutions with respect to decrease of freezing point would be $CaCl_2$, NaCl, CH_3COOH, and $C_{12}H_{22}O_{11}$.

31. **Ans. 3** The *volumes* of *gases* that react or are formed in a chemical reaction at constant temperature and pressure are proportional to the number of *moles* as shown by the numerical coefficients in the equation of that reaction. The reaction is given as:

$$2C_2H_6(g) + 7O_2(g) \rightarrow 4CO_2(g) + 6H_2O(g)$$

We are concerned with the two substances, O_2 and C_2H_6.

Actual volume: 14 liters x

$$\boxed{2C_2H_6} \quad + \quad \boxed{7O_2} \rightarrow$$

Equation volumes: 2 molar volumes   7 molar volumes

Note that according to the equation, 7 volumes of oxygen are required for the complete combustion of 2 volumes of ethane. Thus we can set up a proportion:

$$\frac{14 \text{ liters}}{2 \text{ molar volumes}} = \frac{x}{7 \text{ molar volumes}}$$
$$2x = 98 \text{ liters}$$
$$x = 49 \text{ liters}$$

32. **Ans. 2** The tendency for a system to undergo a spontaneous chemical change is dependent on 2 factors: (1) the change in energy of the system and (2) the change in entropy of the system.

Factor 1: A system always tends to change from a higher energy state to a lower one, thereby releasing energy. This energy is represented mathematically as ΔH. Such a reaction is *exothermic*. For example, when two hydrogen atoms unite to form the hydrogen molecule, the formation of the covalent bond results in a release of energy—an exothermic reaction. Thus a system containing hydrogen atoms would react to form diatomic hydrogen molecules since nature favors a change toward a lower energy state.

Factor 2: The other tendency in nature is to change to a system of more disorder and randomness. The degree of disorder is called *entropy*. For example, a solid crystal is more orderly or organized and thus has less entropy than the liquid phase. The tendency toward higher entropy favors the change from ice to water.

33. **Ans. 4** The K_{sp} of a salt is the product of the concentrations of its ions in a saturated solution at a given temperature. We are given four carbonate salts and asked which is the least soluble. These salts dissociate as follows:

$$XCO_3 = X^{+2} + CO_3^{-2}$$
Therefore $\qquad K_{sp} = [X^{+2}][CO_3^{-2}]$

where the brackets indicate concentration in moles per liter. The least soluble carbonate will have the fewest number of ions in solution. The formula of the K_{sp} above tells us that the concentration of the ions depends on the K_{sp} itself. Thus the carbonate with the smallest K_{sp} is the least soluble in water. Since the smallest exponent is -13, the least soluble salt is $PbCO_3$ with a K_{sp} of 1×10^{-13}.

34. **Ans. 4** When a reversible reaction reaches equilibrium at a given temperature—that is when the rate of the formation of the products is equal to the rate of formation of the reactant in the opposite direction—an equilibrium constant can be derived. This constant is equal to the product of the molar concentrations of the products (on the right) divided by the molar concentration of the reactants (on the left) with each concentration raised to the power equal to the number of moles of that substance appearing in the equation. In expressing the constant mathematically brackets are used to indicate concentrations measured in moles per liter. For the given equation:

$$2A(g) + B(g) = 3C(g)$$

C, the substance on the right, is in the numerator raised to the third power (there are 3 moles of C) and the A and B, substances of the left, are in the denominator with the A raised to the second power. The equilibrium constant would be:

$$K = \frac{[C]^3}{[A]^2[B]}$$

35. **Ans. 1** A reaction is *exothermic* if it gives off heat to its surroundings. We are given the reaction

$$H_2(g) + \tfrac{1}{2}O_2(g) = H_2O(g) + 57.8 \text{ kcal.}$$

Thus we see that as the reaction proceeds to the right, heat is being given off. Thus the given reaction is exothermic. ΔH is the difference in heat content between the final products and the initial reactants or

$$\Delta H = H_{products} - H_{reactants}$$

Since the reaction is exothermic, it is releasing heat to its surroundings. Thus the heat content of the system is decreasing. As a result the heat content of the products is less than the heat content of the reactants and the difference between the heat of the products and the reactants will be negative. ΔH is always negative for an exothermic reaction (one that releases heat and thus *decreases* the energy of the system) and positive for an endothermic reaction (one that absorbs heat and thus *increases* the energy of the system).

36. **Ans. 3** The *equilibrium constant K* is the ratio of the product of the concentrations of the products formed to the product of the concentrations of the reactants. For the reaction $A + B = C$, the equation for the equilibrium constant is:

$$K = \frac{[C]}{[B][A]}$$

where the brackets indicate concentrations in moles per liter. We are told that the original reactants are largely converted to products. This means that the concentration of the product C is high and the concentrations of the reactants A and B are low since they have been consumed in the reaction. With a large value for C in the numerator and low values for A and B in the denominator, the value of K would have to be quite high. Among the choices, the highest value for the equilibrium constant is 10, choice (3).

37. **Ans. 2** *Le Chatelier's principle* states that if a system in equilibrium is subjected to a stress (such as increased temperature or pressure), the equilibrium will be shifted in the direction that relieves the effects of the stress. Here we are asked for the stresses that will drive the reaction

$$2SO_2(g) + O_2(g) = 2SO_3(g) + 44 \text{ kcal}$$

in the direction of an increased SO_3 yield, or to the right. The pressure in a closed container is dependent upon the volume of the gas in that container. Volumes of gases are proportional to the number of moles as shown by the coefficients of the molecules in the equation of the reaction. The reactants $2SO_2$ and O_2 in the container occupy $2 + 1$ or 3 molar volumes. The product $2SO_3$ occupies 2 molar volumes. Thus the lower pressure lies on the right side of the equation. In order to shift the reaction in this direction we must apply the needed stress, or an *increase* in pressure, which will force the reaction to the right, in the direction of decreased pressure.

The given equation is exothermic, that is, it releases heat in proceeding to the right. In order to push the reaction to the right, we must decrease the temperature, forcing the reaction to release heat and thus proceed to the right. Thus increasing the pressure and decreasing the temperature will result in an increase in concentration of SO_3.

38. Ans. **1** When a catalyst is added to a reaction, it changes the pathway of the reaction and lowers (or raises) the *activation energy*. The activation energy is the energy required to transform the reactants to an activated complex, formed at the peak of the energy curve, here points A and A'. An accelerator catalyst lowers the energy requirement at the peak of reaction by forming complexes of lower energy content. Thus the activation energy required

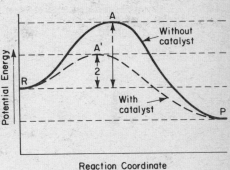

Reaction Coordinate

in the forward reaction is lowered from the larger value *without the catalyst* (arrow 1) to a smaller value *with the catalyst* (arrow 2).

39. Ans. **2** The pH is defined as the logarithm of the reciprocal of the hydrogen ion concentration, symbolized as $[H^+]$.

Thus $pH = \log \dfrac{1}{[H^+]}$

Substituting 2 for pH:

$$2 = \log \frac{1}{[H^+]}$$

antilog $2 = \dfrac{1}{[H^+]}$

Since the antilog of a number is 10 raised to that number:

$$10^2 = \frac{1}{[H^+]}$$

$$[H^+] = \frac{1}{10^2} \quad \text{or} \quad [H^+] = 1 \times 10^{-2}$$

40. Ans. **4** A Brønsted acid is a proton (H^+ ion) donor. Thus the strongest acid would be the substance that most readily gives up protons. Referring to *Table H, Acid-Base Chart,* we see that in the left column (conjugate acid) the acid strength decreases as we read down the column. Of the four choices given, the one highest up in the left column is HSO_4^-.

41. Ans. **3** The conductivity of a solution is directly proportional to the number of freely-moving charged particles present. *Table M* gives us the ionization constants of acids and bases. The higher the ionization constant, the higher is the degree of ionization or dissociation and therefore the higher the number of charged particles present. *Table M* tells us that sulfuric acid is almost completely ionized in dilute solution. Thus, of the substances listed, a 1.0 M solution of sulfuric acid will have the highest conductivity.

42. Ans. **3** The product of the concentrations of the H^+ ion and the OH^- ion in water is a constant represented as K_w. Its value is 1×10^{-14}.

$$K_w = [H^+][OH^-] = 1 \times 10^{-14}$$

The brackets indicate that the concentrations are expressed in moles per liter. If we are given one concentration and asked for the other, all we need do is substitute in the above equation. In this case we are given that the concentration of the OH^- ion in aqueous solution is 1×10^{-6} M. (M stands for molar or moles per liter).

$$[H^+][OH^-] = 1 \times 10^{-14}$$
$$[H^+](1 \times 10^{-6}) = 1 \times 10^{-14}$$
$$[H^+] = \frac{1 \times 10^{-14}}{1 \times 10^{-6}}$$
$$[H^+] = 1 \times 10^{-8} \text{ M}$$

43. Ans. **3** A *conjugate acid-base pair* consists of an acid and the negative ion created by the removal of a proton from that acid. Examples of conjugate pairs as given in *Table H* are HCl, Cl^-; H_2SO_4, HSO_4^-; H_3O^+, H_2O; and NH_3, NH_2^-. Note that each conjugate acid-base pair is related by the transfer of a proton.

$$\text{Acid} - H^+ \rightarrow \text{Base} \quad \text{or} \quad \text{Base} + H^+ \rightarrow \text{Acid}$$

In the reaction given,

$$H_3BO_3(s) + H_2O(l) = H_3O^+ + H_2BO_3^- \text{ (aq)}$$

the H_3BO_3 acts as an acid in the forward reaction, donating a proton to the H_2O. The H_3BO_3 without a proton is now a $H_2BO_3^-$ ion, a base. At the same time the H_2O acts as a base and gains a proton to become an acid, the H_3O^+ ion. Thus the reaction contains two conjugate acid-base pairs—(H_3BO_3, $H_2BO_3^-$) and (H_2O, H_3O^+). Each conjugate pair is related by the transfer of a proton. Therefore choice (3) (H_3BO_3, $H_2BO_3^-$) is the correct one.

44. Ans. **2** Sulfuric acid reacts with sodium hydroxide, a base, a reaction that is typical of a *neutralization* reaction:

$$\text{Acid} + \text{Base} \rightarrow \text{Salt} + \text{Water}$$
Thus, $$H_2SO_4 + 2NaOH \rightarrow Na_2SO_4 + 2HOH$$

In the balanced reaction, as shown above, we see that one mole of sulfuric acid combines with two moles of sodium hydroxide to form two moles of water.

45. Ans. 4 Since a compound as a whole has no charge, the sum of the positive oxidation numbers must equal the sum of the negative oxidation numbers. In the given compound K_2SO_3, each oxygen atom has an oxidation number of -2 and thus the total negative charge for 3 oxygen atoms is $3 \times (-2)$ or -6. Each potassium atom has a charge of $+1$, and thus two potassium atoms have a positive charge of $2 \times (+1)$ or $+2$. The sulfur atom must have a charge of $+4$ to give a total oxidation number of ($+6$ and -6) or zero.

46. Ans. 1 Fused (molten) NaCl consists of freely moving Na^+ ions and Cl^- ions. During the electrolysis of fused NaCl, the positive sodium ion (Na^+) is attracted to the negative electrode, or cathode, where it gains one electron and is thereby *reduced* to the neutral sodium atom (Na^0). The *negative* chloride ion (Cl^-) is attracted to the *positive* electrode, or anode, where it loses one electron, and is thereby *oxidized* to form the neutral chlorine atom (Cl^0). Immediately, two neutral chlorine atoms combine to form a diatomic chlorine molecule, Cl_2. The ion-electron equation for the oxidation reaction at the positive electrode is:

$$2Cl^- - 2e^- \rightarrow Cl_2^0$$

Wrong Choices Explained:

(2) As stated above, when the chloride ion migrates to the positive electrode, it loses one electron. The loss of electrons is oxidation. Chlorine is being oxidized, not reduced.

(3) and (4) We are asked for the reaction at the *positive* electrode. The sodium ion, as stated above, migrates to the *negative* electrode where it gains one electron to form Na^0. The gain of electrons is reduction, and thus sodium ions are being reduced at the negative electrode.

47. Ans. 1 In a balanced redox reaction, the number of electrons lost by one species must equal the number of electrons gained by the other. Using the ion-electron method we can break down the given redox reaction into two half-reactions:
Oxidation:

(1) $\qquad\qquad\qquad 2Cl^- - 2e^- \rightarrow Cl_2^0$

2 electrons must be lost to raise the oxidation state of $2Cl^-$ to Cl_2^0.
Reduction:

(2) $\qquad\qquad Cr_2O_7^{-2} + 14H^+ + 6e^- \rightarrow 2Cr^{+3} + 7H_2O$

In order for the number of electrons lost to equal the number of electrons gained, we must multiply the first equation by 3. We can then add it to equation (2) to obtain the net reaction.

$$6Cl^- \qquad\quad - 6e^- \rightarrow \qquad 3Cl_2$$
$$Cr_2O_7^{-2} + 14H^+ + 6e^- \rightarrow 2Cr^{+3} + 7H_2O$$

Adding: $\qquad Cr_2O_7^{-2} + 6Cl^- + 14H^+ \qquad \rightarrow 2Cr^{+3} + 7H_2O + 3Cl_2$

Therefore the coefficient of Cl^- is 6. Note that the free electrons drop out of the equation.

48. **Ans. 3** Copper is above silver on *Table L, Standard Oxidation Potentials*. It is therefore a stronger reducing agent than silver and will displace silver from its compounds. Each silver atom will be forced to accept an electron from the copper atoms resulting in the displacement of the Ag^+ ions from solution in the form of Ag^0 atoms. Each Cu^0 atom loses 2 electrons to two silver ions and goes into solution as a Cu^{+2} ion. These Cu^{+2} ions are hydrated in solution and become the light blue $Cu(H_2O)_4^{+2}$ ions, which impart a blue color to the solution.

$$Cu^0 + 2Ag^+ \rightarrow Cu^{+2} + Ag^0$$
$$Cu^{+2} + 4H_2O \rightarrow Cu(H_2O)_4^{+2}$$

Wrong Choices Explained:

(1), (2) and (4) Copper is below lead, zinc and cadmium on *Table L* and thus will not displace them from their compounds.

49. **Ans. 1** In a replacement reaction, a more active element replaces a less active element from a compound. We see from *Table L, Standard Oxidation Potentials*, that the zinc atom is above the lead atom, and thus has a greater tendency to lose electrons. Thus a reaction between the lead ion and the zinc atom will occur spontaneously. In the reaction:

$$Zn + Pb^{+2} \rightarrow Zn^{+2} + Pb$$

the zinc atom replaces the lead ion from its compound. The negative ion of the compound is omitted since it is a spectator ion. The zinc atom is oxidized to the zinc ion, losing two electrons to the lead ion and thereby reducing the lead ion to the lead atom.

50. **Ans. 1** The strongest oxidizing agent is the species that tends to gain electrons most readily. On *Table L, Standard Oxidation Potentials*, the lower the position of the species in the table, the less is the tendency of a reducing agent to lose electrons, and the greater is the tendency of an oxidizing agent to gain electrons. Thus the strongest reducing agents are at the top of the chart and the strongest oxidizing agents are at the bottom. Of the choices listed fluorine, F_2, is the one lowest in *Table L* and is therefore the strongest oxidizing agent.

51. **Ans. 4** We are given the reaction:

$$Cu^{+2} (aq) + Ni(s) \rightarrow Cu(s) + Ni^{+2} (aq)$$

This is an oxidation-reduction reaction in which the Ni^0 atom is oxidized to the Ni^{+2} ion and the Cu^{+2} ion is reduced to the Cu^0 atom. The potential (E^0) of the overall reaction can be found by combining the E^0 of the oxidation half-reaction and the E^0 of the reduction half-reaction.

From *Table L* we find that:

  (1) Oxidation: $Ni^0 = Ni^{+2} + 2e^-$; $E^0 = 0.23$ volts
  (2) Oxidation: $Cu^0 = Cu^{+2} + 2e^-$; $E^0 = -0.34$ volts

Equation (2) can be reversed and made the desired reduction half-reaction. In doing so, the E^0 must change its sign since reduction is the opposite of oxidation. Thus equation (2) becomes:

  (3) Reduction: $Cu^{+2} + 2e^- = Cu^0$; $E^0 = 0.34$ volts

In any oxidation-reduction reaction the electrons gained must equal the electrons lost. In this case note that 2 electrons are gained in equation (3) and 2 electrons are lost in equation (1). It is most important to note that the E^0 is constant and does not depend on the number of ions or atoms oxidized or reduced. To obtain the net reaction we add the balanced half-reactions (1) and (3). Note the electrons lost and gained are equal and cancel out. The net equation for the overall reaction is:

$$Cu^{+2} + Ni \rightarrow Cu + Ni^{+2}; E^0 = (0.23 + 0.34) \text{ or } 0.57 \text{ volts}$$

52. Ans. 2 The I.U.C. (International Union of Chemists) rules of nomenclature of organic compounds include the following:

  (1) We name the compound according to the longest chain of carbon atoms using the suffix that indicates the number of bonds between two carbons. Thus we use *ane* for a single bond, *ene* for a double bond, *yne* for a triple bond.

  (2) We use a prefix for all radicals attached to this chain such as methyl for CH_3, ethyl for C_2H_5, chloro for Cl, bromo for Br, and iodo for I.

  (3) We specify to which carbon atom in the chain the radical is bonded by numbering the carbon atoms so that the compound nomenclature has the lowest numbers. Following the above I.U.C. rules for nomenclature, we look for the longest carbon chain, which here is 4 carbons. Since all the carbon-carbon bonds are single bonds the compound is a member of the saturated alk*ane* series. Since there are 4 carbons, the compound is a butane. However, we notice that one of the hydrogen atoms has been replaced by a chlorine atom. Thus, the compound is a chlorobutane. To specify which carbon atom is bonded to the chlorine atom, we must number the carbon atoms from right to left so that the chlorine is bonded to the carbon having the *lowest* number as shown below:

$$
\begin{array}{cccc}
1 & 2 & 3 & 4 \\
C\!-\!C\!-\!C\!-\!C \\
4 & 3 & 2| & 1 \\
 & & Cl &
\end{array}
$$

Choosing the lower number, that is "2" rather than "3," we can call this compound 2-chlorobutane, which is a halogen substitution product.

53. Ans. 1 *Isomers* are compounds having the same molecular formula but different molecular structures. CH_3OCH_3 (dimethyl ether) and CH_3CH_2OH (ethyl alcohol) both have the same molecular formula C_2H_6O. However, their structures are different as shown below:

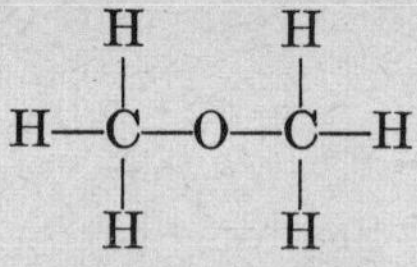

$$
\begin{array}{ccccc}
& H & & H & \\
& | & & | & \\
H\!-\!\!&C\!&-\!O\!-\!&C\!&-\!H \\
& | & & | & \\
& H & & H &
\end{array}
\qquad
\begin{array}{ccccc}
& H & H & \\
& | & | & \\
H\!-\!\!&C\!&-\!C\!&-\!OH \\
& | & | & \\
& H & H &
\end{array}
$$

dimethyl ether 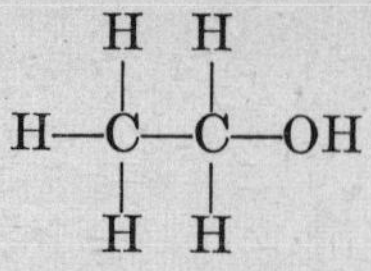   ethyl alcohol

Wrong Choices Explained:

(2) CH_3CH_2Cl. (chloroethane) and C_6H_5Cl (chlorobenzene) do not have the same molecular formula and thus are not isomers. When we condense the formula for chloroethane we get C_2H_5Cl.

(3) CH_3COCH_3 (acetone or dimethyl ketone) and CH_3OCH_3 (dimethyl ether) do not have the same molecular formula and thus are not isomers. The condensed molecular formula of acetone is C_3H_6O and the condensed molecular formula of dimethyl ether is C_2H_6O.

(4) $CH_3(CH_2)_2CH_3$ (butene) and $CH_3(CH)_2CH_3$ (2-butene) do not have the same molecular formula and thus are not isomers Butane has the molecular formula C_4H_{10}, and 2-butene has the formula C_4H_8.

54. Ans. 1 An organic acid is characterized by the functional group —COOH, called the *carboxyl* group which is bonded to an organic radical. Thus CH_3COOH, known as acetic acid, is an organic acid, since it contains the carboxyl group. Structurally, acetic acid is:

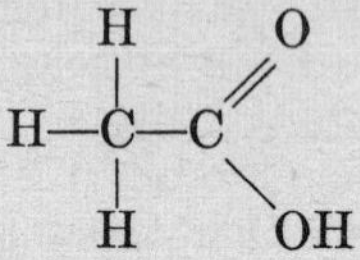

$$
\begin{array}{ccc}
H & & O \\
| & & \diagup \\
H\!-\!C\!-\!C & & \\
| & & \diagdown \\
H & & OH
\end{array}
$$

Wrong Choices Explained:

(2) CH_3COOCH_3, methyl acetate, is an *ester*. Esters are identified by the —COOR group attached to the organic radical. Actually, an ester is an organic acid with the H of —COOH group replaced by an R (organic radical). An ester is formed by the reaction between an organic acid and an alcohol. Methyl acetate is synthesized by reacting methyl alcohol and acetic acid:

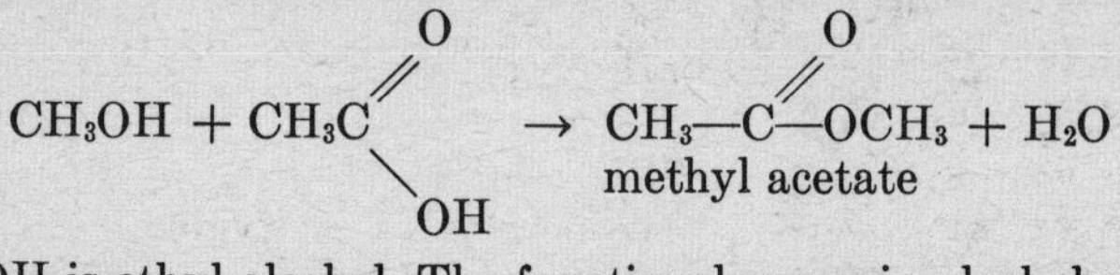

$$
CH_3OH + CH_3C\!\!\overset{\displaystyle O}{\underset{\displaystyle OH}{\diagup\!\!\!\diagdown}} \rightarrow CH_3\!-\!\overset{\displaystyle O}{C}\!-\!OCH_3 + H_2O
$$

methyl acetate

(3) C_2H_5OH is ethyl alcohol. The functional group in alcohols is the —OH or hydroxyl radical.

(4) $CH_3CHOHCH_3$ is isopropyl alcohol, and again is recognized as an alcohol by the —OH radical. The structure of isopropyl alcohol is shown below:

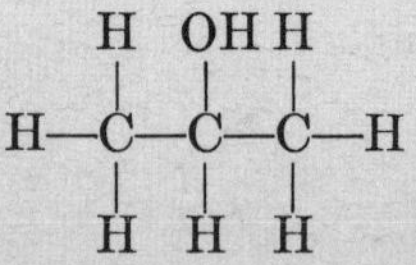

$$
\begin{array}{ccccccc}
& H & & OH & & H & \\
& | & & | & & | & \\
H\!-\!\!&C\!&-\!\!&C\!&-\!\!&C\!&-\!H \\
& | & & | & & | & \\
& H & & H & & H &
\end{array}
$$

55. Ans. 4 The addition of atoms to a compound by the breaking up of a double or triple bond is known as an *addition reaction*. Ethene (ethylene) C_2H_4, is an unsaturated hydrocarbon with one double bond. The double bond can break and form covalent bonds with two additional monovalent atoms such as Br or Cl to form a saturated halogen substitution compound.

Wrong Choices Explained:

(1) *Substitution* means replacement of one kind of atom or group by another kind of atom or group. Saturated compounds undergo substitution reactions. An example of a substitution reaction is the replacement of a hydrogen atom by a halogen atom, such as the reaction between ethane and bromine:

$$C_2H_6 \quad + \quad Br_2 \rightarrow \quad C_2H_5Br \quad + HBr$$

$$H-\underset{\underset{H}{|}}{\overset{\overset{H}{|}}{C}}-\underset{\underset{H}{|}}{\overset{\overset{H}{|}}{C}}-H + Br-Br \rightarrow H-\underset{\underset{H}{|}}{\overset{\overset{H}{|}}{C}}-\underset{\underset{Br}{|}}{\overset{\overset{H}{|}}{C}}-H + H-Br$$

In the given reaction, bromine is being added to ethene without replacing hydrogen atoms

(2) *Hydrogenation* is an addition reaction in which hydrogen is added to an unsaturated substance. An example of hydrogenation is the adding of hydrogen to ethene:

$$\overset{H}{\underset{H}{}}C=C\overset{H}{\underset{H}{}} + H_2 \rightarrow H-\underset{\underset{H}{|}}{\overset{\overset{H}{|}}{C}}-\underset{\underset{H}{|}}{\overset{\overset{H}{|}}{C}}-H$$

In the given reaction we are adding bromine to ethene, not hydrogen to ethene.

(3) *Polymerization* is the formation of large molecules from smaller molecules. For example acetylene can be polymerized to form benzene:

$$3C_2H_2 \rightarrow C_6H_6$$

No addition of atoms to a molecule is taking place by the breaking up of double or triple bonds.

56. Ans. 3 Hydrocarbon classification is simplified by the fact that organic compounds can be classified into groups having related structures and properties. Such groups are called *homologous series*. These series include the *alkane*, the *alkene*, the *alkyne* and the *benzene* series. Each member of an homologous series differs from the preceding one by a methylene or —CH_2 group. The alkane series, also known as the paraffin series, contains hydrocarbons that contain only single bonds. These saturated hydrocarbons can undergo substitution reactions. They contain the maximum number of hydrogen atoms. Their general formula is C_nH_{2n+2}, which means that the number of hydrogen atoms is two more than twice the number of carbon atoms.

Wrong Choices Explained:

(1) C_nH_{2n} is the general formula for the *alkene* series. These hydrocarbons contain one double bond. The members are called unsaturated hydrocarbons and can undergo addition reactions in which two monovalent atoms can be added.

(2) C_nH_{2n-2} is the general formula for the *alkyne* series. These hydrocarbons contain one triple bond and can add up to 4 monovalent atoms.

(4) C_nH_{2n-6} is the general formula for the *benzene* series which are *aromatic* ring hydrocarbons. Benzene has the formula C_6H_6. Its structure can be shown by the resonance formula given below:

57. **Ans. 1** According to Boyle's law, the volume of a given mass of gas varies inversely with the pressure exerted on it. This means that as the volume of a gas increases, the pressure exerted by the gas decreases if the temperature is constant. The reason that the pressure and volume are inversely related can be explained by the *kinetic theory* of gases. As the volume increases, there is more surface area bombarded by a given number of gaseous molecules. Pressure is merely the frequency or force of collisions per unit surface area per unit time. Since there will be fewer impacts per unit surface area per unit time as the volume increases, the pressure exerted by the gas decreases.

58. **Ans. 1** When two atoms of hydrogen combine to form a molecule of hydrogen, the atoms are held together by a covalent bond, which results from the simultaneous attraction of electrons to two nuclei. The sharing of electrons by the two hydrogen atoms enables each of the two atoms to complete its outer shell. Thus each hydrogen atom has a more stable electron configuration. This means that the hydrogen molecule is now at a lower energy level than were the two hydrogen atoms before they combined. In general we can say that nature favors a change toward a lower energy state.

59. Ans. **2** Referring to the *Periodic Table* in the *Reference Tables* we see that the electron configuration of the magnesium atom (Mg^0) is 2–8–2. Since magnesium is a metal (because of its low ionization energy), it loses 2 valence electrons to form the magnesium ion (Mg^{+2}). Since the magnesium ion is missing the outer shell, its radius is smaller than the neutral magnesium atom. Thus when the magnesium ion is changed to an atom, the magnesium ion gains electrons, the valence shell is once more present, and so the radius increases.

60. Ans. **3** *Le Chatelier's principle* states that if a system in equilibrium is subject to a stress (such as increased pressure or temperature), the equilibrium will be displaced in the direction that relieves the stress. Here, an increased pressure is being applied to the reaction. Therefore, we should expect the reaction to go in the direction which creates a lower pressure. The pressure in a closed container is dependent upon the volume of the gas in the container. Volumes are proportional to the coefficients of the molecules as shown in the equation of the reaction. Here the equation is:

$$H_2(g) + I_2(g) \rightleftarrows 2HI(g)$$

The reactants H_2 and I_2 in the container have $1 + 1$ or 2 volumes. The product 2HI has 2 volumes. Since the volumes on each side of the equation are equal, an increase in pressure at the equilibrium point will favor neither side. Thus the number of moles of HI will remain the same.

PART TWO

GROUP 1

61. Ans. **3** A phase curve shows the changes in phase of a substance from solid to liquid to gas as the system *absorbs* energy. As heat is applied to the system, the *temperature rises as long as the substance is in the same phase* for the heat increases the average kinetic energy of the molecules. However, there are two definite points on the temperature scale at which the

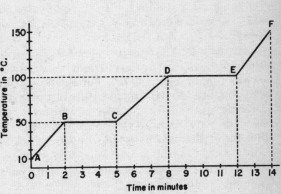

phase changes—the melting point and the boiling point. At these two temperatures the heat absorbed weakens the bonds between the particles (molecules or ions) and increases the potential energy of the system. The *temperature does not change while the phase of the system is changing.*

Now let us identify the various portions of the curve. We start with a solid at a temperature below its melting point as stated in the question. In section AB, the temperature of the solid rises from 10°C to the melting point 50°C in the time interval from 0 to 2 minutes. Then the temperature remains constant in section BC as the solid melts to form the liquid phase from time 2 minutes to 5 minutes. Section CD is the liquid phase. The temperature rises from 50°C to the boiling point, 100°C, at time 8 minutes. Section DE represents the period during which the liquid is changing to a gas with the temperature remaining at 100°C. At time 12 minutes all the liquid has changed to a gas. Any heat that is added to the gas can result only in an increase in its temperature as shown in section EF.

From the discussion above, we see that the sample is undergoing a phase change between points D and E, where it is changing from the liquid to the gas phase. The heat energy that is absorbed is used to break the intermolecular forces and thus the temperature does not change during the phase change.

62. Ans. **2** As stated in the discussion in answer to question 61, the melting point is the temperature at which the solid phase changes to the liquid phase as shown by section BC on the graph. This temperature is 50°C.

63. Ans. **2** The sample begins to melt at point B on the graph, (see answer to question 61 above). The graph tells us that the time to go from A to B is 2 minutes. Since we are told that heat is being delivered to the system at the rate of 100 calories per minute, in 2 minutes the system will have absorbed 2×100 or 200 calories.

64. Ans. **3** As stated in the answer to question 61, the substance is melting between points B and C, from time 2 minutes to time 5 minutes, a time interval of 3 minutes. In three minutes the system will have absorbed 3×100 or 300 calories.

65. Ans. **4** The kinetic energy possessed by a substance is the energy of the molecules due to their motion. Not all the molecules of the substance have the same kinetic energy, but the *average* kinetic energy is proportional to the absolute (Kelvin) temperature of the substance. On the phase diagram, the temperature increases as we go up the curve. The point on the curve at the *highest* temperature is therefore point F. Since, at point F, the temperature is the highest, the molecules must have the highest average kinetic energy.

66. Ans. **4** Ethanol, or ethyl alcohol, has the formula C_2H_5OH and its structural formula is:

$$\begin{array}{cc}
\text{H} & \text{H} \\
| & | \\
\text{H—C—C—OH} \\
| & | \\
\text{H} & \text{H}
\end{array}$$

Ethanol is produced in the *fermentation* of sugar by yeast. The fermentation of sugar produces ethanol and carbon dioxide as shown below:

$$C_6H_{12}O_6 \xrightarrow{\text{yeast}} 2C_2H_5OH + 2CO_2 \uparrow$$

sugar   ethanol

(glucose)

67. Ans. 2 *Saponification* or soap-making is the process by which a fat reacts with a strong alkali such as sodium hydroxide to produce a soap and glycerol. The fat usually used is stearin (glyceryl stearate); the soap is usually a sodium salt of stearic acid, sodium stearate. The saponification equation is

$$C_3H_5(C_{17}H_{35}COO)_3 + 3NaOH \rightarrow 3C_{17}H_{35}COONa + C_3H_5(OH)_3$$

stearin   sodium stearate   glycerol

(glyceryl stearate)

68. Ans. 1 *Esterification* is the process in which an acid reacts with an alcohol to form an ester and water. Methyl acetate is an ester formed by the reaction of methyl alcohol and acetic acid. The equation for this organic reaction is

$$CH_3OH + CH_3COOH \rightarrow CH_3COOCH_3 + H_2O$$

methyl alcohol + acetic acid → methyl acetate + water

69. Ans. 3 Polymerization is the process by which "giant" organic molecules may be produced from smaller molecular units. Ethylene (C_2H_4) polymerizes to form polyethylene, a semi-flexible plastic. The double bonds of the ethylene apparently break open. This leaves free electrons that form covalent bonds with free electrons from other ethylene molecules to produce a high polymer.

70. Ans. 5 Substitution is an organic reaction where an atom or radical in a saturated hydrocarbon is replaced by another atom or radical. Dichloromethane, CH_2Cl_2, is a halogen substitution product formed in the reaction between methane, saturated hydrocarbon, and chlorine:

$$CH_4 + 2Cl_2 \rightarrow CH_2Cl_2 + 2HCl$$

$$
\begin{array}{c}
\quad\quad H \quad\quad\quad\quad\quad\quad\quad\quad H \\
\quad\quad | \quad\quad\quad\quad\quad\quad\quad\quad | \\
H-\!\!\underset{\displaystyle |}{\overset{\displaystyle |}{C}}\!\!-H + 2\ Cl-Cl \rightarrow Cl-\!\!\underset{\displaystyle |}{\overset{\displaystyle |}{C}}\!\!-Cl + 2\ H-Cl \\
\quad\quad H \quad\quad\quad\quad\quad\quad\quad\quad H
\end{array}
$$

dichloromethane

Wrong Choices Explained:

(6) Halogen addition involves the addition of halogen atoms to carbon atoms at the site of a double bond or triple bond of an unsaturated hydrocarbon. An example of a halogen addition reaction is the addition of bromine to ethylene:

$$2C_2H_2 + Br_2 \rightarrow 2C_2H_2Br$$

$$\underset{\substack{| \\ H}}{\overset{\substack{H \\ |}}{C}} = \underset{\substack{| \\ H}}{\overset{\substack{H \\ |}}{C}} + Br\text{—}Br \rightarrow H\text{—}\underset{\substack{| \\ Br}}{\overset{\substack{H \\ |}}{C}}\text{—}\underset{\substack{| \\ Br}}{\overset{\substack{H \\ |}}{C}}\text{—}H$$

GROUP 2

71. Ans. 3 An *orbital* is the region encompassing the probability distribution of an electron of an atom. It is often represented in diagrams as an "electron cloud." Four quantum numbers are needed to describe the most probable location and energy of an electron. The *principal quantum number* or *principal energy level* ($n = 1, 2, 3$, etc.) gives the average distance of the electron from the nucleus. The *secondary quantum number* or sublevel gives the shapes of the orbital and is designated by the letters s, p, d and f. The *magnetic quantum number* gives the spatial orientation of the various shapes indicated by s, p, d and f. There is one spatial orientation for sublevel s, 3 for sublevel p, 5 for d and 7 for f. Finally we have the *spin quantum number* which gives the direction of the spin of the electron, clockwise or counterclockwise. These quantum numbers can be used to identify any electron of an atom since no two electrons have the same four quantum numbers. Most important is the fact that an orbital can have 0, 1 or 2 electrons; but if there are 2, they must have opposite spins. Although an orbital may hold up to 2 electrons, each orbital in a sublevel must be occupied by one electron with parallel spins before a second electron can be added to complete a pair. In the given system of orbital notation, the key is

☐ unoccupied orbital   ↑ orbital with one electron

↑↓ orbital with two electrons (opposite spins)

To illustrate the use of these symbols, let us see how the $2p$ sublevel with 3 orbitals would fill up.

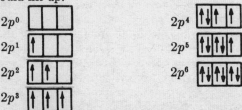

The *Periodic Table* tells us that nitrogen has an atomic number of 7. This means it has 7 protons, and thus the neutral atom has 7 electrons. Two electrons are in the $1s$ orbital, two are in the $2s$ orbital, and 3 are in the $2p$ orbitals. Thus the correct configuration for nitrogen is

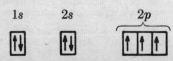

72. Ans. **2** The first *ionization energy* is the energy required to remove the most loosely-held electron from the outer shell of an atom in the gaseous phase. The less tightly an electron is held to an atom, the lower the ionization energy. The electrons are less tightly held in the higher energy levels, since they are farther away from the nucleus. Thus a 3s electron will have a lower ionization energy than a 2s electron. Also, the less positive the nucleus, the less the pull on the outer electrons. Since atoms with 3p electrons have more protons than atoms with only 3s electrons, they have a greater nuclear pull on the valence electrons. Thus an atom with only a 3s valence electron will have a lower ionization energy than one with 3p electrons. Among the given configurations, the atom with the lowest ionization energy would be one that has the fewest number of 3rd energy level electrons, but at least one. That element is choice (2) with one 3s electron.

73. Ans. **5** The valence electrons are the electrons in the outermost principal energy level of an atom. The outermost principal energy level of the atom in choice (5) is the M ($n = 3$) energy level. This atom has 2 electrons in the 3s sublevel and 4 electrons in the 3p sublevel, for a total of $2 + 4$ or 6 electrons in its outer (valence) shell.

74. Ans. **1** A noble gas is an element in Group O of the *Periodic Table*. These elements have complete (stable) outer shells (2 electrons if it is the K($n = 1$) shell and 8 electrons if it is any other shell). They do not readily combine with other elements. Choice (1) shows an element, atomic number 2, with a complete outer (K) shell. This element is He, a noble gas.

75. Ans. **7** The *Group* number of the A groups of elements indicates the number of electrons in the valence shell of that element. Thus an element in Group II A would have two electrons in its valence shell. Choice (7) has 3 principal energy levels. Its outer principal energy level ($n = 3$) contains only the 3s orbital, which is completely filled with 2 electrons. Thus element (7) has 2 electrons in its outer shell and is therefore a member of Group II A.

76. Ans. **3** A nonpolar covalent bond results from the sharing of electrons of equal electronegativities. Since the atoms have equal attraction for the shared electrons, the electrons are shared equally. The diatomic molecule of fluorine, F_2, consists of 2 highly electronegative fluorine atoms. One atom will share a pair of electrons with an identical atom to form a diatomic molecule with a nonpolar covalent bond and stable outer shells of 8 electrons. The electron dot diagram is

$$: \overset{..}{\underset{..}{F}} \overset{xx}{\underset{xx}{:}} \overset{x}{\underset{x}{F}}$$

77. Ans. **1** The ammonia molecule is polar because of the polar covalent bonds between the nitrogen and hydrogen atoms and the nonsymmetrical arrangement of the atoms. Since the electronegativity of nitrogen (3.0) is

greater than that of hydrogen (2.1), the nitrogen atom will have a greater hold on the shared electron pairs. The molecule will be polar with the nitrogen end of the molecule being the negative pole. The electron-dot diagram of the ammonia molecule would be drawn as follows:

$$H^{\delta+}$$
$$\overset{\cdot x\,\delta-}{H^{\delta+}\,{}^{x}_{x}N\,{}^{\cdot}_{x}\,H^{\delta+}}$$

Note that the centers of positive charge and negative charge do not coincide and therefore the NH_3 molecule is a dipole.

78. Ans. **2** An *ionic* compound is one formed from elements whose electronegativity difference is more than 1.7. Such a bond is formed by the *transfer* of electrons from the less electronegative atom to the more electronegative atom. As a result of this transfer the particles are now electrostatically charged. The atom that lost the electron now has an excess positive charge, and the atom that has gained the electron now has excess negative charge. The charged particles are now called ions. Na (electronegativity = 0.9) and Cl (electronegativity = 3.0) have an electronegativity difference of $(3.0 - 0.9)$ or 2.1. Thus the bond in NaCl is ionic, and sodium chloride is called an ionic compound. The electron-dot diagram of NaCl is as follows:

$$[Na]^+[\,{}^{x}\overset{\cdot\cdot}{Cl}:\,]^-$$

79. Ans. **5** Carbon dioxide is a *nonpolar compound*, with polar bonds. The molecules, however, have a linear arrangement of the atoms. The two oxygen atoms are bonded symmetrically to the central carbon atom. Thus, although the carbon-oxygen bond is polar because of the electronegativity difference (C = 2.5, O = 3.5), the centers of positive and negative charge coincide because of the symmetry of the molecules. As a result the molecule as a whole is nonpolar. The electron-dot diagram is as follows:

$$\overset{\delta-}{\underset{\overset{xx}{x}O\,{}^{x}_{x}}{}}:\ \overset{\delta+}{C}\ :\overset{\delta-}{\underset{\overset{xx}{x}O\,{}^{x}_{x}}{}}$$

80. Ans. **6** A *coordinate covalent* bond is one in which both electrons forming the bond are donated by the same single atom. In the case of the ammonium ion, a proton (H^+) forms a coordinate covalent bond with the nitrogen of the dipolar ammonia molecule, using the unshared pair of electrons of the nitrogen atom. The H^+ particle has no electrons. Both electrons shared by the nitrogen atom and H^+ are supplied by the nitrogen atom. The ammonium ion is now positively charged because of the addition of the positively charged proton:

$$H\ {}^{\cdot x}_{x}N\ {}^{x}_{x}H + H^+ \rightarrow \left[\begin{array}{c} H \\ {}^{\cdot x} \\ H\ {}^{x}_{x}N\ {}^{x}_{x}H \\ {}^{\cdot\cdot} \\ H \end{array}\right]^+$$

Note that once the NH_4^+ ion is formed, it is impossible to tell which hydrogen atom was the original free proton.

81. **Ans. 3** A coordinate covalent bond is one in which both electrons forming the bond are donated by the same single atom. To form the hydronium ion, a stripped hydrogen atom or proton forms a coordinate covalent bond with the oxygen of the water molecule, using one of the two unshared pairs of electrons from the oxygen. The result is a hydrated proton or hydronium ion. The hydration of the proton can be shown by the following equation:

$$H^+ + H \stackrel{..}{\underset{\overset{\bullet}{\times}}{O}} : \;\rightarrow\; \left[H \stackrel{..}{\underset{\overset{\bullet}{\times}}{O}} : H \right]^+$$
$$\qquad\qquad H \qquad\qquad\quad H$$

Note that once the H_3O^+ ion is formed, it is impossible to tell which hydrogen atom was the original free proton.

82. **Ans. 5** *Metallic bonding* occurs between atoms which have low ionization energies. A low ionization energy indicates a ready tendency for an atom to lose electrons. A metallic crystal consists of an arrangement of positive ions, located at the crystal lattice points immersed in a "sea" of mobile electrons, given off by the valence shell of each metallic atom. These free electrons can be considered as belonging to the crystal as a whole rather than to individual atoms. The mobility of the electrons distinguishes the metallic bond from an ionic or covalent bond, and accounts for the electrical conductivity of metals in the solid or liquid state.

83. **Ans. 1** An *ionic bond* is formed between two atoms whose electronegativity difference is more than 1.7. Such a bond is formed by the *transfer* of electrons from the less electronegative to the more electronegative atom. After the electron transfer, the atoms are no longer neutral but are electrostatically charged. The atom that has lost electrons has an excess positive charge and is now a *positive ion* or cation. The electronegative atom has gained electrons, acquired a negative charge, and has become a *negative ion* or anion. The positive and negative ions attract each other due to their opposite charges, and thus a strong ionic bond is formed.

Sodium chloride is an ionic compound and in the solid state it has crystals which are composed of positive and negative ions in rigid patterns at the lattice points of the crystal. These ions are not free to move. Thus, they cannot carry an electric current. Crystalline NaCl is thus a poor conductor of electricity.

However, when NaCl is heated to its melting point, the rigid ionic bonds are weakened and the ions are loosened from the lattice points in the crystal.

Thus in the liquid phase, there are freely moving particles (Na^+ ions and Cl^- ions) which are able to conduct electricity.

84. Ans. **6** Van der Waals forces are weak attractive forces that exist between nonpolar molecules, due to an imbalance of electron charge distribution that causes momentary polarization of the molecule. Generally, the more electrons there are in the molecule, the greater the van der Waals forces. Thus, iodine (atomic number 53), which has many electrons in the diatomic molecule has van der Waals forces which are strong enough to make it possible for iodine to exist as a solid at room temperature. However, as iodine is heated, the heat energy increases molecular motion and the van der Waals forces are overcome. The iodine sublimes, which means that molecules from the solid phase enter directly into the gas phase without passing through the liquid phase.

85. Ans. **4** *Hydrogen bonds* are formed between molecules in which hydrogen is covalently bonded to an atom of small atomic radius and high electronegativity such as oxygen and fluorine. The hydrogen atom has a very small share of the electron pair. Acting almost as a bare proton, it is attracted to the electronegative atom of an *adjacent* molecule. This intermolecular attraction accounts for the abnormally high boiling point of hydrogen fluoride as compared to hydrogen chloride, hydrogen bromide and hydrogen iodide. A higher temperature (more heat energy) is needed to overcome the intermolecular forces of attraction created by strong hydrogen bonds. HCl, HBr and HI have weaker hydrogen bonding between molecules because of the increased atomic radius and decreased electronegativity of the Cl, Br and I atoms (see *Table J*). The following table comparing the boiling points of the hydrogen halides will clearly show the effect of hydrogen bonding:

	Boiling Point (°C)
HF	19.9
HCl	−85
HBr	−66.7
HI	−35.35

86. Ans. **Cl** A strong binary acid is a compound which is composed of hydrogen and an active nonmetal. Its solution is highly ionized and thus yields a high concentration of hydronium ions. In looking for an active nonmetal in Period 3, we must remember that an active nonmetal tends to gain electrons because it has a small atomic radius and a large nuclear charge (atomic number). Since Cl has the smallest atomic radius (0.99Å) and the largest nuclear charge (+17) within Period 3, it will gain electrons the most readily, and thus it is the most active nonmetal within the period. It combines with hydrogen to form HCl, a strong binary acid (see *Table M*), which ionizes completely in water:

$$HCl + H_2O \rightarrow H_3O^+ + Cl^-$$

87. Ans. **Na** The atomic radius is the distance in an atom from the nucleus to the outermost electron energy level. Referring to the key in the *Periodic Table*, we see that the atomic radius is the decimal number below the chemical symbol of the element. In Period 3, the element with the largest atomic radius is sodium, Na (1.86 Å). Sodium has the smallest nuclear charge of any element in Period 3. The weaker nuclear pull on the valence shell allows the atom to expand.

88. Ans. **Al** The element in Period 3 that assumes a +3 oxidation state in chemical combination would have 3 electrons in its outer shell. The element with this oxidation state would be found in Group III *A* of the *Periodic Table*. That element is aluminum. Referring to the *Periodic Table* we see that Al has the electronic configuration 2-8-3. In chemical combination, it loses the 3 valence electrons in the outer shell. The Al^{+3} ion is formed which now has a stable configuration, 2-8, because the outer shell is now complete.

89. Ans. **Si** A *metalloid* is an element that has some properties of a metal, such as luster, conductivity, and tendency to lose electrons and form bases. At the same time a metalloid has properties of nonmetals, such as brittleness and tendency to gain electrons and form acids. As we move to the right in the Periodic Table in the direction of increasing atomic number, the electronegativity and ionization energy both increase. This means a gradual change from metallic to nonmetallic characteristics as it becomes more difficult for the elements to lose electrons and easier to gain them. Thus in Period 3, Na and Mg are active metals; Al is a less active metal; Si is a metalloid; P, S, and Cl are relatively active nonmetals; Ar is a noble gas and is almost completely unreactive because of its complete outer shell of 8 electrons.

90. Ans. **Ar** Elements tend to react in order that their atoms attain a lower energy state, a state which is more stable. In general, a *complete* outer shell is the most stable energy state, and atoms of elements lose or gain electrons to achieve a complete outer shell. However, argon, which has 8 electrons in the outer shell is already at a stable energy state. Thus Ar is almost completely unreactive.

GROUP 4

91. Ans. **3** The percentage by mass of sulfur in sulfur dioxide is equal to the gram-atomic mass of sulfur in sulfur dioxide divided by the mole mass of sulfur dioxide. Then multiply the ratio by 100%:

Solution:

Formula for sulfur dioxide = SO_2

Mole mass of SO_2:

$$S = 1 \times 32 = 32$$
$$2O = 2 \times 16 = 32$$

Mole mass of SO_2 = 64 grams

Thus, % sulfur = $\dfrac{\text{mass of sulfur}}{\text{mass of sulfur dioxide}}$

$= \dfrac{32 \text{ grams of sulfur}}{64 \text{ grams of sulfur dioxide}} \times 100\%$

$= 1/2 \times 100\%$

$= 50\%$

Thus, there is 50% of sulfur (by mass) in sulfur dioxide.

92. Ans. 1 A molar (1.00 M) solution of H_2SO_4 contains 1.00 moles of H_2SO_4 in 1000. ml. of solution. A 2.00 M solution therefore contains 2.00 moles in 1000. ml. of solution. In 250 ml. the number of moles is $\frac{250}{1000}$ or $\frac{1}{4}$ of 2.00 moles. This is equal to 0.50 mole.

93. Ans. 4 Using the formula

$$\text{Molarity} = \dfrac{\text{moles of solute}}{\text{liters of solution}}$$

we get

$$1.0 \, \dfrac{\text{moles}}{\text{liter}} = \dfrac{x}{.500 \text{ liters}}$$

$$x = .50 \text{ mole}$$

Thus we have .50 moles of solute in the original solution. If we dilute the original solution to a volume of 1000. ml (1 liter). Since we still have 0.50 moles of solute,

$$\text{Molarity} = \dfrac{0.50 \text{ moles}}{1 \text{ liter}}$$

$$= 0.50 \text{ M}$$

ALTERNATE METHOD:

The volume of the solution is doubled when going from 500. ml. to 1000. ml. Since the amount of solute is the same, the concentration of the resulting solution is halved. Thus the new molarity is $\frac{1}{2}$ of 1.0 or 0.50 M.

94. Ans. 2 A mole is a gram-molecular mass of a substance. We can find the number of moles a substance contains by dividing the mass of the substance by the mass of 1 mole.

$$\text{Moles of CuS} = \dfrac{\text{grams of CuS}}{\text{g. mol. mass of CuS}}$$

In order to find the gram-molecular mass of CuS we add up the atomic masses of the atoms in the compound. The molecular mass of CuS is (64 + 32) or 96 grams.

$$\text{Moles of CuS} = \dfrac{192 \text{ grams}}{96 \, \dfrac{\text{grams}}{\text{mole}}}$$

$$= 2.0 \text{ moles of CuS}$$

The equation tells us that when 2 moles of CuS are oxidized, 2 moles of CuO are produced. Thus the number of moles of CuO formed is 2.0 moles.

95. Ans. **4** The equation tells us that when 2 moles of CuS are consumed, 3 moles of O_2 are required. We found in question 94 that 2.0 moles of CuS were consumed. Thus 3.0 moles of O_2 were used. One mole of any gas at S.T.P. occupies 22.4 liters. Thus 3.0 moles would occupy 3.0×22.4 or 67.2 liters.

96. Ans. **3** One mole or gram-molecular mass of a substance has a mass equal to its molecular mass expressed in grams. The molecular mass of NO is found by adding the atomic masses of N and O. Thus the molecular mass of NO is $(14 + 16)$ or 30. One mole of NO would have a mass of 30 grams. Thus 2 moles of NO would have a mass of 2×30 or 60 grams.

97. Ans. **2** One mole or gram-molecular mass of any gas occupies 22.4 liters at S.T.P. Thus we obtain the formula

$$\text{Moles} = \frac{\text{liters}}{22.4 \frac{\text{liters}}{\text{mole}}}$$

$$\text{Moles of NO} = \frac{33.6 \cancel{\text{liters of NO}}}{22.4 \frac{\cancel{\text{liters of NO}}}{\text{mole of NO}}}$$

$$= 1.50 \text{ moles of NO}$$

98. Ans. **3** One mole of any gas contains 6.02×10^{23} molecules. Therefore 2 moles of NO would contain $2(6.02 \times 10^{23})$ molecules.

99. Ans. **1** The equation

$$2NO + O_2 \rightarrow 2NO_2$$

tells us that two moles of NO combine completely with one mole of oxygen gas to form two moles of NO_2.

100. Ans. **2** One mole of NO gas has a mass of 30 grams (see answer to question 96) and occupies 22.4 liters at S.T.P. Since the density of a substance is its mass per unit volume, we have

$$\text{Density} = \frac{\text{mass of one mole of NO}}{\text{volume of one mole of NO}}$$

$$= \frac{30 \text{ grams}}{22.4 \text{ liters}}$$

$$= 1.34 \frac{\text{grams}}{\text{liter}} \quad \text{or}$$

$$= 1.3 \frac{\text{grams}}{\text{liter}} \text{ correct to 2 significant figures.}$$

If significant figures are not taken into account, we can accept the answer 1.34 g./l. as given in choice (2).

ALTERNATE METHOD:

The density of NO is given in *Table A*. *Table A* tells us that the density of nitrogen monoxide or nitrogen (II) oxide is 1.34 g/l

101. **Ans. 3** The heat of reaction (ΔH) is the heat energy released or absorbed in a chemical reaction. ΔH represents the difference between the heat content (H) of the products and the heat content of the reactants. Thus we get the formula

$$\Delta H = H_{products} - H_{reactants}$$

The heat content of a substance measures the internal energy that is stored during the formation of the substance. Thus the heat content is a form of potential energy. On the graph shown, the heat content of the products is shown at point P and the heat content of the reactants is shown at point R. The heat of reaction is $H_P - H_R$ as shown by

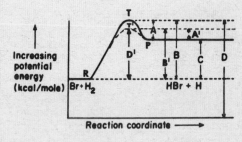

the interval marked C. Note that the energy content of the products at P is more than the energy content of the reactants at R. In other words the system has absorbed or gained energy. This indicates that the reaction shown by the graph is an *endothermic* one.

102. **Ans. 2** A chemical reaction takes place if there is an effective collision between two species, for example two molecules. To be effective the colliding molecules must be able to supply enough energy to break the bonds between the atoms of the molecules so that the atoms can become reactive and form new bonds and new molecular compounds. The energy that supplies the initial boost to the forward reaction to raise the energy content of the reactants (Br and H_2) from point P to point T at the peak of the curve where a reaction can take place is termed the *activation energy*. On the graph the activation energy is shown by interval B which extends the vertical distance from R to T. When the colliding molecules possess this activation energy, an intermediate structure called the *activated complex* is formed. This is located at the top of the curve at T. The activated complex has the maximum heat content of the system. The life of the activated complex is an extremely short one. It is during this brief interval that both molecules have penetrated each other's electron clouds. With old bonds breaking and new bonds forming, the molecular complex shows partial bonding of reactants and products simultaneously. The short-lived activated complex immediately breaks apart, either continuing on to form the products or going back to form the initial reactants.

This property of an activated complex can be shown in the reaction between molecules of AB and CD:

$$AB + CD = A - B = AD + CB$$
$$C-D$$

reactants   activated   products
complex

103.   Ans. **1** The activation energy for the reverse reaction is the minimum energy needed by the products HBr and H to start reacting to form the initial reactants, H_2 and Br. On the diagram, the activation energy of the reverse reaction is the energy needed to get HBr and H up to the top of the curve at T where the activated complex is formed. This is the interval from P to T, or interval A.

Note that the activation energy for the reverse reaction is smaller than that for the forward reaction. This is readily explained by the fact that the heat content of the products is at a higher level than was the heat content of the reactants. Thus less energy is required to bring the energy level to the peak when the activated complex is formed.

104.   Ans. **3** When an accelerator catalyst is added to a reaction, it changes the pathway of the reaction and lowers the activation energy. The potential energy of the original activated complex is shown by interval D. The activated complex that is formed at the top of the new curve (dotted) has a lower potential energy content shown by interval D'. With a lower energy content at the peak, the activation energy required in the forward reaction from R to P is lowered from the larger value without the catalyst shown by interval B to a smaller value with the catalyst shown by interval B'. In the reverse reaction from P to R, the activation energy required is lowered from the larger value without the catalyst shown by interval A to the smaller value with the catalyst shown by interval A'. Thus the only interval that would not change is interval C, the heat of reaction.

Both curves, one representing a reaction involving a catalyst and the other without a catalyst, start at the same point and end at the same point from R to P in the forward reaction and P to R in the reverse reaction. Thus the interval C which represents the energy difference between R and P does not change.

105.   Ans. **4** An increase in temperature increases the rate of all reactions. An increase in temperature provides greater collision frequency and collision efficiency. The collision frequency is increased because the molecules are moving at a greater speed and therefore will collide more often. The collision efficiency is increased since the more energetic molecules have the necessary activation energy for combination. Thus the rate of both the forward and the reverse reactions is increased.

Note: The rate of both forward and reverse reactions are not increased equally. Since the reaction is endothermic, an increase in temperature will greatly in-

crease the forward reaction and only moderately increase the reverse reaction. This drives the equilibrium point to the right as predicted by Le Chatelier's principle. The rate of both reactions is increased, however.

106. Ans. 2 A solution in which the solid phase on the bottom of the flask is in equilibrium with the liquid phase is called a *saturated* solution. A saturated solution cannot hold any more solute at that temperature. Any crystals that are added will simply drop to the bottom of the vessel. If any ions from the ammonium chloride crystal do dissolve, an equal number of ions will come out of solution and deposit on the crystal. Thus the concentration of the dissolved salt will remain the same.

107. Ans. 4 If the stopper is left off the flask for several weeks, some of the water from this saturated solution will evaporate. Thus the level of the liquid will decrease. The smaller volume of water left in solution in the flask will be unable to hold as much dissolved NH_4Cl as before, since a saturated solution can contain only a certain amount of solute per unit volume of H_2O. As the volume of the water decreases, less and less NH_4Cl can remain dissolved. The dissolved NH_4Cl will precipitate gradually, and the amount of solid NH_4Cl will increase.

108. Ans. 2 For most solutions containing a solid solute in a liquid solvent, an increase in temperature causes an increase in solubility of the solute. When solid NH_4Cl dissolves in water, the dipoles of the water molecules pull apart the ions at the surface of the crystal lattice. Thus the ions of the solid NH_4Cl *dissociate*. An increase in temperature increases the motion of solute and solvent molecules and thus hastens the separation of the ions from the solid. In the given question, the flask is cooled. With a decrease in temperature, the solubility of NH_4Cl decreases. The NH_4^+ ions and Cl^- ions combine to form solid NH_4Cl at the bottom of the flask. Thus the amount of solid NH_4Cl increases.

109. Ans. 1 A saturated solution of NH_4Cl has the solid, undissolved NH_4Cl in equilibrium with the NH_4^+ and Cl^- ions in solution. Increasing the amount of water present allows more of the solid NH_4Cl at the bottom of the flask to dissolve. Thus, the mass of solid NH_4Cl at the bottom of the flask decreases.

110. Ans. 1 If a soluble salt yielding Cl^- ions is added to the saturated solution of NH_4Cl, the concentration of Cl^- ions in solution is increased, thus disturbing the equilibrium between solid NH_4Cl and the NH_4^+ and Cl^- ions in solution:

$$NH_4Cl(s) \rightleftarrows NH_4^+(aq) + Cl^-(aq)$$

According to Le Chatelier's principle, if a stress is applied to a system in equilibrium, the system shifts in the direction that will relieve the stress. Here the stress is an increased concentration of Cl^-(aq) ions. Thus, to relieve the stress, the system shifts to the left and the concentration of $Cl^-(aq)$ decreases. But by shifting to the left, the $NH_4^+(aq)$ concentration also decreases, since in the reaction going to the left $Cl^-(aq)$ combines with $NH_4^+(aq)$ to form more solid NH_4Cl.

GROUP 6

111. Ans. **3** The hydronium (H_3O^+) ion is produced when an acid (proton donor) reacts with water. The acid donates the proton to the water, forming the H_3O^+ ion. The solution that contains the largest hydronium ion concentration is the solution containing the strongest acid. *Table H* lists the relative strengths of some acid-base conjugate pairs. Looking at the left-hand column titled "Conjugate acid," we see that the acid strength decreases as we go down the chart. Thus the strongest acid would be HCl, at the top of the chart. The other three choices in order of decreasing strength are $NaHSO_4$, whose HSO_4^- ion is an acid, NH_4Cl, whose NH_4^+ ion is an acid, and NH_3.

112. Ans. **4** According to the *Brønsted-Lowry Theory* an acid is a *proton donor* and a base is a *proton acceptor*. Any acid can lose a proton and become a base. This base can regain the proton to become an acid. The acid and base are related by the transfer of a proton and together are called a *conjugate acid-base pair*. In order to find the conjugate base of a given acid, we simply remove a proton. In the left column of *Table H* we see that the hydrated aluminum ion, $Al(H_2O)_6^{+3}$, is a Brønsted acid. This ion is an Al^{+3} ion surrounded by 6 water molecules. To find its conjugate base we remove a proton:

$$Al(H_2O)_6^{+3} = Al(H_2O)_5(OH)^{+2} + H^+$$
$$\text{or}$$
$$Al(H_2O)_6^{+3} + H_2O = Al(H_2O)_5(OH)^{+2} + H_3O^+$$

Thus the conjugate base of the hydrated aluminum ion is $Al(H_2O)_5(OH)^{+2}$ listed on the right in *Table H*.

113. Ans. **1** A weak acid is one which ionizes only to a small degree in a dilute solution. However, even among the weak acids some ionize to a greater extent than others. The seven substances listed at the top of *Table M, Ionization Constants of Acids and Bases at* 25°C. are all weak acids and bases. The ionization constant for hypochlorous acid is 3.5×10^{-8} and for acetic acid is 1.8×10^{-5} (recall that 10^{-5} is a larger value than 10^{-8}). Nitric acid and hydrochloric acid are listed as completely ionized in dilute solution, that is their ionization constant is very large. Therefore of the four acids listed, the acid that ionizes to the smallest degree is hypochlorous acid.

114. Ans. **2** The pH of a solution will increase if the solution is becoming more basic. Sodium carbonate is a salt produced by the action of weakly-ionized carbonic acid and highly-dissociated sodium hydroxide, as shown by *Table M, Ionization Constants of Acids and Bases*. Salts produced from either weak acids or bases will hydrolyze when placed in water. In the solution of sodium carbonate there are Na^+ ions, CO_3^{-2} ions and H_2O molecules. According

to the Brønsted Theory the carbonate ion is a strong base since it shows a very great tendency to gain protons. Here the carbonate ion gains a proton from the water molecule to form the bicarbonate ion and the hydroxide ion:

$$CO_3^{-2} + H_2O = HCO_3^- + OH^-$$

The hydroxide ions remain in solution since sodium hydroxide remains completely dissociated. The hydroxide ions, present in excess, cause the pH of the solution to rise.

115. Ans. **4** According to the Brønsted-Lowry Theory, a base is a proton acceptor. In the equation

$$NH_3 + H_2O = NH_4^+(aq) + OH^-(aq)$$

the NH_3 accepts a proton from the H_2O, becoming the NH_4^+ ion. Thus the NH_3 acts as a base. In the reverse reaction, the OH^- ion is a Brønsted base since it accepts a proton from the NH_4^+ ion and becomes H_2O. Thus the two bases are NH_3 and OH^-.

116. Ans. **4** In the given reaction, each $Al^0(s)$ atom loses 3 electrons to become an Al^{+3} ion. Thus for every mole of $Al^0(s)$ atoms that is oxidized to Al^{+3} ions, 3 moles of electrons are lost:

$$Al^0(s) \rightarrow Al^{+3}(aq) + 3e^-$$

In the balanced reaction, there are 2 moles of $Al^0(s)$ being oxidized. Therefore 2 × 3 or 6 moles of electrons are being transferred.

117. Ans. **3** An *oxidizing agent* is a particle in a reaction that gains electrons from a second particle. The loss of electrons by this second particle is known as oxidation. In the reaction given:

$$2Al(s) + 3Cu^{+2}(aq) = 2Al^{+3}(aq) + 3Cu(s)$$

the copper ion gains 2 electrons to become the copper atom. We say that the Cu^{+2} is the oxidizing agent. The Al^0 has been oxidized to Al^{+3} by the gain of electrons.

118. Ans. **2** As explained in the answer to question 51 above, we find the E^0 for a reaction by combining the E^0 of the oxidation half-reaction and the E^0 for the reduction half-reaction.

From *Table L* we find that

(1) Oxidation: $Al^0 = Al^{+3} + 3e^-$; $E^0 = 1.66$ volts
(2) Oxidation: $Cu^0 = Cu^{+2} + 2e^-$; $E^0 = -0.34$ volts

Equation (2) can be reversed and made the desired reduction half-reaction.

In doing so, the E^0 must change its sign since reduction is the opposite of oxidation. Thus equation (2) becomes:

(3) Reduction: $Cu^{+2} + 2e^- = Cu^0$; $E^0 = 0.34$ volts

In any oxidation-reduction reaction the electrons gained must equal the electrons lost. Thus we multiply equation (1) by 2 and equation (3) by 3, so that 6 electrons are lost in equation (1) and gained in equation (3). It is most important to note that the E^0 is constant and does not depend on the number of ions or atoms oxidized or reduced. The balanced equations are

(4) Oxidation: $2Al = 2Al^{+3} + 6e^-$; $E^0 = 1.66$ volts
(5) Reduction: $3Cu^{+2} + 6e^- = 3Cu$; $E^0 = 0.34$ volts

We add the two equations. Note the electrons lost equals the electrons gained and they cancel out. The equation for the overall reaction becomes

$$2Al^0 + 3Cu^{+2} = 2Al^{+3} + 3Fe^0; \qquad E^0 = 1.66 + 0.34 = 2.00 \text{ volts}$$

119.   Ans.   **1**   As Al(s) is oxidized to Al^{+3}, each Al^0 atom is losing 3 electrons. The electrons collect at the aluminum electrode and an excessive negative charge builds up. As the Cu^{+2} is reduced to Cu(s), it is gaining 2 electrons from the copper electrode resulting in a deficiency in the number of electrons at the copper electrode. Thus there is a tendency for the excess electrons to flow through the external circuit from the negative aluminum electrode across the wire to the positive copper electrode where there is a deficiency of electrons.

120.   Ans.   **1**   When chemical equilibrium is reached in the cell, the rates of the forward and reverse reactions are equal. Thus, 2Al(s) will be losing 6 electrons to form $2Al^{+3}$(aq) at the same rate that $2Al^{+3}$(aq) is gaining 6 electrons to form 2Al(s) in the reverse reaction. Likewise, $3Cu^{+2}$(aq) will gain 6 electrons to form 3Cu(s) at the same rate that 3Cu(s) is losing 6 electrons to form $3Cu^{+2}$(aq). Thus there is no net electron flow in either direction across the voltmeter and therefore the voltage will be 0.00 volts.

Examination June, 1968 Chemistry

१॰   **PART ONE**   *Answer all 52 questions in this part.*

Directions (1–52): *For each statement or question, write in the space provided the number preceding the word or expression that, of those given, best completes the statement or answers the question.*

1. Which is *not* a form of energy?   (1) light   (2) electricity   (3) temperature   (4) heat   1.........

2. At its normal boiling point of 100° C., the vapor pressure of water in millimeters of mercury is   (1) 0   (2) 100   (3) 373   (4) 760   2.........

3. The heat produced by burning 2 grams of a solid raised the temperature of 10 grams of water 1 degree C. Assuming 100 percent heat transfer to the water, how many calories were produced per gram of solid?   (1) 0.5   (2) 2   (3) 5   (4) 10   3.........

4. The volume of a gas is 400 ml. at 20° C. If the pressure of the gas is held constant and the temperature is changed to 40° C., the final volume of the gas will be equal to 400 ml. multiplied by

(1) $\dfrac{293}{273}$ (3) $\dfrac{293}{313}$

(2) $\dfrac{313}{293}$ (4) $\dfrac{313}{273}$ 4.........

5. Which sublevel represents the *lowest* energy level?   (1) $4s$ (2) $4p$ (3) $4d$ (4) $4f$ 5.........

6. What is the maximum number of electrons that can occupy the p sublevel of an atom?   (1) 6   (2) 2   (3) 8   (4) 10   6.........

7. Which is the electron configuration of an element with a first ionization energy of 11.2 electron-volts?
(1) $1s^2 2s^2 2p^4$ (3) $1s^2 2s^2 2p^6 3s^1$
(2) $1s^2 2s^2 2p^2$ (4) $1s^2 2s^1$ 7.........

8. In the reaction $^{239}_{92}U \rightarrow {}^{239}_{93}Np + X$, X represents   (1) a gamma ray   (2) a hydrogen nucleus   (3) an alpha particle   (4) a beta particle   8.........

9. Which particle has the same electronic configuration as an atom of argon?   (1) Na^+ (2) Cl^0 (3) Ca^{+2} (4) K^0 9.........

10. A sample of iodine-131 contains 10. grams. Approximately how much iodine-131 will remain after 24 days?   (1) 1.3 gm.   (2) 2.5 gm.   (3) 5.0 gm.   (4) 10. gm.   10.........

1

11. The characteristic spectrum of an element is produced when
(1) the energy level of the nucleus is increased
(2) electrons drop back to lower energy levels
(3) electrons are raised to higher energy levels
(4) electrons are emitted by an atom   11........

12. Given a balanced chemical reaction, it is *always* possible to determine
(1) whether a reaction will or will not take place
(2) the conditions necessary for the reaction to take place
(3) the relative number of moles taking part in the reaction
(4) the physical state of the products and reactants   12........

13. Which diagram contains a nonpolar covalent bond?

(1) $: \ddot{Br} : \ddot{Br} :$ (3) $(Na)^+ (: \ddot{Cl} :)^-$

(2) $H : \ddot{Cl} :$ (4) $H : \ddot{N} : H$
                        H 13........

14. Which molecule is a dipole? (1) H_2 (2) N_2 (3) CH_4 (4) HF   14........

15. Which compound exhibits bonds having the *least* ionic character? (1) CsCl (2) RbBr (3) KF (4) NaI   15........

16. Which is the formula for the sodium salt of perchloric acid? (1) NaClO (2) $NaClO_2$ (3) $NaClO_3$ (4) $NaClO_4$ 16........

17. Which elements may have electrons from the two outermost shells involved in a chemical reaction?
(1) transition elements   (3) noble gases
(2) alkali metals   (4) alkaline earth metals   17........

18. Which element in Period 3 of the *Periodic Table* is the strongest oxidizing agent? (1) Na (2) Al (3) S (4) Cl   18........

19. The radius of an oxygen atom is approximately
(1) 0.16 Å   (3) 0.80 Å
(2) 0.66 Å   (4) 1.32 Å   19........

20. If 3 moles of HCl are used in the reaction
$$6HCl + Fe_2O_3 \rightarrow 2FeCl_3 + 3H_2O,$$
then the number of moles of $FeCl_3$ produced is (1) 1 (2) 2 (3) 3 (4) 6   20........

21. The mass in grams of 2.00 moles of SO_2 gas is (1) 48.0 (2) 64.0 (3) 80.0 (4) 128   21........

22. The empirical formula for a compound is CH. If the molecular mass of this compound is 78 grams, then the molecular formula of the compound is (1) CH (2) C_2H_2 (3) C_5H_{18} (4) C_6H_6 22........

23. The percentage of hydrogen in H_2S is approximately (1) 1 (2) 2 (3) 6 (4) 34

23........

24. The density of a gas at S.T.P. is 1.26 grams per liter. What is the molecular mass of this gas in grams per mole? (1) 1.26 (2) 6.02 (3) 17.8 (4) 28.2

24........

25. One liter of a solution of nitric acid contains 126 grams of solute. The molarity of the solution is (1) 1.00 (2) 2.00 (3) 1.26 (4) 0.500

25........

26. Which base listed below is *least* soluble at 25° C.? [K_{sp} values at 25° C.]
  (1) $Mg(OH)_2$ ($K_{sp} = 8.9 \times 10^{-12}$)
  (2) $Ca(OH)_2$ ($K_{sp} = 1.3 \times 10^{-6}$)
  (3) $Sr(OH)_2$ ($K_{sp} = 3.2 \times 10^{-4}$)
  (4) $Ba(OH)_2$ ($K_{sp} = 5.0 \times 10^{-3}$)

26........

27. For the general equilibrium system
$$2A(g) + 3B(g) = 3C(g) + 2D(g)$$
at a constant temperature, K equals

  (1) $\dfrac{[3C] \times [2D]}{[2A] \times [3B]}$ (3) $\dfrac{[3C]^3 \times [2D]^2}{[2A]^2 \times [3B]^3}$

  (2) $\dfrac{[C]^3 \times [D]^2}{[A]^2 \times [B]^3}$ (4) $\dfrac{[2A]^2 \times [3B]^3}{[3C]^3 \times [2D]^2}$

27........

28. In which reaction would an increase in pressure produce an increase in the amount of product? [Temperature remains constant.]
  (1) $CaCO_3(s) = CaO(s) + CO_2(g)$
  (2) $2HgO(s) = 2Hg(s) + O_2(g)$
  (3) $N_2(g) + 3H_2(g) = 2NH_3(g)$
  (4) $H_2(g) + Cl_2(g) = 2HCl(g)$

28........

29. Potassium chloride dissolved in pure water is an example of
  (1) an ionic compound dissolved in an ionic type solvent
  (2) an ionic compound dissolved in a covalent type solvent
  (3) a covalent compound dissolved in an ionic type solvent
  (4) a covalent compound dissolved in a covalent type solvent

29........

30. A change in which factor is most likely to change the value of an equilibrium constant? (1) pressure (2) catalyst (3) concentration (4) temperature

30........

31. Which hydrogen ion concentration indicates the strongest acid solution? (1) 1.0×10^{-4} (2) 2.0×10^{-5} (3) 3.0×10^{-6} (4) 4.0×10^{-7}

31........

32. How many milliliters of 0.200 molar NaOH are needed to neutralize 100 milliliters of 0.100 molar HCl? (1) 40.0 (2) 50.0 (3) 100. (4) 200.

32........

33. Which is an amphoteric (amphiprotic) substance?   (1) H_2O
(2) H_3O^+ (3) NH_4^+ (4) $(OH)^-$ 33........

34. In the reaction $H_2SO_4 + H_2O = HSO_4^- + H_3O^+$, the two Brönsted-Lowry acids are
- (1) H_2SO_4 and H_2O (3) H_2O and H_3O^+
- (2) H_2SO_4 and H_3O^+ (4) HSO_4^- and H_3O^+ 34........

35. What is the oxidation number of sulfur in $H_2S_2O_7$?   (1) -2
(2) $+2$ (3) $+6$ (4) $+4$ 35........

36. In the reaction
$$4HCl + MnO_2 \rightarrow MnCl_2 + 2H_2O + Cl_2,$$
the manganese is
- (1) reduced from $+4$ to $+2$
- (2) oxidized from $+4$ to $+2$
- (3) reduced from $+2$ to $+4$
- (4) oxidized from $+2$ to $+4$ 36........

37. In the reaction
$$Zn(s) + Pb^{+2}(aq) \rightarrow Zn^{+2}(aq) + Pb(s),$$
the net potential (E^0) for the overall reaction is   (1) $+0.89$ volt
(2) $+0.76$ volt   (3) $+0.63$ volt   (4) $+0.13$ volt   37........

38. Which is the ion electron equation for the oxidation that takes place in the reaction
$$Mg + CuSO_4 \rightarrow MgSO_4 + Cu?$$
- (1) $Cu^{+2} + 2e^- \rightarrow Cu^0$
- (2) $Cu^0 \rightarrow Cu^{+2} + 2e^-$
- (3) $Mg^{+2} + 2e^- \rightarrow Mg^0$
- (4) $Mg^0 \rightarrow Mg^{+2} + 2e^-$ 38........

39. On the basis of Table L (Standard Oxidation Potentials), which reaction occurs spontaneously?
- (1) $K^0(s) + Li^+(aq) \rightarrow$
- (2) $Cr^0(s) + Ni^{+2}(aq) \rightarrow$
- (3) $Ag^0(s) + H^+(aq) \rightarrow$
- (4) $F^-(aq) + Cl_2^0(g) \rightarrow$ 39........

40. Which is an oxidation-reduction reaction?
- (1) $NH_3 + H_2O = NH_4^+ + OH^-$
- (2) $H_3O^+ + OH^- \rightarrow 2H_2O$
- (3) $Ba^{+2} + SO_4^{-2} \rightarrow BaSO_4$
- (4) $2H_2O_2 \rightarrow 2H_2O + O_2$ 40........

41. Which formula represents an acid?   (1) CH_3COOCH_3
(2) CH_3OH (3) CH_3COOH (4) $CH_3CH_2CH_3$ 41........

42. Ethyl formate (ethyl methanoate) can be produced by heating concentrated sulfuric acid, ethyl alcohol, and formic acid. This type of reaction is called
(1) fermentation   (3) saponification
(2) esterification   (4) polymerization   42.........

43. Which formula represents a member of the alkene series?
(1) C_3H_6 (2) C_2H_6 (3) C_2H_2 (4) C_6H_6 43.........

44. Each member of a homologous series of hydrocarbons *differs* from the one before it by a   (1) CH group   (2) CH_2 group
(3) CH_3 group   (4) CH_4 group   44.........

45. Compared with inorganic compounds in general, organic compounds usually have
(1) greater solubility in water
(2) a tendency to form ions more readily
(3) more rapid reaction rates
(4) lower melting points   45.........

Note that questions 46 through 52 have only three choices.

46. As one proceeds from left to right across a given period on the *Periodic Table*, the electronegativities of the elements generally
(1) decrease   (2) increase   (3) remain the same   46.........

47. As conjugate acid strength decreases, the strength of conjugate bases   (1) decreases   (2) increases   (3) remains the same   47.........

48. If an ideal gas is heated at constant pressure, its volume
(1) decreases   (2) increases   (3) remains the same   48.........

49. In a saturated solution of AgCl at 25° C.,
$$K_{sp} = [Ag^+][Cl^-].$$
If the temperature is kept constant and the concentration of the $Ag^+(aq)$ is increased, then the concentration of the $Cl^-(aq)$ (1) decreases   (2) increases   (3) remains the same   49.........

50. As the difference in electronegativities decreases, the tendency for elements to form covalently bonded compounds   (1) decreases   (2) increases   (3) remains the same   50.........

51. As a lump of sugar dissolves in a beaker of water, the entropy of the sugar and water system   (1) decreases   (2) increases (3) remains the same   51.........

52. As the pressure above a confined liquid decreases, the boiling point of the liquid   (1) decreases   (2) increases   (3) remains the same   52.........

PART TWO   *This part consists of six groups. Choose four of these six groups. Be sure that you answer all questions in each group chosen.*

GROUP 1

If you choose this group, be sure to answer questions 53–62.

Directions (53–57): *Write the* number *of the word or expression that best completes* each *statement or answers each question.*   [5]

Base your answers to questions 53 through 57 on the information and diagrams below.

Cylinder *A* contains 1 liter of hydrogen gas and cylinder *B* contains 1 liter of carbon dioxide gas. Both gases are originally at S.T.P.

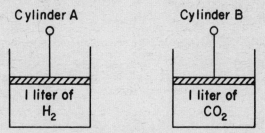

Note that questions 53 through 57 have only three choices.

53. Compared to the number of moles of carbon dioxide in cylinder *B*, the number of moles of hydrogen in cylinder *A* is (1) less   (2) the same   (3) greater   53........

54. Compared to the mass of hydrogen gas in cylinder *A*, the mass of the carbon dioxide gas in cylinder *B* is   (1) less   (2) the same   (3) greater   54........

55. The temperatures of both cylinders are lowered to $-10°$ C. Compared to the pressure exerted by the hydrogen gas in cylinder *A*, the pressure exerted by the carbon dioxide gas in cylinder *B* is (1) less   (2) the same   (3) greater   55........

56. The temperatures of both cylinders are raised to 100° C. Compared to the average kinetic energy of the hydrogen gas molecules in cylinder *A*, the average kinetic energy of the carbon dioxide gas molecules in cylinder *B* is   (1) less   (2) the same   (3) greater   56........

57. The volume of the hydrogen gas is reduced to one-half the volume occupied by the carbon dioxide gas by moving the piston. The temperature in cylinder *A* is the same as the temperature in cylinder *B*. Compared to the pressure exerted by the carbon dioxide gas in cylinder *B*, the pressure exerted by the reduced volume of hydrogen gas in cylinder *A* is (1) less (2) the same (3) greater 57........

Directions (58–62): *For each of questions 58 through 62, write the* number *preceding the structural formula,* chosen from the list below, *which is most closely associated with that question.* [5]

Structural Formulas

(1) 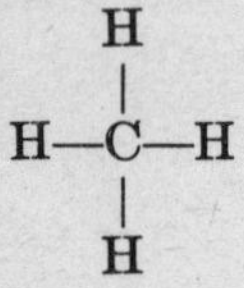
```
     H
     |
H — C — H
     |
     H
```

(5) 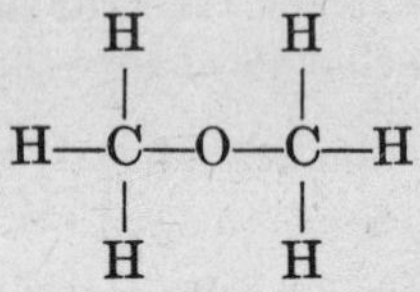
```
     H        H
     |        |
H — C — O — C — H
     |        |
     H        H
```

(2) 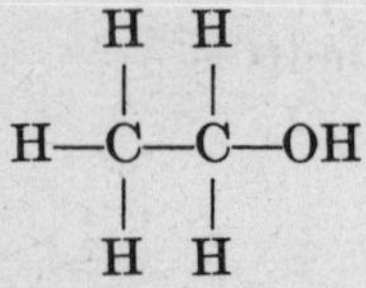
```
     H   H
     |   |
H — C — C — OH
     |   |
     H   H
```

(6) 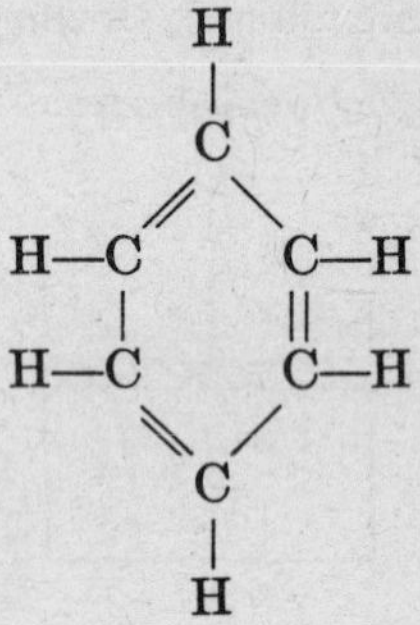
```
          H
          |
          C
         ⁄ ⁢⁢⁢⁢⁢ ╲
   H — C      C — H
      |       ‖
   H — C      C — H
         ╲   ⁄
          C
          |
          H
```

(3) H — C ≡ C — H

(4)
```
     H   H   H
     |   |   |
H — C — C — C — H
     |   |   |
     H   H   H
```

(7) 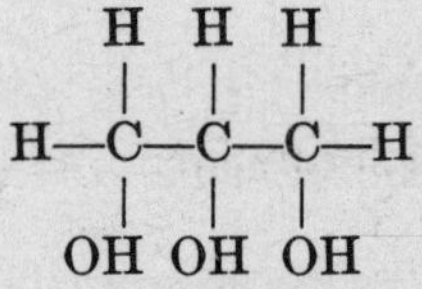
```
      H    H    H
      |    |    |
 H — C —  C —  C — H
      |    |    |
     OH   OH   OH
```

58. A structural formula that cannot correctly represent an organic compound   58........

59. A compound that may be referred to as glycerol   59........

60. The correct structural formula for a saturated hydrocarbon 60........

61. A compound that is an isomer of 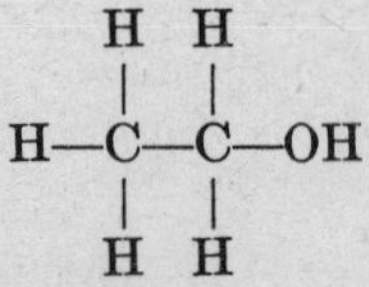 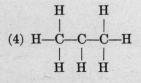 61........

62. A compound that will react most readily with bromine by addition   62........

GROUP 2

If you choose this group, be sure to answer questions 63–72.

Directions (63–67): *For each of questions 63 through 67, write the number of the electron configuration of the neutral atom,* chosen from the list below, *that best answers that question.*   [5]

Electron Configurations
(1) $1s^2 2s^2 2p^5$
(2) $1s^2 2s^2 2p^6$
(3) $1s^2 2s^2 2p^6 3s^1$
(4) $1s^2 2s^2 2p^6 3s^2 3p^3$

63. Which has more than one common oxidation state?   63........

64. Which has the highest electronegativity?   64........

65. Which is the *least* reactive?   65........

66. Which will combine with potassium to form an ionic compound?   66........

67. Which has the *lowest* ionization energy?   67........

Directions (68–72): *For each of questions 68 through 72, write the number of the compound,* chosen from the list below, *which best answers that question.*   [5]

Compounds
(1) CsCl
(2) CO_2
(3) CCl_4
(4) H_2O

68. Which compound best represents a tetrahedral molecule?   68........

69. Which compound would show a bent (V-shaped) molecular structure?   69........

70. Which compound has the highest degree of ionic bonding?   70........

71. Which compound probably has double bonds within its molecular structure?   71........

72. Which compound has polar covalent molecules?   72........

GROUP 3

If you choose this group, be sure to answer questions 73–82.

Directions (73–77): *For each substance or molecule in questions 73 through 77, write the number preceding the bond or binding forces,* chosen from the list below, *which is best illustrated by that substance or molecule.*   [5]

Chemical Terms
(1) Ionic bond
(2) Metallic bond
(3) Nonpolar covalent bond
(4) Van der Waals forces

73. A molecule of a diatomic gaseous element .... 73.........

74. Group *O* gases in the liquid phase .... 74.........

75. Substances that are nonconductors in the solid phase and conductors in the liquid phase .... 75.........

76. A substance with mobile electrons in the solid phase .... 76.........

77. Salts with high melting points .... 77.........

Directions (78–82): *For each of questions 78 through 82, write the* number *of the graph,* chosen from the list below, *which best represents the relationship described in that question.* [5]

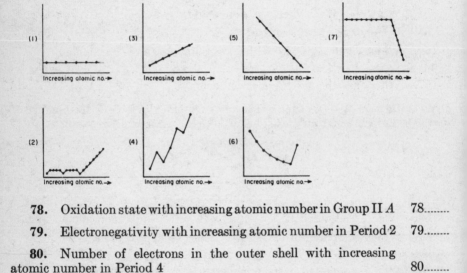

78. Oxidation state with increasing atomic number in Group II *A* 78.........

79. Electronegativity with increasing atomic number in Period 2 79.........

80. Number of electrons in the outer shell with increasing atomic number in Period 4 .... 80.........

81. Atomic radius with increasing atomic number in Period 3 81.........

82. Ionization energy with increasing atomic number in Period 3 82.........

GROUP 4

If you choose this group, be sure to answer questions 83–92.

Directions (83–92): *For each of questions 83 through 92, write the* number *of the word or expression that best completes the statement or answers the question.* [10]

Base your answers to questions 83 through 87 on the information and equation below.

Copper is completely reacted with dilute nitric acid as indicated by the equation

$$3Cu + 8HNO_3 \rightarrow 3Cu(NO_3)_2 + 2NO + 4H_2O.$$

83. If 1 mole of H_2O is produced, how many moles of HNO_3 are used? (1) 1 (2) 2 (3) 8 (4) 4   83........

84. If 1.5 moles of Cu are used, how many moles of NO are produced? (1) 1.0 (2) 2.0 (3) 3.0 (4) 1.5   84........

85. If 2 moles of NO are produced, the mass of the NO is (1) 30 grams (2) 44 grams (3) 60 grams (4) 92 grams   85........

86. Which electronic equation represents the oxidation which takes place in this reaction?
(1) $4O^{-2} - 8e^- \rightarrow 4O^0$
(2) $8H^+ + 8e^- \rightarrow 8H^0$
(3) $2N^{+5} + 6e^- \rightarrow 2N^{+2}$
(4) $3Cu^0 - 6e^- \rightarrow 3Cu^{+2}$ 86........

87. At S.T.P., what volume of NO is produced when 4 moles of HNO_3 are used? (1) 1 liter (2) 2 liters (3) 22.4 liters (4) 44.8 liters   87........

Base your answers to questions 88 through 90 on the information below and on your knowledge of chemistry.

1.00 mole of ethanol has a mass of 46.0 grams. The freezing point depression constant for water is 1.86 C.°.

88. How much ethanol must be added to water to make 1.0 liter of 0.5 molar solution of ethanol? (1) 0.5 gram (2) 23 grams (3) 46 grams (4) 92 grams   88........

89. If 46.0 grams of ethanol are completely dissolved in 1,000. grams of water, the freezing point of the solution is most nearly (1) 3.72° C. (2) 1.86° C. (3) −1.86° C. (4) −3.72° C.   89........

90. If 1 mole of ethanol is dissolved in 1 liter of water, the resulting mixture is (1) an emulsion (2) a colloid (3) a solution (4) a suspension   90........

Base your answers to questions 91 and 92 on the information below.

A hydrocarbon is 80% carbon and 20% hydrogen and has a density of 1.34 grams/liter at S.T.P.

91. What is the empirical formula of this substance? (1) CH_3 (2) CH_4 (3) C_2H_6 (4) C_3H 91........

92. What is the molecular mass of this substance?
(1) 2.2×10^1 grams   (3) 6.0×10^1 grams
(2) 3.0×10^1 grams   (4) 1.0×10^2 grams   92........

GROUP 5

If you choose this group, be sure to answer questions 93–102.

Directions (93–102): *For each of questions 93 through 102, write the* number *of the word or expression that best completes the statement or answers the question.* [10]

Base your answers to questions 93 through 97 on the potential energy diagram and the reaction below.

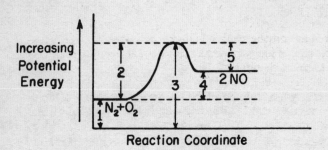

$$N_2(g) + O_2(g) = 2NO(g) \quad \Delta H = +43.2 \text{ kcal.}$$

93. The potential energy of the reactants

$$(N_2(g) + O_2(g))$$

is represented by   (1) 1   (2) 2   (3) 3   (4) 5   93........

94. The energy of activation for the forward reaction is represented by   (1) 1   (2) 2   (3) 3   (4) 4   94........

95. Compared to the potential energy of the product, the potential energy of the reactants is   (1) less   (2) the same   (3) greater   (4) impossible to determine   95........

96. The potential energy of the activated complex is represented by   (1) 1   (2) 5   (3) 3   (4) 4   96........

97. The heat of formation of NO(g), in kilocalories per mole, is (1) −21.6   (2) 21.6   (3) −43.2   (4) 43.2   97........

Base your answers to questions 98 through 102 on the information and equation below.

$SO_2(g)$, $O_2(g)$, and $SO_3(g)$ are in a closed system and have attained equilibrium at a certain temperature according to the reaction

$$2SO_2(g) + O_2(g) = 2SO_3(g) + 45 \text{ kcal.}$$

98. Which would cause the amount of product $SO_3(g)$ to increase? [The temperature of the system remains constant.]

(1) an increase in the concentration of the SO_2

(2) a decrease in the concentration of the O_2

(3) a decrease in the pressure on the system
(4) the addition of a catalyst   98........

99. How would the addition of a catalyst affect the rates of reaction of the system? [The temperature and pressure of the system remain constant.]

(1) It would increase the rate of the forward reaction only.
(2) It would increase the rate of the reverse reaction only.
(3) It would increase the rates of the forward and reverse reactions equally.
(4) It would increase the rates of the forward and reverse reactions unequally.   99........

100. The pressure on the system is increased, while the temperature is kept constant. Which statement can be made about the mass of the gases at the new equilibrium?

(1) SO_3 has increased, and O_2 has increased.
(2) SO_3 has increased, and SO_2 has decreased.
(3) SO_3 has decreased, and SO_2 has decreased.
(4) SO_2 has increased, and O_2 has decreased.   100........

101. The temperature is increased and the pressure is kept constant. Which statement can be made about the new equilibrium concentrations of the gases as compared to the original concentrations?

(1) SO_2 is greater.
(2) SO_2 must be the same.
(3) SO_3 is greater.
(4) SO_3 must be the same.   101........

102. Some $SO_3(g)$ is removed from the system, while temperature and pressure are kept constant. Which statement can be made about the reactants at the new equilibrium as compared to the original equilibrium? (1) SO_2 is unchanged. (2) SO_2 is increased. (3) O_2 is unchanged. (4) O_2 is decreased.   102........

GROUP 6

If you choose this group, be sure to answer questions 103–112.

Directions (103–112): *For each of questions 103 through 112, write the* number *of the word or expression that best completes the statement or answers the question.* [10]

Base your answers to questions 103 through 107 on Table H *of the* Reference Tables for Chemistry *and on your knowledge of chemistry.*

103. Which substance is the strongest acid? (1) NH_3 (2) H_2O (3) $Al(H_2O)_6^{+3}$ (4) H_3O^+ 103........

104. Which substance is a weaker base than water? (1) NH_3 (2) OH^- (3) SO_4^{-2} (4) NO_3^- 104........

105. Which substance can behave as either an acid or a base? (1) H_3O^+ (2) HNO_3 (3) HSO_4^- (4) NH_2^- 105........

106. A solution has a pH of 3. What is the hydrogen ion concentration of this solution in moles per liter?
(1) 1×10^{-3} (3) 1×10^{-11}
(2) 1×10^{3} (4) 1×10^{11} 106........

Base your answer to question 107 *on the expression* $K_w = [H^+] \cdot [OH^-] = 1.0 \times 10^{-14}$ *at* 25° C.

107. If the hydrogen ion concentration is determined to be 1×10^{-2} mole per liter, what is the hydroxide ion concentration?
(1) 1×10^{-12} (2) 1×10^{-10} (3) 1×10^{-7} (4) 1×10^{-2} 107........

Base your answers to questions 108 *through* 112 *on the diagram of the chemical cell and equation below.*

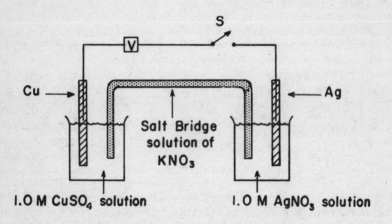

$$Cu(s) + 2Ag^+(aq) \rightarrow Cu^{+2}(aq) + 2Ag(s)$$

108. When the cell reaches equilibrium, the net potential (E^0) for the cell is (1) 0.80 (2) 0.46 (3) 0.00 (4) −0.34   108........

109. The species oxidized is (1) Ag(s) (2) Cu(s) (3) Ag$^+$(aq) (4) Cu^{+2}(aq)   109........

110. When switch S is closed, the maximum net potential (E^0) for the cell is (1) −1.14 (2) −0.34 (3) 0.46 (4) 0.80   110........

111. Which is the electronic equation for the reaction that takes place at the copper electrode?
(1) $Cu^0 - 2e \rightarrow Cu^{+2}$
(2) $Cu^{+2} + 2e \rightarrow Cu^0$
(3) $Cu^0 + 2e \rightarrow Cu^{+2}$
(4) $Cu^{+2} - 2e \rightarrow Cu^0$ 111........

112. The species that acts as a reducing agent is (1) Ag(s) (2) Cu(s) (3) Ag$^+$(aq) (4) Cu^{+2}(aq)   112........

Answers June, 1968 Chemistry

PART ONE

1. Ans. **3** *Energy* is defined as the capacity for doing work. Energy may be stored in a given system by virtue of position (*potential energy*) as, for example, a stone above the earth's surface, or a spring under compression; or by virtue of chemical properties due to arrangement of atoms and electrons within a molecule. Energy may also exist in other forms such as the kinetic energy of a moving ball or molecule. Energy manifests itself in the universe in various forms, some of which are: atomic energy, electromagnetic (*light*) energy, electrical energy, heat energy, mechanical energy, nuclear energy and sound energy. Thus, light, electricity and heat are forms of energy. Temperature is an indicator of the intensity of the heat. Temperature means hotness or coldness. Temperature is not a form of energy.

2. Ans. **4** According to the *kinetic theory* there is a continuous flight of molecules from the surface of a liquid into the free space above it. At the same time, molecules of gas or vapor return to the surface of the liquid at a rate depending upon the concentration of the vapor. *We will consider a confined system.* Eventually a condition of equilibrium is established between the liquid and its vapor, when the rate of escape is exactly equal to the rate of condensation of the vapor. The vapor is said to be saturated. The pressure exerted by vapor which is in equilibrium with the liquid is known as vapor pressure. The equilibrium between a liquid and its vapor is dependent on the temperature. As the temperature increases, the kinetic energy of the molecules increases. As a result more molecules leave the liquid and the vapor pressure of the liquid increases. When the vapor pressure of the liquid equals the atmospheric pressure, the liquid will boil. Thus, the boiling point of a liquid is that temperature at which the vapor pressure is equal to the atmospheric pressure. Standard atmospheric pressure is 760 mm of mercury, or 1 atmosphere. Since the vapor pressure of water at 100°C. is 760 mm of mercury, it will boil at that vapor pressure.

3. Ans. **3** Since the heat produced by burning 2 grams of a solid raised the temperature of 10 grams of water 1 C°., we can determine the heat transferred to the water, *assuming 100% heat transfer*. Since it requires 1 calorie to raise the temperature of 1 gram of water 1 C°., the specific heat of water is 1 cal/gram/C°. Thus we can calculate the heat produced as follows:

Heat produced = mass × change in temperature × specific heat of H_2O

14

Heat produced = 10 grams $\times$ 1 C° $\times$ 1 $\dfrac{\text{calorie}}{\text{gram/C}°}$

= 10 calories produced for 2 grams of solid.

If 2 grams produced 10 calories, 1 gram of solid would produce 5 calories. We can set up a proportion to prove it as follows:

$$\frac{2 \text{ grams}}{10 \text{ calories}} = \frac{1 \text{ gram}}{X} \qquad X = 5 \text{ calories per gram of solid.}$$

4. **Ans. 2** *Charles' Law* states that at constant pressure, the volume of a fixed mass of gas is directly proportional to the Kelvin (absolute) temperature. Also, since the average kinetic energy of the gas molecules is directly proportional to the absolute temperature, an increase in temperature will cause an increase in volume. A decrease in temperature will cause a decrease in volume. We can solve the problem as follows:

$$\text{Charles' Law—} \qquad \frac{V_1}{T_1} = \frac{V_2}{T_2}$$

Where V_1 = original volume = 400 ml.
T_1 = original temperature = C° + 273° = 20° + 273° = 293°K
V_2 = final volume = x
T_2 = final temperature = C° + 273° = 40° + 273° = 313°K

Solving for V_2: $\qquad V_2 = \dfrac{V_1 T_2}{T_1} = 400 \text{ ml.} \times \dfrac{313°\text{K}}{293°\text{K}}.$

Since the question asks the final volume of the gas will be equal to 400 ml.

multiplied by ——, it can be readily seen that the answer is $\dfrac{313}{293}$.

5. **Ans. 1** Sublevels, also called subshells, are subdivisions of the main quantum level. The principal quantum number (n) represents the principal energy level and indicates the average distance of an orbital from the nucleus of an atom. An orbital is a diffuse region around the nucleus in which an electron may be expected to exist. Orbitals are designated by the letters s, p, d, f. Principal energy levels are in order of increasing distance from the nucleus, K $(n = 1)$, L $(n = 2)$, M $(n = 3)$, N $(n = 4)$, etc. Thus, $n = 4$ is a higher energy level than $n = 3$.

For $n = 1$, there is only one sublevel called $1s$
For $n = 2$, there are two sublevels $2s$ and $2p$
For $n = 3$, there are three sublevels $3s$, $3p$ and $3d$
For $n = 4$, there are four sublevels $4s$, $4p$, $4d$ and $4f$

In general, the order of filling orbitals in a particular level starts with the orbital of lowest energy, the s orbital, and proceeds with the p, d, and f orbitals, the f being of highest energy. Thus, in this question concerning the 4th principal energy level, since the $4s$ orbital or sublevel fills up first, it represents the lowest energy level.

6. Ans. **1** The maximum number of electrons that can fill any principal energy level is equal to $2n^2$ where $n = 1, 2, 3, 4$, etc. Thus, in the K level ($n = 1$), we have a maximum of 2 electrons. In the L level, we have a maximum of 8 electrons etc. The maximum number of orbitals in each principal energy level is n^2, where $n = 1, 2, 3, 4$, etc. Thus for $n = 1$, we have 1 orbital; for $n = 2$, we have 4 orbitals, etc. An orbital can have 0, 1, or a maximum of 2 electrons in it. In the atom any s sublevel has 1 orbital with a maximum of 2 electrons. Any p sublevel has 3 orbitals with a maximum of 6 electrons. Any d sublevel has 5 orbitals with a maximum of 10 electrons. Any f sublevel has 7 orbitals with a maximum of 14 electrons. Therefore, the maximum number of electrons that can occupy the p sublevel of an atom is 6.

Wrong Choices Explained:
(2) The s sublevel can have a maximum of 2 electrons.
(3) The L shell ($n = 2$) can have a maximum of 8 electrons.
(4) The d sublevel can have a maximum of 10 electrons.

7. Ans. **2** *Ionization energy* is the minimum energy needed to remove the most loosely bound electron from an isolated gaseous atom. Ionization energy may be measured in electron-volts or Kcal/mole. *Table J* indicates that the element carbon has a value of 11.2 ev. Since carbon has the orbital arrangement $1s^2 2s^2 2p^2$, this is the answer. The orbital arrangement is explained as follows:

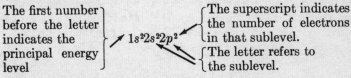

The first number before the letter indicates the principal energy level $1s^2 2s^2 2p^2$ The superscript indicates the number of electrons in that sublevel. The letter refers to the sublevel.

Wrong Choices Explained:
(1) $1s^2 2s^2 2p^4$ is oxygen with an ionization energy of 13.6 ev.
(3) $1s^2 2s^2 2p^6 3s^1$ is sodium with an ionization energy of 5.1 ev.
(4) $1s^2 2s^1$ is lithium with an ionization energy of 5.4 ev.

8. Ans. **4** In this nuclear reaction, a beta particle is emitted from the nucleus. This nuclear reaction could be classified as radioactive decay by beta particle emission. A beta particle is an electron ($_{-1}e^0$). A beta particle is formed when a neutron in the nucleus breaks down into a proton, an electron and a neutrino. The proton is picked up by the nucleus and the electron (*beta particle*) and neutrino are emitted. In solving nuclear equations such as these, the sum of the subscripts for the reacting particles must equal the sum of the subscripts for the products, and the sum of the superscripts for the reacting particles must equal the sum of the superscripts for the products. The reaction is explained as follows:

	U	Np	x
Superscript	239	= 239	+ 0
Subscript	92	= 93	− 1

$$^{239}_{92}U \rightarrow {}^{239}_{93}Np + {}_{-1}e^0$$
$$\text{where } x = {}_{-1}e^0$$

Wrong Choices Explained:

(1) A gamma ray is an electromagnetic wave.
(2) A hydrogen nucleus is a proton, $_1H^1$.
(3) An alpha particle is a helium nucleus, $_2He^4$ or He^{++}.

9. **Ans. 3** The *Periodic Table* of the elements tells us that the electronic structure of the element argon in Group O is 2-8-8. Since the elements in Group 2A lose 2 electrons when they form ions, calcium will have an electron configuration of 2-8-8 as Ca^{+2}. Therefore an atom of argon and the calcium ion are isoelectronic (2-8-8). Isoelectronic means they have identical electronic configurations.

Wrong Choices Explained:

(1) The sodium ion, Na^+, has an electronic configuration of 2-8.
(2) The chlorine atom, Cl^0, has an electronic configuration of 2-8-7.
(4) An atom of potassium, $K°$, has a configuration of 2-8-8-1.

10. **Ans. 1** *Iodine*-131 is a radioactive isotope (*radioisotope*) of *Iodine*-127. An isotope differs in the number of neutrons in the nucleus. Many isotopes are radioactive. Some elements have a few isotopes and others have as many as 20. Radioactive isotopes such as Iodine-131 have half-lives. A half-life of a radioisotope is the time required for half of the atoms of the radioisotope to change into other atoms. The half-life of Iodine-131 listed on *Table G* is 8 days. Thus, after 8 days, only 5 grams of iodine-131 would remain unchanged, after 16 days, 2.5 grams would remain unchanged, and after 24 days, 1.25 or 1.3 grams would remain unchanged. We can set up a chart to solve this problem as follows:

Time	Now	1st half-life 8 days	2nd half-life 16 days	3rd half-life 24 days
Amount unchanged	10 grams	5 grams	2.5 grams	1.25 grams
Amount changed	0 grams	5 grams	7.5 grams	8.75 grams

11. **Ans. 2** The characteristic spectrum of an element is produced when the element is excited by heat, light or electron bombardment producing characteristic lines which identify the element. When an element is excited by heat, light or electron bombardment, some electrons are elevated from their normal (*ground*) state to a higher energy level. The electrons in this higher energy level have absorbed energy and are in an excited state. The electrons in this excited state will drop back to the ground state and will emit their characteristic energy. This energy in the form of spectral lines will have

characteristic wavelengths and can be examined using a spectroscope. The energy emitted by each electron falling back to the ground state can be determined by the formula, Energy $= hv$, where v is the frequency and h is Planck's Constant. Thus, when an electron is raised to an excited state of higher energy, energy is absorbed, and when it drops back to a state of lower energy, energy is released.

Wrong Choices Explained:

(1) The spectrum produced by an atom is not affected by the nucleus. It is caused by energy transitions of the orbital electrons.

(3) A characteristic spectrum is not produced when electrons are raised to higher energy levels.

(4) Electrons are emitted by an atom as a result of adding sufficient energy to remove them (*ionization energy*). Also, in the photoelectric effect electrons are emitted by metallic atoms. In neither case is a characteristic spectrum formed.

12. Ans. **3** A balanced chemical reaction is a method of representing such facts as reacting substances, products, type of chemical reaction, the mole quantities of reactants and products of the reaction. It obeys the *Law of Conservation of Mass*. In our study of chemistry we might know the conditions under which a particular reaction will take place, the physical state of the reactants and products and other factors about a particular reaction. However, an ordinary balanced chemical reaction does not give this information. Since we have millions of chemical reactions, we cannot know all the information by looking at a balanced chemical reaction. However, from a balanced chemical reaction, we can always determine the relative number of moles taking part in the reaction. For example, the balanced chemical reaction for the decomposition of water is:

$$2H_2O \rightarrow 2H_2 + O_2$$

In this reaction, 2 moles of water decomposes to form 2 moles of hydrogen and 1 mole of oxygen.

13. Ans. **1** A nonpolar covalent bond is one in which the electronegativity difference between 2 elements is zero. The diatomic molecules such as F_2, Cl_2, Br_2, H_2, I_2, O_2, and N_2 contain nonpolar covalent bonds. A nonpolar covalent bond is formed when identical atoms or groups share an electron pair equally.

Wrong Choices Explained:

(2) HCl contains a polar covalent bond since the shared electrons are closer to the chlorine. The electronegativity difference is 0.9.

(3) NaCl contains an ionic bond. The electronegativity difference is 2.1.

(4) Ammonia (NH_3) is a polar covalent molecule since the shared electrons are drawn closer to the more electronegative nitrogen atom.

14. Ans. **4** A dipole is a molecule characterized by unequal sharing of an electron pair between atoms. This gives rise to a polar molecule one region of which is positive and the other negative. As we explained in question 13, H_2

and N_2 share electrons equally since they are nonpolar covalent molecules. As a result, N_2 and H_2 are not dipoles. In CH_4, the hydrogen atoms are distributed symmetrically around the carbon atom. CH_4 has a tetrahedral shape with the carbon at the center of the tetrahedron and the four hydrogens at the corners. The bonding electrons are distributed symmetrically around the carbon. As a result, one side of the molecule does not get a greater negative or positive charge than the other side. The molecule is neutral; therefore, CH_4 is not a dipole. In the HF molecule, fluorine having a much greater electronegativity value than hydrogen, attracts the bonding electrons toward itself. As a result, there is a greater number of electrons around the fluorine end of the molecule. The fluorine end of the molecule becomes very negative and the hydrogen end very positive. Therefore, the HF molecule is a dipole. The electron-dot diagram is shown below:

$$^{+\delta}_{} H \quad {}^{xx}_{x}F^{x}_{xx} \, {}^{\delta^-}$$

15. **Ans. 4** The bond with the least ionic character is the one with the smallest difference in electronegativity. *Table J* shows that the electronegativity difference between each compound is:

(1) CsCl is $(3 - 0.7) = 2.3$
(2) RbBr is $(2.8 - 0.8) = 2.0$
(3) KF is $(4.0 - 0.8) = 3.2$
(4) NaI is $(2.5 - 0.9) = 1.6$

Since the compound exhibiting the bond with the least ionic character has the lowest difference in electronegativity, NaI is the answer.

16. **Ans. 4** The formula for perchloric acid is $HClO_4$. The $(ClO_4)^-$ ion is called perchlorate. The perchlorate ion has one more oxygen atom than the chlorate ion $(ClO_3)^-$. If we replace the hydrogen of the perchloric acid with sodium to form a salt, the resulting salt is called sodium perchlorate, $(NaClO_4)$.

Wrong Choices Explained:

Formula	Name	Corresponding acid
1) NaClO	sodium hypochlorite	hypochlorous acid (HClO)
2) NaClO$_2$	sodium chlorite	chlorous acid (HClO$_2$)
3) NaClO$_3$	sodium chlorate	chloric acid (HClO$_3$)

17. **Ans. 1** An element may have electrons from the two outermost shells involved in a chemical reaction if the next to the outer level is incomplete. Elements with incomplete inner energy levels are called transition elements. They are located in the "B" Groups of the *Periodic Table*. Transition elements in Period 4 have a deficiency of electrons in the 3d sublevel. In forming com-

pounds, the transition elements exhibit many oxidation states presumably because some or all of the 3d electrons can also be used with 4s electrons in chemical bonding.

Wrong Choices Explained:

(2) Alkali metals are Group 1A metals. The inner levels of Group 1A are completely filled; thus, they are not available for bonding. The one outer electron is available for bonding.

(3) Noble gases are Group O inert gases. Every energy level is completely filled including the outer level. As a result, they do not ordinarily react with other elements.

(4) Alkaline earth metals are Group 2A metals. In general, they tend to lose their 2 outer electrons in combining with other elements. The inner levels of Group 2A metals are completely filled; therefore, they are not available for bonding purposes.

18. Ans. 4 The strongest oxidizing agent in Period 3 of the *Periodic Table* is chlorine. A strong oxidizing agent has a great tendency to gain electrons. Since chlorine has the greatest tendency to gain electrons in Period 3, it is the strongest oxidizing agent. Chlorine also has a high electron affinity value. On *Table L*, as you go down from lithium to fluorine, the oxidizing ability or role as an oxidizing agent of an element increases. Since chlorine is lower than sodium, aluminum and sulfur, it is the strongest oxidizing agent.

Wrong Choices Explained:

(1) Sodium is a very strong reducing agent.

(2) Aluminum is an excellent reducing agent.

(3) Sulfur can function either as an oxidizing or reducing agent depending upon its role in a redox reaction.

19. Ans. 2 In view of the indefinite size of the electron cloud, the radius of the atom is a somewhat ambiguous quantity. As a result, it is usually determined by taking one-half of the distance of the closest approach of 2 atoms in a molecule or in a crystal. It is convenient for many reasons to assign a radius to each atom called the covalent atomic radius. The covalent atomic radius is measured in units called the *Angstrom* (Å). One *Angstrom* (Å) $= 10^{-8}$ cm. Covalent atomic radii values range from about 0.3 (Å) to 2.7 (Å). The covalent atomic radii values are listed directly under the symbol for each element on the *Periodic Table*. The atomic radius of an oxygen atom as listed is 0.66 (Å).

20. Ans. 1 In a chemical reaction, the number of moles of reactants consumed and the number of moles of products formed are proportional to the numerical coefficients of the substances in the equation. The equation given is:

$$6HCl + Fe_2O_3 \rightarrow 2FeCl_3 + 3H_2O$$

The equation tells us that if we consume 6 moles of HCl, we will get 2 moles of FeCl₃ produced. Thus, the mole ratio of HCl to FeCl₃ is 6:2 or 3:1. We can also set up a proportion to determine how much $FeCl_3$ is produced when we use 3 moles of HCl.

$$\frac{3 \text{ moles HCl}}{6 \text{ moles HCl}} = \frac{x}{2 \text{ moles FeCl}_3}$$

$$6x = 6$$

$$x = 1 \text{ mole of FeCl}_3 \text{ produced.}$$

21. Ans. 4 A mole is a gram-molecular mass of a substance. One mole would contain *Avogadro's number* (6.02×10^{23}) of atoms, molecules or ions of a substance at S.T.P. The gram-molecular mass for SO_2 is 64 grams; thus, 1 mole of SO_2 gas has a mass of 64 grams. If 1 mole has a mass of 64 grams, 2 moles have a mass of 128 grams. We can set up a proportion as follows to solve this problem:

$$\frac{1 \text{ mole}}{64 \text{ grams}} = \frac{2 \text{ moles}}{x}$$

$$x = 128 \text{ grams}$$

22. Ans. 4 The empirical formula represents the constituent elements of a substance and the simplest relative number of atoms of each. Thus, the empirical formula given is a whole-number multiple where the ratio of carbon atoms to hydrogen atoms is 1:1. Since the molecular mass of this compound is 78 grams and the general formula is $(CH)_x$, we can determine the relative number of atoms of each using the following relationship:

$$(CH)_x = 78$$

Carbon   = 12

$$(12 + 1)_x = 78$$

Hydrogen = 1

$$(13)_x = 78$$

$$x = 6 \text{ atoms of each element in the formula.}$$

Substituting $x = 6$, we get $(CH)_6$ or C_6H_6. This is the molecular formula for the compound.

23. Ans. 3 To determine the percentage of hydrogen by mass in H_2S, we can set up the following relationship:

$$\text{Percentage of hydrogen in } H_2S = \frac{\text{Mass of hydrogen}}{\text{Gram-molecular mass of } H_2S} \times 100\%$$

$$\text{Mass of } H_2 = 2 \text{ grams}$$

$$\text{Gram-molecular mass of } H_2S = 34 \text{ grams}$$

$$\text{Percentage of hydrogen in } H_2S = \frac{2 \text{ grams}}{34 \text{ grams}} \times 100\% = 6\%$$

Thus, the percentage of hydrogen in H_2S is approximately 6%.

24. Ans. 4 One mole (gram-molecular mass) of any gas at S.T.P. has a volume of 22.4 liters. The density of a gas is defined as the mass per unit volume. The density of the gas is given as 1.26 grams per liter. Thus, we can determine the mass of 1 mole of the gas using the following formula:

$$\text{Density} = \frac{\text{Mass}}{\text{Volume}}$$

Density = 1.26 grams/liter
Mass = X
Volume = 22.4 liters/mole

$$1.26 \text{ grams/liter} = \frac{X}{22.4 \text{ liters/mole}}$$

$$X = 28.2 \text{ grams/mole}$$

Thus, the molecular mass of this gas in grams per mole is 28.2.

25. Ans. 2 *Molarity* is defined as the number of moles per liter of solution. Molarity is a term used to indicate the concentration of an acid, base or salt solution. A 1 molar solution contains 1 mole of solute dissolved in 1 liter of solution. We can solve this problem using the following formula:

$$\text{Molarity} = \frac{\dfrac{\text{The number of grams given}}{\text{Gram-molecular mass of } HNO_3}}{\text{The number of liters of solution}}$$

Molarity = X
The number of grams given = 126 grams

Gram-molecular mass of HNO_3 = 1H 1 = 63 grams/mole
1N 14
3O 48
——
63

$$\text{Molarity} = X = \frac{\dfrac{126 \text{ grams}}{63 \text{ grams}} \Big/ \text{mole}}{1 \text{ liter}} = 2 \text{ moles/liter or } 2M$$

ALTERNATE METHOD:

If 1 mole of HNO_3 has a mass of 63 grams, 2 moles have a mass of 126 grams.

$$\text{Molarity} = \frac{\text{The number of moles of } HNO_3}{\text{The number of liters of solution}}$$

Molarity = X
The number of moles of HNO_3 = 2 moles $X = \dfrac{2 \text{ moles}}{1 \text{ liter}}$ X = 2 moles/liter
The number of liters of solution = 1 liter

26. Ans. 1 The solubility product constant, K_{sp}, is defined as the product of the molar concentrations of the ions—each molar concentration being raised to a power equal to the number of moles of that particular ion which appears in the balanced equation representing the ionization. The solubility product constant is used for a saturated solution of a slightly soluble salt at a given temperature. The question lists the K_{sp} values for the bases of 4 Group 2A elements. The K_{sp} for each base can be determined by substituting the con-

centration of each ion in moles/liter and raising each to the appropriate power in the following general equation:

$$K_{sp} = [X^{+2}][OH^-]^2$$

Since each Group 2A base dissociates in water to form:

$$X(OH)_2 \rightarrow X^{+2} + 2OH^-$$

This relationship tells us that the higher the concentration of ions, the greater the K_{sp} value, and the greater the solubility. The lower the K_{sp} value, the lower the concentration of each ion hence, the lower the solubility. Since the K_{sp} value for $Mg(OH)_2$ is the smallest value, (8.9×10^{-12}), it would be the least soluble in water at 25°C. $Ba(OH)_2$ (5.0×10^{-3}), would be the most soluble.

27.   Ans. 2   The equilibrium constant K_e is a number referring to a given reversible reaction occurring at a given temperature. It is determined by dividing the product of the concentrations of the products of the reaction (*each raised to that power which is its coefficient in the equation*) by the product of the concentrations of the reactants (*each raised to a power which is its coefficient in the equation*). The equilibrium constant for the following reaction can be determined as follows:

$$aA + bB = cC + dD$$

$$\text{The } K_e = \frac{C^c \times D^d}{A^a \times B^b}$$

In this question, the equilibrium reaction is:

$$2A + 3B = 3C + 2D$$

$$\text{The } K_e = \frac{[C]^3 \times [D]^2}{[A]^2 \times [B]^3}$$

28.   Ans. 3   A change in pressure has a negligible effect on a reaction in which we have solids or liquids involved. A change in pressure affects a reaction in which the reactants and products are all gaseous. Also, the effect of a pressure change on a solid dissolved in a liquid is negligible. Thus, we can eliminate choices (1) and (2), since an increase in pressure will not affect these reactions. Reactions (1) and (2) involve solid materials. According to *Le Chatelier's Principle*, if we place a stress on a system in equilibrium, it will readjust itself to relieve the stress. Increasing the pressure on a gaseous system shifts the equilibrium to the side with the smaller volume. Therefore, an increase in pressure on the reaction $N_{2(g)} + 3H_{2(g)} = 2NH_{3(g)}$ will shift the equilibrium to the side with the smaller volume which is the product side, NH_3. We have 4 volumes for the reactants and 2 volumes for the product. An increase in pressure will not affect reaction (4) since the volumes on each side are equal.

29.   Ans. 2   Potassium chloride is formed from an active metal, potassium, and an active nonmetal, chlorine. In general, all compounds formed from Group 1A elements and Group 7A elements are ionic. The Group 1A elements give an electron to the Group 7A elements to form an ionic bond. The difference

in electronegativity between chlorine and potassium is $3.0 - 0.8 = 2.2$. This is another indication that KCl is ionic. In the water molecule, H_2O, the bonding between the hydrogen and the oxygen is polar covalent since the shared bonding electrons are pulled closer to the oxygen. The difference in electronegativity between oxygen and hydrogen is $3.5 - 2.1 = 1.4$. This also indicates that the bonding in the water molecule is polar covalent. Therefore, water is a polar covalent solvent. Potassium chloride dissolved in pure water is an example of an ionic compound dissolved in a covalent type solvent.

30.   Ans. **4**   According to *Le Chatelier's Principle*, when an equilibrium is subjected to a stress, it is displaced in the direction which will relieve the stress. When the temperature is increased, the equilibrium is displaced in the direction that will absorb the added heat, toward the endothermic reaction. Since all equilibria have an endothermic and an exothermic reaction, changes in temperature always shift the equilibrium in such a way that all the concentrations on one side are increased and all those on the other side are decreased. Thus, the equilibrium constant is always changed with a change in temperature.

Wrong Choices Explained:

(1) Changes in pressure may shift the equilibrium, but they do not alter the equilibrium constant. For example, when the pressure on a system is increased, the volume is decreased, and, therefore, all the concentrations on both sides of the equilibrium are increased. Thus, the equilibrium constant is unaffected.

(2) In general, catalysts do not shift the equilibrium; they only change the rate at which equilibrium is reached. They do not affect the value of the equilibrium constant.

(3) Although changes in concentration shift the equilibrium, they generally do not affect the equilibrium constant. This is illustrated by the following example: $A + B = C$. If A is increased, C is increased and in the process B is consumed so that B is decreased. For this reason, $\dfrac{C}{A \times B}$, the equilibrium constant, remains the same.

31.   Ans. **1**   A strong acid solution has a high concentration of hydrogen ions. Since 1×10^{-4} is the largest number for the hydrogen ion concentration, it is the strongest acid solution of those listed. Using the H^+ ion concentration, we can determine the pH of the solution. The pH of a solution is equal to the logarithm of the reciprocal of the hydrogen ion concentration when this concentration is expressed in moles/liter. Using our answer, 1×10^{-4}, we can determine the pH as follows:

$$[H^+] = 1 \times 10^{-4}$$

$$pH = \log \frac{1}{[H^+]}$$

$$pH = \log \frac{1}{[1 \times 10^{-4}]}$$

$$pH = \log 10^4 = 4$$

Therefore, a solution containing 1×10^{-4} moles/liter of H^+ ion has a pH value of 4. The lower the pH value, the greater the concentration of H^+ ions and the stronger the acid solution. The higher the pH, the weaker is the acid solution. Choices (2), (3) and (4) all have pH values greater than 4.

32. Ans. **2** In a neutralization reaction, the number of equivalents of NaOH must equal the number of equivalents of HCl. The total number of equivalents of solute contained in a definite number of milliliters of solution will be represented as follows:

$$\text{Total Equivalents of Acid or Base} = \text{Milliliters} \times \frac{\text{Equivalents}}{1000 \text{ ml.}}$$

Since Total Equivalents of Acid = Total Equivalents of Base

$$\text{ml. of Acid} \times \frac{\text{Equivalents of Acid}}{1000 \text{ ml.}} = \text{ml. of Base} \times \frac{\text{Equivalents of Base}}{1000 \text{ ml.}}$$

Also,

$$\text{Normality} = \frac{\text{Equivalents}}{1000 \text{ ml.}}$$

Since NaOH is a monohydroxy base and HCl is a monoprotic acid, their molarities equal their normalities. The gram-equivalent mass of each is equal to the gram-molecular mass of each. Therefore, we can solve the problem as follows:

Acid	Base

$$\text{ml.} \times \text{Normality} = \text{ml.} \times \text{Normality}$$

ml. of Acid = 100 ml. $100 \text{ ml.} \times 0.1 = X \times 0.2$

Normality of Acid = 0.1 $2X = 100$

ml. of Base = X $X = 50$ ml. of NaOH needed

Normality of Base = 0.2 to neutralize the HCl

33. Ans. **1** An *amphoteric* (amphiprotic) substance is one that can act either as an acid or as a base, depending on its chemical environment. The hydroxides of some metals such as aluminum, zinc, lead and chromium are amphoteric. In the presence of a strong base they behave as acids, and in the presence of a strong acid they behave as bases. According to the *Brönsted-Lowry Theory*, substances such as H_2O or HSO_4^-, which can either donate or accept a proton are also amphiprotic. The amphiprotic nature of water is shown as follows: Acid: $H_2O \rightarrow H^+ + OH^-$

Base: $H_2O + H^+ \rightarrow H_3O^+$

Wrong Choices Explained:

(2) H_3O^+ can donate a proton; however, it cannot accept a proton.

(3) NH_4^+ can donate a proton; however, it cannot accept a proton.

(4) $(OH)^-$ can accept a proton; however, it cannot donate a proton.

34. Ans. **2** The *Brönsted-Lowry Theory* of acids and bases states that acids are proton donors and bases are proton acceptors. In the reaction listed, $H_2SO_4 + H_2O = HSO_4^- + H_3O^+$, since we have 2 Brönsted-Lowry acids, we must also have 2 Brönsted-Lowry bases. Thus:

$$\text{Acid} + \text{Base} = \text{Base} + \text{Acid}$$
$$H_2SO_4 + H_2O = HSO_4^- + H_3O^+$$

When the reaction is preceding to the right, H_2SO_4 (Acid), donates a proton to H_2O (Base). When the reaction is preceding to the left, H_3O^+ (Acid), donates a proton to the HSO_4^- (Base). Thus, the two Brönsted-Lowry acids are H_3O^+ and H_2SO_4.

Wrong Choices Explained:

(1) H_2SO_4 is a *Brönsted-Lowry* acid and H_2O is a *Brönsted-Lowry* base.

(3) H_2O is a *Brönsted-Lowry* base and H_3O^+ is a *Brönsted-Lowry* acid.

(4) HSO_4^- is a *Brönsted-Lowry* base and H_3O^+ is a *Brönsted-Lowry* acid.

35. Ans. 3   For neutral molecules, the oxidation number of all the atoms must add algebraically up to zero. Hydrogen has an oxidation number of $+1$ in all its compounds except in the metal hydrides such as LiH when it is -1. Oxygen has an oxidation number of -2 in all its compounds except in peroxides such as H_2O_2 when it is -1. Thus, in the molecule $H_2S_2O_7$, hydrogen has a total value of $2 \times (+1) = +2$, oxygen has a total value of $7 \times (-2) = -14$. The total charge on the sulfur is $+12$ in order that the algebraic sum of the oxidation numbers of all atoms add up to zero. Since we have 2 atoms of sulfur, the oxidation number of each sulfur atom is $\dfrac{+12}{2} = +6$. We can summarize this question using the following chart:

Molecular Formula	H_2^{+1}	S_2^{+6}	O_7^{-2}	
Algebraic Sum of Oxidation Numbers	$+2$	$+12$	-14	$= 0$

36. Ans. 1   Using the rules for the oxidation states of oxygen and hydrogen from question 35, we can insert them in the equation given. The halides (7A *elements*) have an oxidation state of -1 when combined with hydrogen. Chlorine gas (Cl_2) has an oxidation number of zero since the electrons shared between the two like atoms are divided equally between the sharing atoms. Now we can determine the oxidation number of manganese since the algebraic sum of the oxidation numbers of a compound is zero. In MnO_2, oxygen has a total value of $2(-2) = -4$. Therefore, manganese must be $+4$. In $MnCl_2$, chlorine has a total value of $2(-1) = -2$. Therefore, manganese must be $+2$. The oxidation numbers or oxidation states are shown in the reaction given as follows:

$$4H^{+1}Cl^{-1} + Mn^{+4}O_2^{-2} \rightarrow Mn^{+2}Cl_2^{-1} + 2H_2^{+1}O^{-2} + Cl_2^0$$

Therefore, manganese changes from $+4$ in MnO_2 to $+2$ in $MnCl_2$. In order for manganese to change from a $+4$ oxidation state to a $+2$ oxidation state, it has to gain 2 electrons. This can be shown by the ion-electron equation as follows:

$$Mn^{+4} + 2e^- \rightarrow Mn^{+2}$$

If an atom gains electrons in a redox reaction, it is reduced. Thus, manganese is reduced from $+4$ to $+2$.

37. Ans. **3** The overall redox reaction is given as:

$$Zn^0_{(s)} + Pb^{+2}_{(aq)} \rightarrow Zn^{+2}_{(aq)} + Pb^0_{(s)}$$

In this reaction the zinc is oxidized by losing 2 electrons to form $Zn^{+2}_{(aq)}$. The lead is reduced by gaining 2 electrons to form $Pb^0_{(s)}$. Thus, we have the ion-electron equations for the oxidation and reduction reactions as follows:

Oxidation: $Zn^0_{(s)} - 2e^- \rightarrow Zn^{+2}_{(aq)}$
Reduction: $Pb^{+2}_{(aq)} + 2e^- \rightarrow Pb^0_{(s)}$

To obtain the E^0 values for each reaction, we consult Table L. Table L lists the E^0 values for the oxidation half-reactions only. For the reduction half-reactions, the sign ($+$ or $-$) for the E^0 value on Table L must be reversed. Thus, the value for the reduction reaction, $Pb^{+2}_{(aq)} + 2e^- \rightarrow Pb^0_{(s)}$, the E^0 value is -0.13 volt. The E^0 value for the oxidation reaction $Zn^0_{(s)} - 2e^- \rightarrow Zn^{+2}_{(aq)}$ is listed as $+0.76$ volt. The total or net E^0 value is determined by adding the E^0 values for the half-reactions. The problem is solved as follows:

Oxidation		
half-reaction:	$Zn^0_{(s)} \rightarrow Zn^{+2}_{(aq)} + 2e^-$	$E^0 = +0.76$ volt
Reduction		
half-reaction:	$Pb^{+2}_{(aq)} + 2e^- \rightarrow Pb^0_{(s)}$	$E^0 = -0.13$ volt
	$Zn^0_{(s)} + Pb^{+2}_{(aq)} \rightarrow Zn^{+2}_{(aq)} + Pb^0_{(s)}$ Net	$E^0 = +0.63$ volt

Thus, the net potential E^0, equals $+0.63$ volts.

38. Ans. **4** In the redox reaction, $Mg + CuSO_4 \rightarrow MgSO_4 + Cu$, metallic magnesium with an oxidation state of 0 replaces the Cu^{+2} ion from $CuSO_4$ to form $MgSO_4$ and metallic copper with an oxidation state of 0. In a single replacement reaction as this, magnesium is more active than copper; therefore, it can replace the copper from $CuSO_4$. Table L tells us that magnesium is above copper; thus, the magnesium is a stronger reducing agent. *The role as a reducing agent decreases as we go down on Table L.* Since a reducing agent always loses electrons, the magnesium would be the species oxidized in this reaction. We can substitute the oxidation numbers and write the oxidation and reduction half-reactions as follows:

Oxidation half-reaction: $Mg^0 - 2e^- \rightarrow Mg^{+2}$ or $Mg^0 \rightarrow Mg^{+2} + 2e^-$
Reduction half-reaction: $Cu^{+2} + 2e^- \rightarrow Cu^0$

Thus, the ion-electron equation for the oxidation that takes place is $Mg^0 \rightarrow Mg^{+2} + 2e^-$

Wrong Choices Explained:
(1) $Cu^{+2} + 2e^- \rightarrow Cu^0$ represents the reduction that takes place in the reaction.

(2) Copper is not oxidized in this reaction; it is reduced.

(3) Magnesium is not reduced in this reaction; it is oxidized.

39. Ans. 2 On the basis of *Table L*, the reaction which occurs spontaneously is the one in which the net E^0 value is positive. We can determine the net E^0 values using the E^0 values on Table L for each half-reaction. Remember that all half-reactions are shown as oxidation reactions on Table L. For the reduction reaction, we must reverse the sign of the E^0 value. The E^0 value does not depend on the number of atoms or ions involved in the redox reaction. The only reaction which gives us a positive E^0 value is the following:

Oxidation
half-reaction: $\qquad 2(Cr^0_{(s)} \rightarrow Cr^{+3}_{(aq)} + 3e^-) \qquad E^0 = +0.74$ volt
Reduction
half-reaction: $\qquad \underline{3(Ni^{+2}_{(aq)} + 2e^- \rightarrow Ni^0_{(s)})} \qquad E^0 = -0.25$ volt
$\qquad 2Cr^0_{(s)} + 3Ni^{+2}_{(aq)} \rightarrow 2Cr^{+3}_{(aq)} + 3Ni^0_{(s)}$ Net $\quad E^0 = +0.49$ volt

Wrong Choices Explained:

Choices (1), (3) and (4) do not occur spontaneously since each net E^0 value is negative.

(1) Oxidation
half-reaction: $\qquad K^0_{(s)} \rightarrow K^+_{(aq)} + e^- \qquad E^0 = +2.93$ volts
Reduction
half-reaction: $\qquad \underline{Li^+_{(aq)} + e^- \rightarrow Li^0_{(s)}} \qquad E^0 = -3.05$ volts
$\qquad K^0_{(s)} + Li^+_{(aq)} \rightarrow K^+_{(aq)} + Li^0_{(s)}$ Net $\quad E^0 = -0.12$ volt

(3) Oxidation
half-reaction: $\qquad 2(Ag^0_{(s)} \rightarrow Ag^+_{(aq)} + e^-) \qquad E^0 = -0.80$ volt
Reduction
half-reaction: $\underline{2H^+_{(aq)} + 2e^- \rightarrow H^0_{2(g)}} \qquad E^0 = -0.00$ volt
$\qquad 2Ag^0_{(s)} + 2H^+_{(aq)} \rightarrow 2Ag^+_{(aq)} + H_{2(g)}$ Net $\quad E^0 = -0.80$ volt

(4) Oxidation
half-reaction: $\qquad 2F^-_{(aq)} \rightarrow F^0_{2(g)} + 2e^- \qquad E^0 = -2.87$ volts
Reduction
half-reaction: $\underline{Cl^0_{2(g)} + 2e^- \rightarrow 2Cl^-_{(aq)}} \qquad E^0 = +1.36$ volts
$\qquad 2F^-_{(aq)} + Cl^0_{2(g)} \rightarrow F^0_{2(g)} + 2Cl^-_{(aq)}$ Net $\quad E^0 = -1.51$ volts

40. Ans. 4 An oxidation-reduction (*redox*) reaction is one in which the oxidation numbers of 2 or more species are changed. Oxidation and reduction occur simultaneously; therefore, total electron loss equals total electron gain. In redox reactions, the increase and decrease of oxidation number results from a transfer of electrons from one atom or ion to another atom or ion. The only reaction in which oxidation-reduction takes place is the following:

$$2H_2^{+1}O_2^{-1} \rightarrow 2H_2^{+1}O^{-2} + O_2^0$$

In this redox reaction, the oxygen in the peroxide ($O_2{}^-$) is both reduced to O^{-2} and oxidized to $O_2{}^0$. The peroxide acts simultaneously as an oxidizing agent and as a reducing agent. This process is called auto-oxidation.

Wrong Choices Explained:

(1) $N^{-3}H_3{}^{+1} + H_2{}^{+1}O^{-2} = (N^{-3}H_4{}^{+1})^+ + (O^{-2}H^{+1})^-$
There is no change in the oxidation state of any element.

(2) $(H_3{}^{+1}O^{-2})^+ + (O^{-2}H^{+1})^- \rightarrow 2H_2{}^{+1}O^{-2}$
There is no change in the oxidation state of any element.

(3) $Ba^{+2} + (S^{+6}O_4{}^{-2})^{-2} \rightarrow Ba^{+2}S^{+6}O_4{}^{-2}$
There is no change in the oxidation state of any element.

41.   **Ans. 3**   The general formula for an organic acid is RCOOH, where R is an alkyl group (except for formic acid which has a formula HCOOH). We can show the general formula for organic acids structurally as follows:

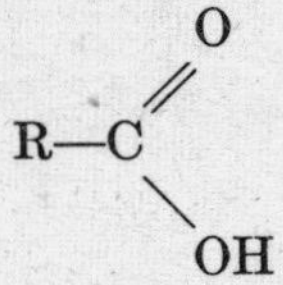

$$R-C\underset{OH}{\overset{O}{\big|\big|}}$$

where $-C\underset{OH}{\overset{O}{\big|\big|}}$ is called the carboxy or carboxyl group. The only molecular formula given which is an organic acid is CH_3COOH, acetic acid. The I.U.C. (*Geneva*) name for acetic acid is ethanoic acid. The structural formula for acetic acid is:

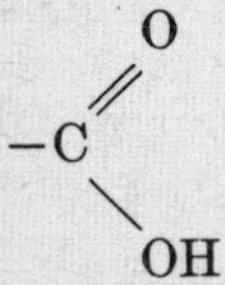

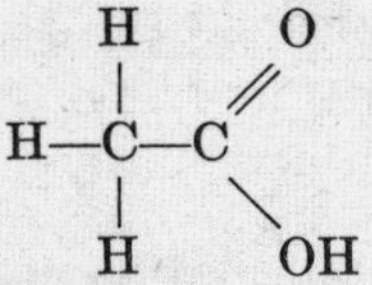

$$H-\underset{H}{\overset{H}{C}}-C\underset{OH}{\overset{O}{\big|\big|}}$$

Wrong Choices Explained:

(1) This formula is an ester since it corresponds to the general formula RCOOR'. The name of the ester CH_3COOCH_3 is methyl acetate or methyl ethanoate. Structurally it is written:

$$H-\underset{H}{\overset{H}{C}}-C\underset{O-CH_3}{\overset{O}{\big|\big|}}$$

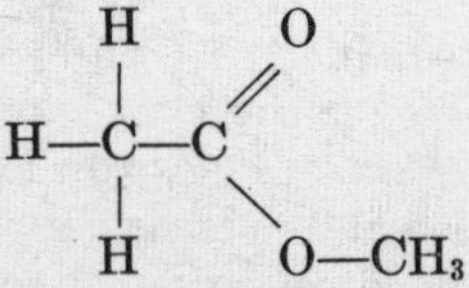

(2) This formula is a primary alcohol since it corresponds to the general formula ROH. It contains the functional group —OH. The name of the alcohol, CH_3OH, is methyl alcohol or methanol. Structurally it is written:

$$
\begin{array}{c}
H \\
| \\
H-C-OH \\
| \\
H
\end{array}
$$

(4) This formula represents a saturated hydrocarbon. The general formula for a saturated hydrocarbon is C_nH_{2n+2}. The saturated hydrocarbon, C_3H_8, is called propane. Structurally it is written:

$$
\begin{array}{ccc}
H & H & H \\
| & | & | \\
H-C- & C- & C-H \\
| & | & | \\
H & H & H
\end{array}
$$

42.   Ans. 2   Ethyl formate or ethyl methanoate (I.U.C.) has the molecular formula, $HCOOC_2H_5$. Since it corresponds to the general formula $RCOOR'$, it is an ester. An ester can be produced in an esterification reaction in which an acid reacts with an alcohol in the presence of concentrated sulfuric acid to yield an ester and water. The concentrated sulfuric acid is a strong dehydrating agent, and, therefore, removes the water from the reaction field. This action increases the yield of the ester. Ethyl formate is formed from ethyl alcohol (ethanol) and formic acid (methanoic acid). In writing an esterification reaction, it is a good practice to write the general equation first and then the regular equation below. This is done as follows:

$$
RCOOH + R'OH \underset{}{\overset{Con.\ H_2SO_4}{\rightleftharpoons}} RCOOR' + HOH
$$

$$
HCOOH + C_2H_5OH \rightleftharpoons HCOOC_2H_5 + HOH
$$

Therefore, the type of reaction in which ethyl formate is formed is called an esterification reaction.

Wrong Choices Explained:

(1) Fermentation is the decomposition of organic compounds into simpler compounds by the action of enzymes. A common fermentation reaction is the fermentation of glucose. The equation for the fermentation of glucose is shown as follows:

$$
C_6H_{12}O_6 \xrightarrow{zymase} 2CO_2 + 2C_2H_5OH
$$

(3) Saponification is the reaction between a fat and a base to form soap and glycerine (glycerol). The following equation illustrates a saponification reaction:

$$
\underset{\text{fat}}{C_3H_5(C_{17}H_{35}COO)_3} + \underset{\text{base}}{3NaOH} \rightarrow \underset{\text{soap}}{3C_{17}H_{35}COONa} + \underset{\text{glycerine}}{C_3H_5(OH)_3}
$$

(4) *Polymerization* involves the chemical combination of a number of identical or similar molecules (monomers) to form a complex molecule of high molecular mass. Polyethylene, a polymer, is formed from basic units of the monomer, ethylene, which in the presence of a suitable catalyst will undergo an addition reaction to form the long chain polymer.

43. Ans. 1 An alkene is an unsaturated hydrocarbon. Alkenes contain one double bond in their structure. The general formula for the alkenes is C_nH_{2n}, where "n" equals the number of carbon atoms. The only molecular formula which corresponds to the general formula C_nH_{2n} is C_3H_6. This alkene is called propene or propylene. Structurally it is shown as follows:

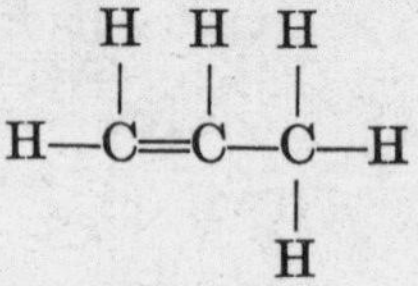

$$
\begin{array}{ccccc}
 & H & H & H & \\
 & | & | & | & \\
H- & C & = C - & C & -H \\
 & & & | & \\
 & & & H &
\end{array}
$$

Wrong Choices Explained:

(2) C_2H_6, ethane is a saturated hydrocarbon. The general formula for the saturated hydrocarbons is C_nH_{2n+2}. The structural formula for ethane is shown as follows:

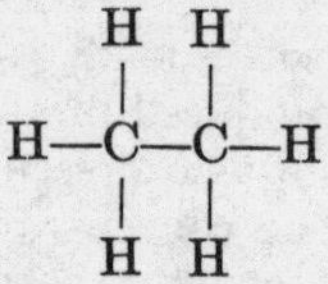

$$
\begin{array}{cccc}
 & H & H & \\
 & | & | & \\
H- & C & - C & -H \\
 & | & | & \\
 & H & H &
\end{array}
$$

(3) C_2H_2 is called acetylene or ethyne. It is an unsaturated hydrocarbon and is a member of the alkyne series. It contains 1 triple bond. The general formula for the alkynes is C_nH_{2n-2}. The structural formula for acetylene is shown as follows:

$$H - C \equiv C - H$$

(4) C_6H_6 is an aromatic cyclic hydrocarbon. C_6H_6 is the formula for benzene. The general formula for the benzene series is C_nH_{2n-6}. The structural formula for benzene is shown as follows:

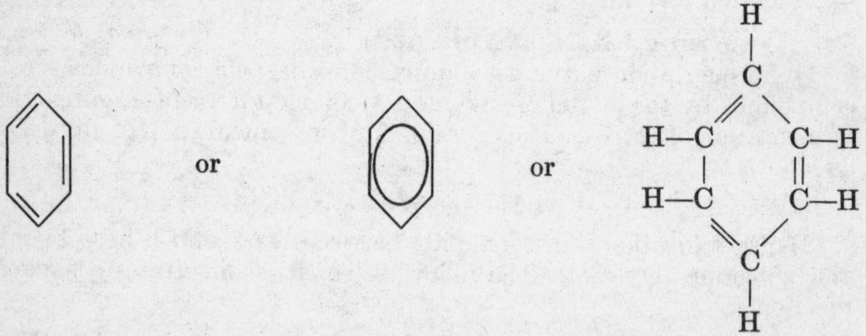

44. Ans. 2 The study of the hydrocarbons is simplified by the fact they can be divided into distinct series in which the composition of the first member of each series *differs* from that of the second by a CH_2 group. This relationship in such a series is called a homologous series. These hydrocarbon series include the alkane, alkene, alkyne and the benzene series. If we take any 2 consecutive members of any one of these series, they would differ by a CH_2 group. For instance in the alkane series, CH_4, methane, differs from C_2H_6, ethane, by a CH_2 group, in the alkyne series, C_2H_2, acetylene, differs from C_3H_4, propyne, by a CH_2 group.

45. **Ans. 4** The properties of organic compounds compared to inorganic compounds are listed as follows:

1) In general, organic compounds have lower melting and lower boiling points than inorganic compounds. In many inorganic or ionic solids, the forces of attraction are those between a positive and a negative charge and are high. Hence, ionic solids have high melting points.

2) In general, most organic compounds are insoluble in water. Many organic compounds have a non-polar nature, whereas water has a polar nature. Most inorganic compounds are soluble in water.

3) In general, most organic compounds are soluble in nonaqueous liquids. This is due to the non-polar nature of each. Inorganic compounds are generally insoluble in nonaqueous liquids.

4) In solution and in the molten state, organic compounds are non-conducting. They do not form ions. Inorganic compounds conduct electric current in the molten state and in solution since they dissociate or ionize to form ions.

5) Organic reactions have slower reaction rates than do inorganic reactions. Many inorganic reactions are instantaneous because of the ions formed during the solution process. Many organic reactions take hours for completion because the covalent bonds of organic compounds are not easily broken.

Wrong Choices Explained:

(1) It is explained in (2) and (3) above.

(2) It is explained in (4) above.

(3) It is explained in (5) above.

46. **Ans. 2** The *electronegativity* values for each *Period* on the *Periodic Table* are listed on *Table J*. In all *Periods*, the electronegativity values increase from left to right (from Group 1A to Group 7A). Group 1A elements have low electronegativity values, whereas Group 7A elements have high values. Group 7A elements strongly attract shared pairs of electrons whereas Group 1A elements do not attract shared electrons as strongly. Two factors which influence electronegativity are the ionization energy and the electron affinity. Since Group 7A have high ionization energy values and high electron affinity values, they have high electronegativity values. Group 1A elements have low values in all cases.

47. **Ans. 2** The strength of a conjugate acid-conjugate base pair is listed on *Table H*. Each pair is made up of an acid and a base related by the transfer of a proton. The table tells us as we go down in the conjugate acid column, the acid strength decreases. Thus, NH_3 is a very weak acid and HCl is a very strong acid. In the conjugate base column, we see that the conjugate base of NH_3 is NH_2^- which is a very strong base. The conjugate base of HCl is Cl⁻

which is a very weak base. Therefore the strongest acids have the weakest conjugate bases and the strongest bases have the weakest conjugate acids.

48. Ans. 2 If we heat an ideal gas at constant pressure, its volume increases. For an ideal gas, we assume that there are no attractive forces between molecules. *Charles' Law* states that at constant pressure, the volume of a fixed mass of gas is directly proportional to the absolute temperature. Therefore, if we increase the temperature of a gas, we also increase the volume of this gas. The reason is that the increased temperature increases the average kinetic energy of the molecules which results in more vigorous collisions. The more vigorous collisions cause an increase in volume.

49. Ans. 1 The solubility product constant, K_{sp}, was explained in question 26. In a saturated solution of AgCl at 25°C, the $K_{sp} = [Ag^+] \cdot [Cl^-]$. The brackets [ ] indicate the concentrations are expressed in moles per liter. The K_{sp} value for AgCl at 25°C is a constant. The product of the molar concentrations of the Ag^+ ion and the Cl^- ion must equal the K_{sp} values in a saturated solution. If we increase the concentration of the $Ag^+_{(aq)}$, the concentration of $Cl^-_{(aq)}$ is decreased since the product of $[Ag^+] \cdot [Cl^-]$ at 25°C is a constant (K_{sp}).

50. Ans. 2 In general, if the difference in electronegativity between 2 elements is greater than 1.7 the chemical bond has a greater ionic character. If the difference in electronegativity is less than 1.7, the chemical bond has a greater covalent character. As the electronegativity difference increases above 1.7, the ionic character increases. As the electronegativity difference decreases below 1.7, the covalent character increases. Thus, as the difference in electronegativity decreases, the tendency for elements to form covalently bonded compounds increases. A compound with an electronegativity difference of 0.5 has a 94% covalent character, whereas a compound with an electronegativity difference of 1.5 has a 57% covalent character.

51. Ans. 2 *Entropy* is a measure of the disorder or randomness of a system. The more the molecules in a system are distributed in a disordered or random manner, the greater is the entropy. The change from the solid state which is well ordered to the random gaseous state is accompanied by an increase in entropy. There is a tendency for processes to occur which lead to the highest possible state of disorder. There will always be an entropy increase when a solution is formed because the mixed components are in a more random state than the separate components. The tendency toward maximum randomness tends to cause solids to dissolve.

52. Ans. 1 A liquid will boil at the temperature at which the vapor pressure of the liquid equals the pressure on the liquid. The normal boiling point is the temperature at which the vapor pressure of the liquid equals 1 atmosphere. At the boiling point, the vapor pressure of the liquid is high enough so that the atmosphere can be pushed aside. The bubbles which form

in the boiling liquid and rise to the top are, of course, bubbles of saturated vapor, and since these do not collapse the pressure inside them must equal the external pressure. If we decrease the pressure above a confined liquid, the boiling point of the liquid decreases. If we increase the pressure above a confined liquid, the boiling point of the liquid increases.

PART TWO

GROUP 1

Base your answers to questions 53 through 57 on the information and diagrams below.

Cylinder A contains 1 liter of hydrogen gas and cylinder B contains 1 liter of carbon dioxide gas. Both gases are originally at S.T.P.

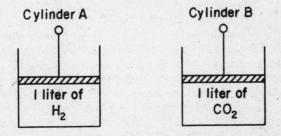

53.   Ans. 2   *Avogadro's Law* states that under similar conditions of temperature and pressure equal volumes of all gases contain equal numbers of molecules. Since we have equal volumes of H_2 and CO_2 at S.T.P., they contain equal numbers of molecules. One mole (22.4 liters) of any gas at S.T.P. contains 6.02×10^{23} molecules. One liter of any gas at S.T.P. would contain 2.7×10^{22} molecules. Since the gases in cylinder A and cylinder B contain equal numbers of molecules, the number of moles of CO_2 and H_2 is the same.

54.   Ans. 3   We do have an equal number of moles of H_2 and CO_2 in the cylinders. However, since the mass of 1 mole of H_2 is 2 grams and the mass of 1 mole of CO_2 is 44 grams, the CO_2 gas would have the greater mass. Actually the mass of 1 liter of CO_2 is 1.98 grams and that of hydrogen is 0.09 gram.

55.   Ans. 2   The pressure exerted by a gas depends only on the number of molecular impacts per unit wall area per second at constant temperature. Since we have equal volumes of H_2 and CO_2, we will have an equal number of molecular impacts per unit wall area per sec. Since the temperature in each cylinder is constant at $-10°C.$, the pressure of the hydrogen gas in cylinder A is the same as the pressure of CO_2 in cylinder B.

56. **Ans. 2** The average kinetic energy of the molecules in the cylinder is directly proportional to the absolute temperature. Since the temperature for each cylinder is the same (100°C.), the average kinetic energy of the H_2 molecules in cylinder A compared to the CO_2 molecules in cylinder B is the same.

57. **Ans. 3** As we stated in question 55, the pressure exerted by a gas depends only on the number of molecular impacts per unit wall area per second, at constant temperature. If the volume of H_2 is decreased to $\frac{1}{2}$ its volume compared to the volume of CO_2, there will be more molecular impacts per unit area per second; thus, the pressure will be greater. Also from *Boyle's Law*, since the volume of a gas is inversely proportional to the pressure, a decrease in the volume of H_2 will cause an increase in pressure in the H_2 cylinder.

58. **Ans. 4**

$$
\begin{array}{ccc}
 & H & H \\
 & | & | \\
H{-}C{-} & C{-} & C{-}H \\
 & | & | \\
 & H & H \quad H
\end{array}
$$

In any organic compound, the number of bond lines around carbon should always be 4. Since the middle carbon in this formula has only three lines, this formula cannot correctly represent an organic compound. If it had a hydrogen atom or another functional group connected to the middle carbon, it would represent an organic compound.

59. **Ans. 7**

$$
\begin{array}{ccc}
H & H & H \\
| & | & | \\
H{-}C{-} & {-}C{-} & {-}C{-}H \\
| & | & | \\
OH & OH & OH
\end{array}
$$

Glycerol or glycerine, $C_3H_5(OH)_3$ is the product of a saponification reaction where a fat and NaOH react to yield soap and glycerol. Glycerol is a trihydroxy alcohol.

60. **Ans. 1**

$$
\begin{array}{c}
H \\
| \\
H{-}C{-}H \\
| \\
H
\end{array}
$$

A saturated hydrocarbon is one in which carbon is attached to other carbon and hydrogen atoms by single valence bonds. The paraffins (*alkanes*) and other compounds like paraffins which have only single valence bonds in their molecules are known as saturated compounds. A hydrocarbon is a compound containing carbon and hydrogen. If the hydrocarbon is saturated, it is a member of the alkane series (C_nH_{2n+2}) where n = the number of carbon atoms. The only molecular formula given that is a saturated hydrocarbon is CH_4 (methane). It is the first member of the alkane series.

61. Ans. 5

$$\begin{array}{c} \text{H} \quad\quad \text{H} \\ | \quad\quad\quad | \\ \text{H—C—O—C—H} \\ | \quad\quad\quad | \\ \text{H} \quad\quad \text{H} \end{array}$$

Two or more compounds with the same molecular formula but different structural formulas are called isomers. Ethyl alcohol has the formula, C_2H_5OH. It contains 2 carbon atoms, 6 hydrogen atoms and 1 oxygen atom (C_2H_6O). The only formula listed that has the same molecular formula (C_2H_6O) but a different structural formula is choice 5—dimethyl ether.

62. Ans. 3

$$\text{H—C}\equiv\text{C—H}$$

An addition reaction is one in which atoms (*usually chlorine or bromine*) are added to an unsaturated organic molecule. An unsaturated organic molecule contains a double or triple bond. The compounds listed containing double or triple bonds include (3) acetylene and (6) benzene. However, since we cannot add to the benzene ring without replacing one hydrogen atom, benzene (C_6H_6) cannot be involved in an addition reaction. Acetylene (C_2H_2) can be involved in an addition reaction.

63. Ans. 4   The answers to questions 5, 6, and 7 give adequate information to explain the orbital designations for questions 63 to 67. In answering questions 63 to 67, it is best to first identify the elements using the electron configurations given. The electron configurations of the elements given are:

1) $1s^2 2s^2 2p^5$—fluorine
2) $1s^2 2s^2 2p^6$—neon
3) $1s^2 2s^2 2p^6 3s^1$—sodium
4) $1s^2 2s^2 2p^6 3s^2 3p^3$—phosphorus

The common oxidation state is a number assigned to each element to indicate the number of electrons assumed to be gained, lost, or shared in the formation of a compound. The common oxidation states are listed in the upper right-hand corner of each box on the *Periodic Table*. Elements with more than 1 oxidation state include the "B" group elements and elements in Groups 4A, 5A, 6A and 7A except fluorine. The elements sodium in Group 1A and neon in Group O have only one oxidation state. Thus, the element phosphorus in Group 5A is the only element of the four given that has more than one oxidation state.

64. Ans. 1   Electronegativity is a measure of the attraction an atom has for a shared pair of electrons. Elements such as fluorine, oxygen, chlorine and nitrogen have high electronegativity values. If we consult *Table J*, we see that fluorine has the highest electronegativity value, 4.0. Neon is not assigned a value. Sodium has a value of 0.9 and phosphorus 2.1.

65. Ans. 2   The least reactive elements are elements which do not ordinarily combine with other elements. They have a completed outer energy level

and are listed in Group O. These elements are helium, neon, argon, krypton, xenon and radon. Although some of these noble gases have reacted with elements, they are generally the least reactive of all elements. Neon is an element with a complete electronic configuration in the K and L levels; thus, it is the least reactive. Sodium and fluorine are extremely reactive and phosphorus is quite reactive.

66. **Ans. 1** Potassium, an element in Group 1A, is a very active element. It forms ionic compounds when it combines with elements of Group 6A and 7A, which are active non-metals. Fluorine is in Group 7A. Potassium will react with fluorine to form the ionic compound, potassium fluoride. The difference in electronegativity between K and F is 3.2. The electron-dot diagram for KF is:

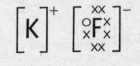

67. **Ans. 3** Ionization energy is the energy needed to remove the most loosely bound electron from an isolated gaseous atom. Ionization energy values are listed on *Table J*. Elements which lose electrons easily are in Groups 1A and 2A. Their ionization energy values are low, whereas elements in Groups 6A, 7A and Group O have high ionization energy values. Since sodium is in Group 1A, it has the lowest value, 5.1 ev. Fluorine has a very high ionization energy value of 17.3 ev. Neon, although not listed, has a very high value of 21.6 ev. Phosphorus has a rather high value of 10.9 ev.

68. **Ans. 3** The four covalent bonds of a carbon atom are directed in space toward the four vertices of a regular tetrahedron. In the CCl_4 molecule, a carbon atom is covalently and symmetrically bonded to 4 chlorine atoms. The carbon atom is in the center of the tetrahedron. The structural formula for CCl_4 is shown as:

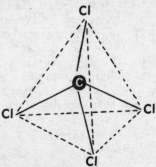

69. **Ans. 4** A compound which would show a bent structure would usually be a dipole. The only dipole listed is H_2O. As we explained in question 14, a dipole is a molecule characterized by unequal sharing of an electron pair between atoms. The more electronegative oxygen pulls the bonding electrons closer to itself. The electron-dot diagram for H_2O is:

70. **Ans. 1** The compound having the highest degree of ionic bonding would be the one with the greatest difference in electronegativity. In general, active metals combining with active nonmetals have a high degree of ionic bonding. Since cesium is a very active metal and chlorine is a very active nonmetal, these two would have the highest degree of ionic bonding. The electronegativity difference is (Cl − Cs) 3.0 − 0.7 = 2.3, which is 74% ionic character. The other choices listed are covalent. In the formation of CsCl, cesium gives an electron to chlorine. The electron-dot formula for CsCl is:

$$\left[\text{Cs} \right]^+ \left[{\overset{\text{X X}}{\underset{\text{X X}}{\text{o}\text{Cl}\text{X}}}} \right]^-$$

71. **Ans. 2** As we have explained in the answers to 68, 69 and 70, the bonding in CsCl, CCl$_4$ and H$_2$O does not involve a double bond. The bonding for CO$_2$ indicates that the structure probably has double bonds within its molecular structure. The electron-dot diagram for CO$_2$ is:

$$\overset{\text{o o}}{\underset{\text{o o}}{\text{o}\text{O}\text{o}}} \quad \overset{\text{X}}{\underset{\text{X}}{\text{X}\text{C}\text{X}}} \quad \overset{\text{o o}}{\underset{\text{o o}}{\text{o}\text{O}\text{o}}}$$

72. **Ans. 4** A compound that has polar covalent molecules is a dipole. As we explained in question 69, water is a dipole because the bonding electrons are closer to the oxygen due to its higher electronegativity. Thus, we have a separation of electric charge, the oxygen end-negative and the hydrogen ends-positive.

73. **Ans. 3** An example of a molecule of a diatomic gaseous element is either F$_2$, Cl$_2$, H$_2$, O$_2$ or N$_2$. The bonding between the diatomic gaseous atoms is non-polar covalent since the difference in electronegativity is zero.

74. **Ans. 4** The Group O gases have low boiling points. This is due to the fact that the only binding forces between noble gases are weak *van der Waal's Forces*. The noble or inert gases do not combine with themselves since they all have a completed outer energy level. *Van der Waal's Forces* appear to be due to chance distribution of electrons resulting in momentary dipole attractions. These weak attractions cause the noble gas molecules to come closer together to form a liquid. Of course, the change from a gas to a liquid occurs at rather

low temperatures for the noble gases. Since *van der Waal's Forces* increase with an increasing number of electrons, xenon would have greater attractive forces between molecules than helium. As a result, xenon has a higher boiling point ($-107°C$) than helium ($-272°C$).

75.   Ans. 1   In order for a substance to conduct electricity, it must contain ions or electrons that are free to move. In the solid phase, ionic compounds have neither free electrons nor free ions to cause conductivity. Ionic compounds have a strong crystal structure, and consequently, the ions in the crystal are not free to move. Therefore, an ionic crystal will not conduct electricity. However, if we melt an ionic crystal, the lattice structure is broken and the ions are free to move. The molten salt will then become a good conductor of electricity.

76.   Ans. 2   We can picture a metal such as magnesium or sodium as an array of positive ions located at the crystal lattice sites and immersed in a *cloud* of mobile electrons. The metal is held together by the attraction between the positive metallic ions and a *cloud* of negative electrons. This attraction in metals is called a metallic bond. Since electrons can move at will throughout the metal, a metallic solid is characterized by high electrical conductivity.

77.   Ans. 1   A salt is an ionic compound containing positive ions other than hydrogen and negative ions other than hydroxide. In an ionic solid, the positive and negative ions occupy the lattice points of the crystal. The forces of attraction are strong electrostatic bonds between the positive and negative ions. Thus, in general ionic solids are hard and have high melting points.

78.   Ans. 1   The oxidation state for each element is listed in the upper right-hand corner of each box on the *Periodic Table*. In Group 2A the oxidation state of each element is $+2$. There is no change in the oxidation state with increasing atomic number in Group 2A. The graph that best represents the relationship described in this question is graph 1.

79.   Ans. 3   The electronegativity values are listed on *Table J*. As the atomic number in Period 2 increases from 3 for lithium to 9 for fluorine, the electronegativity values also increase from 1 for lithium to 4 for fluorine. The electronegativity values for increasing atomic numbers are: 1, 1.5, 2, 2.5, 3, 3.5, and 4. There is a regular increase for each element of 0.5, for increasing atomic number. The graph which best represents this relationship is 3.

80.   Ans. 2   In Period 4, the number of electrons in the outer shell of each element with increasing atomic number from potassium to krypton is: 1, 2, 2,

2, 2, 1, 2, 2, 2, 2, 1, 2, 3, 4, 5, 6, 7, and 8. Since Group B transition elements add electrons to the inner 3d level, there is little change in the number of outer electrons. The graph should show a rather straight line from calcium to zinc with the exception of elements chromium and copper which have 1 electron in their outer level. The graph should then gradually increase to krypton. The graph which best represents this relationship is 2.

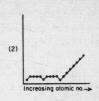

81. Ans. **6** The covalent atomic radius values for the elements in Period 3 are listed directly below each symbol on the *Periodic Table*. Thus, for the elements sodium to argon, the covalent atomic radius values in *Angstrom* (Å) units are: 1.86, 1.60, 1.43, 1.17, 1.10, 1.04, 0.99 and 1.54. These numbers indicate a general decrease in covalent atomic radius from sodium to chlorine and an increase for argon. Within a given Period, the atomic radius decreases with increasing atomic number due to the effect of increasing the nuclear charge without increasing the number of principal energy levels. The graph which best represents this relationship is 6.

82. Ans. **4** The ionization energy values are listed on *Table J*. The ionization energy values for the elements from sodium to chlorine in Period 3 are: 5.1, 7.6, 6.0, 8.1, 10.9, 10.3 and 13 ev. The general increase in ionization energy with the exception of aluminum and sulfur is due to the increased nuclear charge and the decreased atomic radius. The graph which best represents this general ionization increase from sodium to chlorine with the exception of aluminum and sulfur is 4.

83. Ans. **2** The coefficient before each formula in the balanced equation indicates the number of moles of the reactants and products. The balanced equation given tells us that the ratio of moles of HNO_3 to H_2O is 8:4 or 2:1. Thus, if one mole of water is produced, 2 moles of HNO_3 must be used up. We can also set up a proportion to solve this problem as follows:

$$\frac{X}{8 \text{ moles}} = \frac{1 \text{ mole of } H_2O \text{ produced}}{4 \text{ moles}}$$

$$4X = 8 \qquad X = 2 \text{ moles of } HNO_3 \text{ used up.}$$

84. Ans. **1** The balanced equation tells us that the ratio of moles of Cu to NO is 3:2 or 1.5:1. Therefore, if 1.5 moles of copper are used, 1 mole of NO is produced. We can also set up a proportion to solve this problem as follows:

$$\frac{1.5 \text{ moles of copper used}}{3 \text{ moles}} = \frac{X}{2 \text{ moles}}$$

$$3X = 3 \qquad X = 1 \text{ mole of NO produced.}$$

85.   Ans. **3**   A mole is equal to a gram-molecular mass of a substance. One mole of NO has a mass of 30 grams (14 *for nitrogen and* 16 *for oxygen*). If 1 mole has a mass of 30 grams, 2 moles have a mass of 60 grams. We can also set up a proportion to solve the problem, as follows:

$$\frac{1 \text{ mole of NO}}{30 \text{ grams/mole}} = \frac{2 \text{ moles of NO}}{X}$$

$$X = 60 \text{ grams/mole}$$

86.   Ans. **4**   In this oxidation-reduction reaction, 2 elements change in oxidation state. Metallic copper with an oxidation state of 0 is oxidized to the cupric ion, Cu^{+2} in $Cu(NO_3)_2$. Nitrogen with an oxidation state of $+5$ in HNO_3 is reduced to an oxidation state of $+2$ in NO. We can now set up the ion-electron partial equations for the oxidation and reduction reactions as follows:

Oxidation reaction: $3(Cu^0 - 2e^- \rightarrow Cu^{+2})$
Reduction reaction: $2(N^{+5} + 3e^- \rightarrow N^{+2})$

In order to cancel the electrons we have to multiply the oxidation reaction by 3 and the reduction reaction by 2. Thus, total electron loss will equal total electron gain. The electronic equation which represents the oxidation reaction is $3Cu^0 - 6e^- \rightarrow 3Cu^{+2}$. Choice (3) represents the reduction reaction. Choices (1) and (2) do not take place in this reaction.

87.   Ans. **3**   According to the equation given, the mole ratio of HNO_3 to NO is 8:2 or 4:1. Therefore, if 4 moles of HNO_3 are used, 1 mole of NO would be produced. Since NO is a gas at S.T.P., 1 mole of a gas occupies 22.4 liters. Therefore, 22.4 liters of NO gas are produced when 4 moles of HNO_3 are used up.

88.   Ans. **2**   Molarity is defined as the concentration of a solution expressed in moles of solute per liter of solution. Molarity can be expressed using the formula:

$$\text{Molarity} = \frac{\text{Number of moles}}{\text{Number of liters of solution}}$$

Molarity = 0.5 moles/liter
Number of moles = X $0.5 \text{ moles/liter} = \dfrac{X}{1 \text{ liter}}$
Number of liters of solution = 1 liter

$$X = 0.5 \text{ mole.}$$

Since 1 mole of ethanol has a mass of 46 grams, 0.5 mole of ethanol has a mass of 23 grams.

89.   Ans. **3**   The presence of a solute lowers the freezing point of the solvent by an amount that is proportional to the concentration of the dissolved solute particles. One mole of a nonelectrolyte (*such as ethanol*) per 1000 grams of water lowers the freezing point of the water by 1.86 C°. This temperature

interval is called the molal freezing point depression of water. Since most all organic compounds are nonelectrolytes, ethanol is classified in this category. One mole of ethanol has a mass of 46 grams. According to our explanation, 1 mole of ethanol (46 *grams*) will lower the freezing point by 1.86 C°. Thus, the freezing point of the solution is most nearly −1.86°C. The freezing point of pure water is 0°C.

90.   Ans. 3   When ethanol is added to water, the two substances mix to give a liquid similar in appearance to the original liquids. If 1 mole of ethanol is dissolved in 1 liter of water, the resulting mixture is a solution. Alcohol-water mixtures are called solutions. The alcohol and water will mix since their molecules are somewhat related in composition and structure.

Wrong Choices Explained:

(1) An emulsion is a system of two immiscible liquids, one of which is dispersed throughout the other in small drops. Immiscible liquids do not mix with one another.

(2) A colloid is a two-phase system having dispersed particles suspended in a dispersing medium. The particle size lies between 10^{-7} cm. and 10^{-5} cm. In colloidal sols, a solid is dispersed through a liquid. The solid should not settle out. There are also many other types of colloids.

(4) In a suspension, the solid particles can be seen by the unaided eye, they can be separated from the liquid by filtration, and they will settle on standing. The solid particles are insoluble in the liquid medium. The liquid will usually appear to be cloudy.

91.   Ans. 1   The empirical formula represents the constituent elements of a substance and the simplest relative number of atoms of each. The empirical formula for any compound is determined by the following procedure:

Step 1.   The hydrocarbon contains 80% carbon and 20% hydrogen. This means 100 grams of the compound would contain 80 grams of carbon and 20 grams of hydrogen. The number of gram-atoms or moles of each element contained in 100 grams of the compound is determined by dividing the amount (percentage × 100 grams) of each element by its atomic mass. Step 1 is solved as follows:

$$\text{Carbon} = \frac{80 \text{ grams}}{12 \text{ grams/gram-atom}} = 6.67 \text{ gram-atoms or moles}$$

$$\text{Hydrogen} = \frac{20 \text{ grams}}{1 \text{ gram/gram-atom}} = 20 \quad \text{gram-atoms or moles}$$

Step 2.   Divide each of the above gram-atom ratios by the smallest common divisor (6.67). Step 2 is solved as follows:

$$\text{Carbon} = \frac{6.67}{6.67} = 1$$

$$\text{Hydrogen} = \frac{20}{6.67} = 3$$

Step 3. Using the atomic ratios determined in Step 2, it is obvious that the empirical formula for this hydrocarbon is CH_3.

92. **Ans. 2** To determine the molecular mass of this substance when the density is given at S.T.P., we use the formula, Density $= \dfrac{Mass}{Volume}$. The volume of 1 molecular mass (mole) of this substance at S.T.P. is 22.4 liters. We can now solve this problem as follows:

Density = 1.34 grams/liter

Density $= \dfrac{Mass}{Volume}$

Mass $= X$
Volume = 22.4 liters

Therefore: Mass = Density × Volume
Mass = 1.34 grams/liter × 22.4 liters
Mass = 30 grams or $3.0 \times 10'$ grams.

Base your answers to questions 93 through 97 on the potential energy diagram and the reaction below.

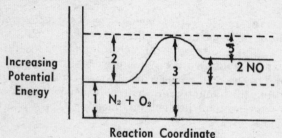

$$N_2(g) + O_2(g) = 2NO(g) \quad \triangle H = +43.2 \text{ kcal.}$$
Forward Reaction →

The relationship between activation energy and heat of reaction for a given reaction can be shown graphically in a potential energy diagram by plotting potential energy against a reaction coordinate representing the progress of the reaction. In answering questions pertaining to a potential energy diagram, I feel it is a good practice to list the identity or significance of the numbered arrows on the potential energy diagram. The arrows are identified as follows:

Arrow 1 indicates the potential energy of the reactants of the forward reaction.

Arrow 2 indicates the energy of activation of the forward reaction.

Arrow 3 indicates the potential energy of the activated complex.

Arrow 4 indicates the heat of reaction.

Arrow 5 indicates the energy of activation of the reverse reaction.

93. **Ans. 1** The potential energy of the reactants is the vertical distance from the X axis, *Reaction Coordinate*, to the reactants of the forward reaction. Arrow 1 indicates the potential energy of the forward reaction.

94. **Ans. 2** The energy of activation is the minimum energy required to initiate a chemical reaction. The energy of activation represents the difference

between the highest point in the curve and the initial potential energy of the reactants. The energy of activation for the forward reaction is represented by arrow 2.

95. Ans. **1** Since the $\triangle H$ value for the forward reaction is +43.2 kcal., this reaction is an endothermic reaction. In an endothermic reaction, the products have a higher potential energy than the reactants. The diagram tells us that the potential energy of the reactants is represented by arrow 1. The potential energy of the products is represented by arrow 1 + arrow 4. Obviously the potential energy of the products is higher than the potential energy of the reactants.

96. Ans. **3** The highest point in the curve represents the potential energy of the intermediate products which are called activated complexes. Therefore, an activated complex represents the highest point in the potential energy curve. The activated complex is a transitory arrangement resulting from an effective collision of reactant particles and persisting while old bonds are breaking and new bonds are forming. Therefore, the potential energy of the activated complex is represented by arrow 3.

97. Ans. **2** Heat of formation, *also called heat of reaction,* is the heat energy released or absorbed in the formation of the products. It represents the difference in heat content between the products and the reactants. $\triangle H = H_{(products)} - H_{(reactants)}$. In an endothermic reaction, the products have a higher potential energy than the reactants, and the $\triangle H$ value is positive. In the endothermic reaction in this question,

$$N_2(g) + O_2(g) = 2NO(g) \quad \triangle H = +43.2 \text{ kcal.}$$

Since 2 moles of NO gas have a $\triangle H$ value of +43.2 kcal, 1 mole of NO gas has a value of $\frac{43.2}{2} = +21.6$ kcal/mole. Therefore, the heat of formation of NO gas, in kilocalories per mole, is +21.6.

98. Ans. **1** *Le Chatelier's Principle* states—when an equilibrium is subjected to a stress, it is displaced in the direction that relieves the stress. If more SO_2 is added to the system, the equilibrium will shift to the right to use up the added SO_2 and thereby relieve the stress of the increased concentration of SO_2. Since the equilibrium is shifted toward the right (*toward the formation of the products*), the concentration of SO_3 increases.

Wrong Choices Explained:
(2) A decrease in concentration of O_2 will shift the equilibrium toward the left to relieve the stress. Thus, the concentration of SO_3 would decrease and the concentration of SO_2 and O_2 would increase.

(3) A decrease in pressure on the system will shift the equilibrium toward the side with the larger volume (*more molecules*). Thus, the concentration of SO_3 would decrease and the concentration of SO_2 and O_2 would increase.

(4) The addition of a catalyst has no effect on an equilibrium system. A

catalyst increases the rate of both the forward and reverse reactions equally and produces no net change in equilibrium concentrations.

99. Ans. 3 In a system in equilibrium, a catalyst increases the rate of both the forward and reverse reactions equally and produces no net change in the equilibrium concentrations. A catalyst may cause equilibrium to be reached in a shorter time, but it does not affect the equilibrium reached.

100. Ans. 2 Again using *Le Chatelier's Principle,* an increase in pressure will shift the equilibrium toward the side with the smaller molar volume (*number of moles of gas*). Since the number of moles of gas is shown by the coefficients of the molecules in the equation, we have 3 molar volumes on the left side (*2 for SO₂ and 1 for O₂*) and 2 volumes on the right side for SO₃. Since the smaller volume is on the right side, SO₃ will increase in mass. Thus, the stress of the added pressure is lessened by the formation of SO₃ in the given reaction. Since the equilibrium is shifted to the right side, there is an increase in the mass of SO₃ and a decrease in the mass of SO₂ and O₂.

101. Ans. 1 Using *Le Chatelier's Principle,* when the temperature of a system in equilibrium is increased, the equilibrium is displaced to the side which absorbs heat. The reaction given is:

$$2SO_2(g) + O_2(g) = 2SO_3(g) + 45 \text{ kcal.}$$

This reaction is exothermic therefore, heat is released on the right side. In every system in equilibrium, an endothermic and an exothermic reaction are taking place simultaneously. A decrease in temperature of this system would favor the exothermic side. The endothermic reaction is favored by an increase in temperature. In the reaction given, the endothermic reaction would proceed to the left or toward the formation of SO₂ and O₂. Therefore, the concentrations of SO₂ and O₂ are greater and SO₃ is smaller.

102. Ans. 4 Using *Le Chatelier's Principle,* removal of one of the products of a reaction results in the decrease of its concentration and will cause the reaction to go in such a direction as to increase the concentration of the products. Therefore, at the new equilibrium as compared to the old equilibrium, the concentration of the product SO₃, will be increased and the concentrations of O₂ and SO₂ will be decreased.

103. Ans. 4 Using *Table H,* the conjugate acid-conjugate base chart, the acid strength decreases as we go from HCl to NH₃ in the conjugate acid column. Therefore, HCl is the strongest of all the 9 acids listed. In this question, H₃O⁺ is the strongest acid of the 4 choices given since it is higher than the other 3 choices on the chart.

104. Ans. 4 In the conjugate base column, the strength of the base decreases as you go from bottom to top. Therefore, NH₂⁻ is the strongest base of the 9 bases listed. The higher you rise in the column, the weaker is the base.

A substance which is a weaker base than H_2O has to be higher than H_2O in the column. The only base of the 4 choices given which is higher than H_2O in the conjugate base column is NO_3^-. Thus, NO_3^- is a weaker base than water.

105. **Ans. 3** According to the *Brönsted-Lowry Theory* of acids and bases, an acid is a proton donor and a base is a proton acceptor. A substance which can behave as either an acid or a base could donate or accept a proton. This substance would be both a conjugate acid and a conjugate base. The only one of the four choices that is in both the conjugate acid and conjugate base column is HSO_4^-. It can accept or donate a proton as follows:

Accept a proton: $HSO_4^- + H^+ \rightarrow H_2SO_4$
Donate a proton: $HSO_4^- \rightarrow SO_4^{-2} + H^+$

Wrong Choices Explained:
(1) H_3O^+ can donate a proton, but it cannot accept a proton.
(2) HNO_3 can donate a proton, but it cannot accept a proton.
(4) NH_2^- can accept a proton, but it cannot donate a proton.

106. **Ans. 1** If a solution has a pH of 3, the hydrogen ion concentration of the solution in moles per liter can be determined as follows:

$$pH = Log \frac{1}{[H^+]}$$

Therefore, $[H^+] = 10^{-pH}$
If pH = 3 $[H^+] = 10^{-3}$

Therefore, the H^+ ion concentration in moles per liter is 1×10^{-3}.

107. **Ans. 1** The expression for the ionization constant of water, K_w, is given as: $K_w = [H^+] \cdot [OH^-] = 1 \times 10^{-14}$ at 25°C. This expression tells us that the product of the molar concentrations of H^+ and OH^- must equal 1×10^{-14}. If we substitute the H^+ ion concentration, 1×10^{-2} mole/liter in the expression, we can determine the OH^- ion concentration. The problem is solved as follows:

$$[H^+] = 1 \times 10^{-2} \qquad [H^+] \cdot [OH^-] = 1 \times 10^{-14}$$
$$[OH^-] = X \qquad 1 \times 10^{-2}\, X = 1 \times 10^{-14}$$

$$OH^- = X = \frac{1 \times 10^{-14}}{1 \times 10^{-2}} = 1 \times 10^{-12}$$

Therefore, the hydroxide ion concentration is 1×10^{-12}.

108. **Ans. 3** When the electrochemical cell reaches equilibrium, the net potential (E^0) for the cell is 0.00. When the cell reaches equilibrium, the reverse reaction, $Cu_{(aq)}^{+2} + 2Ag_{(s)} \rightarrow 2Ag_{(aq)}^+ + Cu_{(s)}$ proceeds at a rate equal to that of the forward reaction. The E^0 value for the reverse reaction is -0.46 volt and that for the forward reaction is $+0.46$ volt. (The E^0 for the forward reaction is determined in the answer to question 110.) When the opposing reactions become equal, the total cell potential is zero. This occurs at equilibrium.

109.   Ans. **2**   The species oxidized is the element which has lost electrons. Using the reaction given, we can set up the ion-electron partial equations for the oxidation and reduction reactions as follows:

Oxidation half-reaction: $Cu^0_{(s)} - 2e^- \rightarrow Cu^{+2}$
Reduction half-reaction: $2Ag^+_{(aq)} + 2e^- \rightarrow 2Ag^0_{(s)}$

Thus, the species that is oxidized is the metallic copper, $Cu^0_{(s)}$, since it has lost 2 electrons.

Wrong Choices Explained:

(1) Metallic silver, $Ag^0_{(s)}$, is a product of the reduction reaction.
(3) The silver ion, $Ag^+_{(aq)}$, is reduced to metallic silver.
(4) The copper ion, $Cu^{+2}_{(aq)}$, is a product of the oxidation reaction.

110.   Ans. **3**   As we explained in question 37, the maximum net potential (E^0) for an electrochemical cell can be determined by adding the E^0 of the oxidation half-reaction to the E^0 for the reduction half-reaction. To solve this problem, we set up the ion-electron equation for each half-reaction and determine the E^0 values from *Table L*. This is done as follows:

Oxidation
   half-reaction: $Cu^0_{(s)} \rightarrow Cu^{+2}_{(aq)} + 2e^-$ $E^0 = -0.34$ volt
Reduction
   half-reaction: $2Ag^+_{(aq)} + 2e^- \rightarrow 2Ag^0_{(s)}$ $E^0 = +0.80$ volt
(Reverse E^0 sign
   for reduction
   half-reaction) $Cu^0_{(s)} + 2Ag^+_{(aq)} \rightarrow Cu^{+2}_{(aq)} + 2Ag^0_{(s)}$

Net potential $E^0 =$ 0.46 volt

Thus, the maximum net potential for the cell is 0.46 volt.

111.   Ans. **1**   As we explained in question 109, the metallic copper, $Cu^0_{(s)}$, is oxidized to the $Cu^{+2}_{(aq)}$ ion. Oxidation occurs at the positive electrode, the anode. Electrons flow through the external wire to the silver electrode which is the cathode. The electronic equation for the reaction that takes place at the copper electrode is: $Cu^0_{(s)} - 2e \rightarrow Cu^{+2}_{(aq)}$.

Wrong Choices Explained:

(2) This represents a reaction in which copper is reduced.
(3) If metallic copper gained 2 electrons, it would not have a charge of $+2$. It would probably be -2.
(4) If the copper ion lost 2 electrons, it would not become metallic copper.

112.   Ans. **2**   The species that acts as a reducing agent is the species that is oxidized. The substance oxidized loses electrons and is always the reducing agent. As we explained in the answer to questions 109 and 111, the species or element that loses electrons is metallic copper, $Cu^0_{(s)}$. The equation for the oxidation is: $Cu^0_{(s)} - 2e \rightarrow Cu^{+2}_{(aq)}$. Since the metallic copper loses 2 electrons, it is oxidized. It is also the reducing agent.

Wrong Choices Explained:

(1) Metallic silver, $Ag^0_{(s)}$, is the product of the reduction reaction.

(3) The silver ion, Ag^+, is reduced to metallic silver, $Ag^0_{(s)}$. It is the oxidizing agent.

(4) The copper ion Cu^{+2}, is the product of the oxidation reaction.

Examination June, 1969   Chemistry

PART ONE   *Answer all 60 questions in this part.*

DIRECTIONS (1–60):   *For each statement or question, write in the space provided the* number *preceding the word or expression that, of those given, best completes the statement or answers the question.*

1. During an experiment to determine the heat of a reaction ($\triangle H$), 500 grams of water in a calorimeter increased in temperature from 18° C. to 28° C. The approximate number of calories given off by the reaction was   (1) 10   (2) 500   (3) 5,000   (4) 50,000

1.............

2. Which conditions generally cause the characteristics of a gas to deviate most from the ideal gas laws?
(1) low temperature and low pressure
(2) low temperature and high pressure
(3) high temperature and low pressure
(4) high temperature and high pressure

2.............

3. At standard temperature, the volume occupied by 1.00 mole of gas is 11.2 liters. The pressure exerted on this gas is (1) 1.00 atm.   (2) 2.00 atm.   (3) 0.50 atm.   (4) 1.50 atm.

3.............

4. Which is an example of an endothermic reaction?
(1) $H_2(g) + \frac{1}{2}O_2(g) \rightarrow H_2O(g)$
(2) $S(s) + O_2(g) \rightarrow SO_2(g)$
(3) $\frac{1}{2}N_2(g) + O_2(g) \rightarrow NO_2(g)$
(4) $C(s) + O_2(g) \rightarrow CO_2(g)$

4.............

5. What is the boiling point of water when the atmospheric pressure is 23.8 mm. of mercury?   (1) 0° C.   (2) 25° C. (3) 100° C.   (4) 200° C.

5.............

6. If atom X is represented as $^{210}_{84}X$ and atom Y is represented as $^{211}_{84}Y$, then atoms X and Y are   (1) isotopes of the same element   (2) isotopes of different elements   (3) allotropes of the same element   (4) allotropes of a different element

6.............

7. The ionization energy required to remove the first electron from a barium atom is   (1) 0.9 electron-volt   (2) 5.2 electron-volts   (3) 5.3 electron-volts   (4) 9.3 electron-volts

7.............

1

8. An element in its ground state has 5 valence electrons. Which is the correct distribution of these electrons?

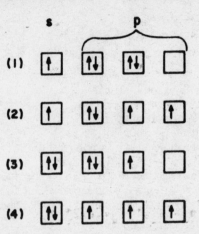

8............

9. Of the elements listed below, which has the highest electronegativity? (1) $1s^2 2s^2 2p^2$ (2) $1s^2 2s^2 2p^6 3s^1$ (3) $1s^2 2s^2 2p^6 3s^2 3p^1$ (4) $1s^2 2s^2 2p^6 3s^2 3p^5$

9............

10. Which energy level transition represents the greatest absorption of energy? (1) $1s$ to $3p$ (2) $2p$ to $3s$ (3) $3s$ to $3p$ (4) $3s$ to $4s$

10............

11. An originally pure radioactive sample of $^{232}_{90}$Th now contains atoms of $^{232}_{91}$Pa. This results because some atoms of $^{23}_{90}$Th each emitted (1) a neutron (2) a beta particle (3) an alpha particle (4) a gamma ray

11............

12. A sample of two naturally occurring isotopes contains 4×10^{23} atoms of isotope ^{24}X and 2×10^{23} atoms of isotope ^{25}X. The average atomic mass of the element is equal to

(1) $(24 \times 4) + (25 \times 2)$

(2) $(24 \times 2) + (25 \times 4)$

(3) $\dfrac{(24 \times 2) + (25 \times 4)}{6}$

(4) $\dfrac{(24 \times 4) + (25 \times 2)}{6}$

12............

13. Which property best accounts for the conductivity of metals? (1) the protons in metallic crystals (2) the malleability of most metals (3) the filled inner electron shells of most metals (4) the free electrons in metallic crystals

13............

14. The correct formula for mercury (I) chloride is (1) $HgCl_2$ (2) $HgCl_3$ (3) Hg_2Cl_2 (4) Hg_3Cl

14............

15. Given the unbalanced equation

$$\_Al_2(SO_4)_3 + \_Ca(OH)_2 \rightarrow \_Al(OH)_3 + \_CaSO_4.$$

The sum of the coefficients for the balanced equation is (1) 5 (2) 9 (3) 3 (4) 4

15............

16. Which is characteristic of ionic solids?
(1) They conduct electricity in the solid state.
(2) They have a high vapor pressure.
(3) They have high melting points.
(4) They dissolve to form molecules in a polar solution.

16............

17. Which type of bonding accounts for the high boiling point of H_2O as compared with the relatively low boiling point of H_2S? (1) *Van der Waals' Forces* (2) hydrogen bonds (3) covalent bonds (4) electrovalent bonds

17............

18. In which compound does the bond have the *least* degree of ionic character? (1) KBr (2) HF (3) MgO (4) BrCl

18............

19. Pure nitrogen combines directly with an active metal to form a (1) nitrate (2) nitride (3) nitrite (4) pernitrate

19............

20. Which is an example of a metalloid? (1) Fe (2) La (3) Mg (4) Si

20............

21. Which type of element frequently forms colored compounds and generally exhibits more than one positive oxidation state? (1) alkaline earths (2) alkali metals (3) transition elements (4) noble gases

21............

22. Which group in the *Periodic Table* contains the alkali metals? (1) I A (2) II A (3) III A (4) IV A

22............

23. A Ca^0 atom *differs* from a Ca^{+2} ion in that the atom has (1) a greater nuclear charge (2) a smaller radius (3) a smaller mass number (4) two 4s electrons

23............

24. An atom of fluorine is smaller than an atom of oxygen. One possible explanation is that, compared with oxygen, fluorine has (1) a smaller oxidation number (2) a smaller atomic number (3) a greater nuclear charge (4) more unpaired electrons

24............

25. According to the balanced equation

$$Cu + 4HNO_3 \rightarrow Cu(NO_3)_2 + 2H_2O + 2NO_2 \uparrow,$$

how many moles of nitric acid are necessary to react with 3.0 moles of copper? (1) 0.75 (2) 12 (3) 3.0 (4) 4.0   25...........

26. Fourteen grams of a gas occupy 11.2 liters at *S.T.P.* The gas may be (1) carbon monoxide (2) hydrogen sulfide (3) hydrogen chloride (4) sulfur dioxide   26...........

27. A compound is found by analysis to consist of 5% hydrogen and 95% fluorine. What is its empirical formula? (1) HF (2) H_2F (3) H_2F_2 (4) H_3F 27...........

28. At S.T.P., which gas is *least* dense? (1) HCl (2) NO (3) NH_3 (4) H_2S 28...........

29. The number of molecules present in 70 grams of nitrogen gas is equal to

(1) $70 \times 6 \times 10^{23}$ (3) $\dfrac{70 \times 6 \times 10^{23}}{28}$

(2) $\dfrac{70}{6 \times 10^{23}}$ (4) $\dfrac{70 \times 6 \times 10^{23}}{14}$ 29...........

30. What mass of NaOH (formula mass —40 g.) is needed to prepare 500 ml. of 0.50 M solution? (1) 10. grams (2) 20. grams (3) 25 grams (4) 40. grams   30...........

31. The activation energy of a system may be lowered by (1) increasing the concentration of the reactants (2) increasing the pressure (3) decreasing the pressure (4) adding a catalyst   31...........

32. Which silver salt is most soluble in water?
(1) silver chloride—K_{sp} at 25° C. = 1.1×10^{-10}
(2) silver bromide—K_{sp} at 25° C. = 7.7×10^{-13}
(3) silver iodide—K_{sp} at 25° C. = 1.5×10^{-16}
(4) silver sulfide—K_{sp} at 25° C. = 1.0×10^{-50} 32...........

33. Which compound is *least* soluble in 100 milliliters of water at 10° C.? (1) $Ce_2(SO_4)_3$ (2) NaCl (3) KI (4) $KClO_3$ 33...........

34. Consider the system $N_2(g) + 3H_2(g) = 2NH_3(g)$ at a constant temperature. An increase in pressure on this system will (1) shift the equilibrium to the left (2) shift the equilibrium to the right (3) have no effect on the equilibrium (4) change the value of the equilibrium constant   34...........

35. Given the reaction:
$$2Al(s) + \tfrac{3}{2}O_2(g) = Al_2O_3(s)$$
$$\triangle H = -399 \text{ kcal./mole}$$

The number of kilocalories of energy liberated by the oxidation of 27 grams of aluminum is approximately (1) 100 (2) 200 (3) 300 (4) 400   35............

36. A chemical reaction must be spontaneous if it results in an energy
  (1) gain and an entropy increase
  (2) gain and an entropy decrease
  (3) loss and an entropy increase
  (4) loss and an entropy decrease   36............

37. In the reaction $H_2SO_4 + HOH \rightarrow H_3O^+ + X$, the species represented by X may be (1) SO_3^{-2} (2) $H_3SO_4^+$ (3) HSO_4^- (4) OH^- 37............

38. During acid-base neutralization, how many moles of hydroxide ions will react with one mole of hydrogen ions? (1) 1.0 mole (2) 0.5 mole (3) 17.007 moles (4) 22.4 moles   38............

39. How many milliliters of 0.20 M H_2SO_4 are required to completely titrate 40 ml. of 0.10 M $Ca(OH)_2$? (1) 10 (2) 20 (3) 40 (4) 80   39............

40. Which is the weakest acid? (1) acetic (2) boric (3) carbonic (4) phosphoric   40............

41. According to the Brönsted-Lowry theory, which species is amphoteric (amphiprotic)? (1) Cl^- (2) H_3O^+ (3) NH_3 (4) NH_4^+ 41............

42. In the reaction $NH_3 + H_2SO_4 = NH_4^+ + HSO_4^-$, the two bases are (1) NH_3 and HSO_4^- (2) NH_3 and NH_4^+ (3) NH_4^+ and H_2SO_4 (4) H_2SO_4 and HSO_4^- 42............

43. A water solution of KCl would have a pH closest to (1) 5 (2) 7 (3) 3 (4) 9   43............

44. Which halogen would *not* be expected to have a positive oxidation state when combined with oxygen? (1) F (2) Cl (3) Br (4) I   44............

45. In the reaction
  $$Cl_2(g) + 2Br^-(aq) = 2Cl^-(aq) + Br_2(l),$$
the E° value is equal to (1) −2.42 volts (2) −0.29 volts (3) 0.29 volts (4) 2.42 volts   45............

46. What is the algebraic sum of the oxidation numbers of all the atoms in the compound $K_2Cr_2O_7$? (1) 0 (2) -5 (3) $+9$ (4) -14

46..............

47. Which reaction occurs at the negative electrode during the electrolysis of fused (molten) calcium fluoride?
(1) $CaF_2 \rightarrow Ca^{+2} + F_2 \uparrow$
(2) $Ca^{+2} + 2e^- \rightarrow Ca^0$
(3) $2F^- \rightarrow F_2 + 2e^-$
(4) $Ca^0 \rightarrow Ca^{+2} + 2e^-$

47..............

48. Which reaction will occur spontaneously at room temperature? (1) $Co^{+2} + Pb^0 \rightarrow$ (2) $2Cl^- + I_2^0 \rightarrow$ (3) $Sr^{+2} + Ag^0 \rightarrow$ (4) $2I^- + Br_2^0 \rightarrow$

48..............

49. Which is the ion-electron equation for the reduction that takes place in the reaction below?

$$2KBr + 3H_2SO_4 + MnO_2 \rightarrow 2KHSO_4 + MnSO_4 + 2H_2O + Br_2$$

(1) $Mn^{+4} + 2e^- \rightarrow Mn^{+2}$
(2) $2Br^- \rightarrow Br_2^0 + 2e$
(3) $Mn^{+2} + 2e^- \rightarrow Mn^{+4}$
(4) $2Br^- + 2e^- \rightarrow 2Br^{-2}$

49..............

50. The structural formula for 1, 2-dichloropropane is

(1)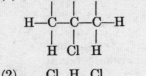

(3)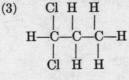

(2)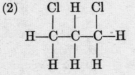

(4)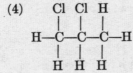

50..............

51. The organic compound $C_3H_3(OH)_3$ is classified as (1) a carbohydrate (2) an ester (3) an alcohol (4) an organic acid

51..............

52. Which compound can have isomers? (1) C_2H_4 (2) C_2H_2 (3) C_2H_6 (4) C_4H_8

52..............

53. In the alkane series, the formula of each member of the series *differs* from its preceding member by   (1) CH   (2) CH_2 (3) CH_3 (4) CH_4 53..............

54. Which type of reaction occurs between C_2H_4 and bromine?   (1) polymerization   (2) substitution   (3) addition   (4) esterification   54..............

NOTE: *That questions 55 through 60 have only three choices.*

55. As the number of particles oxidized during a chemical reaction increases, the number of particles reduced   (1) decreases   (2) increases   (3) remains the same   55..............

56. As the temperature of ethyl alcohol decreases, its vapor pressure   (1) decreases   (2) increases   (3) remains the same   56..............

57. As a sulfur atom becomes a sulfide ion, the radius   (1) decreases   (2) increases   (3) remains the same   57..............

58. As the rate of a given reaction increases due to an increase in the concentration of the reactants, the activation energy for that reaction   (1) decreases   (2) increases   (3) remains the same   58..............

59. As the elements in Group II *A* are considered in order of increasing atomic number, the tendency of each successive atom to form a positive ion generally   (1) decreases   (2) increases   (3) remains the same   59..............

60. Consider the system $AgCl(s) = Ag^+(aq) + Cl^-(aq)$ at equilibrium. As chloride ions are added to this system and the temperature is kept constant, the value of the equilibrium constant   (1) decreases   (2) increases   (3) remains the same   60..............

PART TWO   *This part consists of nine groups. Choose six of these nine groups. Be sure that you answer all questions in each group chosen.*

GROUP 1

DIRECTIONS (**61–65**):   *Write the number of the word or expression that best completes each statement or answers each question.*   [5]

Base your answers to questions 61 through 65 on the graph below, which represents the relationship between the equilibrium vapor pressure and temperature of four liquids.

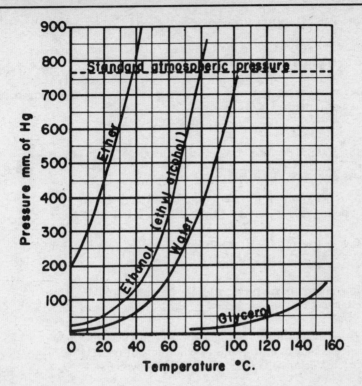

61. The vapor pressure of which liquid would increase the most of its temperature were changed from 20° C. to 40° C.? (1) ether   (2) ethanol   (3) water   (4) glycerol   61...........

62. When the pressure exerted on the surface of glycerol equals that of 100 mm. of Hg, its boiling point will be   (1) 25° C. (2) 140° C.   (3) 145° C.   (4) 160° C.   62...........

63. The liquid whose molecules exert the strongest attractive force upon each other is   (1) glycerol   (2) alcohol   (3) water (4) ether   63...........

64. Water will boil at a temperature of 80° C. when the pressure exerted on its surface is equal to   (1) 300 mm. Hg   (2) 370 mm. Hg   (3) 400 mm. Hg   (4) 760 mm. Hg   64...........

65. The normal boiling point of ether is   (1) 38° C. (2) 42° C.   (3) 100° C.   (4) 760° C.   65...........

GROUP 2

DIRECTIONS (66–70): *Write the number of the word or expression that best completes the statement or answers the question.* [5]

Base your answers to questions 66 through 70 on the following electron configuration of a neutral atom:

$$1s^2 2s^1 2p^3$$

66. How many protons are in the nucleus of this atom? (1) 6 (2) 2 (3) 3 (4) 5

66............

67. In which group of the *Periodic Table* would this element most likely be found? (1) I *A* (2) II *A* (3) III *A* (4) IV *A*

67............

68. How many principal energy levels are in this electron structure? (1) 1 (2) 2 (3) 3 (4) 4

68............

69. How many incomplete orbitals are indicated by this electron configuration? (1) 1 (2) 2 (3) 3 (4) 4

69............

70. When this element combines with chlorine, the bond between this element and an atom of chlorine will be (1) ionic (2) metallic (3) polar covalent (4) nonpolar covalent

70............

GROUP 3

DIRECTIONS (71–75): *For each of questions 71 through 75, write the number of the type of bond,* chosen from the list below, *which is found between the atoms described in that question.* [5]

Bonds

(1) Ionic bond   (3) Nonpolar covalent bond
(2) Metallic bond   (4) Polar covalent bond

71. The hydrogen and chlorine atoms in $HCl(g)$ 71............

72. The magnesium and chlorine particles in $MgCl_2$ 72............

73. The nitrogen and hydrogen atoms in NH_3 73............

74. The nitrogen atoms in N_2 74............

75. The atoms in Cu wire   75............

GROUP 4

DIRECTIONS (76-80): *Write the number of the word or expression that best completes the statement or answers the question.* [5]

Base your answers to questions 76 through 80 on the partial *Periodic Table* shown below.

Group

	I_A	II_A	III_A	IV_A	V_A	VI_A	VII_A	O
2	A				E			
3		J		D		M		R
4			L				G	

(Period on vertical axis: 2, 3, 4)

76. Which two elements would be *least* likely to react to form a compound?   (1) A and G (2) D and G (3) J and M (4) L and R 76.............

77. Which two elements would form the most highly ionic compound?   (1) A and G (2) D and M (3) J and G (4) L and M 77.............

78. What would be the probable formula for a compound formed from elements L and M?   (1) L_4M (2) LM_3 (3) L_2M_3 (4) L_3M_2 78.............

79. Which element could form a compound that is normally called a hydride?   (1) A (2) E (3) M (4) G 79.............

80. Which element has the lowest melting point?   (1) R (2) J (3) G (4) D 80.............

GROUP 5

DIRECTIONS (81-85): *Write the number of the word or expression that best completes the statement or answers the question.* [5]

Base your answers to questions 81 through 83 on the information below.

One mole of potassium permanganate reacts completely with hydrochloric acid according to the following reaction:

$$16HCl + 2KMnO_4 \rightarrow 2KCl + 2MnCl_2 + 5Cl_2 + 8H_2O$$

81. How many moles of water are produced? (1) 1 (2) 2
(3) .5 (4) 4   81............

82. How many grams of potassium chloride are produced?
(1) 1 (2) 37 (3) 74 (4) 148   82............

83. How many liters of chlorine measured at S.T.P. are
produced? (1) 11.2 (2) 22.4 (3) 56.0 (4) 112   82............

Base your answers to questions 84 and 85 on the information below.

A compound is found by analysis to consist of 85.7% carbon and 14.3%
hydrogen by mass.

84. The empirical formula of the compound is (1) CH
(2) CH_2 (3) CH_3 (4) C_2H 84............

85. The number of molecules in one mole of this compound is
(1) 12.04×10^{23} (2) 9.03×10^{23} (3) 6.02×10^{23} (4) 3.01×10^{23} 85............

GROUP 6

DIRECTIONS (86–90): *Write the number of the word or expression that best
completes the statement or answers the question.* [5]

Base your answers to questions 86 through 88 on the information below.

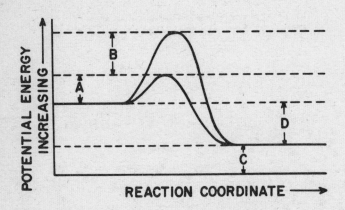

86. Which represents the energy of activation for the uncatalyzed forward reaction? (1) $A + B$ (2) B (3) $C + D$ (4) D 86............

87. Compared to the potential energy of the reactants,
the potential energy of the products is (1) less (2) the same
(3) greater (4) impossible to determine   87............

88. Which represents the heat of reaction for the catalyzed reverse reaction? (1) *A*   (2) *B*   (3) *C*   (4) *D*   88............

Base your answers to questions 89 and 90 on the information below.

	Heat of Reaction $\triangle H$ kcal./mole	Free Energy of Formation $\triangle G$ kcal./mole
Reaction *A:*	−94.05	−94.26
Reaction *B:*	21.60	20.72
Reaction *C:*	−70.96	−71.79
Reaction *D:*	54.19	50.00

89. Which reactions are endothermic? (1) *A* and *B*   (2) *A* and *C*   (3) *C* and *D*   (4) *B* and *D*   89............

90. Which reactions occur spontaneously? (1) *A* and *B*   (2) *A* and *C*   (3) *B* and *D*   (4) *C* and *D*   90............

GROUP 7

DIRECTIONS (91–95): *Write the number of the word or expression that best completes the statement or answers the question.* [5]

Base your answers to questions 91 through 93 on the information below.

Beaker *A* contains 200 ml. of 0.10 M HCl.
Beaker *B* contains 200 ml. of 0.10 M NaOH.

91. The pH of the solution in beaker *A* is closest to (1) 1   (2) 2   (3) 7   (4) 10   91............

92. If the contents of beakers *A* and *B* were mixed, the pH of the resulting solution would be closest to (1) 1   (2) 5   (3) 7   (4) 9   92............

93. When the solutions in beakers *A* and *B* are mixed, the reaction goes essentially to completion because of the formation of (1) HCl   (2) NaOH   (3) NaCl   (4) H_2O 93............

Base your answers to questions 94 and 95 on the information below.

Beaker *A* contains 100 ml. of 0.1 M H_2SO_4.
Beaker *B* contains 100 ml. of 0.1 M $Ba(OH)_2$.

NOTE: *That questions 94 and 95 have only three choices.*

94. As the contents of beaker B are poured into beaker A, the pH of the resulting mixture in beaker A (1) decreases (2) increases   (3) remains the same   94...............

95. As the contents of beaker B are poured into beaker A, the conductivity of the resulting mixture in beaker A (1) decreases (2) increases   (3) remains the same   95...............

GROUP 8

DIRECTIONS (**96–100**): *Write the* number *of the word or expression that best completes the statement or answers the question.*   [5]

Base your answers to questions 96 through 100 on the diagram and equation below.

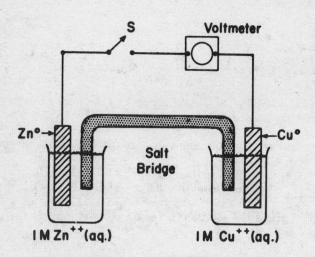

$$Zn(s) + Cu^{+2}(aq) \rightarrow Zn^{+2}(aq) + Cu(s)$$

96. If the salt bridge were removed and switch S closed, the voltage would be   (1) 0.00 volts   (2) 0.34 volt   (3) 0.76 volt (4) 1.10 volts   96...............

97. When the reaction reaches chemical equilibrium, the cell voltage will be   (1) 0.00 volts   (2) 0.34 volt   (3) 0.76 volt (4) 1.10 volts   97...............

98. What will be the maximum voltage in the cell when switch S is closed?   (1) 0.00 volts   (2) 0.34 volt   (3) 0.76 volt (4) 1.10 volts   98...............

99. Which species supplies the electrons which flow through the wire? (1) Cu   (2) Zn   (3) Cu^{+2} (4) Zn^{+2} 99.............

100. In this reaction, the substance reduced is (1) Cu (2) Zn   (3) Cu^{+2} (4) Zn^{+2} 100.............

GROUP 9

DIRECTIONS (**101–105**): *Write the number of the word or expression that best completes the statement or answers the question.* [5]

101. Which organic compound is a product of a fermentation reaction? (1) CCl_2F_2 (2) C_2H_2 (3) C_2H_5OH (4) $C_2H_5OC_2H_5$ 101.............

102. Which is an example of a primary alcohol?

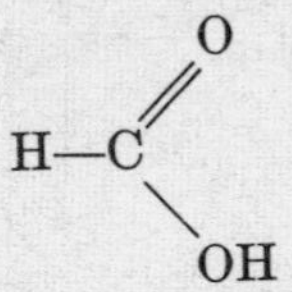

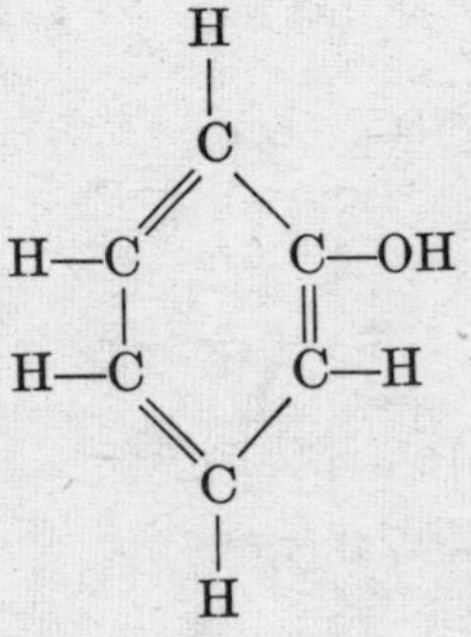

102.............

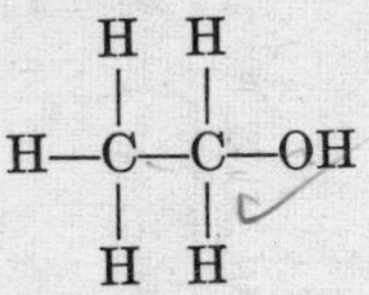

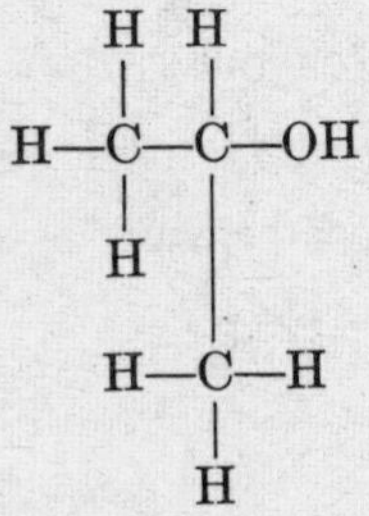

103. Which is the general formula for the benzene series? (1) C_nH_{2n+2} (2) C_nH_{2n} (3) C_nH_{2n-2} (4) C_nH_{2n-6} 103.............

104. Which organic compound is a product of an esterification reaction? (1) C_3H_8 (2) C_3H_7OH (3) CH_3COOH (4) CH_3COOCH_3 104.............

105. Which organic compound is a product of a saponification reaction? (1) CCl_4 (2) $C_3H_5(OH)_3$ (3) C_6H_6 (4) $C_6H_{12}O_6$ 105.............

Answers June, 1969 Chemistry

PART ONE

1. Ans. **3** The question asks us to determine the heat of reaction ($\triangle H$) in calories for an experiment using a calorimeter. A calorimeter is an instrument used to measure the heat of a reaction. A diagram of the calorimeter is shown at the right. We are told that 500 grams of water in the calorimeter increased in temperature from 18° C. to 28° C. To determine the approximate number of calories given off by the reaction, we use the following relationship: Heat given off by reaction is equal to the heat gained by the water in the calorimeter.

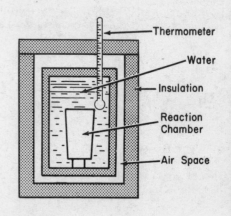

Thermometer

Water

Insulation

Reaction Chamber

Air Space

CALORIMETER

Heat gained by water = Mass of water × change in temperature of water × specific heat of water

Heat gained = Mass × $\triangle T$ × Specific heat of water

$$\text{Mass} = 500 \text{ grams}$$
$$\triangle T = 28° \text{ C.} - 18° \text{ C.} = 10 \text{ C.}°$$
$$\text{Specific heat} = 1 \text{ calorie/gram/C.}°$$

Heat gained = 500 grams × 10 C.° × 1 calorie/gram/C.°
Heat gained = 5,000 calories

2. Ans. **2** The conditions which generally cause the characteristics of a gas to deviate most from the ideal gas laws are low temperature and high pressure. The ideal gas law is a mathematical formula, $\dfrac{P_1 V_1}{T_1} = \dfrac{P_2 V_2}{T_2}$ which expresses the relation among pressure, volume, and temperature. Deviations from this gas law have been experimentally shown to occur at low temperatures and high pressures. An ideal gas approximates a real gas at high temperatures and low pressures where molecules are far apart. A gas that behaves as though

15

the molecules exert no force on each other is called an ideal gas or a perfect gas. In a real gas, the molecules do exert force on each other. The condensation (gas to liquid) of every gas on cooling shows that there are always attractive forces. These forces are not very important when the molecules are far apart (that is, at low pressures) but they become noticeable at higher pressures. The increased pressure forces the molecules closer together. Also, the lower the temperature, the lower is the kinetic energy. As a result of lower temperature, the molecules of the gas are moving more slowly. This decrease in speed means that the molecules will not have sufficient kinetic energy ($\frac{1}{2}mv^2$) to overcome the van der Waals' forces between the molecules. The *Van der Waals'* Forces will liquefy the gas.

3. **Ans.** **2** The problem states that at standard temperature (0° C.), the volume occupied by 1 mole of a gas is 11.2 liters. We know that 1 mole (gram-molecular mass) of a gas at standard temperature (0° C.) and standard pressure (1 atmosphere) occupies 22.4 liters. If the same gas (1 mole) were to occupy 11.2 liters, the pressure must be increased according to *Boyle's Law* ($PV = K$) (at constant temp.). The question asks us to determine the pressure exerted on this gas at standard temperature, 0° C. We use *Boyle's Law* to solve this problem since the temperature is constant. Keep in mind 1 mole of a gas occupies 22.4 liters at *S.T.P.* We solve the problem as follows:

$$P_1V_1 = P_2V_2$$

P_1 = 1 atmosphere
V_1 = 22.4 liters
P_2 = x
V_2 = 11.2 liters

solving for P_2

$$P_2 = \frac{P_1V_1}{V_2}$$

$$P_2 = \frac{1 \text{ atm.} \times 22.4 \text{ liters}}{11.2 \text{ liters}}$$

$$P_2 = 2.00 \text{ atmospheres}$$

4. **Ans.** **3** An endothermic reaction absorbs heat as it progresses. The $\triangle H$ value is positive, since the potential energy of the product is greater than the potential energy of the reactants. Since the heat of reaction values are not listed for any of the four choices on the test, we must consult Table I to determine whether the heat of reaction ($\triangle H$) is positive or negative. If the $\triangle H$ value is positive, the reaction is endothermic. On the other hand if the $\triangle H$ value is negative, the reaction is exothermic. Using *Table I*, we can list the $\triangle H$ value for each of the four choices as follows:

(1) $H_2(g) + \frac{1}{2}O_2(g) \rightarrow H_2O(g)$ $\triangle H = -57.8$ kcal./mole
(2) $S(s) + O_2(g) \rightarrow SO_2(g)$ $\triangle H = -71.0$ kcal./mole
(3) $\frac{1}{2}N_2(g) + O_2(g) \rightarrow NO_2(g)$ $\triangle H = +8.1$ kcal./mole
(4) $C(s) + O_2(g) \rightarrow CO_2(g)$ $\triangle H = -94$ kcal./mole

Obviously, since equation 3 has a heat of reaction of $\triangle H = 8.1$ kcal./mole, this is the endothermic reaction.

The other choices 1, 2, and 4 are exothermic.

5. Ans. 2 The question asks us to determine the boiling point of water when the atmospheric pressure is 23.8 mm. of mercury. Atmospheric pressure is measured by a barometer. The height of the mercury column of the barometer in this question would be 23.8 mm. *Table O* on the Reference Tables for Chemistry tells us that at 25° C., the pressure of water vapor in mm. of Hg is 23.8 mm. When the vapor pressure of the liquid equals the atmospheric pressure, the liquid will boil. Thus, the boiling point of a liquid is that temperature at which the vapor pressure just exceeds the atmospheric pressure. Under standard conditions of temperature (0° C.) and pressure (760 mm.) (*S.T.P.*), water will boil at 100° C. Obviously the vapor pressure of the water under these conditions is 760 mm. In this question the atmospheric pressure on the water is reduced considerably (23.8 mm.) so that the water will boil at a lower temperature (25° C.).

Wrong choices explained:
(1) Table O tells us that at 0° C., the vapor pressure of water is 4.6 mm.
(3) It is explained above.
(4) A considerable amount of atmospheric pressure on the surface of the water would be needed for water to boil at 200° C.

6. Ans. 1 The question tells us that:

$$\text{Atom } X \text{ is represented as: } {}^{210}_{84}X$$
$$\text{Atom } Y \text{ is represented as: } {}^{211}_{84}Y$$

The subscripts (84) refer to the atomic numbers.
The superscripts (210, 211) refer to the atomic weights or mass numbers. Since the atomic numbers are the same and the mass numbers are different, they are considered isotopes of the same element. An isotope is defined as one of two or more forms of atoms with the same atomic number but with different mass number. Recall that if we subtract the atomic number from the mass number, we get the number of neutrons in the nucleus. An isotope of an element differs in the number of neutrons in the nucleus. Therefore, atom X listed in this problem would have 126 neutrons in the nucleus (210 − 84). Element Y would have 127 neutrons in the nucleus (211 − 84).

Wrong choices explained:
(2) If they were isotopes of different elements, they would have different atomic numbers.
(3) Allotropes are two or more forms of the same element. These forms have different energy contents, therefore they have different physical properties. Allotropy is shown by many elements. It is due to the existence of two or more kinds of molecules (containing different numbers of atoms) or to the existence of two or more different crystalline forms. The allotropes of oxygen include O_2 and O_3 (ozone). The allotropic forms of carbon include diamond and graphite. In an allotrope there is no change in the mass number of the element.
(4) It is explained above.

7. Ans. **2** The question asks us to determine the *ionization energy* required to remove the first electron from a barium atom. Ionization energy is the minimum energy needed to remove the most loosely bound electron from an isolated gaseous atom. Ionization energy (also called ionization potential) may be measured in electron-volts or kcal./mole. *Table J* lists the first ionization energy of atoms. Since barium is in Group 2A, we see on *Table J* that its first ionization energy value is 5.2 electron-volts.

Wrong choices explained:
(1) No element has a first ionization energy of 0.9 electron-volts. The number 0.9 refers to the electronegativity value for barium.
(3) Radium has a first ionization energy value of 5.3 electron-volts.
(4) Beryllium has a first ionization energy value of 9.3 electron-volts.

8. Ans. **4** The question asks us to give the correct electron distribution for an element in its ground state with five valence electrons. Valence electrons are the electrons in the outer shell or energy level of the atom. Let us evaluate each diagram, as follows:

(1) According to *Hund's Rule* (explained in choice 4) each p orbital should have at least 1 electron before the extra electrons add to the p_x or p_y orbital. Also an s electron will not be promoted to the p_x or p_y if the p_z orbital is not filled. This will occur if an electron is in the excited state. (Remember we are dealing with an atom in the ground state.) If we have 1 to 8 electrons in the second energy level (L level), in general the order of filling is shown as follows:

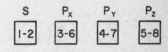

(2) An s electron will not be promoted to the p orbital if the atom is in the ground state. This will take place only when the electron is in the excited state.

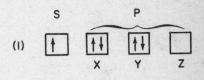

(3)   The electrons will avoid pairing as long as possible to stay in the state of lowest energy. *Hund's Rule* in choice 4 will explain why choice 3 is wrong.

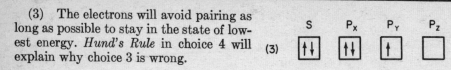

(4)

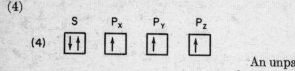

An unpaired electron is indicated by one arrow in a box.

Hund's Rule states—when electrons occupy levels of the same energy in atoms, the most stable arrangement is one where the maximum possible number of unpaired electrons are present with parallel spins. It can also be stated that electrons remain unpaired with parallel spins in orbitals of equal energy until each such orbital has at least one electron in it. In choice 4 we have the most stable arrangement since we have the maximum possible number of unpaired electrons with parallel spins in the p level, p_x, p_y, p_z. The maximum number of unpaired electrons is produced when all equal-energy orbitals are used. Since each orbital corresponds to a preferred direction in space, electrons apparently prefer to move away from each other when they can do so.

9.   Ans.   4   The question asks to determine which element has the highest electronegativity value. Electronegativity is a measure of the attraction an atom has for a shared pair of electrons. Electronegativity values are listed on *Table J*. We have to identify each element first, based on the orbital arrangement given:

(1)   The orbital arrangement is explained as follows:

The first number before the letter indicates the principal energy level. $1s^2 2s^2 2p^2$ The superscript indicates the number of electrons in that sublevel. The letter refers to the sublevel.

The orbital arrangement $1s^2 2s^2 2p^2$ is for the element carbon. Carbon has an electronegativity value of 2.5.

(2) $1s^2 2s^2 2p^6 3s^1$ —This element is sodium. Sodium has an electronegativity value of 0.9.

(3) $1s^2 2s^2 2p^6 3s^2 3p^1$—This element is aluminum. It has an electronegativity value of 1.5.

(4) $1s^2 2s^2 2p^6 3s^2 3p^5$—This element is chlorine. It has an electronegativity value of 3.0. This is the highest electronegativity value of the four choices.

10. Ans. **1** The question asks us to determine which energy level transition represents the greatest absorption of energy. According to the *Bohr Theory* the greatest absorption of energy will occur when $E_2 - E_1 = hv$ has the greatest value. The symbols of the *Bohr Equation* are explained as follows: E_2 = level of higher energy
E_1 = level of lower energy
h = Planck's constant
v = frequency of the absorbed or emitted radiation
hv = energy of a quanta.

The diagram (right) shows the energy of each sublevel. From this diagram we can see that the energy level transition which represents the greatest absorption of energy is from $1s$ to $3p$. The other choices $2p$ to $3s$, $3s$ to $3p$, and $3s$ to $4s$ represent lower values for absorption of energy.

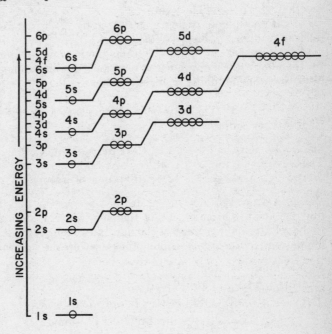

11. Ans. **2** The statement tells us that a pure radioactive sample of $^{232}_{90}$Th now contains atoms of $^{232}_{91}$Pa. The question asks us to determine what particle was emitted by $^{232}_{90}$Th to produce the element $^{232}_{91}$Pa. In this nuclear reaction, a beta particle is emitted from the nucleus. This nuclear reaction could be classified as radioactive decay by beta particle emission. A *beta particle* is an electron ($_{-1}e^0$). A beta particle is formed when a neutron in the

nucleus breaks down into a proton, an electron (beta particle), and a neutrino. The proton is picked up by the nucleus and the electron and neutrino are emitted. In solving nuclear equations such as this one, the sum of the subscripts for the reacting particles must equal the sum of the subscripts for the products, and the sum of the superscripts for the reacting particles must equal the sum of the superscripts for the products. The reaction is explained as follows:

	Th	Pa	x
SUPERSCRIPT	232	= 232 + 0	
SUBSCRIPT	90	= 91 − 1	

$$^{232}_{90}\text{Th} \rightarrow \, ^{232}_{91}\text{Pa} + \, _{-1}e^0$$

Wrong choices explained:

(1)   If a neutron were emitted by $^{232}_{90}\text{Th}$, we would get the following nuclear reaction: $^{232}_{90}\text{Th} \rightarrow \, ^{231}_{90}\text{Th} + \, _0n^1$.

(3)   If an alpha particle were released by $^{232}_{90}\text{Th}$, we would get the following nuclear reaction: $^{232}_{90}\text{Th} \rightarrow \, ^{228}_{88}\text{Ra} + \, _2\text{He}^4$.

(4)   A *gamma ray* is an electromagnetic wave. Gamma rays are emitted by the nucleus in many nuclear reactions. An electromagnetic wave does not alter the atomic number or mass number.

12.   Ans.   4   The statement tells us that a sample of 2 naturally occurring isotopes contains:

$$4 \times 10^{23} \text{ atoms of isotope } ^{24}X$$
and
$$2 \times 10^{23} \text{ atoms of isotope } ^{25}X$$

We have a total of 6×10^{23} atoms of isotopes ^{24}X and ^{25}X. We are asked to find the average atomic mass of the element. The atomic mass of an element is the relative *average* mass of the naturally occurring isotopes of that element. To determine the *average* atomic mass, set up the following relationship:

$$\frac{24 \times \text{Number of atoms of } ^{24}X}{\text{Total number of atoms}}$$

$$+ \frac{25 \times \text{Number of atoms of } ^{25}X}{\text{Total number of atoms}} = \text{Average atomic mass}$$

$$\frac{24 \times 4 \times 10^{23}}{6 \times 10^{23}} + \frac{25 \times 2 \times 10^{23}}{6 \times 10^{23}} = \text{Average atomic mass}$$

$$\frac{24 \times 4}{6} + \frac{25 \times 2}{6} = \text{Average atomic mass}$$

$$\frac{(24 \times 4) + (25 \times 2)}{6} = \text{Average atomic mass.}$$

13.   Ans.   **4**   The property that best accounts for the conductivity of metals is the free electrons in metallic crystals. The metal is held together by the attraction between the positive metallic ions and a cloud of negative electrons. This attraction in metals is called a metallic bond. Since electrons can move at will throughout the metal, a metallic solid is characterized by high electrical conductivity.

Wrong choices explained:

(1)   All atoms contain protons in the nucleus. They do not account for the conductivity of metals.

(2)   Malleability means capable of being shaped by hammering or rolling. This property of metals does not account for the conductivity of metals.

(3)   The filled inner electron shells of most metals does not provide the sea of mobile electrons which accounts for the conductivity of metals.

14.   Ans.   **3**   The correct formula for mercury (I) chloride is Hg_2Cl_2. Hg_2Cl_2 is also called mercurous chloride. In its compounds, mercury shows both $+1$ (mercurous) and $+2$ (mercuric) oxidation states. The mercurous compounds are unusual because they all contain two mercury atoms bound together. In water solutions, the ion is a double ion $(Hg_2)^{++}$ in which there is a covalent bond between the two mercury atoms. In combination with a halide such as the chloride ion, we need 2 chloride ions so that the algebraic sum of the oxidation numbers will equal zero. The formula is worked out as follows:

$$(Hg_2)^{++}Cl_2^{-} \quad (+2 - 2 = 0)$$

Wrong choices explained:

(1) $HgCl_2$ is the formula for mercury (II) chloride. It is also called mercuric chloride.

(2) and (4)   I do not believe the compounds $HgCl_3$ and Hg_3Cl exist. However we do have a complex ion, $HgCl_3^{-}$.

15.   Ans.   **2**   We are given the unbalanced equation:

$$Al_2(SO_4)_3 + Ca(OH)_2 \rightarrow Al(OH)_3 + CaSO_4$$

We are asked to determine the sum of the coefficients for the balanced equation. In order to balance the equation we must write the necessary coefficients before the symbols or formulas, so that there will be the same number of atoms of each element on either side of the arrow. When the equation is balanced properly, it will conform to the *Law of Conservation of Matter*. To balance the equation it is usually best to start balancing with the most complex formula in the equation and then complete the balancing of the other formulas. Since we have 3, SO_4^{-2} radicals, we can place a "3" in front of the $CaSO_4$. Since we have $3Ca^{++}$ on the right side, we must place a "3" in front of $Ca(OH)_2$ to balance the Ca^{++} on the left side. We now have 6 $(OH)^{-}$ groups on the left, so we place a "2" in front of $Al(OH)_3$ to get 6 $(OH)^{-}$ groups on the right side. Now the equation is balanced as follows:

ANSWERS JUNE, 1969 Chemistry** 23

$$Al_2(SO_4)_3 + 3Ca(OH)_2 \rightarrow 2Al(OH)_3 + 3CaSO_4$$

Coefficients → 1 + 3 + 2 + 3 = 9

Therefore the sum of the coefficients is 9.

16. **Ans. 3** The question asks us to determine a characteristic of an ionic solid. Ionic solids or salts have 2 kinds of particles arranged in the crystalline solid—positive and negative ions. In the ionic solid, NaCl, there occurs a strong electrostatic attraction between each sodium ion and every chloride ion in its area. In general, elements of Group 1 and Group 2 metals combined with the Group 6 and Group 7 nonmetals and nonmetallic radicals to form ionic crystals. Some of the characteristics of ionic solids or crystals include the following:

(1) Ionic crystals are relatively hard but also brittle. The hardness of the crystals is due to the strong electrostatic attraction between oppositely charged ions.
(2) Since ionic bonding is strong, these solids or crystals have relatively high melting points and high boiling points.
(3) Ionic crystals, with their ions in fixed positions do not conduct electricity. However, ionic crystals do conduct electricity in the molten state and in solution since the ions are free to move to conduct electricity. In aqueous solution the polar water molecules break down the crystal lattice and the ions are free to move. Remember that ionic solids do not form molecules in a polar (water) solution. They dissociate into ions.
(4) Normal solids which are regarded as non-volatile have infinitesimally small vapor pressures at ordinary temperatures.

Wrong choices explained:
(1) It is explained in statement (3) above.
(2) It is explained in statement (4) above.
(4) It is explained in statement (3) above.

17. **Ans. 2** The type of bonding which accounts for the high boiling point of H_2O as compared with the relatively low boiling point of H_2S is hydrogen bonding. Liquid water contains aggregated groups of the type $(H_2O)_n$. Such aggregates influence any property of water which is related to molecular motion because of additional energy requirements for the destruction of such aggregates. These aggregated groups are due to hydrogen bonding. The comparatively high melting points, high boiling point, low vapor pressure and large heat of fusion and large heat of vaporization are due to hydrogen bonding between water molecules. Hydrogen bonds seem to be formed only between small electronegative atoms like fluorine, oxygen and nitrogen (small in size and high in electronegativity value). A hydrogen bond is a weak chemical bond between a hydrogen atom in one polar molecule and the more electronegative atom in a second polar molecule of the same substance. For example:

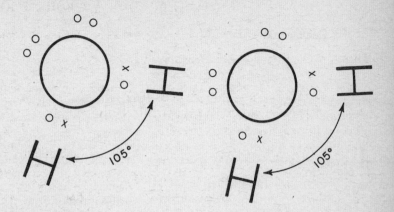

The unexpectedly high boiling point (shown in the graph below) of H_2O in the series H_2O, H_2S, H_2Se, H_2Te is attributed to hydrogen bonding.

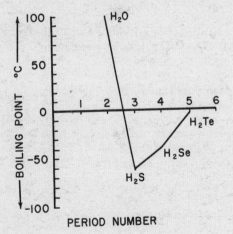

	Boiling Point
H_2O	100° C.
H_2S	−61° C.
H_2Se	−42° C.
H_2Te	−2° C.

Wrong choices explained:

(1) *Van der Waals' Forces* appear to be due to chance distribution of electrons resulting in momentary dipole attractions. These weak forces do not affect the boiling point nearly as much as the hydrogen bonds.

(3) Covalent bonds occur between the hydrogen and oxygen atoms in the water molecule.

(4) Electrovalent or ionic bonds do not enter the picture in this question.

18. Ans. **4** The bond with the least ionic character is the one with the smallest difference in electronegativity value between the elements in the compound. *Table J* lists the electronegativity values for the elements in this question. The electronegativity difference of each compound is listed as follows:

		% Ionic Character
(1)	KBr is $(2.8 - 0.8) = 2.0$	63%
(2)	HF is $(4.0 - 2.1) = 1.9$	59%
(3)	MgO is $(3.5 - 1.2) = 2.3$	74%
(4)	BrCl is $(3.0 - 2.8) = 0.2$	1%

Since the compound exhibiting the bond with the least ionic character has the lowest difference in electronegativity, BrCl is the answer.

19. **Ans. 2** Pure nitrogen combines directly with an active metal to form a nitride. The nitrogen in the nitride has an oxidation number of -3. Examples include:

(A) $3Mg + N_2 \rightarrow Mg_3N_2$ magnesium nitride
(B) $2Al + N_2 \rightarrow 2AlN$ aluminum nitride
(C) $6Na + N_2 \rightarrow 2Na_3N$ sodium nitride

The other choices 1, 3, and 4 cannot be formed when pure nitrogen reacts with an active metal. There is no oxygen involved.

Wrong choices explained:
(1) The nitrate radical is NO_3^-
(3) The nitrite radical is NO_2^-
(4) The pernitrate radical is NO_4^-

20. **Ans. 4** The elements that occupy the zone between the metallic and nonmetallic elements exhibit intermediate properties and are called metalloids. If we draw a stepwise line from boron to polonium we will pass through the metalloids. (Remember this stepwise line separates the metals from the nonmetals on the periodic chart.) The elements which are metalloids include the following: boron, silicon, germanium, arsenic, antimony, tellurium, and polonium. Therefore silicon is a metalloid.

Wrong choices explained:
(1) Fe (iron) is a transition element. All the transition elements are classified as metals.
(2) La (Lanthanum) is another transition element.
(3) Mg (Magnesium) is an active metal. The alkaline earth metals (Group 2A) are active metals.

21. **Ans. 3** The type of element which frequently forms colored compounds and generally exhibits more than one positive oxidation state are the transition elements. Transition elements are located in the "B" Groups and Group VIII of the *Periodic Table*. Transition elements have a deficiency of electrons in the d or f sublevel. In forming compounds, the transition elements (for example Period 4) exhibit many oxidation states presumably because some or all of the $3d$ electrons can also be used with $4s$ electrons in chemical bonding. A typical transition element, nickel, exhibits oxidation states of $+2$ and $+3$. In aqueous solution the Ni^{++} ion gives the solution a green color. In its normal

state, nickel has 8 electrons in the 3d sublevel. The Cu^{++} aqueous ion imparts a blue color to a solution. In its normal state, copper has 10 electrons in 3d sublevel for Cu^+ and 9 electrons in the 3d sublevel for Cu^{++}.

Wrong choices explained:
(1) Alkaline earth metals are Group 2A metals. In general, they tend to lose their 2 outer electrons in combining with other elements. The inner sublevels of Group 2A metals are completely filled; therefore, they are not available for bonding purposes.

(2) Alkali metals are Group 1A metals. The inner sublevels of Group 1A are completely filled; therefore, they are not available for bonding. The one valence electron in the outer level is readily available for bonding purposes.

(4) Noble gases are Group O inert gases. Every energy sublevel is completely filled including the outer level. As a result, they do not ordinarily react with other elements.

22. Ans. 1 The Group in the *Periodic Table* which contains the alkali metals is 1A. The word *alkali* is derived from the Arabic word—al,qili— meaning ashes of the plant saltwort. This substance has marked basic properties since it contains sodium carbonate and potassium carbonate. Thus the first family on the left of the *Periodic Table* is the 1A family also called the alkali metal family. It consists of the elements Li, Na, K, Rb, Cs, and Fr. Because of their strong tendency to form compounds, no member of this family of elements is ever found free in nature.

Wrong choices explained:
(2) The Group II *A* elements are called the alkaline earth metals.
(3) The Group III *A* elements have no special name.
(4) The Group IV *A* elements have no special name.

23. Ans. 4 A Ca^0 atom differs from a Ca^{++} ion in that the atom has a larger radius. When elements in Group 2A such as calcium form ions, they lose electrons since they are metallic. Elements in Group 2A lose 2 electrons to become an ion with a charge of +2. The atomic structure of the neutral calcium atom and the calcium ion are shown as follows:

In the neutral atom we have the same number of protons and electrons (20 protons and 20 electrons). The atomic radius is 1.97 Å.

However in the calcium ion we have 20 protons in the nucleus and 18 electrons in the energy levels. As a result the nuclear charge is more effective

and the electron cloud about the nucleus is drawn in and the atomic radius decreases. Obviously the electrons are pulled toward the nucleus with a greater force. The ionic radius for the Ca^{++} ion is 0.99 Å.

Wrong choices explained:

(1)   We have the same nuclear charge in each case, $+20$ (20 protons).

(2)   As we stated earlier, the Ca^0 atom has an atomic radius of 1.97 Å. The Ca^{++} ion has an ionic radius of 0.99 Å.

(3)   Even though the Ca^{++} ion has lost 2 electrons, the mass number is practically the same since the mass of the electron is *negligible* in comparison to the mass of the protons and neutrons. It is shown as follows:

$$\text{mass of } Ca^{++} \text{ ion} = \text{mass of } Ca^0 - \text{mass of 2 electrons}$$
$$\text{mass of electron} = \tfrac{1}{1837} \times \text{mass of proton}$$
$$= 40.08 - 2(\tfrac{1}{1837})$$
$$= 40.08 - 0.0011$$
$$= 40.0799$$

24.   Ans.   **3**   An atom of fluorine is smaller than an atom of oxygen since fluorine has a greater nuclear charge. The atomic structures for oxygen and fluorine are shown as follows:

$_8O^{16}$ (8P 8N))))   2 6   K L $_9F^{19}$ (9P 10N))))   2 7   K L

Covalent atomic radius = 0.66 Å   Covalent atomic radius = 0.64 Å

In Period 2 of the *Periodic Table*, the electrons are added to the L level as the atomic number increases. However the atomic size continues to decrease as we go from lithium to fluorine. The reason for the decrease in atomic size is that the nuclear charge due to the protons in the nucleus increases causing a greater force of attraction for the L shell electrons. This force of attraction draws the electrons closer to the nucleus. Also as the nuclear charge increases, the ionization energy increases because the nucleus exerts a greater attractive force on the valence electrons in the L shell.

Wrong choices explained:

(1)   An oxidation number is assigned to each element to indicate the number of electrons assumed to be gained, lost or shared in the formation of a compound. This question does not deal with compound formation.

(2)   Fluorine has a larger atomic number (9) than oxygen (8).

(4)   Oxygen has more unpaired electrons according to the following orbital configurations:

Oxygen: $1s^2 2s^2 2p_x^2 \boxed{2p_y^1 2p_z^1}$ unpaired electrons   Oxygen has 2 unpaired electrons.

Fluorine: $1s^2 2s^2 2p_x^2 2p_y^2 \boxed{2p_z^1}$ unpaired electron   Fluorine has 1 unpaired electron.

25. Ans. **2** In a chemical reaction, the number of moles of reactants consumed and the number of moles of products formed are proportional to the numerical coefficients of the substances in the balanced equation. The balanced equation given is:

$$Cu + 4HNO_3 \rightarrow Cu(NO_3)_2 + 2H_2O + 2NO_2$$

The equation tells us that the mole ratio for the reactants $Cu:HNO_3$ is 1:4. The question asks us to determine how many moles of nitric acid are necessary to react with 3 moles of copper. Since the ratio of Cu to HNO_3 is 1:4, 3 moles of copper will react with 12 moles of HNO_3. We can also solve the problem as follows:

$$\frac{\text{mole ratio of Cu}}{\text{mole ratio of HNO}_3} = \frac{\text{moles of Cu used}}{\text{moles of HNO}_3 \text{ used}}$$

$$\frac{1}{4} = \frac{3}{x}$$

$$x = 12 \text{ moles of HNO}_3$$

26. Ans. **1** The statement tells us that fourteen grams of a gas occupies 11.2 liters at *S.T.P.* The problem is to identify the gas. If we determine the density of the gas, we can identify the gas on *Table A*. *Table A* lists the density of some gases in grams/liter at *S.T.P.* To determine the density, we use the following formula:

Density = x
Mass = 14 grams
Volume = 11.2 liters

$$\text{Density} = \frac{\text{Mass}}{\text{Volume}} = x$$

$$= \frac{14 \text{ grams}}{11.2 \text{ liters}} = 1.25 \text{ grams/liter}$$

Table A tells us that nitrogen (N_2) and carbon monoxide (CO) have densities of 1.25 grams/liter. Since nitrogen is not listed as one of the four choices, carbon monoxide is the answer.

ALTERNATE METHOD:

We know that 1 mole of a gas at *S.T.P.* occupies 22.4 liters. If we are told that 14 grams of a gas occupies 11.2 liters, then 28 grams of the gas will occupy 22.4 liters. We can set up a proportion to solve the problem as follows:

$$\frac{11.2 \text{ liters}}{14 \text{ grams}} = \frac{22.4 \text{ l.}}{x} = x = 28 \text{ grams} = 1 \text{ mole}$$

The only gas of the 4 listed which has a molecular weight of 28 is carbon monoxide.

Wrong choices explained:
(2) Hydrogen sulfide (H_2S) has a density of 1.54 g./l. and a molecular weight of 34.

(3)   Hydrogen chloride (HCl) has a density of 1.64 g./l. and a molecular weight of 36.5.

(4)   Sulfur dioxide (SO_2) has a density of 2.93 g./l. and a molecular weight of 64.

27.   Ans.   **1**   The empirical formula represents the constituent elements of a substance and the simplest relative number of atoms of each. The empirical formula for any compound is determined by the following procedure:

STEP 1   The hydrogen halide contains 5% hydrogen and 95% fluorine. This means 100 grams of the compound would contain 5 grams of hydrogen and 95 grams of fluorine. The number of gram-atoms or moles of each element contained in 100 grams of the compound is determined by dividing the amount (percentage × 100 grams) of each element by its atomic mass. Step 1 is solved as follows:

$$\text{Hydrogen} = \frac{5 \text{ grams}}{1 \text{ gram/gram-atom}} = 5.0 \text{ gram-atoms or moles}$$

$$\text{Fluorine} = \frac{95 \text{ grams}}{19 \text{ grams/gram-atom}} = 5.0 \text{ gram-atoms or moles}$$

STEP 2   Divide each of the above gram-atom ratios by the smallest common divisor (5). Step 2 is solved as follows:

$$\text{Hydrogen} = \frac{5.0}{5.0} = 1$$

$$\text{Fluorine} = \frac{5.0}{5.0} = 1$$

STEP 3   Using the atomic ratios determined in Step 2, it is obvious that the empirical formula for this hydrogen halide is HF.

28.   Ans.   **3**   The question asks us to determine which gas is least dense at *S.T.P.* As we pointed out in question 26, the densities of gases are listed on *Table A*. We will set up a list of densities for each gas listed as follows:

Gas	Formula	Density in grams/liter
Hydrogen Chloride	HCl	1.64
Nitrogen Monoxide	NO	1.34
Ammonia	NH_3	0.77
Hydrogen Sulfide	H_2S	1.54

It is obvious that ammonia is the least dense gas of the 4 listed with a value of 0.77 grams/liter.

29. Ans. **3** The number of molecules present in 1 mole of a gas is 6.023×10^{23}. A mole is a gram-molecular mass of a substance. One mole contains *Avogadro's Number* (6.023×10^{23}) of atoms, molecules or ions of a substance at *S.T.P.* One mole of nitrogen (N_2) gas has a mass of 28 grams. Therefore 70 grams would represent $70/28$ moles = 2.5 moles. 2.5 moles of molecules would be equivalent to:

$$2.5 \times 6.023 \times 10^{23} \quad \text{or} \quad \frac{70}{28} \times 6.023 \times 10^{23} \text{ molecules}$$

We can also solve the problem as follows:
(Remember that 1 mole of N_2 has a mass of 28 grams and contains 6.023×10^{23} molecules)

$$\frac{28 \text{ grams}}{6.023 \times 10^{23} \text{ molecules}} = \frac{70 \text{ g.}}{x} \therefore x = \frac{70}{28} \times 6.023 \times 10^{23} \text{ molecules.}$$

30. Ans. **1** The question asks us to determine the mass of NaOH (formula mass-40 grams) needed to prepare 500 ml. of 0.50 molar solution. Molarity is defined as the number of moles of solute per liter of solution. Molarity is a term used to indicate the concentration of an acid, base or salt solution. We can solve this problem using the following formula:

$$\text{Molarity} = \frac{\dfrac{\text{The number of grams given}}{\text{Gram-formula mass of NaOH}}}{\text{The number of liters of solution}} = 0.5 \text{ mole/l.} = \frac{\dfrac{x}{40} \text{ grams/mole}}{\frac{1}{2} \text{ liter}}$$

Molarity = 0.5 mole/liter
The number of grams given = X
Gram-formula mass of NaOH = 40 grams/mole
Number of liters = 500 ml. = $\frac{1}{2}$ liter

$$0.5 = \frac{x}{20}$$
$$x = 10 \text{ grams.}$$

ALTERNATE METHOD:

$$\text{Molarity} = \frac{\text{The number of moles of NaOH}}{\text{The number of liters of solution}}$$

$$0.5 \text{ moles/l.} = \frac{x}{\frac{1}{2} \text{ liter}} = x = \frac{1}{4} \text{ mole.}$$

If 1 mole has a mass of 40 grams, $\frac{1}{4}$ mole has a mass of 10 grams.

31. Ans. **4** The activation energy of a system may be lowered by adding a catalyst. Question 88 of Group 6 in this exam gives an example of a catalyzed reaction. In a catalyzed reaction, there is a change of path or mechanism. Since the rate is now faster, the activation energy for the new path must be lower than for the old path. It is believed that a catalyst somehow provides an alternate pathway or reaction mechanism by which the potential energy barrier between the reactants and products is lowered.

Wrong choices explained:
(1) According to the *Law of Mass Action*, increasing the concentration of

the reactants will increase the rate of the reaction. It will not affect the activation energy of the system.

(2) and (3)   Increases or decreases in pressure do not affect the energy of activation.

32.   **Ans.   1**   The solubility product constant, K_{sp}, is defined as the product of the molar concentrations of the ions each molar concentration being raised to a power equal to the number of moles of that particular ion which appears in the balanced equation representing the ionization. The solubility product constant is used for a saturated solution of a *slightly soluble* salt at a given temperature. The question lists the K_{sp} values of four silver salts. The K_{sp} for each silver salt can be determined by substituting the concentration of each ion in moles/liter and raising each to the appropriate power in the following general equation: (For AgCl, AgBr and AgI)

$$K_{sp} = [Ag^{+1}][X^{-1}]$$

Since each silver halide ionizes slightly in water to form:

$$X = Cl, Br \text{ or } I \mid AgX \rightleftharpoons Ag^+ + X^-$$

For Ag_2S: $\qquad\qquad K_{sp} = [Ag^{+1}]^2[S^{-2}]$

Silver sulfide ionizes very slightly in water to form:

$$Ag_2S \rightleftharpoons 2Ag^+ + S^{-2}$$

These relationships tell us that the higher the concentration of ions, the greater the K_{sp} value, and the greater the solubility. The lower the K_{sp} value, the lower the concentration of each ion, hence the lower the solubility. Since the K_{sp} value for AgCl is the greatest number (1.1×10^{-10}), it would be the most soluble in water. Ag_2S (1.0×10^{-50}) would be the least soluble.

33.   **Ans.   4**   The compound $KClO_3$ is least soluble in 100 ml. of water at 10° C. Using *Table B* as shown at the right, we can list each salt with its corresponding solubility in grams/100 ml. of H_2O at 10° C.

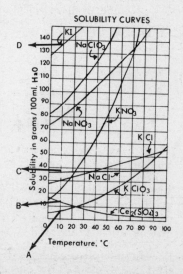

	Salt	Approximate Solubility in grams/100 ml. of H_2O
A	$KClO_3$	5 grams
B	$Ce_2(SO_4)_3$	14 grams
C	NaCl	37 grams
D	KI	137 grams

Therefore $KClO_3$ is the least soluble salt at 10° C. The others are obviously more soluble at 10° C.

34. Ans. **2** We are asked to consider the effect of increased pressure on the following system in equilibrium at a constant temperature.

$$N_2(g) + 3H_2(g) = 2NH_3(g)$$

$$\downarrow \text{ Reactants} = 4 \quad \downarrow \text{Product} = 2$$

Molar Volumes = 1   3   2

According to *Le Chatelier's Principle*, when an equilibrium is subjected to a stress, it is displaced in the direction which will relieve the stress. Therefore, an increase in pressure on this system will shift the equilibrium to the side with the smaller molar volume (number of moles of gas) which is the product side, NH_3. We have 4 molar volumes for the reactants and two molar volumes for the product.

Wrong choices explained:

(1) A decrease in pressure will shift the equilibrium to the left.

(3) Increased pressure will have no effect on the equilibrium when the molar volumes on each side are the same.

(4) An increase in pressure on this system does not change the value of the equilibrium constant. The only factor that affects the value of the equilibrium constant is the temperature.

35. Ans. **2** We are given the following reaction:

$$2Al(s) + \tfrac{3}{2}O_2(g) = Al_2O_3(s)$$

$$\triangle H = -399 \text{ kcal./mole}$$

We are asked to determine the number of kilocalories of energy liberated by the oxidation of 27 grams of aluminum. 1 mole of aluminum has a mass of 27 grams. The equation tells us if 2 moles or 54 grams of aluminum are oxidized, we have an exothermic $\triangle H$ value of -399 kcal./mole. Therefore, if 1 mole of aluminum is oxidized we will have a $\triangle H$ value of $\dfrac{-399}{2}$ = approximately -200 kcal./mole. We can set up a proportion to solve the problem as follows:

$$\frac{2 \text{ moles of aluminum}}{399 \text{ kcal./mole of } Al_2O_3} = \frac{1 \text{ mole of aluminum}}{x}$$

$$2x = 399$$

$$x = \text{approximately } 200 \text{ kcal./mole of energy}$$

36. Ans. **3** A chemical reaction must be spontaneous if it results in an energy loss and an entropy increase. The word *spontaneous* means to have the potential to proceed without the assistance of an external agent. A spontaneous reaction depends on the balance between 2 fundamental tendencies in nature; (1) Toward a lower energy state, and (2) Toward randomness. A system always tends to change from a state of higher energy to a state of lower energy. For chemical systems this energy is represented mathematically as $\triangle H$. This tendency in nature favors the exothermic reaction, in which $\triangle H$ is negative. Entropy is a measure of the disorder of randomness of a system. The more

the molecules in a system are distributed in a disordered or random manner, the greater is the entropy. There is a tendency for processes to occur which lead to the highest possible state of disorder.

37. Ans. **3** In the reaction $H_2SO_4 + HOH \rightarrow H_3O^+ + X$, the species represented by X may be HSO_4^-. Since H_2SO_4 (sulfuric acid) is a diprotic acid, it ionizes in 2 steps as follows:

STEP 1 $H_2SO_4 + H_2O \rightarrow H_3O^+ +$ | X |
                                                | HSO_4^- |

where $X = HSO_4^-$

STEP 2 $HSO_4^- + H_2O \rightarrow H_3O^+ + SO_4^{-2}$

Since the question deals with step 1, $X = HSO_4^-$. The H_2SO_4 is a proton donor and the H_2O is a proton acceptor. The species SO_3^{-2}, $H_3SO_4^+$ and OH^- are not involved in this reaction.

38. Ans. **1** During acid-base neutralization, the number of moles of hydroxide ions (OH^-) that will react with one mole of hydrogen ions is one. An acid-base neutralization is a reaction where an acid and base combine to form a salt and water. A neutralization reaction goes to completion because water is formed. The net ionic equation for neutralization is shown as follows:

$$H^+ + OH^- \rightarrow H_2O$$

The mole ratio of $H^+:OH^-$ is 1:1. Thus, if we use 1 mole of H^+ ions, 1 mole of OH^- will react with it. For any neutralization reaction, the mole ratio of $H^+:OH^-$ is always 1:1.

39. Ans. **2** The question asks us to determine how many milliliters of 0.20 M H_2SO_4 are required to completely titrate 40 ml. of 0.10 M $Ca(OH)_2$. Titration is the process of determining the volume or weight of the reagent solution just required for complete reaction with the sample. The solution used for the titration is of known strength and is called a standard solution. The neutralization reaction in this question is shown as follows:

$$H_2SO_4 + Ca(OH)_2 \rightarrow CaSO_4 + 2H_2O$$

To solve the problem, we must first determine the number of moles of $Ca(OH)_2$ formed in the reaction.

molarity = 0.1 M
number of liters = 40 ml. = 0.04 liter
number of moles = x

$$\text{molarity} = \frac{\text{number of moles}}{\text{number of liters}}$$

$$0.1 \text{ mole/l.} = \frac{x}{0.04 \text{ l.}}$$

$$x = 0.004 \text{ mole.}$$

The number of moles of $Ca(OH)_2$ formed is 0.004. In our balanced equation we see that the mole ratio of $H_2SO_4 : Ca(OH)_2$ is $1:1$. Therefore 0.004 moles of H_2SO_4 are also formed. We can now proceed to find the number of milliliters of 0.2 M H_2SO_4 are needed. We solve the problem as follows:

$$molarity = \frac{number\ of\ moles}{number\ of\ liters}$$

molarity = 0.2 M
number of moles = 0.004
number of liters = x

$$0.2\ mole/l. = \frac{0.004\ mole}{x} = 0.2x = 0.004$$

$$x = 0.02\ liter = 20\ milliliters$$

ALTERNATE SOLUTION:

We can simplify this problem in the following way. Since the total positive valence of the hydrogen in H_2SO_4 is +2 and the total positive valence of calcium in $Ca(OH)_2$ is +2, the normality = 2 × molarity in each case. Using this equation we can solve the problem as follows:

$$\text{Acid} \qquad\qquad \text{Base}$$
$$\text{milliliters} \times \text{Normality} = \text{milliliters} \times \text{Normality}$$
$$x \qquad\times\qquad 0.4 \quad = \quad 40\ ml. \times \qquad 0.2$$

milliliters of H_2SO_4 = x
Normality of H_2SO_4 $2 \times M = 2 \times 0.2 = 0.4$
milliliters of $Ca(OH)_2$ = 40 ml.
Normality of $Ca(OH)_2$ $2 \times M = 2 \times 0.1 = 0.2$

$$0.4x = 8.0$$
$$x = \frac{80}{4} = 20\ ml.$$

40. **Ans. 2** The weakest acid is boric acid. Weak electrolytes (such as we have in this question) in aqueous solution attain an equilibrium between ions and the undissociated compound. Remember that weak electrolytes are only slightly ionized. The equilibrium constant for such systems is called the ionization constant. The ionization constant for the ionization of acids is a convenient method for comparing the relative strength of acids. Ionization constants can be calculated for all acids that are not completely ionized. The larger the ionization constant, the stronger the acid. Also, the smaller the ionization constant the weaker the acid. Since 5.8×10^{-10} is the smallest value of the 4 acids listed, boric acid is the weakest acid. Phosphoric is the strongest. *Table M* lists the ionization constant of these 4 acids as follows:

Acid	Formula	Ionization Constant
Acetic	CH_3COOH	1.8×10^{-5}
Boric	H_3BO_3	5.8×10^{-10}
Carbonic	H_2CO_3	4.3×10^{-7}
Phorphoric	H_3PO_4	7.5×10^{-3}

41. Ans. **3** According to the *Brönsted-Lowry Theory*, the species that is amphoteric (amphiprotic) is NH_3. The *Brönsted-Lowry Theory* states that acids are proton donors and bases are proton acceptors. An amphoteric (amphiprotic) substance is one which can act either as an acid or as a base, depending on its chemical environment. According to the *Brönsted-Lowry Theory*, substances such as H_2O, HSO_4^-, and NH_3, which can either donate or accept a proton are also amphiprotic. The amphiprotic nature of NH_3 is shown as follows:

$$\text{Acid (proton donor):} \quad NH_3 \rightarrow NH_2^- + H^+$$
$$\text{Base (proton acceptor):} \quad NH_3 + H^+ \rightarrow NH_4^+$$

Also, *Table H* tells us that NH_3 can function either as an acid or as a base: Notice that NH_3 is listed in the conjugate acid column as well as in the conjugate base column. H_2O and HSO_4^- are also listed in both columns.

Wrong choices explained:
(1) According to *Table H*, Cl^- is a *Brönsted-Lowry* base since it can accept a proton. It cannot donate a proton.
(2) According to *Table H*, H_3O^+ is a *Brönsted-Lowry* acid, since it can donate a proton. It cannot accept a proton.
(4) According to *Table H*, NH_4^+ is a *Brönsted-Lowry* acid, since it can donate a proton. It cannot accept a proton.

42. Ans. **1** In the reaction given, the two bases are NH_3 and HSO_4^-. The reaction is given as:

$$\xleftarrow{\quad\quad\quad\quad\quad}$$
$$\boxed{\text{TO THE LEFT}}$$

			Acid_1		Base_2
			Proton Donor		Proton Acceptor
NH_3	$+$	H_2SO_4 $=$	NH_4^+	$+$	HSO_4^-
Proton Acceptor		Proton Donor			
Base_1		Acid_2			

$$\boxed{\text{TO THE RIGHT}}$$
$$\xrightarrow{\quad\quad\quad\quad\quad}$$

The *Brönsted-Lowry Theory* states acids are proton donors and bases are proton acceptors. In the reaction listed above, we have 2 *Brönsted-Lowry* acids and 2 *Brönsted-Lowry* bases. When the reaction is preceding to the right, H_2SO_4 (Acid_2) donates a proton to NH_3 (Base_1). When the reaction is preceding to the left NH_4^+ (Acid_1) donates a proton to the HSO_4^- (Base_2). Thus the two *Brönsted-Lowry* bases are NH_3 and HSO_4^-.

Wrong choices explained:
(2) NH_3 is a *Brönsted-Lowry* base and H_2SO_4 is a *Brönsted-Lowry* acid.
(3) NH_4^+ and H_2SO_4 are *Brönsted-Lowry* acids.
(4) H_2SO_4 is a *Brönsted-Lowry* acid and HSO_4^- is a *Brönsted-Lowry* base.

43.   Ans.   **2**   A water solution of KCl would have a pH closest to 7. The pH of a solution is equal to the logarithm of the reciprocal of the hydrogen ion concentration when this concentration is expressed in moles/liter. It is shown as follows:

$$pH = \log \frac{1}{H^+} \quad \text{also} \quad H^+ = 10^{-pH}$$

When the pH is lower than 7, the solution is acidic since we have more H^+ than OH^- ions. At pH 7, the solution is neutral since we have equal numbers of H^+ and OH^- ions. Above pH 7, the solution is basic since we have more OH^- than H^+ ions. When the salt KCl is dissolved in water, it dissociates completely as follows:

$$KCl(s) \xrightarrow[\text{Dissociates}]{\text{in } H_2O} K^+(aq) + Cl^-(aq)$$

$$H_2O \underset{\text{Slightly ionizes}}{\overrightarrow{\qquad\qquad}} \underset{\underset{KOH}{\uparrow}}{OH^-} + \underset{\underset{HCl}{\uparrow}}{H^+}$$

Table M tells us that HCl is completely ionized and KOH is also completely ionized or dissociated in dilute solution. Therefore we get the maximum number of H^+ and OH^- formed. Since the acid and base ionize to the same extent, we get equal numbers of H^+ and OH^- ions. Therefore the solution is neutral and the pH is 7.

44.   Ans.   **1**   The halogen which would not be expected to have a positive oxidation state when combined with oxygen is fluorine. The halogens are Group 7A elements. The oxidation states for each element are listed in the upper right-hand corner of every box on the *Periodic Table*. The oxidation number or oxidation state of an element is assigned to each element to indicate the number of electrons assumed to be gained, lost or shared in the formation of a compound. Fluorine is the most electronegative of all elements with a value of 4.0. It has an oxidation state of -1. Therefore any element (such as oxygen, electronegativity value, 3.5) combining with fluorine would be less electronegative and would have a positive oxidation state. The elements chlorine, bromine and iodine would have positive oxidation states when combined with oxygen since their electronegativities are all lower than oxygen (chlorine 3.0, bromine 2.8, iodine 2.5).

45.   Ans.   **3**   The overall redox reaction is given as:

$$Cl_2(g) + 2Br^-(aq) = 2Cl^-(aq) + Br_2(l)$$

In this reaction the bromine is oxidized by losing one electron per ion to form liquid bromine (Br_2). The chlorine is reduced by gaining one electron per atom to form the chloride ions, $2Cl^-$. The ion-electron equations for the oxidation and reduction reactions are shown as follows:

Oxidation half-reaction:
$$2Br^- - 2e^- \rightarrow Br_2(l)$$

Reduction half-reaction:
$$Cl_2(g) + 2e^- \rightarrow 2Cl^-$$

To obtain the E° values for each half-reaction, we consult *Table L*. *Table L* lists the E° values for the oxidation half-reactions only. For the reduction half-reaction, the sign (+ or −) for the E° value on *Table L* must be reversed. Thus the value for the reduction half-reaction:

$$Cl_2(g) + 2e^- \rightarrow 2Cl^- \text{ is } +1.36 \text{ volts.}$$

The E° value for the oxidation reaction:

$$2Br^- - 2e^- \rightarrow Br_2(l)$$

is listed as −1.07 volts. The total or net E° value is determined by adding the E° values for the half-reactions. The problem is solved as follows:

Oxidation half-reaction:	$2Br^-(aq) - 2e^- \rightarrow Br_2(l)$	E° = −1.07 volts
Reduction half-reaction:	$Cl_2(g) + 2e^- \rightarrow 2Cl^-(aq)$	E° = +1.36 volts
	$2Br^-(aq) + Cl_2(g) \rightarrow Br_2(l) + 2Cl^-(aq)$	E° = +0.29 volt

Thus, the net potential E°, equals +0.29 volt.

46. **Ans. 1** For neutral molecules such as $K_2Cr_2O_7$, the oxidation numbers of all the atoms must add algebraically up to zero. Potassium has an oxidation number of +1 in all compounds. Oxygen has an oxidation number of −2 in all compounds except in peroxides such as H_2O_2 when it is −1. Thus in the compound $K_2Cr_2O_7$, potassium has a total value of $2 \times (+1) = +2$, oxygen has a total value of $7 \times (-2) = -14$. The total charge on the chromium is +12 in order that the algebraic sum of the oxidation numbers of all atoms add up to zero. Since we have 2 atoms of chromium (Cr_2), the oxidation number of each chromium atom is $+\frac{12}{2} = +6$. We can summarize this question using the following chart:

Molecular Formula	K_2^{+1}	Cr_2^{+6}	O_7^{-2}	
Algebraic Sum of the Oxidation Numbers	+2	+ 12	− 14	= 0

47.   Ans.   **2**   During the electrolysis of fused (molten) calcium fluoride the following action takes place. It is described in the diagram below:

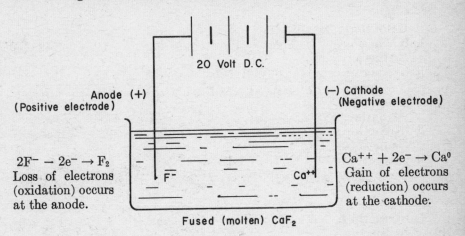

$$CaF_2 \xrightarrow[\text{Dissociates}]{\text{in molten state}} Ca^{++} + 2F^-$$

Final reaction at electrodes: $CaF_2 \rightarrow Ca^0 + F_2{}^0$
The diagram tells us that the fluoride ion (F^-) (an anion) is attracted to the anode. At the anode it loses an electron to become atomic fluorine. At the cathode the calcium ion Ca^{++} (a cation) gains 2 electrons to become atomic calcium, Ca^0.

Wrong choices explained:
(1)   The reaction does not occur since calcium is not oxidized.
(3)   This reaction occurs at the anode.
(4)   Calcium is not oxidized in this reaction, it is reduced.

48.   Ans.   **4**   On the basis of *Table L*, the reaction which occurs spontaneously is the one in which the net E° value is positive. We can determine the net E° values using the E° values on *Table L* for each half-reaction. Remember that all half-reactions are shown as oxidation reactions on *Table L*. For the reduction reaction, we must reverse the sign of the E° value. The E° value does not depend on the number of atoms or ions involved in the redox reaction. The only reaction which gives us a positive E° value is the following:

Oxidation half-reaction: $2I^-(aq) - 2e^- \rightarrow I_2(s)$ $E° = -0.53$ volts

Reduction half-reaction: $Br_2{}^0(l) + 2e^- \rightarrow 2Br^-(aq)$ $E° = +1.07$ volt

$2I^-(aq) + Br_2{}^0(l) \rightarrow I_2(s) + 2Br^-(aq)$ Net $E° = +0.54$ volt

Wrong choices explained:
Choices (1), (2) and (3)   do not occur spontaneously since each net E° value is negative.

(1)   **Oxidation**
    half-reaction: $Pb^0(s) \rightarrow Pb^{++}(aq) + 2e^-$ $E° = +0.13$ volt
    Reduction
    half-reaction: $Co^{+2}(aq) + 2e^- \rightarrow Co^0(s)$ $E° = -0.28$ volt

$$Pb^0(s) + Co^{+2}(aq) \rightarrow Co^0(s) + Pb^{++}(aq) \quad \text{Net } E° = -0.15 \text{ volt}$$

(2)   **Oxidation**
    half-reaction: $2Cl^-(aq) - 2e^- \rightarrow Cl_2(g)$ $E° = -1.36$ volts
    Reduction
    half-reaction: $I_2^0(s) + 2e^- \rightarrow 2I^-(aq)$ $E° = +0.53$ volt

$$2Cl^-(aq) + I_2^0 \rightarrow Cl_2(g) + 2I^-(aq) \quad \text{Net } E° = -0.83 \text{ volt}$$

(3)   **Oxidation**
    half-reaction: $Ag^0(s) - 2e^- \rightarrow 2Ag^+(aq)$ $E° = -0.80$ volt
    Reduction
    half-reaction: $Sr^{+2}(aq) + 2e^- \rightarrow Sr^0(s)$ $E° = -2.89$ volts

$$Ag^0(s) + Sr^{+2}(aq) \rightarrow 2Ag^+(aq) + Sr^0(s) \quad \text{Net } E° = -3.69 \text{ volts}$$

49.   **Ans. 1** Using the rules for the oxidation states of oxygen and hydrogen from question 46, we can insert them in the given equation. The halides (Group 7A elements) have an oxidation state of -1 when combined with the Group 1A elements. Bromine (Br_2) has an oxidation number of zero since the electrons shared between the two like atoms are divided equally between the sharing atoms. The sulfur in the sulfate ion always has an oxidation number of $+6$. Now we can determine the oxidation number of manganese since the algebraic sum of the oxidation numbers of a compound is zero. In MnO_2, oxygen has a total value of $2(-2) = -4$. Therefore, manganese must be $+4$. In $MnSO_4$, the sulfate ion has an oxidation state of -2. Therefore manganese must be $+2$. The oxidation numbers are shown in the reaction given as follows:

$$2K^{+1}Br^{-1} + 3H_2^{+1}S^{+6}O_4^{-2} + Mn^{+4}O_2^{-2} \rightarrow$$
$$2K^{+1}H^{+1}S^{+6}O_4^{-2} + Mn^{+2}S^{+6}O_4^{-2} + 2H_2^{+1}O^{-2} + Br_2^0$$

Therefore, manganese changes from $+4$ in MnO_2 to $+2$ in $MnSO_4$. In order for manganese to change from a $+4$ oxidation state to a $+2$ oxidation state, it has to gain 2 electrons. This can be shown by the ion-electron equation as follows:

$$Mn^{+4} + 2e \rightarrow Mn^{+2}$$

If an atom gains electrons in a redox reaction, it is reduced. Thus, manganese is reduced from $+4$ to $+2$.

50. Ans. 4 The structural formula for 1,2 dichloropropane is:

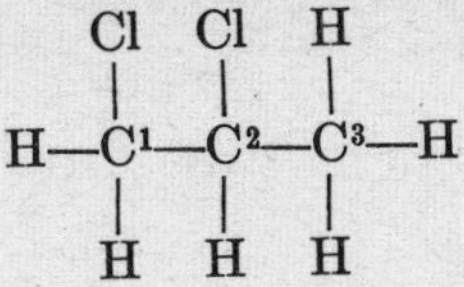

$$\begin{array}{ccccc} Cl & & Cl & & H \\ | & & | & & | \\ H-C^1 & - & C^2 & - & C^3-H \\ | & & | & & | \\ H & & H & & H \end{array}$$

The Geneva or (I.U.C.) (International Union of Chemists) rules for the naming of organic compounds include the following:

(1) We name the compound according to the longest parent chain of carbon atoms using the suffix that indicates the number of bonds between two carbons. We use the suffix *ane* for a single bond, *ene* for a double bond and *yne* for a triple bond.

(2) We use a prefix for all radicals or halide groups attached to this chain such as methyl for CH_3, chloro for Cl, etc.

(3) We indicate the position of the radical or halide group on the carbon chain by numbering the carbon atom so that the name of the compound has the lowest numbers.

According to the rules, 1,2 dichloropropane is set up as follows: The longest parent chain of carbon atoms is propane. Propane is an alkane with 3 carbons. An alkane has all single bonds. 1,2 dichloro means to the first and second carbon atoms, we have one Cl atom attached to each.

Wrong choices explained:

(1) 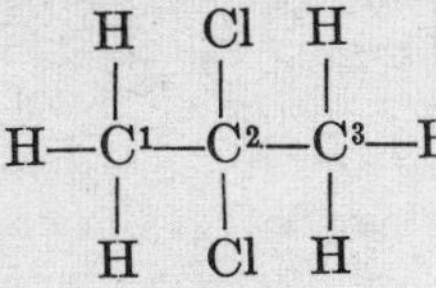 $\begin{array}{ccccc} H & & Cl & & H \\ | & & | & & | \\ H-C^1 & - & C^2 & - & C^3-H \\ | & & | & & | \\ H & & Cl & & H \end{array}$ is 2,2 dichloropropane

---

(2) 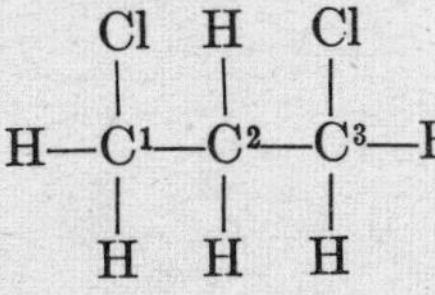 $\begin{array}{ccccc} Cl & & H & & Cl \\ | & & | & & | \\ H-C^1 & - & C^2 & - & C^3-H \\ | & & | & & | \\ H & & H & & H \end{array}$ is 1,3 dichloropropane

---

(3) 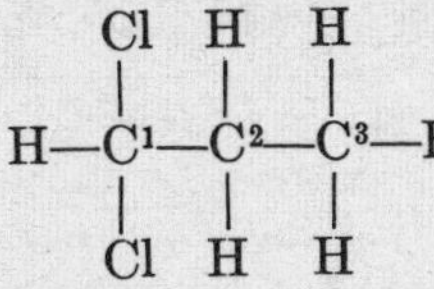 $\begin{array}{ccccc} Cl & & H & & H \\ | & & | & & | \\ H-C^1 & - & C^2 & - & C^3-H \\ | & & | & & | \\ Cl & & H & & H \end{array}$ is 1,1 dichloropropane

51. Ans. 3 The organic compound $C_3H_5(OH)_3$ is classified as an alcohol. It is called glycerol or glycerine. It is a polyhydroxy alcohol. The structural formula for glycerol is shown as follows:

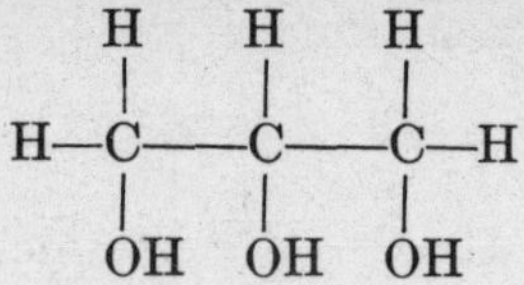

$$
\begin{array}{ccccc}
 & H & & H & & H \\
 & | & & | & & | \\
H- & C & - & C & - & C & -H \\
 & | & & | & & | \\
 & OH & & OH & & OH \\
\end{array}
$$

Wrong choices explained:

(1)   A carbohydrate contains the elements carbon, hydrogen and oxygen. The ratio of hydrogen to oxygen is almost always 2:1. Examples include glucose, $C_6H_{12}O_6$ and sucrose, $C_{12}H_{22}O_{11}$.

(2)   An ester has the general formula RCOOR'. It is the product of an esterification reaction (explained in question 104 of this exam) CH_3COOCH_3— methyl acetate (methyl ethanoate) is an example.

(4)   An organic acid has the general formula RCOOH. Examples include the following:

Formula	Common Name	Geneva Name
HCOOH	Formic acid	Methanoic acid
CH_3COOH	Acetic acid	Ethanoic acid

52.   Ans.   4   Two or more compounds with the same molecular formula but different structural formulas are called isomers. The only molecular formula that can have isomers is C_4H_8. The isomers include 1-butene, 2-butene and methylpropene. The structural formulas are shown as follows:

(a) 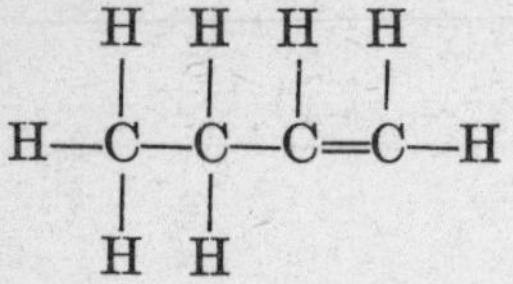 $H-C-C-C=C-H$ is 1-Butene

(b) 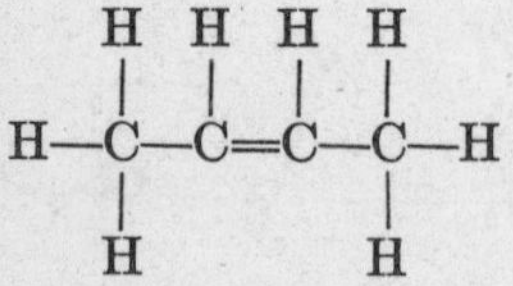 $H-C-C=C-C-H$ is 2-Butene

(c) 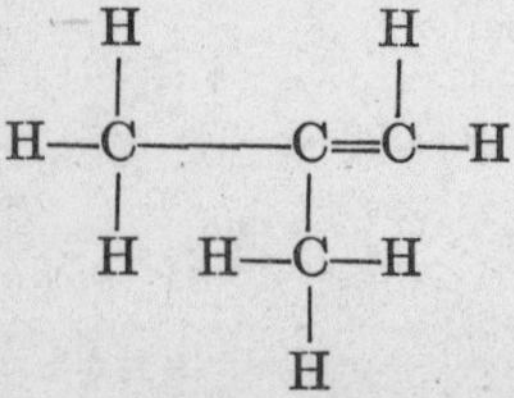 $H-C——C=C-H$ is methylpropene.

Wrong choices explained:

(1) C_2H_4
     (ethene)

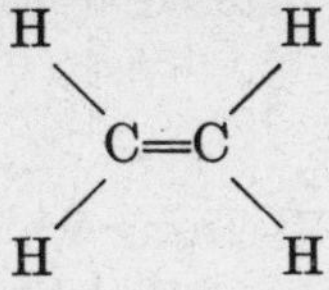

$$\begin{matrix} H & & H \\ & \diagdown & \diagup & \\ & C = C & \\ & \diagup & \diagdown & \\ H & & H \end{matrix}$$

It can have only 1 structural formula.

(2) C_2H_2
     (ethyne)

H—C≡C—H

It can have only 1 structural formula.

(3) C_2H_6
     (ethane)

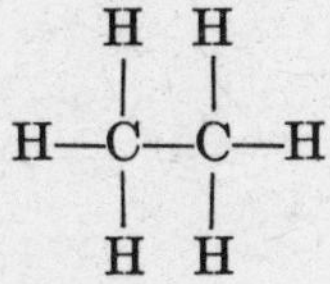

$$\begin{matrix} & H & H \\ & | & | \\ H—&C—&C—H \\ & | & | \\ & H & H \end{matrix}$$

It can have only 1 structural formula.

53. Ans. **2** The study of the hydrocarbons is simplified by the fact that they can be divided into distinct series in which the composition of the first member of each series differs from that of the second by a CH_2 group. This relationship in such a series is called a homologous series. These hydrocarbon series include the alkane, alkene, alkyne and the benzene series. If we take any 2 consecutive members of any one of these series, they would differ by a CH_2 group. For example in the alkane series, CH_4, methane, differs from C_2H_6, ethane, by a CH_2 group. Propane, C_3H_8 differs from butane, C_4H_{10} by a CH_2 group.

54. Ans. **3** The type of reaction which occurs between C_2H_4 (*ethene*) and bromine (Br_2) is an addition reaction. An addition reaction is one in which atoms (*usually chlorine or bromine*) are added to an unsaturated organic molecule. An unsaturated organic molecule contains a double or triple bond. The reaction for the addition of bromine to ethene is shown as follows:

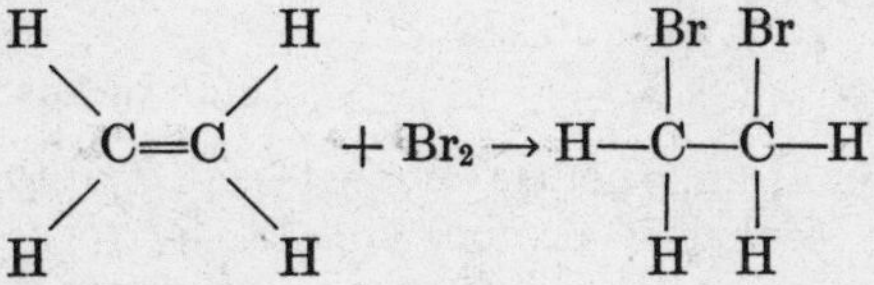

$$\begin{matrix} H & & H \\ & \diagdown & \diagup & \\ & C = C & \\ & \diagup & \diagdown & \\ H & & H \end{matrix} \quad + Br_2 \rightarrow \begin{matrix} & Br & Br \\ & | & | \\ H—&C—&C—H \\ & | & | \\ & H & H \end{matrix}$$

Wrong choices explained:

(1) Polymerization involves the chemical combination of a number of identical or similar molecules (monomers) to form a complex molecule of high molecular weight. Polyethylene, a polymer, is formed from basic units of the monomer, ethylene, which in the presence of a suitable catalyst will undergo an addition reaction to form the long chain polymer.

(2) Substitution is a reaction in which an atom or radical group in a saturated hydrocarbon is replaced by another atom or radical.

(4) Esterification is a reaction in which an alcohol reacts with an acid (in the presence of concentrated sulfuric acid) to yield an ester and water.

55. Ans. **2** As the number of particles oxidized during a chemical reaction increases, the number of particles reduced also increases. Oxidation and reduction occur simultaneously; therefore total electron loss equals total electron gain. In redox reactions, the increase or decrease of oxidation numbers results from a transfer of electrons from one atom or ion to another atom or ion. Therefore as the number of particles oxidized (losing electrons) increases, the number of particles reduced (gaining electrons) also increases.

56. Ans. **1** As the temperature of ethyl alcohol decreases, its vapor pressure decreases. This is shown on the vapor pressure-temperature graph below. Vapor pressure is defined as the pressure exerted by vapor which is in equilibrium with the liquid. The equilibrium between a liquid and its vapor is dependent on the temperature. The vapor pressure curve for ethanol is also shown in the graph for questions 61 to 65. The graph tells us that a temperature decrease will result in a decrease in vapor pressure. Also, an increase in temperature will result in a vapor pressure increase.

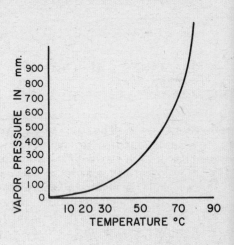

57. Ans. **2** As the sulfur atom becomes a sulfide ion, the radius increases. The atomic structure of the atom and the ion is shown as follows:

Sulfur atom (S^0)   *Sulfide ion* (S^{-2})

Atomic radius = 1.27Å   Ionic radius = 1.84Å

Notice that the sulfur atom is neutral since it has 16 protons and 16 electrons. However the sulfide ion has 16 protons and 18 electrons. Therefore the ionic radius is larger than the atomic radius because the same nuclear charge ($+16$) has a weaker attractive force on the 18 electrons compared to the 16 electrons in the neutral atom. As a result the size of the particle increases.

58. Ans. **3** As the rate of a chemical reaction increases due to an increase in the concentration of the reactants, the activation energy for that reaction remains the same. It is true according to the *Law of Mass Action* that an increase in concentration will increase the rate of a chemical reaction. However the increase in concentration of the reactant will not affect the energy of activation. I believe the only factor which affects the energy of activation is a catalyst.

59. **Ans. 2** As the elements in Group 2A are considered in order of increasing atomic number, the tendency of each successive atom to form a positive ion generally increases. Two factors related to this increase are the ionization potential and the atomic radius. The ionization potentials and covalent atomic radii values for the Group 2A elements are shown as follows:

Element	Ionization Potential in electron-volts	Covalent atomic radius in Angstrom units
Beryllium	9.3	1.12
Magnesium	7.6	1.60
Calcium	6.1	1.97
Strontium	5.7	2.15
Barium	5.2	2.17
Radium	5.3	2.20

Ionization potential is defined as the minimum energy needed to remove an electron from an isolated gaseous atom. In Group 2A, as the atomic number increases the ionization potential decreases; therefore as the atomic number increases it is easier to remove an electron. As a result, it is easier to form a positive ion. Also, as the atomic radius increases with increasing atomic number, the outer electrons are easier to remove since the nuclear attraction for these valence electrons is diminished.

60. **Ans. 3** As chloride ions are added to the following system at equilibrium (at constant temperature)

$$AgCl_{(s)} = Ag^+_{(aq)} + Cl^-_{(aq)}$$

the value of the equilibrium constant remains the same. The equilibrium constant for this system can be determined as follows:

$$K_e = \frac{[Ag^+][Cl^-]}{[AgCl_{(s)}]}$$

therefore $[Ag^+][Cl^-] = K_e[AgCl_{(s)}] = K_{sp}$

According to LeChatelier's Principle, a stress on a system in equilibrium will cause it to change in such a way as to relieve the stress. As more chloride ions are added to the system, the stress produced will shift the equilibrium to the left forming more solid AgCl. Thus, there will be an increase in both the concentration of Cl^- and AgCl and a decrease in the concentration of the Ag^+. These changes will not change the equilibrium constant which is also called the solubility product constant, K_{sp}. (K_{sp} is explained in the answer to question 32.) The solubility product constant (K_{sp}) tells us that the product of the concentrations of the solute ions in a saturated solution of a very slightly soluble ionic solid is constant at a given temperature. The only factor that will change the equilibrium constant is temperature. Temperature will cause a shift in the reaction only one way with nothing being replenished. The direction of the shift would depend upon whether it is an exothermic or endothermic reaction.

PART TWO

GROUP 1

Base your answers to questions 61 through 65 on the graph below, which represents the relationship between the equilibrium vapor pressure and temperature of four liquids.

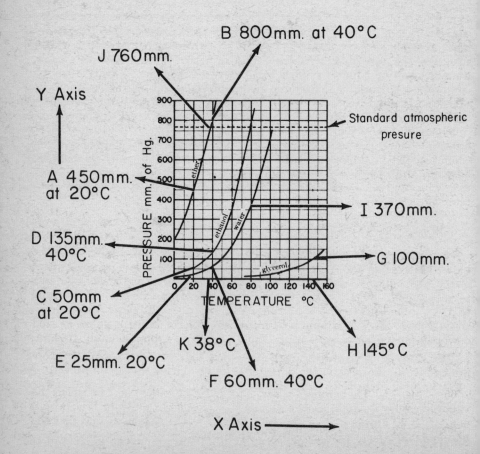

61. Ans. 1 The question asks us to determine the greatest increase in vapor pressure from 20° C. to 40° C. Vapor pressure of a liquid means the partial pressure of vapor in equilibrium with the liquid. Vapor pressures increase with rising temperature. The vapor pressure diagram for this group indicates this fact. Using our labeled diagram on the right, we see that the vapor pressure of ether would increase the most if its temperature were changed from 20° C. to 40° C. From point A to point B we have an increase of $(B - A) = 800 - 450 = 350$ mm. for ether. For ethanol we have a change from C to D. The difference $(D - C) = 135 - 50 = 85$ mm. For water we have a change from E to F. The difference $(F - E) = 60 - 25 = 35$ mm. The curve for glycerol is not shown for the 20° C. - 40° C. range. However if it were it would be a very small change based on the curve given.

62. Ans. 3 Recall from question 5 that the boiling point of a liquid is defined as the point at which the vapor pressure of the liquid equals the atmospheric pressure. If the atmospheric pressure on the surface of the glycerol equals 100 mm. of Hg, its boiling point at 100 mm. will be 145° C. On our labeled graph point G refers to the atmospheric pressure (100 mm.) on the surface of the glycerol. If we draw a vertical line from point G to the X axis, we will have the boiling point of glycerol, point H. Point H equals 145° C.

63. Ans. 1 The liquid whose molecules exert the strongest attractive force upon each other is glycerol. Strong intermolecular forces hold the molecules together in a liquid. These intermolecular forces are due to hydrogen bonding. Molecules which have large mutual attraction have a small tendency to escape into the vapor phase. Such a liquid has a low vapor pressure at room temperature.

64. Ans. 2 As we discussed in question 5, water will boil when the vapor pressure of water is equal to the atmospheric pressure on the surface of the water. The statement in question 64 tells us that water will boil at a temperature of 80° C., when the pressure exerted on its surface is equal to ___?___ . On the graph point I refers to water at 80° C. If we draw a horizontal line to the Y axis from point I, we can determine the pressure exerted on the surface of the water, point L. Point L is equal to approximately 370 mm.

65. Ans. 1 The normal boiling point of ether is the point at which the vapor pressure is equal to the standard atmospheric pressure (760 mm.), point J. If we draw a vertical line from point J to the X axis, we find that the normal boiling point of ether is 38° C. (point K).

GROUP 2

The answers to questions 66 to 70 are based on the following electron configuration of a neutral atom:

$$1s^2 2s^1 2p^3 = {}_6C^{12}$$

Most of the bonds formed by carbon originate from an *excited* carbon atom with the $1s^2 2s^1 2p^3$ electronic structure that has four unpaired electrons and forms four shared-pair bonds. When carbon forms four covalent bonds three of its unpaired electrons are in p orbits while one is in an s orbit. The one $2s$ electron and the $3p$ electrons hybridize and form an sp^3 orbital.

The bonds formed are directed toward the corners of a tetrahedron. Thus we have 4 bonds for carbon as in CCl_4 (shown in question 70). In the case of carbon the four bonds are referred to as sp^3 bonds.

66. Ans. 1 Since the atomic number is 6, we have 6 protons in the nucleus of the carbon atom. The atomic number of the neutral carbon atom tells us the number of protons in the nucleus.

67. Ans. 4 Carbon has an electron configuration of two electrons in the K level and 4 in the L level. Elements with 4 valence electrons are found in Group 4A of the *Periodic Table*.

68. Ans. 2 As we stated in the answer to question 67, we have 2 principal energy levels in the electron structure of carbon, the K level and the L level.

69. Ans. 4 The electron configuration given is:

$$1s^2 2s^1 2p^3$$

As we stated in the introduction to Group 2, carbon forms four covalent bonds since three of its unpaired electrons are in p orbits while one is in an s orbit. Under the influence of other atoms, one of the $2s$ electrons may acquire energy and be promoted to a $2p$ orbital so that the valence electron structure becomes $2s^1$, $2p^3$. Thus, the carbon atom can form 4 electron-pair bonds either with its own kind or with atoms of other elements, especially with hydrogen, fluorine or chlorine. An s^1p^3 or $s^1 p_x{}^1 p_y{}^1 p_z{}^1$ indicates that we have 4 incomplete orbitals.

70. Ans. 3 When carbon combines with chlorine, the bond between carbon and an atom of chlorine will be polar covalent. The more electronegative chlorine will draw the shared bonding electrons closer to itself. This is an example of a polar covalent bond. The electron-dot diagram for CCl_4 is:

The structural formula for CCl_4 is:

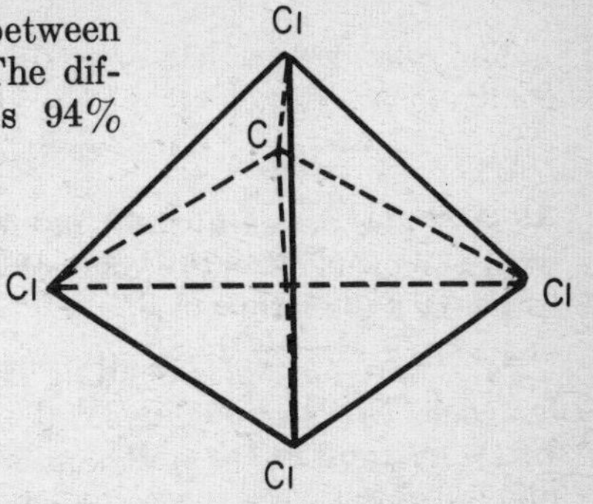

Also the difference in electronegativity between chlorine and carbon is $(3.0 - 2.5) = 0.5$. The difference of 0.5 indicates that the bond is 94% covalent.

Wrong choices explained:

(1)   In general, an ionic bond would have an electronegativity difference of 1.7 or greater.

(2)   There are no metals involved in this question.

(4)   A nonpolar covalent bond is formed between the diatomic molecules such as F_2, Cl_2, Br_2, I_2, O_2, N_2, H_2. The electronegativity difference is zero.

71.   Ans.   4   The bond formed between hydrogen and chlorine in HCl is polar covalent. The electron-dot diagram for HCl indicates that the shared bonding electrons are closer to the chlorine. The electron-dot diagram for HCl is shown as follows:

$$H \: {}_{\times} \overset{\times \times}{\underset{\times \times}{Cl}} {}_{\times}^{\times}$$

Also the difference in electronegativity between Cl and H is $3.0 - 2.1 = 0.9$. The difference 0.9 indicates that we have a bond that is 81% covalent.

72.   Ans.   1   The bond formed between magnesium (an active metal) and chlorine particles (active nonmetals) in $MgCl_2$ is ionic. In general, bonds formed between active metals and active nonmetals are ionic. The electron-dot diagram for $MgCl_2$ is shown as follows:

$$\overset{-1}{\underset{}{}} \qquad \overset{+2}{\underset{}{}} \qquad \overset{-1}{\underset{}{}}$$
$$\overset{\times \times}{\underset{\times \times}{{}_{\times}^{\times} Cl}} \: {}^{\circ}_{\times} \: Mg \: {}_{\times} \overset{\times \times}{\underset{\times \times}{Cl}} {}_{\times}^{\times}$$

Also the difference in electronegativity between Cl and Mg is $3.0 - 1.3 = 1.8$ which is 55% ionic.

73.   Ans.   4   The bond that is formed between the nitrogen and the hydrogen in the ammonia molecule, NH_3 is a polar covalent bond. Since the nitrogen atom is more electronegative, it will draw the shared bonding electrons closer to itself. The electron-dot diagram for NH_3 is shown as follows:

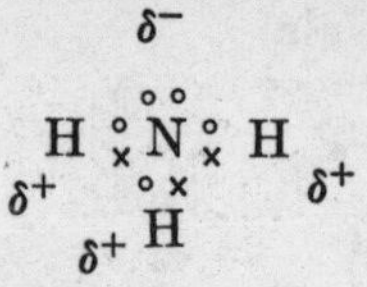

$$\overset{\delta^-}{\underset{\delta^+}{\overset{}{\text{H}}}} \overset{\circ\;\circ}{\underset{\circ\;\times}{\text{N}}} \overset{}{\underset{\delta^+}{\text{H}}} \;\;\delta^+$$

$$\underset{\delta^+}{\text{H}}$$

As a result, the ammonia molecule is a dipole. The difference in electronegativity between nitrogen and hydrogen is $3.0 - 2.1 = 0.9$. An electronegativity difference of 0.9 indicates that the bond is 81% covalent.

74. **Ans. 3** The bonding between the nitrogen atoms in the diatomic molecule N_2, is nonpolar covalent. Diatomic molecules such as F_2, Cl_2, Br_2, I_2, O_2, N_2 and H_2 exhibit nonpolar covalent bonding. The electronegativity difference between the nitrogen atoms in the nitrogen molecule is obviously zero. The electron-dot diagram for N_2 indicates that it has a triple covalent bond. It is shown as follows:

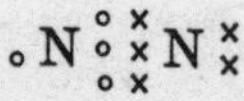

$$\circ\,\text{N}\,\overset{\circ\;\times}{\underset{\circ\;\times}{\times}}\,\text{N}\,\overset{\times}{\underset{}{\times}}$$

75. **Ans. 2** The bonds found between the copper atoms in copper wire are metallic. In metallic crystals such as copper, the atoms are in a regular geometric arrangement with overlapping energy levels so that the electrons can move freely from atom to atom. The copper wire is held together by the attraction between the positive metallic ions and a cloud of negative electrons. This attraction in metals is called a metallic bond.

GROUP 4

The answers to questions 76 through 80 are based on the partial *Periodic Table* shown below:

	I_A	II_A	III_A	IV_A	V_A	VI_A	VII_A	O
2	A				E			
3		J		D		M		R
4			L			G		

It is a good practice to identify the elements which correspond to the letters on this partial *Periodic Table*. This is done as follows:

Letter		Element	Letter		Element
A	=	Li	E	=	N
J	=	Mg	M	=	S
L	=	Ga	G	=	Br
D	=	Si	R	=	Ar

Group

	I_A	II_A	III_A	IV_A	V_A	VI_A	VII_A	O
2	Li				N			
3		Mg		Si		S		Ar
4			Ga				Br	

Period

76. Ans. 4 The two elements which would be least likely to react to form a compound are L and R. The elements corresponding to L and R are gallium and argon respectively. These two elements are least likely to combine since argon is an inert gas. Inert or noble gases do not combine with other elements under ordinary conditions. The other combinations; A (Li) and G (Br), D (Si) and G (Br), J (Mg) and M (S) *do combine* under ordinary conditions.

77. Ans. 1 The two elements which would form the most highly ionic compound are A (Li) and G (Br). Since the elements lithium and bromine have the greatest difference in electronegativity, this combination of elements would be the most highly ionic. The table below lists the information in order to explain this question:

Symbols	Corresponding Elements	Difference in Electronegativity	% Ionic Character
A-G	LiBr	$2.8 - 1.0 = 1.8$	55%
D-M	SiS	$2.5 - 1.8 = 0.7$	12%
J-G	MgBr	$2.8 - 1.2 = 1.6$	47%
L-M	GaS	$2.5 - 1.6 = 0.9$	19%

78. Ans. 3 The probable formula for a compound formed from the elements L and M is L_2M_3. The corresponding elements for the symbols L and M are Ga and S respectively. The element Ga has an oxidation number of +3 and S has an oxidation number of −2. When gallium combines with sulfur, the compound gallium sulfide is formed. Gallium sulfide has the formula Ga_2S_3. The formula is determined as follows:

$$Ga_2^{+3}S_3^{-2}$$

$$\boxed{+6 \ -6 = 0}$$

Since the algebraic sum of the oxidation numbers must equal zero, we have to place a subscript 2 after the gallium and a subscript 3 after the sulfide. The formula is Ga_2S_3 or L_2M_3. We must convert the symbols to the letters used in the question.

79. Ans. **1** The element which could form a compound that is normally called a hydride is A (Li). The oxidation state of a hydride is -1. Thus it will ordinarily combine with an element which has a positive oxidation state. It will combine with metals to form hydrides such as NaH and LiH. The hydrogen in them behaves to some extent like a halogen or electronegative element. The elements E (N), M (S), and G (Br) will not form hydrides since they are more electronegative than hydrogen. The table below indicates that hydrogen has a *positive* oxidation state with choices 2, 3 and 4.

Letter	Symbol of Element	Compound with Hydrogen	Oxidation States
A	Li	LiH	$Li^{+1}H^{-1}$
E	N	NH_3	$N^{-3}H_3^{+1}$
M	S	H_2S	$H_2^{+1}S^{-2}$
G	Br	HBr	H^+Br^-

80. Ans. **1** The element which has the lowest melting point is R (Ar). In general elements at room temperature which are solid have the highest melting points, liquids have lower melting points and gases have the lowest melting points. The choices listed in this question include the following: R (Ar) a gas, J (Mg) and D (Si) are solids, and G (Br) a liquid. The melting points are summarized as follows:

Letter	Element	Melting Point	State at room temperature (25° C.)
R	Ar	$-189.4°$ C.	Gas
J	Mg	650° C.	Solid
G	Br	$-7.2°$ C.	Liquid
D	Si	1410° C.	Solid

Obviously R (argon) has the lowest melting point.

GROUP 5

81. Ans. 4 The statement tells us that one mole of potassium permanganate reacts completely with hydrochloric acid according to the following reaction:

$$16HCl + 2KMnO_4 \rightarrow 2KCl + 2MnCl_2 + 5Cl_2 + 8H_2O$$

The coefficient before each formula in the balanced equation indicates the number of moles of the reactants and products. The balanced equation tells us that the ratio of moles of $KMnO_4$ to H_2O is 2:8 or 1:4. Thus, if we use 1 mole of $KMnO_4$ we will get 4 moles of water. We can also set up a proportion to solve the problem as follows:

$$\frac{1 \text{ mole } KMnO_4}{2 \text{ moles}} = \frac{x}{8 \text{ moles}}$$

$$2x = 8$$

$$x = 4 \text{ moles of water produced.}$$

82. Ans. 3 The balanced equation tells us that the number of moles of $KMnO_4$ to KCl is 2:2 or 1:1. Therefore, if we use 1 mole of $KMnO_4$ we will get 1 mole of KCl. One mole of KCl has a formula weight of:

$$\begin{array}{r} K = 39 \\ Cl = \underline{35} \\ 74 \end{array}$$

Therefore 74 grams of KCl are produced.

83. Ans. 3 The balanced equation tells us that the ratio of moles of $KMnO_4$ to Cl_2 is 2:5 or $1:2\frac{1}{2}$. Thus, if we use 1 mole of $KMnO_4$ we will get $2\frac{1}{2}$ moles of chlorine gas (Cl_2). Since one mole of chlorine gas at $S.T.P.$ occupies 22.4 liters, $2\frac{1}{2}$ moles of Cl_2 gas occupies 56 liters. We can set up a proportion to solve the problem as follows:

$$\frac{1 \text{ mole of } Cl_2}{22.4 \text{ l.}} = \frac{2\frac{1}{2} \text{ moles of } Cl_2}{x}$$

$$x = 22.4 \times 2\frac{1}{2} = 56 \text{ liters.}$$

84. Ans. 2 The empirical formula of the compound is CH_2. The empirical formula represents the constituent elements of a substance and the simplest number of atoms of each. The empirical formula for any compound is determined by the following procedure:

STEP 1 The compound contains 85.7% carbon and 14.3% hydrogen by mass. This means 100 grams of the compound would contain 85.7 grams of carbon and 14.3 grams of hydrogen. The number of gram-atoms or moles of each element contained in 100 grams of the compound is determined by dividing the amount (percentage × 100 grams) of each element by its atomic mass. Step 1 is solved as follows:

$$\text{Carbon} = \frac{85.7 \text{ grams}}{12 \text{ grams/gram-atom}} = 7.15 \text{ gram atoms or moles}$$

$$\text{Hydrogen} = \frac{14.3 \text{ grams}}{1 \text{ gram/gram-atom}} = 14.3 \text{ gram-atoms or moles}$$

STEP 2　Divide each of the above gram-atom ratios by the smallest common divisor (7.15). Step 2 is solved as follows:

$$\text{Carbon} = \frac{7.15}{7.15} = 1$$

$$\text{Hydrogen} = \frac{14.3}{7.15} = 2$$

STEP 3　Using the atomic ratios determined in Step 2, it is obvious that the empirical formula for this compound is CH_2.

85.　Ans.　**3**　The number of molecules in one mole of this compound is 6.023×10^{23}. The number of molecules in one mole of any compound at *S.T.P.* is 6.023×10^{23}.

GROUP 6

Base your answers to questions 86 through 88 on the information below.

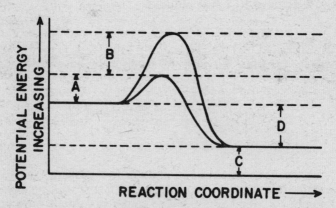

The relationship between activation energy and heat of reaction for a given reaction can be shown graphically in a potential energy diagram by plotting potential energy against a reaction coordinate representing the progress of the reaction. In answering questions pertaining to a potential energy diagram, I feel it is a good practice to list the identity or significance of the numbered arrows on the potential energy diagram. The arrows are identified as follows:

ARROW **A** indicates the energy of activation of the catalyzed forward reaction.

ARROW **B** indicates the difference in potential energy between the catalyzed and uncatalyzed reaction.

ARROW **A** + ARROW **B** = Energy of activation of the uncatalyzed forward reaction.

ARROW **C** indicates the potential energy of the products.

ARROW **D** indicates the heat of reaction.

86. Ans. **1** The energy of activation is the minimum energy required to initiate a chemical reaction. The energy of activation represents the difference between the highest point in the curve and the initial potential energy of the reactants. The energy of activation for the forward reaction is represented ARROWS (**A** + **B**).

87. Ans. **1** Compared to the potential energy of the reactants (bottom of arrow **A**), the potential energy of the products (bottom of arrow **D**) is less. This is always the case in an exothermic reaction.

88. Ans. **4** ARROW **D** represents the heat of reaction for the catalyzed reverse reaction. The difference in potential energy between the final products and the initial reactants represents the heat of reaction. Notice that arrow **D** does not change whether the reaction is forward, reverse or catalyzed. Of course the heat of reaction ($\triangle$H) is negative for the forward reaction since it is exothermic and positive for the reverse reaction since it is endothermic. A catalyst alters the speed of a reaction but does not affect the heat of the reaction.

Base your answers to questions 89 and 90 on the information below.

	Heat of Reaction $\triangle$H kcal./mole	Free Energy of Formation $\triangle$G kcal./mole
Reaction A:	−94.05	−94.26—EXOTHERMIC
Reaction B:	21.60	20.72—ENDOTHERMIC
Reaction C:	−70.96	−71.79—EXOTHERMIC
Reaction D:	54.19	50.00—ENDOTHERMIC

89. Ans. **4** Endothermic reactions are reactions in which the heat of reaction ($\triangle$H) is positive and the free energy of formation ($\triangle$F) is also positive. Reactions B and D are endothermic since they have positive ($\triangle$H) and ($\triangle$F) values.

90. Ans. **2** For a spontaneous reaction to occur in a system, the free energy change ($\triangle$F) must be negative. The free energy change

$$\triangle G = \triangle H - T\triangle S \quad \text{where} \quad \triangle G = \text{Free energy change}$$
$$\triangle H = \text{Heat of reaction}$$
$$T\triangle S = \text{Entropy}$$

Since reactions A and C have negative values for $\triangle G$, these reactions occur spontaneously. A chemical reaction will proceed spontaneously if it is accompanied by a decrease in free energy, that is, if the free energy of the products is less than that of the reactants. In such a case the free-energy change $\triangle G$ in the system is said to be negative.

GROUP 7

91. Ans. 1 The pH (explained in question 43) of the solution in beaker A is closest to 1. Beaker A contains 200 ml. of 0.1 M HCl. Table K tells us that the pH value for a 0.1 N (same as 0.1 M) solution of HCl is 1.1.

92. Ans. 3 If the contents of beakers A & B were mixed, the pH of the resulting solution would be closest to 7. HCl and NaOH react chemically according to the following equation:

neutralization: strong acid + strong base → salt + water
                   HCl   +   NaOH   → NaCl + H_2O

A neutralization reaction involving a strong acid and a strong base will produce equal numbers of H^+ and OH^- ions since the acid and base are completely ionized. At a pH of 7, the hydrogen ion concentration equals the hydroxide ion concentration.

93. Ans. 4 When the solutions in beakers A & B are mixed, the reaction goes essentially to completion because of the formation of water. As we explained in the answer to question 92, a neutralization reaction involves the reaction of an acid and a base to form a salt and water. A neutralization reaction will go to completion if one of the products is very slightly ionized. Since the water formed is very slightly ionized, the reaction will go to completion.

94. Ans. 2 As the contents of beaker B are poured into beaker A, the pH of the resulting mixture in beaker A increases. Strong acids such as H_2SO_4 have a pH value about 1. $Ba(OH)_2$ a strong base has a pH value of 12 or 13. When we add beaker B ($Ba(OH)_2$) to beaker A containing H_2SO_4, we are adding more OH^- ions to the solution. The addition of hydroxide ions makes the solution more basic, therefore the pH increases.

95. Ans. 1 As the contents of beaker B are poured into beaker A, the conductivity of the resulting mixture in beaker A decreases. The chemical equation for the reaction between H_2SO_4 and $Ba(OH)_2$ is shown as follows:

Precipitate
$$H_2SO_4 + Ba(OH)_2 \rightarrow BaSO_4 \downarrow + 2H_2O$$

The conductivity of a solution can be determined using a conductivity apparatus. The conductivity of a solution tells us whether it will conduct electricity or not. In order for a solution to conduct electricity, the materials in the water such as acids, bases and salts should furnish ions. Since the products of the reaction are BaSO₄, a very slightly soluble salt and H₂O, also slightly ionized, we have very few ions in solution. As a result of these slightly ionized compounds, being formed when we add beaker B to beaker A, the conductivity of the resulting mixture decreases.

GROUP 8

96. Ans. 1 If the salt bridge were removed and the switch S closed, the voltage would be 0.00. In order for the circuit to be complete the salt bridge is needed. The salt bridge provides a path for the ions to migrate and carry electricity from one beaker to another. The salt bridge contains a saturated solution of NaCl with cotton plugs at each end. The function of the salt bridge is to keep the two solutions separate. If we remove the salt bridge we break the circuit and the electrons cannot flow through the circuit.

97. Ans. 1 When the reaction reaches chemical equilibrium, the cel voltage will be 0.00 volts. When the cell reaches equilibrium, the reverse reaction, $Cu_{(s)} + Zn^{+2}_{(aq)} \rightarrow Cu^{++}_{(aq)} + Zn_{(s)}$ proceeds at a rate equal to that of the forward reaction. The E^0 for the reverse reaction is -1.10 volts and that for the forward reaction is $+1.10$ volts. (The E^0 value for the forward reaction is determined in the answer to question 98). When the opposing reactions become equal, the total cell potential is zero. This occurs at equilibrium.

98. Ans. 4 The maximum voltage in the cell when switch S is closed is $+1.10$ volts. As we explained in question 45, the maximum net potential (E^0) for an electrochemical cell can be determined by adding the E^0 of the oxidation half-reaction to the E^0 for the reduction half-reaction. To solve this problem, we set up the ion-electron equation for each half-reaction and determine the E^0 values from *Table L*. This is done as follows:

Oxidation **half-reaction:**	$Zn^0(s) - 2e^- \rightarrow Zn^{++}(aq)$	$E^0 = +0.76$ volt
Reduction **half-reaction:**	$Cu^{++}(aq) + 2e^- \rightarrow Cu^0(s)$	$E^0 = +0.34$ volt

(Reverse E sign for reduction)

$$Zn^0(s) + Cu^{++}(aq) \rightarrow Zn^{++}(aq) + Cu^0(s) \quad E^0 = +1.10 \text{ volts}$$

Therefore the maximum voltage in the cell is $+1.10$ volts.

99. **Ans. 2** The species which supplies the electrons which flow through the wire is zinc (Zn^0). At the positive zinc electrode, each zinc atom loses 2 electrons and goes into solution as $Zn^{++}(aq)$. As a result, the positive electrode will get a high density of electrons since an excessive negative charge builds up. At the cathode, each $Cu^{++}(aq)$ ion is gaining 2 electrons from the cathode to become Cu^0. This results in a deficiency in the number of electrons at the cathode (copper electrode). Since the electrons flow from an area of high electron density to an area of low electron density, the excess electrons on the anode will flow through the external wire to the cathode where there is a deficiency of electrons.

100. **Ans. 3** In this reaction, the substance reduced is $Cu^{++}(aq)$. When a substance is reduced, it gains electrons. The ion-electron equation for the reaction is shown as follows:

$$Cu^{++}(aq) + 2e^- \rightarrow Cu^0(s)$$

GROUP 9

101. **Ans. 3** The organic compound that is a product of a fermentation reaction is C_2H_5OH. Fermentation is a reaction in which organic compounds are decomposed into simpler compounds by the action of enzymes. A common fermentation reaction is the fermentation of glucose. The equation for the fermentation of glucose is shown as follows:

$$\underset{\text{(glucose)}}{C_6H_{12}O_6} \xrightarrow{\text{Zymase}} \underset{\text{(ethanol)}}{2C_2H_5OH} + 2CO_2$$

Wrong choices explained:

(1) CCl_2F_2 is called dichlorodifluoromethane or freon. It is the product of a substitution reaction.

(2) C_2H_2 is called acetylene or ethyne. It is formed when calcium carbide reacts with water.

(4) $C_2H_5OC_2H_5$ is called diethyl ether or ethoxyethane. It can be prepared in a variety of ways, one of which is the *Sulfuric Acid Process* using ethyl alcohol and sulfuric acid.

102. **Ans. 1** An example of a primary alcohol is:

It is called ethyl alcohol or ethanol.

$$\begin{array}{ccc} H & H & \\ | & | & \\ H-C-C-OH \\ | & | & \\ H & H & \end{array}$$

Alcohols with 1 hydroxy (OH) group attached can be separated into three categories. They are *primary* alcohols, *secondary* alcohols and *tertiary* alcohols. Each is described as follows:

Primary alcohols: (The alpha carbon (α) is connected to the OH group.) If the alpha carbon (α) is connected to only one other carbon atom, it is a primary alcohol. Ethanol or 1-butanol shown below with the general formula are examples:

General Formula:

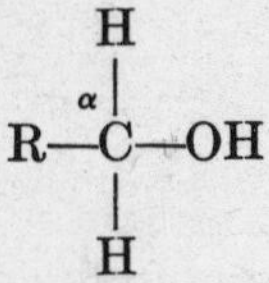

R is an alkyl group.

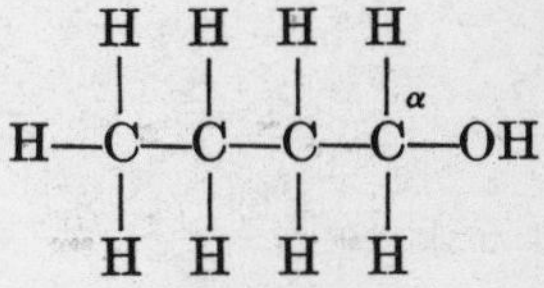

1-butanol
or
n-butyl alcohol

Secondary alcohols: If the alpha carbon is connected to two other carbon atoms, it is a secondary alcohol. Secondary butyl alcohol (2-butanol) is an example. Choice 2 in this question is also an example of a secondary alcohol. The examples and the general formula are shown as follows:

General Formula:

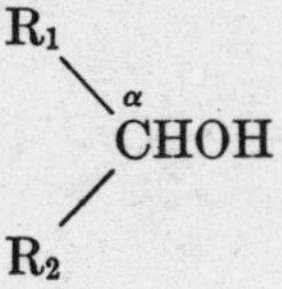

(2)

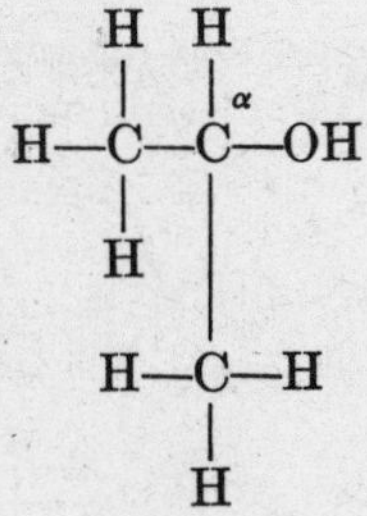

2-propanol
or
isopropyl alcohol

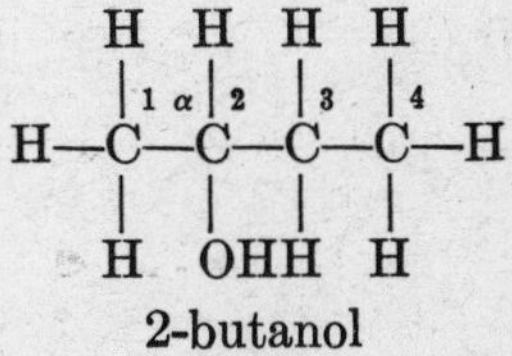

2-butanol
or
secondary butyl alcohol

Tertiary alcohols: If the alpha carbon is connected to 3 other carbon atoms, it is a tertiary alcohol. An example is tertiary butyl alcohol. The general formula and the formula for tertiary butyl alcohol are shown as follows:

General Formula: *Formula for a tertiary alcohol:*

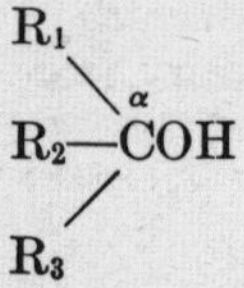

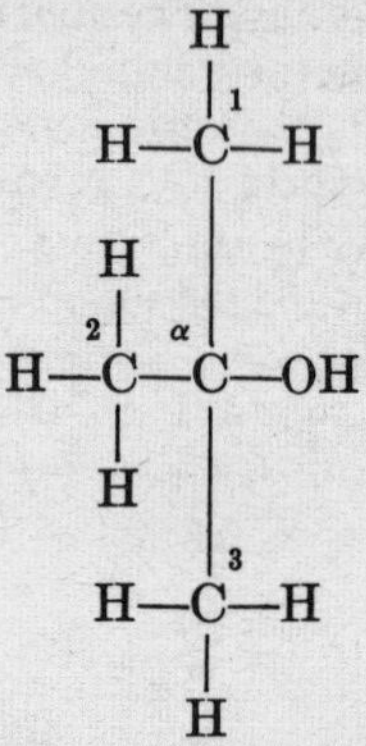

$$R_2-\underset{R_3}{\overset{R_1}{\underset{|}{\overset{|}{C}}}}\overset{\alpha}{}OH$$

tertiary butyl alcohol
or
2-methyl-2-propanol

Wrong choices explained:
(2) It is explained above under secondary alcohols.

(3) 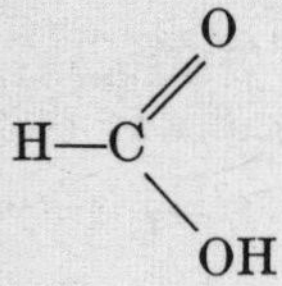   This is the structural formula for formic acid or methanoic acid. Organic acids have the general formula RCOOH.

(4) 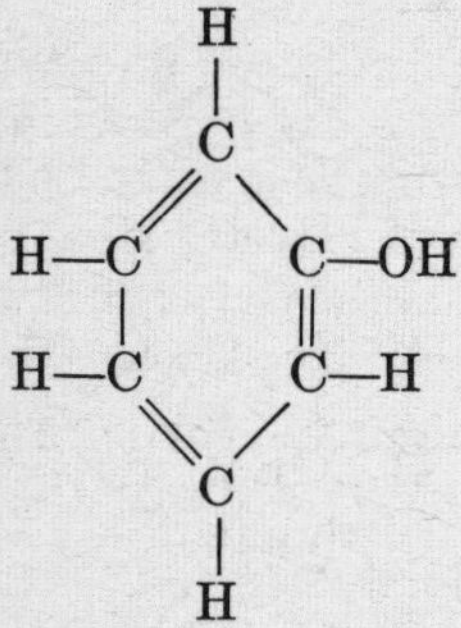   This is the structural formula for phenol. It is also called carbolic acid. It is a monohydroxy derivative of benzene.

103.   Ans.   **4**   The general formula for the benzene series is C_nH_{2n-6} where n = the number of carbon atoms. The benzene series of hydrocarbons starts with benzene, C_6H_6. If we substitute 6 for n in the general formula C_nH_{2n-6}, we get C_6H_6.

Wrong choices explained:
(1) C_nH_{2n+2} is the general formula for the alkanes. The alkanes are saturated, single-bond, hydrocarbons. The first member of the series is methane CH_4.

(2) C_nH_{2n} is the general formula for the alkenes. The alkenes are unsaturated and contain 1 double bond. Ethylene or ethene (C_2H_4) is the first member of this series.

(3) C_nH_{2n-2} is the general formula for the alkyne series. The alkynes are also unsaturated, and contain 1 triple bond. Acetylene or ethyne, C_2H_2, is the first member of the series.

104. Ans. **4** The organic compound which is a product of an esterification reaction is CH_3COOCH_3. The name of this ester is methyl acetate or methyl ethanoate. Since methyl acetate corresponds to the general formula RCOOR′, it is an ester. An ester can be produced in an esterification reaction in which an acid reacts with an alcohol in the presence of concentrated sulfuric acid to yield an ester and water. The concentrated sulfuric acid is a strong dehydrating agent therefore, it removes the water from the field of action. This action increases the yield of the ester. Methyl acetate is formed from methyl alcohol (methanol) and acetic acid (ethanoic acid). In writing an esterification reaction, it is a good practice to write the general equation first and then the regular equation below. This is done as follows:

$$RCO\underline{OH} + R'O\underline{H} \xrightleftharpoons{\text{Con } H_2SO_4} RCOOR' + \underline{HOH}$$

$$CH_3CO\underline{OH} + CH_3O\underline{H} \xrightleftharpoons{\text{Con } H_2SO_4} CH_3COOCH_3 + \underline{HOH}$$

acetic acid + methanol — methyl acetate + water

Therefore, the type of reaction in which methyl acetate is formed is esterification reaction.

105. Ans. **2** The organic compound which is a product of a saponification reaction is $C_3H_5(OH)_3$. $C_3H_5(OH)_3$ is called glycerine or glycerol. It is a product of a saponification reaction in which a fat and NaOH react to yield soap and glycerol. Glycerol is a trihydroxy alcohol. A saponification reaction is summarized as follows:

$$\begin{array}{ccccc}
\text{Fat} & + & \text{lye} & \to & \text{soap} & + & \text{glycerol} \\
\text{Glyceryl Tristearate} & + & \text{NaOH} & \to & \text{sodium stearate} & + & C_3H_5(OH)_3 \\
C_3H_5(C_{17}H_{35}COO)_3 & + & 3NaOH & \to & 3NaC_{17}H_{35}COO & + & C_3H_5(OH)_3
\end{array}$$

Examination June, 1970 Chemistry

PART ONE *Answer all 60 questions in this part.*

DIRECTIONS (1–60): *For each statement or question, write in the space provided the* number *preceding the word or expression that, of those given, best completes the statement or answers the question.*

1. The change from the solid phase directly to the gaseous phase is called (1) sublimation (2) evaporation (3) condensation (4) crystallization   1..............

2. A sample of hydrogen has a volume of 100 milliliters at a pressure of 1 atmosphere. If the temperature is kept constant and the pressure is raised to 2 atmospheres, the volume will now be (1) 25 ml. (2) 50 ml. (3) 100 ml. (4) 200 ml.   2..............

3. A liquid which evaporates rapidly at room temperature would most likely have a high (1) vapor pressure (2) boiling point (3) melting point (4) attraction between molecules   3..............

4. Exothermic reactions are usually self-sustaining because
(1) exothermic reactions usually require low activation energies
(2) exothermic reactions usually require high activation energies
(3) the energy released is sufficient to maintain the reaction
(4) the products contain more potential energy than the reactants   4..............

5. Which gas contains 3.0×10^{23} molecules at S.T.P.?
(1) 38 grams of F_2 (2) 14 grams of N_2 (3) 2.0 grams of H_2
(4) 70. grams of Cl_2 5..............

6. Twenty calories of heat are added to 2 grams of water at a temperature of $10°$ C. The resulting temperature of the water will be (1) $5°$ C. (2) $20°$ C. (3) $30°$ C. (4) $40°$ C.   6..............

7. If the temperature of a substance changes 40 Celsius degrees, how many degrees would its temperature change on the Kelvin scale? (1) 40 (2) 233 (3) 273 (4) 313   7..............

8. What is the number of sublevels in the third principal energy level? (1) 1 (2) 2 (3) 3 (4) 4   8..............

9. A nonmetal would most likely have an ionization energy of (1) 5.1 e.v. (2) 7.4 e.v. (3) 8.5 e.v. (4) 11.8 e.v.   9..............

10. Which is the electron configuration of the element having the highest ionization energy? (1) $1s^2 2s^2 2p^1$ (2) $1s^2 2s^2 2p^2$
(3) $1s^2 2s^2 2p^4$ (4) $1s^2 2s^2 2p^5$ 10..............

11. Which electron configuration represents an atom in the ground state?   (1) $1s^2 2p^1$ (2) $1s^2 2s^2 3p^2$ (3) $1s^2 2s^2 2p^6 3s^2$ (4) $1s^2 2s^2 2p^6 4s^1$

11..............

12. Which electron configuration is characteristic of a noble gas?   (1) $1s^2$ (2) $1s^2 2s^2$ (3) $1s^2 2s^2 2p^2$ (4) $1s^2 2s^2 2p^6 3s^2$

12..............

13. What is the maximum number of electrons that can occupy the $3d$ sublevel?   (1) 6   (2) 8   (3) 10   (4) 14

13..............

14. Which pair has the same electron configuration?   (1) Ca and Ca^{+2} (2) Cl^- and F^- (3) Na^+ and K^+ (4) S^{-2} and Ar

14..............

15. Given the *unbalanced* equation:

$$\underline{\quad}Sb + \underline{\quad}Cl_2 \rightarrow \underline{\quad}SbCl_3$$

What is the coefficient of antimony (III) chloride in the balanced equation?   (1) 1   (2) 2   (3) 3   (4) 4

15..............

16. The attractive forces between nonpolar molecules are called   (1) dipole attraction   (2) hydrogen bonding   (3) molecule-ion attraction   (4) van der Waals

16..............

17. What is the most likely formula for the compound formed when magnesium reacts with nitrogen?   (1) Mg_2N (2) Mg_3N_2 (3) Mg_2N_3 (4) Mg_5N_2

17..............

18. Which best explains why a methane (CH_4) molecule is nonpolar?
(1) Each carbon-hydrogen bond is polar.
(2) Carbon and hydrogen are both nonmetals.
(3) Methane is an organic compound.
(4) The methane molecule is symmetrical.

18..............

19. Which is the smallest particle of a covalent compound that has the chemical properties of that compound?   (1) ion (2) atom   (3) electron   (4) molecule

19..............

20. A solid which is soft, a nonconductor, and which melts at a low temperature is most likely   (1) an ionic solid   (2) a network solid   (3) a metallic solid   (4) a molecular solid

20..............

21. Which is the correct electron-dot formula for the ammonia molecule?

21..............

(1)
$$
\begin{array}{c}
H \\
\cdot \\
H \cdot N \cdot H
\end{array}
$$

(2)
$$
\begin{array}{c}
H \\
\cdot\cdot \\
H : N : H \\
\cdot\cdot
\end{array}
$$

(3)
$$
\begin{array}{c}
H \\
\cdot\cdot \\
H : N : N
\end{array}
$$

(4)
$$
\begin{array}{c}
H \\
\cdot\cdot \\
H : N : H \\
\cdot\cdot \\
H
\end{array}
$$

22. As one proceeds from left to right across Period 3 of the *Periodic Table*, there is a decrease in   (1) ionization energy (2) electronegativity   (3) metallic characteristics   (4) valence electrons

22..............

23. What is the basis for the arrangement of our present *Periodic Table?*
(1) number of neutrons in the nucleus of an atom
(2) number of nucleons in the nucleus of an atom
(3) atomic number of an atom
(4) atomic mass of an atom

23..............

24. Which period of the *Periodic Table* contains elements which may combine chemically by losing electrons from more than one principal energy level?   (1) 1   (2) 2   (3) 3   (4) 4

24..............

25. Which element has the greatest tendency to lose electrons?   (1) barium   (2) magnesium   (3) calcium (4) strontium

25..............

26. Which element is a metalloid?   (1) arsenic   (2) neon (3) potassium   (4) bromine

26..............

27. What is the percent by mass of oxygen in $CaCO_3$? (1) 16%   (2) 32%   (3) 48%   (4) 60%

27..............

28. Given the reaction $H_2(g) + I_2(s) \rightarrow 2HI(g)$. What is the volume of hydrogen required to produce 22.4 liters of HI at S.T.P.?   (1) 1.00 liter   (2) 2.00 liters   (3) 11.2 liters (4) 22.4 liters

28..............

29. The density of a gas at S.T.P. is 1.25 grams per liter. What is the molecular mass of this gas?   (1) 44.0   (2) 28.0 (3) 22.4   (4) 1.25

29..............

30. Two liters of a solution of sulfuric acid contain 98 grams of H_2SO_4. The molarity of this solution is   (1) 1.0   (2) 2.0 (3) 0.50   (4) 1.5

30..............

31. One hundred milliliters of water at 10° C. contains 60 grams of $NaNO_3$. In order to form a saturated solution at 10° C., how many additional grams of $NaNO_3$ must be added?   (1) 20 (2) 40   (3) 60   (4) 80

31..............

32. The number of atoms of hydrogen in 1.00 mole of NH_3 is equal to
(1) 6.02×10^{23} (3) $3(6.02 \times 10^{23})$
(2) $2(6.02 \times 10^{23})$ (4) $4(6.02 \times 10^{23})$

32..............

33. What is the volume occupied by 2.00 grams of helium at S.T.P.? (1) 11.2 liters (2) 2.00 liters (3) 22.4 liters (4) 4.00 liters

33.............

34. Which statement best explains why an increase in temperature usually increases the rate of a chemical reaction?
(1) The activation energy of the reaction is decreased.
(2) The ΔH of the reaction is increased.
(3) The free energy of the reaction is decreased.
(4) The effectiveness of collisions between particles is increased.

34.............

35. Which reaction is represented by the equilibrium expression $K = \dfrac{[C]^2}{[A]^3[B]}$?
(1) $2C(g) = 3A(g) + B(g)$ (3) $3A(g) + B(g) = 2C(g)$
(2) $2C(g) = 3AB(g)$ (4) $3AB(g) = 2C(g)$

35.............

36. Which gas is most soluble at S.T.P.? (1) CO (2) CO_2 (3) NH_3 (4) NO

36.............

37. In the reaction $HC_2H_3O_2 + H_2O = H_3O^+ + C_2H_3O_2^-$, the addition of solid sodium acetate ($Na^+C_2H_3O_2^-$) results in a decrease in the concentration of (1) $C_2H_3O_2^-$ (2) H_3O^+ (3) Na^+ (4) $HC_2H_3O_2$

37.............

38. A solution has a pH of 3. The hydronium ion concentration of this solution, in moles per liter, is (1) 1×10^{-3} (2) 1×10^4 (3) 3×10^{-1} (4) 3×10^1

38.............

39. In the reaction $NH_4^+ + H_2O = NH_3 + H_3O^+$, the two Brönsted acids are
(1) NH_4^+ and NH_3 (3) H_2O and H_3O^+
(2) H_2O and NH_3 (4) NH_4^+ and H_3O^+

39.............

40. A Brönsted base which is stronger than $Al(H_2O)_5(OH)^{+2}$ is (1) SO_4^{-2} (2) OH^- (3) H_2O (4) $Al(H_2O)_6^{+3}$

40.............

41. How many milliliters of 0.2 M KOH are needed to neutralize 20 milliliters of 0.1 M HCl? (1) 10 (2) 20 (3) 30 (4) 40

41.............

42. Which compound is an electrolyte? (1) CH_3OH (2) C_2H_5OH (3) $C_3H_5(OH)_3$ (4) $Ca(OH)_2$

42.............

43. Which half-reaction is the standard for the measurement of the voltages on Table L?
(1) $Na = Na^+ + e^-$ (3) $Li = Li^+ + e^-$
(2) $H_2 = 2H^+ + 2e^-$ (4) $2F^- = F_2 + 2e^-$

43.............

44. How many moles of Ag^+ will be reduced when 1 mole of Fe^{+2} changes to Fe^{+3}? (1) 1 (2) 2 (3) 3 (4) 4

44.............

45. What is the oxidation number of phosphorus in Na_2HPO_4? (1) $+1$ (2) $+5$ (3) $+3$ (4) $+7$

45.............

46. In the reaction $2Cr(s) + 3Cu^{+2}(aq) \rightarrow 3Cu(s) + 2Cr^{+3}(aq)$, the net potential ($E^0$) for the overall reaction is
(1) $+0.40$ volt (3) $+1.08$ volts
(2) $+0.46$ volt (4) $+2.50$ volts

46.............

47. Which will occur when Sr is oxidized?
(1) It will form an isotope.
(2) It will attain a positive oxidation number.
(3) It will become a negative ion.
(4) It will become radioactive.

47.............

48. Given the reaction: $Fe + Cl_2 \rightarrow FeCl_2$, the half-reaction that represents reduction in this reaction is
(1) $Fe^0 + 2e^- \rightarrow Fe^{+2}$ (3) $2Cl^{-1} - 2e^- \rightarrow Cl_2^0$
(2) $Fe^{+2} + 2e^- \rightarrow Fe^0$ (4) $Cl_2^0 + 2e^- \rightarrow 2Cl^{-1}$

48.............

49. Which metal will *not* react with a dilute HCl solution?
(1) Al (2) Ag (3) Mg (4) Zn

49.............

50. Which is an example of a homologous series?
(1) CH_4, C_2H_4, C_3H_8 (3) CH_4, C_2H_6, C_3H_6
(2) CH_4, C_2H_2, C_3H_6 (4) CH_4, C_2H_6, C_3H_8

50.............

51. Which hydrocarbon is saturated? (1) C_2H_6 (2) C_3H_4 (3) C_4H_6 (4) C_2H_2

51.............

52. The structural formula of 1, 3- dichlorobutane is

52.............

53.   Esterification is the reaction of an acid with   (1) a base
(2) an alcohol   (3) water   (4) a hydrocarbon   53.............

NOTE: *That questions 54 through 60 have only three choices.*

54.   A light bulb conductivity apparatus is suspended in a
beaker containing 100 milliliters of 0.1 M H_2SO_4. As 95 milliliters of 0.1 M $Ba(OH)_2$ is added to the beaker, the intensity of
the light   (1) decreases   (2) increases   (3) remains the same   54.............

55.   When calcium carbonate decomposes according to the
equation $CaCO_3(s) \rightarrow CaO(s) + CO_2(g)$, the entropy of the system   (1) decreases   (2) increases   (3) remains the same   55.............

56.   When a catalyst lowers the activation energy, the rate
of a reaction   (1) decreases   (2) increases   (3) remains the
same   56.............

57.   As the number of carbon atoms in the members of the
alkene series increases, the ratio of carbon atoms to hydrogen
atoms   (1) decreases   (2) increases   (3) remains the same   57.............

58.   As one proceeds from left to right across Period 3 on
the *Periodic Table*, the number of electrons in the 2p subshell
(1) decreases   (2) increases   (3) remains the same   58.............

59.   When a metallic atom becomes an ion, its radius   (1) decreases   (2) increases   (3) remains the same   59.............

60.   As sodium hydroxide is added to a solution of sulfuric
acid, the hydrogen ion concentration of the solution   (1) decreases   (2) increases   (3) remains the same   60.............

PART TWO *This part consists of nine groups. Choose six of these nine groups. Be sure that you answer all questions in each group chosen.*

GROUP 1

DIRECTIONS (**61–65**): *Write the number of the word or expression that best completes each statement or answers each question.* [5]

Base your answers to questions 61 and 62 on the information and diagram below and the *Periodic Table*.

Three samples of gas are contained in separate flasks. All flasks are the same size.

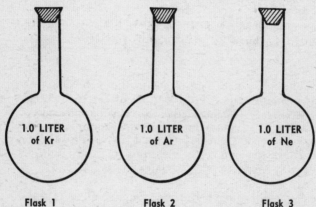

Flask 1   Flask 2   Flask 3

61. If each sample is at S.T.P., then the number of molecules in (1) flask number 1 is greatest (2) flask number 2 is greatest (3) flask number 3 is greatest (4) each flask is the same   61............

62. If each sample is at S.T.P., then the mass of the contents of (1) flask number 1 is greatest (2) flask number 2 is greatest (3) flask number 3 is greatest (4) each flask is the same   62............

63. Which would be found in a closed vessel partially filled with pure water at 25° C. and 760 mm.? (1) $H_2O(g)$, only (2) $H_2O(\ell)$, only (3) $H_2O(g)$ and $H_2O(\ell)$ (4) $H_2O(\ell)$ and $H_2O(s)$ 63............

64. Which is characteristic of a compound?
(1) It can consist of a single element.
(2) It is homogeneous.
(3) Its chemical composition can be varied.
(4) It can be decomposed by a physical change.   64............

65. A sample of a gas has a volume of 100 milliliters at S.T.P. The volume of the gas could remain the same if the temperature
(1) decreases and the pressure decreases
(2) remains the same and the pressure increases
(3) increases and the pressure decreases
(4) decreases and the pressure remains the same

65..............

GROUP 2

DIRECTIONS (66–70): *Write the* number *of the word or expression that best completes the statement or answers the question.* [5]

Base your answers to questions 66 and 67 on the graph below, which represents the first 7 elements in Period 3.

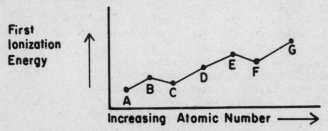

66. The ionization energy of element C is less than that of element B because element C has a (1) larger atomic radius (2) smaller atomic mass (3) smaller electronegativity value (4) more loosely held outer electron

66..............

67. The element with the greatest tendency to gain electrons is most likely (1) A (2) G (3) C (4) D

67..............

68. How many grams of an 8-gram sample of ^{131}I would remain after 24 days? (1) 1 (2) 2 (3) 3 (4) 4

68..............

69. The number of neutrons in ^3_1H is (1) 1 (2) 2 (3) 3 (4) 4

69..............

70. In which way does a Na^+ ion *differ* from a Na^0 atom?
(1) atomic number (2) mass number (3) particle size
(4) nuclear charge

70..............

GROUP 3

DIRECTIONS (71–72): *For each of questions 71 and 72, write the* number *of the compound,* chosen from the list below, *that best answers that question.* [2]

Compounds

(1) CCl_4 (2) $MgCl_2$ (3) H_2O

71. Which compound has the highest degree of ionic bonding?   71..............

72. Which compound has polar molecules?   72..............

DIRECTIONS (73-75): *Write the* number *of the word or expression that best completes the statement or answers the question.*   [3]

73. Element X has an electron configuration of $1s^22s^1$, and element Y has an electron configuration of $1s^22s^22p^4$. The most probable formula for a compound of these two elements is
(1) X_2Y (2) XY_2 (3) X_4Y_3 (4) X_4Y 73..............

74. When compared to hydrogen chloride (HCl), hydrogen fluoride (HF) has an unusually high boiling point. This is due to the magnitude of the
(1) hydrogen bonds   (3) coordinate covalent bonds
(2) *van der Waals* forces   (4) nonpolar covalent bonds   74..............

75. All chemical bonds are the result of the
(1) elevation of electrons to higher energy levels
(2) transfer of electrons from one atom to another
(3) attraction of electrons to each other
(4) simultaneous attraction of electrons to two nuclei   75..............

GROUP 4

DIRECTIONS (76-80): *Write the* number *of the word or expression that best completes the statement or answers the question.*   [5]

76. Silicon is most similar in chemical activity to   (1) carbon
(2) lead   (3) sulfur   (4) nitrogen   76..............

77. Which element in the ground state has a valence electron in a p subshell?   (1) Na   (2) Mg   (3) Al   (4) Be   77..............

78. Which elements would form the strongest bases?   (1) halogens   (2) alkali metals   (3) alkaline earths   (4) transition elements   78..............

79. Magnesium has a smaller atomic radius than sodium because the magnesium atom has more   (1) valence electrons
(2) energy levels   (3) protons   (4) neutrons   79..............

80. Which element in Period 4 of the *Periodic Table* is most likely to form a colored compound?   (1) calcium   (2) krypton
(3) gallium   (4) nickel   80..............

GROUP 5

DIRECTIONS (81–85): *Write the* number *of the word or expression that best completes the statement or answers the question.* [5]

81. The volume occupied by 6.02×10^{23} atoms of argon at S.T.P. is approximately   (1) 6.00 liters   (2) 11.2 liters   (3) 22.4 liters   (4) 44.8 liters

81...........

82. A compound contains carbon and hydrogen in the mole ratio C:H = 2:3. The molecular mass of this compound could be   (1) 5   (2) 26   (3) 38   (4) 54

82...........

83. How many moles of $AgNO_3$ are dissolved in 10 ml. of a 1 M $AgNO_3$ solution?   (1) 1   (2) 0.1   (3) 0.01   (4) 0.001

83...........

84. NaOH is added to one beaker of distilled water, and C_2H_5OH is added to another beaker of distilled water. Both of the solutions that are formed will
(1) be strong electrolytes
(2) turn litmus paper blue
(3) have a lower boiling point than pure water
(4) have a lower freezing point than pure water

84...........

85. Which 1 molal solution will have the highest boiling point?   (1) KNO_3 (2) $Mg(NO_3)_2$ (3) $Al(NO_3)_3$ (4) NH_4NO_3

85...........

GROUP 6

DIRECTIONS (86–90): *Write the* number *of the word or expression that best completes the statement or answers the question.* [5]

Base your answers to questions 86 through 88 on the information and equation below.

$$A(g) + B(g) \rightleftharpoons AB(g) + \text{heat}$$
$$\text{Equilibrium constant } (K) \text{ at } 25° \text{ C.} = 0.50$$

NOTE: *That questions 86 through 88 have only three choices.*

86. If a catalyst is added to the system at equilibrium with temperature and pressure remaining constant, the concentration of A would   (1) decrease   (2) increase   (3) remain the same

86...........

87. When chemical equilibrium is reached, the concentration of AB, compared to the concentration of A times the concentration of B, is   (1) less   (2) greater   (3) the same

87...........

88. As the concentration of B is increased *at constant temperature*, the value of K will   (1) decrease   (2) increase   (3) remain the same   88..............

89. At 23° C., 100 milliliters of a saturated solution of NaCl is in equilibrium with 1 gram of solid NaCl. The concentration of the solution will be changed most when
(1) 80 ml. of water is added to the solution
(2) additional solid NaCl is added to the solution
(3) the pressure on the solution is increased
(4) the temperature of the solution is decreased 5 C.°   89..............

90. Carbon dioxide is most soluble in water under conditions of
(1) high pressure and high temperature
(2) high pressure and low temperature
(3) low pressure and low temperature
(4) low pressure and high temperature   90..............

GROUP 7

DIRECTIONS (**91–92**): *For each solution in questions 91 and 92 write the* number *of the phrase* chosen from the list below, *that best describes the relative concentration of* H_3O^+ and OH^- *in that solution.*   [2]

Relative Concentration of H_3O^+ and OH^-

      (1) $[H_3O^+]$ is greater than $[OH^-]$.
      (2) $[H_3O^+]$ is less than $[OH^-]$.
      (3) $[H_3O^+]$ is equal to $[OH^-]$.

91. A solution of Na_2CO_3 91..............

92. A solution with a H_3O^+ concentration of 1×10^{-2} M   92..............

DIRECTIONS (**93–95**): *Write the* number *of the word or expression that best completes the statement or answers the question.*   [3]

93. Which is the conjugate base of the H_3O^+ ion?   (1) H_2O
(2) OH^- (3) H_2 (4) H^+ 93..............

94. If a water solution at 25° C. has an H_3O^+ concentration of 1×10^{-4} mole/liter, what is the concentration of the OH^-?
(1) 1×10^{-10} (2) 1×10^{-7} (3) 1×10^{-4} (4) 1×10^{-3} 94..............

95. According to Table M, which 0.1 M solution contains the lowest concentration of hydrogen ions?   (1) H_2SO_4 (2) H_3PO_4
(3) $HC_2H_3O_2$ (4) H_2CO_3 95..............

GROUP 8

DIRECTIONS (96–100): *Write the number of the word or expression that best completes the statement or answers the question.* [5]

Base your answers to questions 96 through 98 on the diagrams of the half-cells below and on the information in Table *L*.

Half-Cells

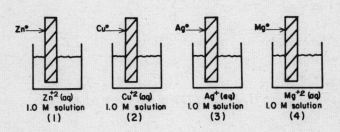

96. Which half-cell contains a metal electrode that is the strongest reducing agent? (1) 1 (2) 2 (3) 3 (4) 4   96.............

97. Half-cell 2 is connected to half-cell 3 by means of a wire and a salt bridge. When the cell reaches equilibrium, the voltage will be (1) 1.14 v. (2) 0.80 v. (3) 0.46 v. (4) 0.00 v.   97.............

98. Half-cell 3 is connected to half-cell 4 by means of a wire and a salt bridge. Which electronic equation represents the oxidation reaction that occurs?
(1) $Mg^0 + 2e^- \rightarrow Mg^{+2}$ (3) $Mg^{+2} + 2e^- \rightarrow Mg^0$
(2) $Mg^0 - 2e^- \rightarrow Mg^{+2}$ (4) $Mg^{+2} - 2e^- \rightarrow Mg^0$ 98.............

99. In the half-reaction $Mn^{+2} + 4H_2O \rightarrow MnO_4^- + 8H^+$, the substance oxidized is (1) Mn^{+2} (2) H_2O (3) MnO_4^- (4) H^+ 99.............

100. Which reaction will take place spontaneously?
(1) $Cu^0 + 2H^+ \rightarrow Cu^{+2} + H_2$
(2) $Cu^0 + Zn^{+2} \rightarrow Cu^{+2} + Zn^0$
(3) $Zn^0 + 2H^+ \rightarrow Zn^{+2} + H_2$
(4) $2Cl^- + Br_2^0 \rightarrow Cl_2^0 + 2Br^-$ 100.............

GROUP 9

DIRECTIONS (101–105): *Write the* number *of the word or expression that best completes the statement or answers the question.* [5]

Base your answers to questions 101 and 102 on the structural formula below.

$$
\begin{array}{c}
\quad\ \ \ \text{H}\ \ \text{H} \\
\quad\ \ \ | \ \ \ | \\
\text{H—C—C—OH} \\
\quad\ \ \ | \ \ \ | \\
\quad\ \ \ \text{H}\ \ \text{H}
\end{array}
$$

101. This compound is (1) an acid (2) an alcohol (3) an ester (4) a hydrocarbon

101..............

102. When this compound burns completely in oxygen, the products are (1) C and H_2O (2) CO and H_2 (3) CO_2 and H_2 (4) CO_2 and H_2O

102..............

103. Which compound will react most readily with bromine? (1) methane (2) ethene (3) propane (4) butane

103..............

104. Which is an isomer of 2-methyl butane? (1) pentane (2) propane (3) 2-methyl propane (4) 2-methyl pentane

104..............

105. What is the name of the compound represented by the formula C_4H_8? (1) butanol (2) butyne (3) butene (4) butane

105..............

Answers June, 1970 Chemistry

1. Ans. **1** The change from the solid phase directly to the gaseous phase is called sublimation. It is shown as follows:

$$\text{Solid} \xrightarrow{\text{Sublimation}} \text{Vapor}$$

Some solid substances when heated under atmospheric pressure, do not melt but change directly from the solid to the vapor state. In these solids, the intermolecular forces are weak and they exhibit measurable vapor pressures at room temperature. Because of these low intermolecular forces, many of them such as iodine and naphthalene (mothballs) evaporate rather easily. Sublimation might also be described as the complete process of a solid passing directly into the vapor state without melting and recondensation of the vapor into the solid state.

Wrong choices explained:
(2) Evaporation is the escape of molecules from the liquid state to the gas or vapor state. It is shown as follows:

$$\text{Liquid} \xrightarrow{\text{Evaporation}} \text{Vapor}$$

The escaping molecules have a higher kinetic energy compared to those in the liquid.
(3) Condensation—The transition from vapor (gas) to liquid or the process of converting a gas into a liquid. It is shown as follows:

$$\text{vapor (gas)} \xrightarrow{\text{Condensation}} \text{liquid}$$

(4) Crystallization is the process of building a solid structure from a liquid in which small crystal aggregates are formed at a small number of points and larger crystals shoot out from these centers until the whole is a solid. A crystal is a solid with a natural geometric form.

ALSO The physical change of a liquid to a solid is called freezing or crystallization and involves a loss of energy by the liquid. It may be shown as follows:

$$\text{liquid} \rightarrow \text{solid} + \text{energy}$$

(2) Ans. **2** The problem states that a sample of hydrogen has a volume of 100 ml. at a pressure of 1 atmosphere and asks us to determine the volume at 2 atmospheres of pressure, temperature remaining constant. *Boyle's Law* states that at constant temperature the volume of a fixed mass of gas is inversely proportional to the pressure ($v = 1/p$). Thus, if the pressure increases the volume decreases.

ALSO: $PV = K$ (constant) at a fixed temperature. This principle may be illustrated by the following diagram:

14

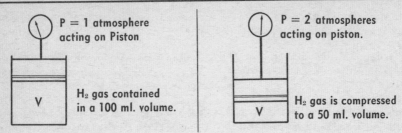

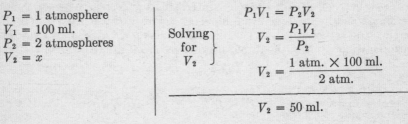

We solve the problem as follows:

$P_1 = 1$ atmosphere
$V_1 = 100$ ml.
$P_2 = 2$ atmospheres
$V_2 = x$

Solving for V_2

$$P_1V_1 = P_2V_2$$

$$V_2 = \frac{P_1V_1}{P_2}$$

$$V_2 = \frac{1 \text{ atm.} \times 100 \text{ ml.}}{2 \text{ atm.}}$$

$$V_2 = 50 \text{ ml.}$$

3. **Ans. 1** A liquid which evaporates rapidly at room temperature would most likely have a high vapor pressure. A high rate of evaporation is favored by:

(1) High temperature of the liquid
(2) Small attractive forces in the liquid
(3) Low atmospheric pressure above the liquid
(4) A large surface area
(5) Movement of the atmosphere above the liquid.

In order for molecules to leave the surface of a liquid and become vapor, they have to overcome the forces of attraction of the other molecules in the liquid. The vapor pressure of a liquid is the pressure exerted by the vapor that is in equilibrium with the liquid at a definite temperature. The vapor pressure depends on the temperature and on the nature of the liquid. At 20°C., H_2O has a vapor pressure of 17.5 mm.; CCl_4 has a vapor pressure of 91 mm. and chloroform, $CHCl_3$ has a vapor pressure of 160 mm. These values of the vapor pressure tell us that chloroform will evaporate faster than either H_2O or CCl_4 since it has a higher vapor pressure. In general organic liquids such as ethanol, benzene and acetone etc., have high vapor pressures.

Wrong choices explained:
(2) A liquid with a high boiling point would have strong attractive forces between molecules, thus it would have a low vapor pressure.
(3) The melting point of a solid is equivalent to the freezing point of a liquid. A liquid with a high freezing point would have a low vapor pressure.
(4) A liquid which has strong attractive forces between molecules would have a low vapor pressure.

4. Ans. **3** Exothermic reactions are usually self-sustaining because the energy released is sufficient to maintain the reaction. In a chemical reaction, energy is required to break bonds in molecules so they can become reactive. This energy is called energy of activation. We shall consider the formation of water from oxygen and hydrogen molecules. By some reaction mechanism, the bonds of hydrogen and oxygen molecules must be broken and new bonds between oxygen and hydrogen must be formed. Once the reaction is started, the energy released is enough to sustain the reaction. When new bonds are formed in the water molecule, energy is released. Bond breaking is an endothermic process and bond forming is an exothermic process. The net process in the formation of water is exothermic. *Table F* tells us that the heat of formation of H_2O, $\Delta H = -68$ Kcal/mole (an exothermic reaction). The following potential energy diagram describes the pathway for an exothermic reaction:

Heat of Reaction for water
$H_2 + \frac{1}{2}O_2 = H_2O$

ΔH = Heat of Reaction
$\Delta H = -68$ Kcal/mole

Wrong choices explained:

(1) Some exothermic chemical reactions require more activation energy than others. Energy of activation is not responsible for sustaining a chemical reaction.

(2) Likewise, some exothermic chemical reactions require less activation energy than others. As we stated above, energy of activation is not responsible for sustaining a chemical reaction.

(4) If the products contain more potential energy than the reactants, the reaction is endothermic. Endothermic reactions are not self-sustaining.

5. Ans. **2** The mass of gas which contains 3×10^{23} molecules at S.T.P. is 14 grams of N_2. We know that 1 mole of a gas at S.T.P. contains 6×10^{23} molecules and has a mass of one gram molecular weight. One mole of N_2 gas has a gram molecular weight of 28 grams at S.T.P. It contains 6×10^{23} molecules. This problem can be solved as follows:

$$\frac{28 \text{ grams of } N_2}{6 \times 10^{23} \text{ molecules}} = \frac{x \text{ grams}}{3 \times 10^{23} \text{ molecules}}$$

Solving for x $\qquad\qquad x = 14$ grams of N_2

14 grams of N_2 ($\frac{1}{2}$ mole) would have a volume of 11.2 liters at S.T.P.

Wrong choices explained:

(1) 38 grams of F_2 = 1 gram molecular weight = 1 mole

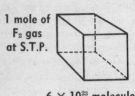

1 mole of F_2 gas at S.T.P.

22.4 liters
1 mole

6×10^{23} molecules of F_2 gas.

The gram molecular mass of F_2 gas at S.T.P. is 38 grams. This is equivalent to 1 mole which contains 6×10^{23} molecules.

(2) 2 grams of H_2 = 1 gram molecular weight = 1 mole

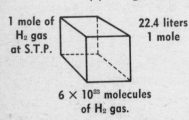

1 mole of H_2 gas at S.T.P.

22.4 liters
1 mole

6×10^{23} molecules of H_2 gas.

The gram molecular mass of H_2 gas at S.T.P. is 2 grams. This is equivalent to 1 mole which contains 6×10^{23} molecules.

(4) 70 grams of Cl_2 = 1 gram molecular weight = 1 mole

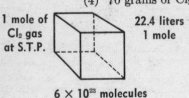

1 mole of Cl_2 gas at S.T.P.

22.4 liters
1 mole

6×10^{23} molecules of Cl_2 gas.

The gram molecular mass of Cl_2 gas at S.T.P. is 70 grams. This is equivalent to 1 mole which contains 6×10^{23} molecules.

6. **Ans. 2** The problem tells us that 20 calories of heat are added to 2 grams of water at a temperature of 10° C. and asks us to determine the resulting temperature of the water. The problem can be analyzed using the following diagram:

BEFORE ADDITION OF HEAT

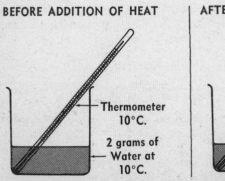

Thermometer 10°C.

2 grams of Water at 10°C.

AFTER ADDITION OF HEAT

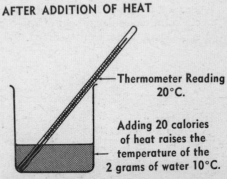

Thermometer Reading 20°C.

Adding 20 calories of heat raises the temperature of the 2 grams of water 10°C.

We can solve the problem mathematically as follows:

Heat gained by water
= Mass of water × Change in temperature of water × Specific heat of water

or: Heat gained = Mass × ΔT × Specific heat

Heat gained = 20 calories
$\Delta T = x$
Mass = 2 grams
Specific heat = 1 calorie/gram/C°.

$$\Delta T = \frac{\text{Heat gained}}{\text{Mass} \times \text{Specific heat}}$$

$$\Delta T = \frac{20 \text{ calories}}{2 \text{ grams} \times 1 \text{ calorie/gram/C°}}$$

$$\Delta T = 10C°$$

Since the change of temperature is 10C°, the final temperature is 10° C. + 10C° = 20° C.

7. Ans. 1 If the temperature of a substance changes 40 Celsius degrees, the number of degrees change in temperature on the Kelvin scale is 40°. We can use the following relationship to determine change in Kelvin degrees since we know the increases in Celsius degrees.

$$°K = °C + 273$$

This relationship tells us that the Kelvin reading is directly proportional to the Celsius reading. Therefore, if there is a change of 40° on the Celsius scale, there will be a similar increase on the Kelvin scale. We can solve the problem as follows:

at 0° C.
$°K. = °C. + 273$
$°K. = °C. + 273$
$°K. = 0° + 273$
$°K. = 273.$

We now increase the temperature of a substance from 0° C. to 40° C. This is an increase of 40 Celsius degrees. Let us determine the Kelvin reading corresponding to 40° C.

at 40° C.
$°K. = °C. + 273$
$°K. = 40° + 273$
$°K. = 313° K.$

°K.	°C.
273°	0°
313°	40°

Therefore, an increase of 40° on the Celsius scale is equal to an increase of 40° on the Kelvin scale. Using the temperature scales, we can analyze the problem as follows:

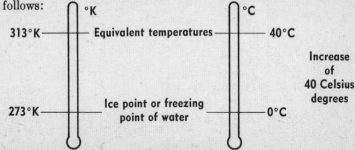

°K   °C

313°K —— Equivalent temperatures —— 40°C

273°K —— Ice point or freezing point of water —— 0°C

Increase of 40 Celsius degrees

It can be seen that an increase of 40 Celsius degrees is equal to an increase of 40 Kelvin degrees.

8. Ans. **3** The number of sublevels in the third principal energy level is 3. They are the s, p and d sublevels. Sublevels, also called subshells, are subdivisions of the main quantum level. The principal quantum number (n) represents the principal energy level and indicates the average distance of an orbital from the nucleus of the atom. An orbital is a diffuse region around the nucleus in which an electron may be expected to exist. Orbitals are designated by the letters s, p, d and f. Principal energy levels are in order of increasing distance from the nucleus, K ($n = 1$), L ($n = 2$), M ($n = 3$), N ($n = 4$), etc. The sublevels are outlined as follows for the first four principal energy levels:

For $n = 1$, there is only one sublevel called $1s$
For $n = 2$, there are two sublevels $2s$ and $2p$
For $n = 3$, there are three sublevels $3s$, $3p$ and $3d$
For $n = 4$, there are four sublevels $4s$, $4p$, $4d$ and $4f$

The diagram below shows the energy and the number of sublevels in each principal quantum level. Notice that the third quantum level has three sublevels.

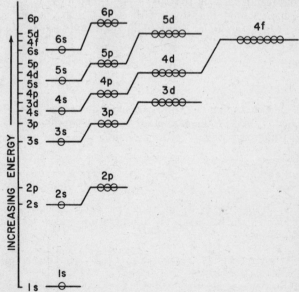

Wrong choices explained:
(1) As stated above, the first principal energy level has one sublevel.
(2) As stated above, the second principal energy level has two sublevels.
(4) As stated above, the fourth principal energy level has four sublevels.

9. **Ans. 4**   A nonmetal would most likely have an ionization energy of 11.8 electron-volts (e.v.). Ionization energy is the minimum energy needed to remove the most loosely bound electron from an isolated gaseous atom. Ionization energy (also called ionization potential) may be measured in electron volts or kcal/mole. *Table J* lists the first ionization energy of atoms. Using *Table J*, we can set up the following chart for the choices 1 to 4:

Choice	Electron-Volts	Element
1	5.1	Na
2	7.4	Pb
3	8.5	Sb
4	11.8	Br

Choices 1, 2 and 3 are metals.
Choice 4 is a nonmetal.

In general, metals have lower ionization potential values. Nonmetals have higher values, since it is harder to remove the outer electrons. In this question we see that bromine has the highest ionization value. Elements in Groups VIA, VIIA and O have high ionization potential values.

Nonmetals are located to the right of the stepwise line running from boron to astatine. Sodium (Na), lead (Pb) and antimony (Sb) are metals whereas bromine (Br) is a nonmetal. (Of course the metals are located to the left of the stepwise line.) Bromine is located in Group 7A. Group 7A contains very active nonmetals. The wrong choices are explained in the table above.

10. **Ans. 4**   The electron configuration of the element having the highest ionization energy is $1s^2 2s^2 2p^5$. Ionization energy is explained in the previous question, #9. Ionization energy values are listed in *Table J*. The orbital arrangement is explained as follows:

The first number before the letter indicates the principal energy level.

$1s^2 2s^2 2p^5$

The superscript indicates the number of electrons in that sublevel. The letter refers to the sublevel.

The orbital designation $1s^2 2s^2 2p^5$ is for the element fluorine.

As we explained in question 9, elements in Group 7A have high ionization energy values. Fluorine has the highest ionization potential value in Group 7A. One of the reasons it has such a high value is that it is small in size, since the electrons are strongly attracted by nuclear charge. The stronger the nonmetallic properties, the higher is the ionization potential value. The table below summarizes the electron configuration and the ionization energy values of the elements in this question:

Choice	Electron Configuration	Element	Ionization Energy
1	$1s^22s^22p^1$	Boron	8.3 e.v.
2	$1s^22s^22p^2$	Carbon	11.2 e.v.
3	$1s^22s^22p^4$	Oxygen	13.6 e.v.
4	$1s^22s^22p^5$	Fluorine	17.3 e.v.

Since fluorine has the highest value, $1s^22s^22p^5$ is the answer.
The wrong choices are explained in the table above.

11. Ans. **3** The electron configuration which represents an atom in the ground state is $1s^22s^22p^63s^2$. The other configurations represent configurations in excited states. Atoms become excited when electrons are raised to higher energy levels by absorption of energy. The ground state is the most stable state of the atom. If we consider the elements from atomic number 1 to 20 in the ground state, they fill up the orbitals as follows: (numbers indicate order of filling.)

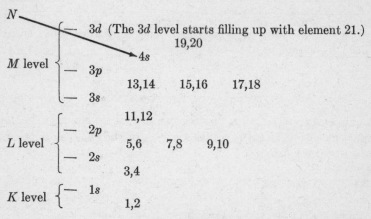

```
N
        ⌐ —  3d  (The 3d level starts filling up with element 21.)
        │                  19,20
M level ┤      —  4s
        │   — 3p
        │           13,14     15,16     17,18
        ⌐ — 3s
                 11,12
        ⌐ — 2p
L level ┤       5,6     7,8     9,10
        │ — 2s
        ⌐        3,4
        ⌐ — 1s
K level ┤
        ⌐     1,2
```

We see that the answer to this question follows our diagram for filling of orbitals in numerical order since it is in the ground state.

Wrong choices explained:
(1) $1s^22p^1$ is in the excited state. The $2s$ level should fill up before the $2p$.
(2) $1s^22s^23p^2$ is an excited atom. If it were in the ground state, the $3s$ orbital should fill up before the $3p$ orbital.
(4) $1s^22s^22p^64s^1$ is another excited atom. If it were in the ground state, the $3s^1$ should fill up before the $4s^1$.

12. Ans. **1** The electron configuration for a noble gas is $1s^2$. Noble gases are located in Group O of the *Periodic Table*. Noble gases are stable

since their outer energy levels are complete. Noble gases do not ordinarily combine with other elements however we do have the compound XeF_4. The electron configurations for the noble gases are listed as follows:

Element	Electron Configuration
Helium	$1s^2$
Neon	$1s^2 2s^2 2p^6$
Argon	$1s^2 2s^2 2p^6 3s^2 3p^6$
Krypton	$1s^2 2s^2 2p^6 3s^2 3p^6 3d^{10} 4s^2 4p^6$
Xenon	$1s^2 2s^2 2p^6 3s^2 3p^6 3d^{10} 4s^2 4p^6 4d^{10} 5s^2 5p^6$
Radon	Xenon $+ 4f^{14} 5d^{10} 6s^2 6p^4$

Wrong choices explained:

Choice	Electron Configuration	Element	Group
2	$1s^2 2s^2$	Be	2A
3	$1s^2 2s^2 2p^2$	C	4A
4	$1s^2 2s^2 2p^6 3s^2$	Mg	2A

13. **Ans. 3** The maximum number of electrons that can occupy the $3d$ sublevel is 10. The maximum number of electrons that can fill any principal energy level is equal to $2n^2$ where $n = 1,2,3,4$, etc. Thus, in the K level ($n = 1$), we have a maximum of 2 electrons. In the L level, we have a maximum of 8 electrons etc. An orbital can have 0, 1, or a maximum of 2 electrons. In the atom any s sublevel has 1 orbital with a maximum of 2 electrons. Any p sublevel has 3 orbitals with a maximum of 6 electrons. Any d sublevel has 5 orbitals with a maximum of 10 electrons. Any f sublevel has 7 orbitals with a maximum of 14 electrons. Therefore, the maximum number of electrons that can occupy the $3d$ sublevel is 10.

Wrong choices explained:
(1) The p sublevel can have a maximum of 6 electrons.
(2) The second principal energy level can have a maximum of 8 electrons.
(4) The f sublevel can have a maximum of 14 electrons.

14. **Ans. 4** The pair which has the same electron configuration is S^{-2} and Ar^0. The *Periodic Table* tells us that the electron configuration of the element argon in Group O is 2-8-8. In order for the sulfur atom (2-8-6) to become the sulfide ion S^{-2} 2-8-8, the atom has to gain 2 electrons. Therefore, an atom of argon and the sulfide ion are *isoelectronic*. Isoelectronic means they have identical electronic configurations, (2-8-8).

We can summarize the electron configurations of all the atoms and ions in this question as follows:

Choice	Atom or Ion	Electron Configuration	Explanation
1	Ca^0	2-8-8-2	It is a neutral atom of calcium.
	Ca^{+2}	2-8-8	When Ca^0 becomes the Ca^{++} ion, it loses 2 electrons.
2	Cl^-	2-8-8	When the chloride ion, Cl^- is formed from the atom, it gains an electron.
	F^-	2-8	When the F^- ion is formed from the atom, it gains an electron.
3	Na^+	2-8	When the sodium ion is formed, it loses one electron.
	K^+	2-8-8	When the potassium ion is formed, it loses one electron.
4	S^{-2}	2-8-8	When the sulfide S^{-2} ion is formed from the sulfur atom it gains 2 electrons.
	Ar^0	2-8-8	This is the configuration for an atom of argon.

Choice 4 is the correct answer since S^{-2} and Ar are isoelectronic.

15. **Ans. 2** We are given the unbalanced equation:

$$Sb + Cl_2 \rightarrow SbCl_3$$

We are asked to determine the coefficient of antimony (111) chloride in the balanced equation. In order to balance the equation, we must write the necessary coefficients before the symbols or formulas, so that there will be the same number of atoms of each element on either side of the arrow. When the equation is balanced properly, it will conform to the *Law of Conservation of Matter*. To balance the equation it is usually best to start balancing with the most complex formula in the equation and then complete the balancing of the other formulas. Since we have 3 Cl atoms on the right side and 2 Cl atoms on the left side, placing a "3" in front of Cl_2 on the left side and a "2" on the right side in front of $SbCl_3$ will balance the Cl atoms. Now we have 2 atoms of Sb on the right side. We now place a "2" in front of the Sb on the left side and the equation is balanced. The answer to the question is 2, since it is the coefficient of $SbCl_3$. The balanced equation is listed as follows:

$$2Sb + 3Cl_2 \rightarrow 2SbCl_3$$

16. **Ans. 4** The attractive forces between nonpolar molecules are called *van der Waal's forces*. Examples of nonpolar molecules include molecules such as F_2, Cl_2, H_2, O_2, and N_2. The bonding between these diatomic gaseous atoms is nonpolar covalent since there is equal sharing of the electron pair between atoms. For example:

H $\overset{\circ}{\underset{\times}{}}$ H   The Hydrogen Molecule shows Equal Sharing of the bonding electrons

The electronegativity difference between diatomic gaseous atoms is zero. Since these molecules are nonpolar, the only attractive forces between these molecules are *van der Waal's forces*. *Van der Waal's forces* appear to be due to chance distribution of electrons resulting in momentary dipole attractions. These weak *van der Waal's* attractions cause the nonpolar molecules to liquefy when the pressure and temperature conditions are proper for each gas.

Wrong choices explained:

(1) *Dipole attraction* The asymmetric distribution of electrical charge in a molecule gives rise to a molecule which is polar in nature and is called a dipole. Dipoles attract one another with electrostatic forces. Examples of dipoles include polar covalent molecules such as H_2O, HCl, NH_3.

(2) *Hydrogen bonding* Hydrogen bonds are formed between molecules in which hydrogen is covalently bonded to an element of small atomic radius and highly electronegative. Hydrogen bonding occurs between water molecules, ammonia (NH_3) molecules and HF molecules.

(3) *Molecule-ion attraction* Polar covalent compounds when interacting with ionic compounds, attract ions from these compounds and form a solution. Example—negative end of the water molecule for the sodium ion.

17. **Ans. 2** The most likely formula for the compound formed when magnesium reacts with nitrogen is Mg_3N_2. Pure nitrogen combines with an active metal to form a nitride. The nitride ion has an oxidation number of -3. The equation for the reaction is:

$$3Mg + N_2 \rightarrow Mg_3N_2$$

The formula below shows that the algebraic sum of the oxidation numbers adds up to zero.

$$Mg_3{}^{+2}N_2{}^{-3} \qquad (+6 - 6) = 0$$

Choices 1, 3 and 4 will not give us an algebraic sum of zero. I do not believe that choices 1, 3 and 4 could exist under ordinary conditions.

18. **Ans. 4** The methane molecule is nonpolar and this can be best explained by

the fact that the methane molecule is symmetrical. In the methane molecule, the four covalent bonds of the carbon atom are directed (oriented) in space toward the four vertices of a regular tetrahedron. A tetrahedron is a regular four-sided pyramid whose four faces are equilateral triangles. In this molecule, a carbon atom is covalently bonded to 4 hydrogen atoms. In other words, all bonds are equidistant. The angles between the C—H are 109°. The carbon atom is in the center of the tetrahedron. The structural formula for CH_4 is shown as follows:

CH_4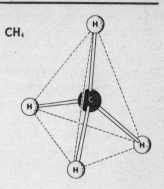

Wrong choices explained:

(1)   The fact that the carbon-hydrogen bond is slightly polar does not explain why the CH_4 molecule is nonpolar. We must take into consideration the 4 carbon-hydrogen bonds in the molecule.

(2)   The fact that carbon and hydrogen have nonmetallic properties does not explain why the CH_4 molecule is nonpolar.

(3)   The fact that methane is an organic compound does not explain why it is nonpolar. Some organic compounds are polar and some are nonpolar.

19.   Ans.   **4**   The smallest particle of a covalent compound that has the chemical properties of that compound is a molecule. A molecule is the smallest chemical unit of a substance which is capable of stable existence and which retains the properties of that substance. Thus one molecule of H_2 contains 2 hydrogen atoms covalently bonded to one another. In the water molecule, H_2O, 2 atoms of hydrogen are covalently bonded to the oxygen atom.

Wrong choices explained:

(1)   An ion is an atom or group of atoms with an unbalanced electrostatic charge. Examples include the sodium ion, Na^+, the sulfate ion, SO_4^{-2}, etc.

(2)   An atom is the smallest particle of an element which has all the chemical properties of that element and which may enter into chemical combination.

(3)   An electron is a negatively charged particle found in the atom.

20.   Ans.   **4**   A solid which is soft, a nonconductor, and which melts at a low temperature is most likely a molecular solid. Below we have prepared a list of properties and examples of the 4 types of solids listed in this question.

(1)   Ionic solids have high melting points, but as solids they do not conduct electricity. They conduct electricity in the molten state and in solution. Examples of ionic solids are NaCl and MgO.

(2)   Network solids are hard, electrical insulators, poor conductors of heat, and have high melting points. Examples of network solids are mica, asbestos, graphite, diamonds and silicon dioxide.

(3)   Metallic solids generally have high melting points and great strength Metallic solids are good conductors of heat and electricity. Examples include Mg, Fe, Ag etc.

(4)   In general molecular solids are soft, electrical insulators (nonconductors), poor heat conductors, and have low melting points. Examples include solid carbon dioxide (dry ice); sucrose, $C_{12}H_{22}O_{11}$; and paraffin wax (a mixture of hydrocarbons). This fourth statement explains the answer to this question. Wrong choices 1, 2, and 3 have been explained above.

21.   Ans.   2   The correct electron-dot formula for the ammonia molecule is:

$$H$$
$$\overset{\cdot\cdot}{H : N : H}$$
$$\underset{\cdot\cdot}{}$$

The ammonia molecule has the formula NH_3. An electron-dot formula shows the bonding arrangement as well as the number of valence electrons. Valence electrons are all the electrons in the outermost principal energy level of an atom. The hydrogen atom has a single electron in its electron configuration. The electron-dot configuration for the hydrogen atom is $(H \cdot)$. The electron configuration of the nitrogen atom (Group 5A of the *Periodic Table*) shows 5 electrons in its valence shell. The electron-dot diagram for the nitrogen atom is: $\dot{N}$. . As shown above, the electron-dot formula should show 8 valence electrons, 5 for the nitrogen atom and 1 for each of three hydrogen atoms. The proper bonding arrangement should also be shown.

Wrong choices explained:
(1)   This electron-dot diagram is incorrect since it shows only 3 valence electrons.
(3)   This electron-dot diagram is incorrect since it shows only 6 valence electrons for NH_3.
(4)   The formula for ammonia is NH_3 and not NH_4.

22.   Ans.   3   As one proceeds from left to right across Period 3 of the *Periodic Table*, there is a decrease in metallic characteristics. Metallic characteristics are governed by:

(1)   Low ionization energy. The lower the ionization energy, the more metallic is the element. Ionization energy is explained in the answers to questions 9 and 10.
(2)   Low electronegativity values. The lower the electronegativity value, the more metallic is the element. Electronegativity is a measure of the attraction an atom has for a shared pair of electrons. Electronegativity values are listed on *Table J*.
(3)   A small number (1, 2 or 3) of electrons in the outer or valence shell.
(4)   Other factors include electrical conductivity, heat conductivity, melting point, etc.
The ionization energy, electronegativity and valence electron values for Period 3 of the *Periodic Table* are shown as follows:

Element	Na	Mg	Al	Si	P	S	Cl	Ar
Ionization Energy	5.1	7.6	6.0	8.1	10.9	10.3	13	15.7
Electronegativity	0.9	1.2	1.5	1.8	2.1	2.5	3.0	—
Valence Electrons	1	2	3	4	5	6	7	8

Metallic Properties are decreasing ⟶

It can be seen that the ionization energy, electronegativity and valence electron values are increasing as we go from left to right. These factors indicate that the metallic properties are decreasing as we go from left to right. The wrong choices are analyzed above.

23. **Ans. 3** The basis for the arrangement of our present *Periodic Table* is the atomic number. The original *Periodic Table* set up by *Mendeleyev* in 1869 was based on atomic weight. However in 1914, *Henry Moseley* used different elements as targets for a stream of electrons in an X-ray tube. He then studied the pattern of X-rays given off by each element. Moseley noticed that as the atomic number of the element increased the wave length of the X-ray decreased. Moseley's results showed that the atomic number is a property of the atom more fundamental than the atomic weight, and he suggested that this was the positive charge on the nucleus of the atom. Moseley showed that the properties of the elements are periodic functions of their atomic numbers. This is the basis for the *Periodic Law*. As a result of Moseley's work, the elements are now arranged according to their atomic number.

Wrong choices explained:
(1) The number of neutrons in an atom is not the basis for our present *Periodic Table*. It is based on the number of protons in the nucleus of the atom.
(2) A nucleon is either a proton or neutron. These particles make up the nucleus of the atom. The number of nucleons in the nucleus is not the basis for the arrangement of our present *Periodic Table*. The protons are the basis for the table.
(4) As we discussed above, the atomic mass was the basis for the arrangement of the first *Periodic Table* set up by Mendeleyev in 1869.

24. **Ans. 4** The period of the *Periodic Table* which contains elements that may combine chemically by losing electrons from more than one principal energy level is period 4. The type of element in which electrons are lost from more than one principal energy level in chemical bonding is a transition element. Transition elements are located in the "B" Groups and Group 8 of the *Periodic Table*. Transition elements have a deficiency of electrons in the d or f sublevel. In forming compounds, the transition elements (for example Period 4) exhibit many oxidation states presumably because some or all of the $3d$ electrons can also be used with the $4s$ electrons in chemical bonding.

Wrong choices explained:
Periods 1, 2, and 3 of the *Periodic Table* do not contain transition elements.

25. **Ans. 1** The element which has the greatest tendency to lose electrons is barium. In this question, we are dealing with Group 2A metals. For metals in Group 2A, the element with the larger atomic radius would have a smaller ionization energy. Ionization energy was explained in the answers to questions 9 and 10. The element having the lowest ionization energy value would have the greatest tendency to lose electrons. Since barium has the largest covalent atomic radius of the 4 elements and the smallest ionization energy value of the 4, it would have the greatest tendency to lose electrons. We can compare the covalent atomic radii values and the ionization energy values for these elements in the chart below:

	Magnesium	Calcium	Strontium	Barium
Covalent atomic radius	1.60 Å	1.97 Å	2.15 Å	2.17 Å
Ionization energy	7.6 e.v.	6.1 e.v.	5.7 e.v.	5.2 e.v.

Since barium has the largest radius and the smallest ionization energy values, it has the greatest tendency to lose electrons.

Wrong choices explained:
The table above shows that choices 2, 3 and 4 have a lesser tendency to lose electrons compared to barium. Their radii values are smaller and their ionization energy values are larger.

26. **Ans. 1** The element that is a metalloid is arsenic. The elements that occupy the zone between metallic and nonmetallic elements exhibit intermediate properties and are called metalloids. If we draw a stepwise line from boron to polonium we pass through the metalloids. (Remember this stepwise line separates the metals from the nonmetals on the chart.) The elements which are metalloids include the following: boron, silicon, germanium, arsenic, antimony, tellurium and polonium. Therefore arsenic is a metalloid.

Wrong choices explained:
(2) Neon is located in Group O of the *Periodic Table*. Group O elements are called noble gases.
(3) Potassium is located in Group 1 of the *Periodic Table*. Group 1 elements are called alkali metals. They are active metals.
(4) Bromine is located in Group 7A of the *Periodic Table*. Group 7A elements are called halogens. They are active nonmetals.

27. **Ans. 3** To determine the percentage of oxygen by mass in $CaCO_3$, we can set up the following relationship:

$$\text{Percentage of oxygen in } CaCO_3 = \frac{\text{Mass of oxygen}}{\text{Gram-Formula Mass of } CaCO_3} \times 100\%$$

$$\text{Mass of oxygen} = O_3 = 3 \times 16 = 48 \text{ grams}$$
$$\text{Gram-Formula Mass of } CaCO_3 = 100 \text{ grams}$$

$$\text{Percentage of oxygen in } CaCO_3 = \frac{48 \text{ grams}}{100 \text{ grams}} \times 100\% = 48\%$$

Thus, the percentage of oxygen in $CaCO_3$ is 48%.

28.   Ans.   **3**   The volume of hydrogen required to produce 22.4 liters of HI at S.T.P. is 11.2 liters. We are given the reaction:

$$H_{2(g)} + I_{2(g)} \rightarrow 2HI_{(g)}$$

The equation tells us that the mole ratio of H_2 to HI is 1:2. Therefore, if we use 1 mole of H_2, we will get 2 moles of HI. If we want to produce 1 mole (22.4 liters) of HI, we must use $\frac{1}{2}$ mole (11.2 liters) of H_2. We can also solve the problem as follows:

$$\frac{\text{liters of } H_2}{\text{moles of } H_2 \text{ in equation}} = \frac{\text{liters of HI}}{\text{moles of HI in equation}}$$

$$\frac{x}{1 \text{ mole}} = \frac{22.4 \ \ell.}{2 \text{ moles}} \qquad \begin{aligned} 2x &= 22.4 \ \ell. \\ x &= 11.2 \text{ liters} \end{aligned}$$

Therefore, in order to produce 22.4 liters of HI, we must use 11.2 liters of H_2.

29   Ans.   **2**   The molecular mass of a gas which has a density of 1.25 grams per liter at S.T.P. is 28. To determine the mass of gas when we are given the density, we use the following formula:

Density = 1.25 grams/liter
Mass = x
Volume = 22.4 liters = 1 mole

$$\text{Density} = \frac{\text{Mass}}{\text{Volume}}$$
$$\therefore \text{Mass} = \text{Density} \times \text{Volume}$$
$$\text{Mass} = 1.25 \text{ g.}/\ell. \times 22.4 \ \ell.$$
$$\text{Mass} = 28 \text{ grams}$$

ALSO: *Table A* tells us that nitrogen and carbon monoxide each have a density of 1.25 grams per liter. The molecular mass of N_2 is 28 and so is the molecular weight of CO-28.

30.   Ans.   **3**   The question asks us to determine the molarity of a solution which contains 98 grams of H_2SO_4 dissolved in 2 liters of solution. Molarity is defined as the number of moles of solute per liter of solution. Molarity is a term used to indicate the concentration of an acid, base or salt solution. We can solve this problem using the following formula:

$$\text{Molarity} = \frac{\dfrac{\text{The number of grams given}}{\text{Gram-molecular mass of } H_2SO_4}}{\text{The number of liters of solution}}$$

Molarity = x
The number of grams given = 98 = 1 mole
Gram-molecular mass of H_2SO_4 = 98
Number of liters = 2 liters

$$x = \frac{\dfrac{98}{98}}{2} = \frac{1}{2} = x$$
$$x = \tfrac{1}{2} \text{ or } 0.5 \text{ molar solution.}$$

ALTERNATE METHOD:

$$\text{Molarity} = \frac{\text{The number of moles of } H_2SO_4}{\text{The number of liters of solution}}$$

$$\text{Molarity} = \frac{1 \text{ mole}}{2 \text{ liters}} = 0.5 \text{ molar solution of } H_2SO_4$$

31. Ans. **1** The problem states that 100 ml. of water at 10° C. contains 60 grams of NaNO₃. We are asked to determine how many additional grams of NaNO₃ have to be added to form a saturated solution. *Table B* (shown below) tells us that at 10° C., 80 grams of NaNO₃ in 100 ml. of water are needed to make a saturated solution. If we have only 60 grams in the beaker, we have to add 20 more grams. (Remember that every point on the curve is a saturated solution).

SOLUBILITY CURVES

A saturated solution of NaNO₃ at 10°C would contain 80 grams.

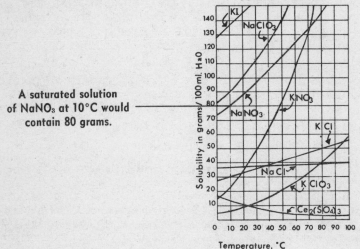

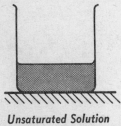

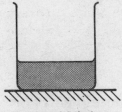

80 grams
−60 grams
20 grams
have to be added
for a saturated solution.

Unsaturated Solution
60 grams of NaNO₃
in 100 ml of water

Saturated Solution
80 grams of NaNO₃
in 100 ml. of water

32. Ans. **3** The number of atoms of hydrogen in 1 mole of NH₃ is 3(6 × 10²³). *Avogadro's Law* was explained in question 5. One mole of NH₃

contain 6×10^{23} molecules. Since NH_3 contains 1 nitrogen atom and 3 hydrogen atoms per molecule, the number of nitrogen atoms in 1 mole of NH_3 is 6×10^{23}. The number of hydrogen atoms is $3(6 \times 10^{23})$. This problem might also be explained using the following diagram:

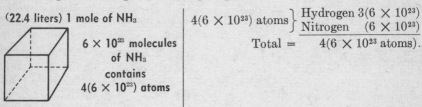

(22.4 liters) 1 mole of NH_3

6×10^{23} molecules of NH_3 contains $4(6 \times 10^{23})$ atoms

$$4(6 \times 10^{23}) \text{ atoms} \left\} \begin{array}{l} \text{Hydrogen } 3(6 \times 10^{23}) \\ \text{Nitrogen } \quad (6 \times 10^{23}) \end{array} \right.$$

$$\text{Total} = \quad 4(6 \times 10^{23} \text{ atoms}).$$

33. Ans. 1 The volume occupied by 2 grams of helium at S.T.P. is 11.2 liters. As we stated in the answer to question 5, 1 mole of a gas at S.T.P. occupies 22.4 liters and contains 6×10^{23} molecules. One mole of helium gas has a mass of 4 grams at S.T.P. and has a volume of 22.4 liters. 2 grams of helium is equivalent to $\frac{1}{2}$ mole and would have a value of 11.2 liters. We can also solve the problem as follows:

$$\boxed{1 \text{ mole}} \qquad \boxed{\tfrac{1}{2} \text{ mole}}$$

$$\frac{4 \text{ grams}}{22.4 \text{ liters}} = \frac{2 \text{ grams}}{x}$$

$$4x = 88.8$$
$$x = 11.2 \text{ liters}$$

34. Ans. 4 An increase in temperature usually increases the rate of a chemical reaction because the effectiveness of collisions between particles is increased. In order for reactions to occur between substances, the particles must collide and the collisions must result in interactions. An increase in temperature increases the average kinetic energy of the molecules. In other words, an increase in temperature makes molecules move faster. Therefore, they collide more frequently with other particles and are more likely to cause reaction. The curves below show that an increase in temperature shifts a greater majority of particles to higher energies so that a larger fraction of the particles are highly energetic. As a result, more of the collisions are effective at high temperatures. In other words, more particles will possess the required energy of activation at the higher temperature. The curves are shown as follows:

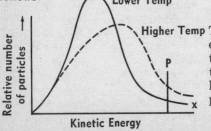

Lower Temp

Higher Temp

Relative number of particles

Kinetic Energy

P

x

This point (P) represents the minimum energy required for a reaction. Notice that a greater fraction of particles have the required activation energy at the higher temperature (This is shown by point x between the curves).

35. Ans. **3** The reaction which is represented by the equilibrium constant expression $K = \dfrac{[C]^2}{[A]^3[B]}$ is $3A_{(g)} + B_{(g)} = 2C_{(g)}$. The equilibrium constant K_e is a number referring to a given reversible reaction occurring at a given temperature. It is determined by dividing the product of the concentrations of the products of the reaction (each raised to that power which is its coefficient in the equation) by the product of the concentrations of the reactants (each raised to a power which is its coefficient in the equation). The equilibrium constant for the following reaction can be determined as follows:

$$aA + bB = cC + dD$$

The $\qquad$ $K_e = \dfrac{[C]^c \times [D]^d}{[A]^a \times [B]^b}$ $\qquad$ [ ] $\begin{cases}\text{Square brackets} \\ \text{indicate concentration} \\ \text{in moles per liter.}\end{cases}$

In this question we are given the following K_e equation:

$$K_e = \dfrac{[C]^2}{[A]^3[B]}$$

and we are asked to determine the reaction corresponding to this K_e equation. The reaction corresponding to this equation is:

$$3A_{(g)} + B_{(g)} = 2C_{(g)}$$

36. Ans. **3** The gas which is most soluble at S.T.P. is NH_3. *Table A* lists the solubility of gases at S.T.P. An analysis of *Table A* will indicate that ammonia (NH_3) is the most soluble. *Table A* is shown as follows:

DENSITY AND SOLUBILITY OF SOME COMMON GASES		
Name	*Density* grams/liter 0° C. 760 mm.	*Solubility**
Air	1.29	——
Ammonia	0.77	89.5
Carbon dioxide	1.98	0.3346
Carbon monoxide	1.25	0.0044
Chlorine	3.21	0.9972†
Nitrogen monoxide	1.34	0.0098
Hydrogen	0.09	0.0002
Hydrogen chloride	1.64	82.3
Hydrogen sulfide	1.54	0.7066
Nitrogen	1.25	0.0029
Oxygen	1.43	0.0069
Sulfur dioxide	2.93	22.83

NH_3 is the most soluble gas.

$\left.\begin{array}{l}CO_2 \\ CO \\ NO\end{array}\right\}$ are less soluble.

* mass of gas in grams dissolved in 100 grams of water at 0° C. and 760 mm.
† at 10° C.

Wrong choices explained:
The table reveals that CO, CO_2 and NO are less soluble than ammonia.

37. Ans. **2** In the reaction, $HC_2H_3O_2 + H_2O = H_3O^+ + C_2H_3O_2^-$ the addition of solid sodium acetate ($NaC_2H_3O_2$) results in a decrease in the concentration of H_3O^+. Solutions of weak electrolytes such as acetic acid ($HC_2H_3O_2$) represents an equilibrium system and it is possible to vary the concentration of an equilibrium mixture by increasing the concentration of one of the components of the weak electrolyte. *Le Chatelier's Principle* states if a system at equilibrium is subjected to a stress, the system will be displaced in such a direction as to relieve the stress. If we add $NaC_2H_3O_2$ to the solution, the $NaC_2H_3O_2$ dissociates completely as follows: $NaC_2H_3O_2 \rightarrow Na^+ + C_2H_3O_2^-$. The addition of the extra $C_2H_3O_2^-$ ions to the solution causes an increase in the $C_2H_3O_2^-$ ion concentration. The Na^+ ion does not affect the equilibrium. As a result, the equilibrium is subjected to a stress according to *Le Chatelier's Principle*. As a result, the system will alter itself to relieve the stress. The system will shift to the left to increase the concentration of $HC_2H_3O_2$ and H_2O. The concentration of H_3O^+ is decreased in this shift to the left. The type of reaction just described is called the common ion effect. The common ion effect is defined as the addition of an ion in common with an ion of a weak electrolyte which suppresses the ionization of the weak electrolyte. We can summarize the action taking place in this question as follows:

Shift to the left

Common ion

The addition of excess acetate ion shifts the equilibrium to the left to form more $HC_2H_3O_2 + H_2O$.

$$HC_2H_3O_2 + H_2O \underset{\text{slightly}}{\overset{\text{Ionizes}}{\rightleftharpoons}} H_3O^+ + C_2H_3O_2^-$$

$$NaC_2H_3O_2 \xrightarrow{\text{Dissociates}} Na^+ + + C_2H_3O_2^-$$

The H_3O^+ ion concentration decreases.

Wrong choices explained:
(1) As shown above, the acetate ion concentration increases.
(3) The addition of the Na^+ ions (from $NaC_2H_3O_2$) causes an increase of the Na^+ ion concentration.
(4) As shown above, the $HC_2H_3O_2$ concentration increases.

38. Ans. **1** If a solution has a pH of 3, the hydronium ion concentration of this solution in moles per liter is 1×10^{-3}. The pH of a solution is equal to the logarithm of the reciprocal of the hydrogen ion (hydronium ion) concentration when this concentration is expressed in moles/liter. It is shown as follows:

The brackets [ ]
indicate concentration
in moles/liter.

$$pH = \log \frac{1}{[H_3O^+]}$$
$$pH = -\log [H_3O^+]$$
$$= \log [H_3O^+] = -pH$$
$$[H_3O^+] = 10^{-pH}$$
$$pH = 3 [H_3O^+] = 10^{-3}$$

Therefore, if the pH is 3, the H_3O^+ ion concentration in moles per liter is 10^{-3} or 1×10^{-3}.

39.   Ans.   **4**   In the reaction $NH_4^+ + H_2O = NH_3 + H_3O^+$, the 2 Brönsted acids are: NH_4^+ and H_3O^+. The reaction is analyzed as follows: The *Brönsted-Lowry Theory* states that acids are proton donors and bases are proton acceptors.

$$\overleftarrow{\boxed{\text{TO THE LEFT}}}$$

			Base$_1$		Acid$_2$
			Proton Acceptor		Proton Donor
NH_4^+	$+$	H_2O	$= \quad NH_3$	$+$	H_3O^+
Proton Donor		Proton Acceptor			
Acid$_1$		Base$_2$			

$$\overrightarrow{\qquad\qquad\qquad}$$
$$\boxed{\text{TO THE RIGHT}}$$

Wrong choices explained:

(1) NH_4^+ is a *Brönsted-Lowry* acid and NH_3 is a Brönsted-Lowry base in this reaction.

(2) H_2O and NH_3 are *Brönsted-Lowry* bases in this reaction.

(3) H_2O is a *Brönsted-Lowry* base and H_3O^+ is a Brönsted-Lowry acid in this reaction.

40.   Ans.   **2**   A *Brönsted* base which is stronger than $Al(H_2O)_5(OH)^{+2}$ is OH^-. (Refer to *Table H*). In the conjugate base column, the strength of the base decreases as you go from bottom to top. Therefore, NH_2^- is the strongest of the 9 bases listed. The higher you rise in the column, the weaker is the base. Therefore, a substance which is a stronger base than $Al(H_2O)_5(OH)^{+2}$ is a species that is lower than $Al(H_2O)_5OH^{+2}$ on the conjugate base side. Of the 4 choices listed, OH^- is the only one lower than $Al(H_2O)_5(OH)^{+2}$, therefore it is a stronger base.

Wrong choices explained:

(1),(3)   On *Table H*, SO_4^{-2} and H_2O are weaker bases compared to $Al(H_2O)_5(OH)^{+2}$.

(4) $Al(H_2O)_6^{+3}$ is not a base. It is the conjugate acid of the conjugate base $Al(H_2O)_5(OH)^{+2}$.

41.   Ans.   **1**   The question asks us to determine how many milliliters of 0.2 molar KOH are needed to neutralize 20 milliliters of 0.1 molar HCl. A neutralization reaction is explained as follows:

$$\text{Acid} + \text{Base} \rightarrow \text{Salt} + \text{Water}$$
$$\text{HCl} + \text{KOH} \rightarrow \text{KCl} + H_2O$$

The problem is solved as follows:

Since the total positive valence (TPV) of HCl is +1 and the (TPV) of KOH is +1, we can determine the normality by multiplying the molarity × TPV. Using the equation below we can solve the problem as follows:

Acid   Base

milliliters × Normality = milliliters × Normality

20 ml.   ×   0.1   = x ×   0.2

milliliters of HCl = 20 ml.	$2 = 0.2x$
Normality of acid = 0.1 molar × 1(TPV) = 0.1 N	$20 = 2x$
milliliters of KOH = x	$10\ \text{ml.} = x$
Normality of base = 0.2 molar × 1(TPV) = 0.2 N	

Therefore it requires 10 ml. of 0.2 Normal KOH to neutralize 20 ml. of 0.1 Normal HCl.

42. **Ans. 4** The compound which is an electrolyte is $Ca(OH)_2$. Electrolytes are compounds that conduct electricity in solution. In general, acids, bases and salts are electrolytes. Acids, bases and salts ionize or dissociate in water solution to form ions. The ions conduct electricity. Compounds such as CH_3OH, C_2H_5OH, and $C_3H_5(OH)_3$ which do not conduct electricity are called nonelectrolytes. Nonelectrolytes do not form ions in water solution. In general, organic compounds are nonelectrolytes. CH_3OH, C_2H_5OH and $C_3H_5(OH)_3$ are organic compounds. This question can be summarized using the following table:

Choice	Compound	Electrical Conductivity	Ions Conducting
1	CH_3OH	No	None
2	C_2H_5OH	No	None
3	$C_3H_5(OH)_3$	No	None
4	$Ca(OH)_2$	Yes	Ca^{++} and OH^-

43. **Ans. 2** The half-reaction which is the standard for the measurement of the voltages on *Table L* is $H_2^0 \rightleftharpoons 2H^+ + 2e^-$. The absolute potential between a metal and its ions in solution cannot be measured directly, but it can be measured indirectly by comparison with a standard electrode, such as the hydrogen electrode. For this purpose, it is customary to use solutions in which the concentration of the ions is one molal, that is, 1 mole in 1000 grams of water. The standard hydrogen electrode consists of a piece of platinum foil on which has been deposited electrolytically a coating of finely divided platinum which, due to its color, is called "platinum black." The platinized foil is introduced into a solution of HCl which is 1 molal with respect to the hydrogen ions and a temperature of 25° C. A slow current of hydrogen under a pressure of 1 atmosphere is bubbled over the platinum in order to stir the solution around the electrode and to keep the latter thoroughly saturated with the gas.

The platinum black adsorbs large quantities of hydrogen and catalyzes the transformation of the molecular hydrogen into atomic hydrogen. Some of the hydrogen atoms give up their valence electrons to the platinum and pass into the solution as hydrogen ions. The accumulation of electrons on the hydrogen electrode charges it negatively, but to what extent is unknown. For convenience, however, the potential of the standard hydrogen electrode has been assigned the arbitrary value of zero.

Wrong choices explained:
Obviously choices 1, 3 and 4 are not standards. Oxidation potentials are based on hydrogen as the standard. Table L lists their position and E^0 values in volts.

44. Ans. **1** When 1 mole of Fe^{+2} is oxidized to Fe^{+3}, 1 mole of Ag^+ will be reduced to one mole of Ag^0. The oxidation-reduction reactions are shown as follows:

(LEO) **Loss of electrons-Oxidation**
$$1 \text{ mole } Fe^{+2} - 1 \text{ mole electrons} \rightarrow 1 \text{ mole } Fe^{+3}$$

(GER) **Gain of electrons-Reduction**
$$\underline{1 \text{ mole } Ag^{+1} + 1 \text{ mole electrons} \rightarrow 1 \text{ mole } Ag^0}$$
$$1 \text{ mole } Fe^{+2} + 1 \text{ mole } Ag^{+1} \rightarrow 1 \text{ mole } Fe^{+3} + 1 \text{ mole } Ag^0$$

One mole of Fe^{+2} contains 6×10^{23} ions. Therefore, Fe^{+2} will lose 6×10^{23} electrons when it is oxidized to Fe^{+3}. (6×10^{23} electrons is equivalent to one mole of electrons). One mole of Ag^+ will gain 1 mole of electrons to form 1 mole of Ag^0.

45. Ans. **2** The oxidation number of phosphorus in Na_2HPO_4 is $+5$. For neutral molecules such as Na_2HPO_4, the oxidation numbers of all the atoms must add algebraically up to zero. Sodium has an oxidation number of $+1$ in all compounds. Oxygen has an oxidation number of -2 in all compounds except in peroxides such as H_2O_2 when it is -1. Hydrogen has an oxidation number of $+1$ in all its compounds except in metal hydrides such as LiH where it is -1. Thus, in the compound Na_2HPO_4, sodium has a total value of $2 \times (+1) = +2$, hydrogen has a value of $+1$, oxygen has a total value of $4 \times (-2) = -8$. Therefore the charge on the phosphorus is $+5$ in order that the algebraic sum of the oxidation numbers of all the atoms adds up to zero. We can summarize this question using the following chart:

Molecular Formula	Na_2^{+1}	H^{+1}	P^{+5}	O_4^{-2}	Na_2HPO_4
Algebraic sum of the oxidation numbers	$+2$	$+1$	$+5$	-8	$= 0$

46. Ans. **3** In the reaction $2Cr(s) + 3Cu^{+2}(aq) \rightarrow 3Cu(s) + 2Cr^{+3}(aq)$, the net potential ($E^0$) for the overall reaction is $+1.08$ volts.
In this reaction, chromium is oxidized by losing 3 electrons per atom to form the Cr^{+3} ion. The Cu^{++} ion is reduced by gaining 2 electrons per ion to

form metallic copper Cu^0. The ion-electron half-reactions for the oxidation and reduction are shown as follows:

LEO-**Oxidation** $2Cr(s) - 6e^- \rightarrow 2Cr^{+3}(aq)$
GER-**Reduction** $3Cu^{+2}(aq) + 6e^- \rightarrow 3Cu^0(s)$

To obtain the E^0 values for each half-reaction, we consult *Table L. Table L* lists the E^0 values for the oxidation half-reactions only. For the reduction half-reaction, the sign ($+$ or $-$) for the E^0 value on *Table L* must be reversed. Thus the value for the reduction is shown as follows:

$$Cu^{+2} + 2e^- \rightarrow Cu^0 \qquad E^0 = +0.34 \text{ Volt}$$

The E^0 value for the oxidation half-reaction is:

$$Cr^0 \rightarrow Cr^{+3} + 3e^- \qquad E^0 = +0.74 \text{ Volt}$$

The total or net E^0 value is determined by adding the E^0 values for the half-reactions. The problem is solved as follows:

		E^0
Oxidation: **half-reaction:**	$2Cr(s) - 6e^- \rightarrow 2Cr^{+3}(aq)$	$+0.74$ Volt
Reduction **half-reaction:**	$3Cu^{+2}(aq) + 6e^- \rightarrow 3Cu^0(s)$	$+0.34$ Volt
	$2Cr(s) + 3Cu^{+2}(aq) \rightarrow 2Cr^{+3}(aq) + 3Cu^0(s)$	$+1.08$ Volts

Thus, the net potential E^0, equals $+1.08$ volts.

47. Ans. **2** When strontium (Sr) is oxidized, it will attain a positive oxidation number. When an element is oxidized, it loses electrons. The oxidation of strontium is shown as follows:

$$Sr^0(s) - 2e^- \rightarrow Sr^{+2}(aq)$$

or $Sr^0(s) \rightarrow Sr(aq)^{+2} + 2e^-$.   {This oxidation reaction is shown on Table L.

Wrong choices explained:

(1)   An isotope of strontium would have a different atomic mass. It would have a different number of neutrons in the nucleus. When an atom is oxidized, the neutrons in the nucleus are not involved.

(3)   When strontium is oxidized it becomes a positive ion not a negative ion.

(4)   Strontium will not become radioactive when it is oxidized. Radioactive changes are caused by changes in the nucleus of the atom.

48. Ans. **4** Given the reaction $Fe + Cl_2 \rightarrow FeCl_2$, the half-reaction that represents reduction is: $Cl_2^0 + 2e^- \rightarrow 2Cl^-$.

As we stated in question 46, if an element is reduced, it gains electrons. The ion-electron equations for the oxidation and reduction reactions are shown as follows:

(LEO) **Loss of electrons-Oxidation** $Fe^0 - 2e^- \rightarrow Fe^{+2}$
(GER) **Gain of electrons-Reduction** $Cl_2^0 + 2e^- \rightarrow 2Cl^-$

Wrong choices explained:

(1),(2) and (3)   These half-reactions do not take place in this reaction.

49.   Ans.   **2**   The metal which will not react with a dilute HCl solution is Ag. On *Table L*, the metals listed above hydrogen will replace hydrogen from acids, while those listed below hydrogen, will not replace hydrogen from acids. The reaction for each choice is listed as follows:

Choice	Reaction
1	$2Al + 6HCl \rightarrow 2AlCl_3 + 3H_2$
2	$Ag + HCl \rightarrow$ No Reaction
3	$Mg + 2HCl \rightarrow MgCl_2 + H_2$
4	$Zn + 2HCl \rightarrow ZnCl_2 + H_2$

50.   Ans.   **4**   An example of a homologous series is CH_4, C_2H_6, C_3H_8. The study of hydrocarbons is simplified by the fact that they can be divided into distinct series in which the composition of the first member of each series differs from that of the second by a CH_2 group. This relationship in such a series is called a homologous series. These hydrocarbon series include the alkane, alkene, alkyne and the benzene series. If we take any 2 consecutive members of any one of these series, they would differ by a CH_2 group. For example, in the alkane series, CH_4, methane, differs from C_2H_6, ethane, by a CH_2 group. Ethane, C_2H_6, differs from propane, C_3H_8, by a CH_2 group. Propane, C_3H_8, differs from butane, C_4H_{10}, by a CH_2 group. Choices 1, 2 and 3 are not examples of homologous series since they do not differ in each case by a CH_2 group.

51.   Ans.   **1**   The hydrocarbon which is saturated is C_2H_6. A saturated hydrocarbon has all single bonds. The general formula for the saturated hydrocarbons is C_nH_{2n+2}. The structural formula for ethane, C_2H_6, is shown as follows:

$$
\begin{array}{c}
\quad H \quad\ H \\
\quad | \quad\ | \\
H-C-C-H \\
\quad | \quad\ | \\
\quad H \quad\ H
\end{array}
$$

Wrong choices explained:
(2) C_3H_4 is called propyne. It is an unsaturated hydrocarbon and is a member of the alkyne series. It contains one triple bond. The general formula for the alkynes is C_nH_{2n-2}. The structural formula for propyne is shown as follows:

$$
\begin{array}{c}
\qquad\quad H \\
\qquad\quad | \\
H-C\equiv C-C-H \\
\qquad\quad | \\
\qquad\quad H
\end{array}
$$

(3) C_4H_6 is called butyne. It is a member of the alkyne which we explained in choice 2. The structural formula for butyne is shown as follows:

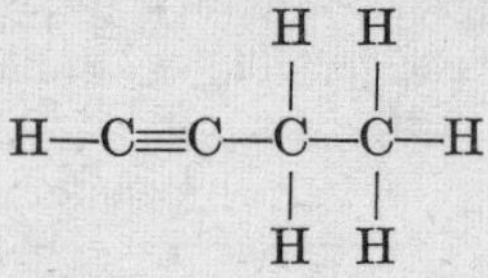

$$
\begin{array}{c}
\text{H}\ \ \text{H} \\
| \ \ \ | \\
\text{H--C}\equiv\text{C--C--C--H} \\
| \ \ \ | \\
\text{H}\ \ \text{H}
\end{array}
$$

(4) C_2H_2 is called acetylene or ethyne. It is a member of the alkyne series which we explained in choice 2. The structural formula for ethyne is shown as follows:

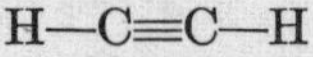

$$\text{H--C}\equiv\text{C--H}$$

52. Ans. **3** The structural formula of 1,3- dichlorobutane is

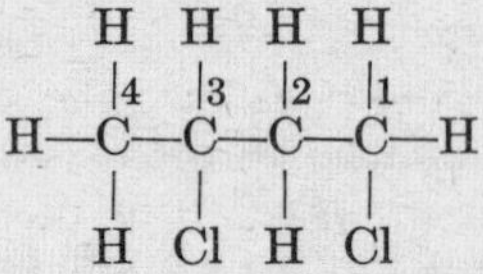

$$
\begin{array}{c}
\text{H}\ \ \text{H}\ \ \text{H}\ \ \text{H} \\
|4\ \ |3\ \ |2\ \ |1 \\
\text{H--C--C--C--C--H} \\
|\ \ \ |\ \ \ |\ \ \ | \\
\text{H}\ \ \text{Cl}\ \ \text{H}\ \ \text{Cl}
\end{array}
$$

The Geneva or (I.U.C.) (International Union of Chemists) rules for the naming of organic compounds include the following:

(1) We name the compound according to the longest parent chain of carbon atoms using the suffix that indicates the number of bonds between two carbons. We use the suffix *ane* for a single bond, *ene* for a double bond and *yne* for a triple bond.

(2) We use a prefix for all radicals or halide groups attached to this chain such as methyl for CH_3, chloro for Cl, etc.

(3) We indicate the position of the radical or halide group on the carbon chain by numbering the carbon atom so that the name of the compound has the lowest numbers.

According to the rules, 1,3- dichlorobutane is set up as follows: The longest parent chain of carbon atoms is butane. Butane is an alkane with 4 carbon atoms. An alkane has all single bonds. 1,3- dichloro means to the first and third carbon atoms, we have one Cl atom attached to each.

Wrong choices explained:

(1) 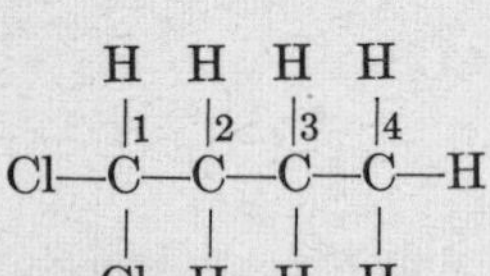
$$
\begin{array}{c}
\ \ \ \text{H}\ \ \text{H}\ \ \text{H}\ \ \text{H} \\
\ \ \ |1\ \ |2\ \ |3\ \ |4 \\
\text{Cl--C--C--C--C--H} \\
\ \ \ |\ \ \ |\ \ \ |\ \ \ | \\
\ \ \ \text{Cl}\ \ \text{H}\ \ \text{H}\ \ \text{H}
\end{array}
$$
is 1,1- dichlorobutane

(2) 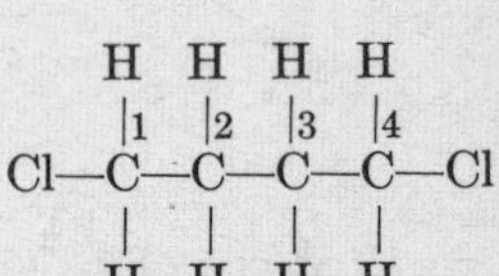
$$
\begin{array}{c}
\ \ \ \text{H}\ \ \text{H}\ \ \text{H}\ \ \text{H} \\
\ \ \ |1\ \ |2\ \ |3\ \ |4 \\
\text{Cl--C--C--C--C--Cl} \\
\ \ \ |\ \ \ |\ \ \ |\ \ \ | \\
\ \ \ \text{H}\ \ \text{H}\ \ \text{H}\ \ \text{H}
\end{array}
$$
is 1,4- dichlorobutane

(4) 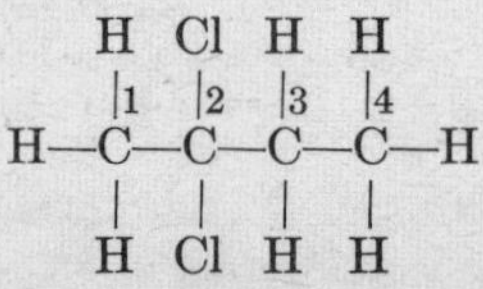
$$
\begin{array}{c}
\text{H}\ \ \text{Cl}\ \ \text{H}\ \ \text{H} \\
|1\ \ |2\ \ |3\ \ |4 \\
\text{H--C--C--C--C--H} \\
|\ \ \ |\ \ \ |\ \ \ | \\
\text{H}\ \ \text{Cl}\ \ \text{H}\ \ \text{H}
\end{array}
$$
is 2,2- dichlorobutane

53. **Ans. 2** Esterification is a reaction in which an acid reacts with an alcohol to yield an ester and water in the presence of concentrated H_2SO_4. The concentrated-sulfuric acid is a strong dehydrating agent therefore, it removes the water from the field of action. This action increases the yield of the ester. An esterification reaction is summarized as follows:

$$\text{Acid} + \text{Alcohol} \xrightleftharpoons{\text{Con } H_2SO_4} \text{Ester} + \text{Water}$$

$$RCOOH + R^1OH \xrightleftharpoons{\text{Con } H_2SO_4} RCOOR^1 + H\text{OH}$$

54. **Ans. 1** As the 95 ml. of $Ba(OH)_2$ is added to the beaker containing 100 milliliters of 0.1 M H_2SO_4, the intensity of the light decreases. An analysis of this question is shown in the diagram below:

As $Ba(OH)_2$ is added, the intensity of the light bulb decreases.

When the conductivity apparatus is placed in the 0.1 M solution of H_2SO_4, the light will be bright since the H_2SO_4 is completely ionized in solution. It is a strong electrolyte. As we add 0.1 M $Ba(OH)_2$ to the solution, the following reaction takes place:

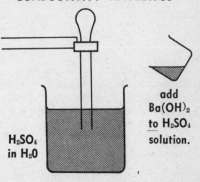

CONDUCTIVITY APPARATUS

add $Ba(OH)_2$ to H_2SO_4 solution.

H_2SO_4 in H_2O

$$H_2SO_4 + Ba(OH)_2 \rightarrow BaSO_4 \downarrow + 2H_2O$$

Table D tells us that $BaSO_4$ is insoluble in water. H_2O is only very slightly ionized and is classified as a very weak electrolyte or a nonelectrolyte. The precipitate $BaSO_4$ leaves the field of action and falls to the bottom of the beaker as a white solid. When $BaSO_4$ is formed, it removes Ba^{++} ions and SO_4^{-2} ions from the solution. Since the conductivity of the solution is based on the number of ions in solution, a decrease in the ion concentration of SO_4^{-2} and Ba^{++} ions will decrease the conductivity of the solution. Thus, the intensity of the bulb decreases.

55. **Ans. 2** When $CaCO_3$ decomposes according to the equation:

$$CaCO_3(s) \rightarrow CaO(s) + CO_2(g),$$

the entropy of the system increases. In decomposing $CaCO_3$ using heat, we get a solid CaO and a gas CO_2. Therefore with the gas formed as one of the products, we have a more random state. Substances are more ordered or most organized in the solid state and least organized in the gaseous state. There is a tendency for processes to occur which lead to the highest possible state of disorder. The property which describes the state of disorder of a system is called entropy. The change from the solid state which is well ordered to the random gaseous state is accompanied by an increase in entropy.

56. **Ans. 2** When a catalyst lowers the activation energy, the rate of a reaction increases. A diagram showing the lowering of the activation energy

by a catalyst is shown in the answer to question 86. A catalyst is a substance which alters the rate (speed) of a chemical reaction without itself being permanently altered. Catalysts affect the rate (speed) of chemical reactions. In general catalysts provide a suitable surface for the reactants to meet. As a result, the reaction is speeded up by more effective collisions. The process of increasing the rate of a chemical reaction using catalysts is called catalysis.

57. Ans. **3** As the number of carbon atoms in the members of the alkene series increases, the ratio of carbon atoms to hydrogen atoms remains the same. The alkene series of hydrocarbons has the general formula C_nH_{2n} where n equals the number of carbon atoms. The alkene series contains 1 double bond. The following chart analyzes this question:

Formula	Common Name	Geneva Name	Ratio Carbon:Hydrogen
C_2H_4	ethylene	ethene	2:4 or 1:2
C_3H_6	propylene	propene	3:6 or 1:2
C_4H_8	butylene	butene	4:8 or 1:2
C_5H_{10}	amylene	pentene	5:10 or 1:2

Notice that the ratio of carbon atoms to hydrogen atoms remains the same.

58. Ans. **3** As one proceeds from left to right across Period 3 of the *Periodic Table*, the number of electrons in the 2p subshell remains the same. In Period 3, the 2p sublevel is completely filled. The 3s and the 3p levels are being filled. The electron configuration for the elements in Period 3 are shown as follows:

Element	Electron Configuration	Orbital Configuration
Na	2-8-1	$1s^22s^22p^63s^1$
Mg	2-8-2	$1s^22s^22p^63s^2$
Al	2-8-3	$1s^22s^22p^63s^23p^1$
Si	2-8-4	$1s^22s^22p^63s^23p^2$
P	2-8-5	$1s^22s^22p^63s^23p^3$
S	2-8-6	$1s^22s^22p^63s^23p^4$
Cl	2-8-7	$1s^22s^22p^63s^23p^5$
Ar	2-8-8	$1s^22s^22p^63s^23p^6$

Notice that the 2p level is completely filled. The 3s and 3p levels are being filled.

59. Ans. **1** When a metallic atom becomes an ion, its radius decreases. (We will take the metal, Na, as an example.) The structure of the atom and the ion is shown as follows:

Sodium atom (Na°)

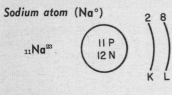

In the neutral atom we have the same number of protons and electrons (11 protons and 11 electrons). The atomic radius is 1.90 Å.

Sodium ion

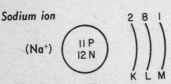

In the sodium ion, we have 11 protons in the nucleus and 10 electrons in the energy levels. The electrons are pulled toward the nucleus with a greater force.

The nuclear charge is more effective and exerts a greater attraction on the 10 electrons than it would on 11 electrons. This increased attraction decreases the size of the radius of the atom in forming the ion. The ionic radius for the sodium ion is 0.95 Å.

60. Ans. **1** As sodium hydroxide is added to a solution of sulfuric acid, the hydrogen ion concentration of the solution decreases. As we explained in question 38, the pH of a solution is based on H^+ ion concentration. If the $H^+(H_3O^+)$ ion concentration is high, we have a low pH (about 1 or 2). Whereas if the H^+ ion concentration is low, we have a pH of 11, 12 or 13. As we add OH^- ions to the solution of sulfuric acid, the OH^- will combine with H^+ ions to form slightly ionized water. As a result the H^+ ion concentration will decrease and the pH will increase. The question can be analyzed and summarized using the following diagram:

Before adding NaOH

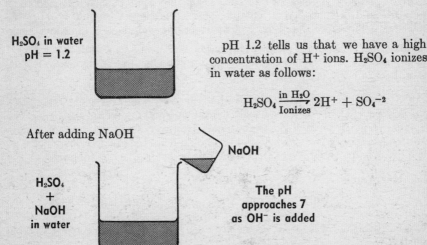

H_2SO_4 in water
pH = 1.2

pH 1.2 tells us that we have a high concentration of H^+ ions. H_2SO_4 ionizes in water as follows:

$$H_2SO_4 \xrightarrow[\text{Ionizes}]{\text{in } H_2O} 2H^+ + SO_4^{-2}$$

After adding NaOH

NaOH

H_2SO_4
+
NaOH
in water

The pH approaches 7 as OH^- is added

When NaOH is added to a solution of sulfuric acid, the following chemical reaction takes place:

$$H_2SO_4 + 2NaOH \rightarrow Na_2SO_4 + 2H_2O$$

The net ionic equation for neutralization is $H^+ + OH^- \rightarrow H_2O$. As the OH^- ion is added to the solution, the OH^- ion combines with the H^+ ion to form slightly ionized water. As a result the hydrogen ion concentration decreases.

PART TWO

GROUP 1

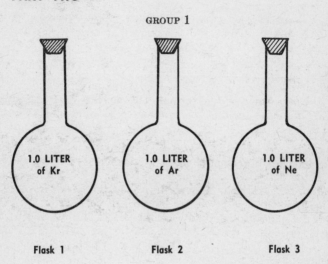

| Flask 1 | Flask 2 | Flask 3 |

61. Ans. 4 *Avogadro's Law* states that under similar conditions of temperature and pressure, equal volumes of all gases contain equal numbers of molecules. Therefore the number of molecules in each flask is the same, since we have equal volumes of krypton, argon and neon. One mole (22.4 liters) of any gas at S.T.P. contains 6×10^{23} molecules. One liter of any gas at S.T.P. would contain 2.7×10^{22} molecules.

62. Ans. 1 The mass of the contents in flask number 1 is greatest. Since the gases in each of the three flasks contain an equal number of molecules, the number of moles of each gas is the same. However, since the mass of 1 mole of each gas is different, the krypton gas would have the greatest mass per unit volume. The mass per liter of each gas can be determined as follows:

For Krypton

$$\text{the Mass of 1 liter} = \frac{\text{Mass}}{\text{Volume}} = \frac{\text{1 Gram Molecular Weight}}{\text{1 Molar Volume}} = \frac{83.8 \text{ g.}}{22.4 \text{ l.}}$$

$$= 3.73 \text{ grams/liter}$$

For Argon

the Mass of 1 liter $= \dfrac{\text{G.M.W.}}{1 \text{ M.V.}} = \dfrac{40 \text{ g.}}{22.4 \text{ l.}} = 1.79$ grams /liter

For Neon

the Mass of 1 liter $= \dfrac{\text{G.M.W.}}{1 \text{ M.V.}} = \dfrac{20 \text{ g.}}{22.4 \text{ l.}} = 0.89$ grams /liter

Therefore, the 1 liter of Krypton gas would have the greatest mass.

63. **Ans. 3** In a closed vessel partially filled with pure water at 25° C. and 760 mm., we would find $H_2O(g)$ and $H_2O(\ell)$. At equilibrium, we have an exchange of molecules between liquid and gas. Dynamic equilibrium between a liquid and its vapor exists when the rate of escape from the liquid equals the rate of return from the gas. *Table O* tells us we have a vapor pressure of 23.8 mm. for water at 25° C. Therefore we would find both $H_2O(g)$ and $H_2O(\ell)$ in the closed vessel.

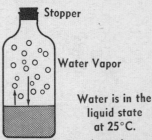

Stopper

Water Vapor

Water is in the liquid state at 25°C.

Diagram showing the exchange of molecules between liquid and gas in a closed system.

64. **Ans. 2** A characteristic of a compound is that it is homogeneous. A compound can be decomposed by a chemical change but not by a physical change. A compound is a chemical combination of two or more elements united in a definite proportion by weight, for example, NaCl, H_2O. The word "homogeneous" means uniform throughout. A compound such as NaCl or H_2O would be uniform throughout. NaCl would contain sodium and chloride ions and H_2O would contain oxygen and hydrogen atoms.

Wrong choices explained:
(1) A compound contains 2 or more elements.
(3) A compound is governed by the law of definite proportions which states that every compound has a definite composition by weight.
(4) A compound cannot be decomposed by a physical change. It can be decomposed by a chemical change.

65. **Ans. 1** The problem states that a sample of a gas has a volume of 100 ml. at S.T.P. It asks us to determine the conditions of temperature and pressure under which the volume of the gas would remain the same. The conditions would be a temperature decrease and a pressure decrease. The combined gas law equation is listed as follows:

P = pressure
V = volume
T = absolute temperature

$$\frac{P_1 V_1}{T_1} = \frac{P_2 V_2}{T_2}$$

If the volume remains constant we have,

$$\frac{P_1}{T_1} = \frac{P_2}{T_2} \qquad \textit{Amontons' Law}$$

Thus $P_1 \propto T_1$

Amontons' Law states that the pressure of a fixed mass and volume of a gas is directly proportional to the absolute temperature. Therefore, if the pressure increases so does the temperature. Also, if the pressure decreases the temperature decreases as well. Choice 1 is the only correct answer.

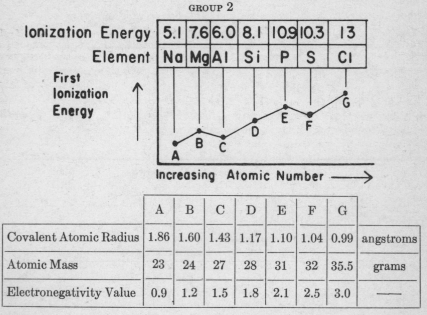

GROUP 2

Ionization Energy	5.1	7.6	6.0	8.1	10.9	10.3	13
Element	Na	Mg	Al	Si	P	S	Cl

	A	B	C	D	E	F	G	
Covalent Atomic Radius	1.86	1.60	1.43	1.17	1.10	1.04	0.99	angstroms
Atomic Mass	23	24	27	28	31	32	35.5	grams
Electronegativity Value	0.9	1.2	1.5	1.8	2.1	2.5	3.0	——

66. Ans. 4 The ionization energy of element C is less than that of element B because element C has a more loosely held outer electron. Ionization energy has been explained in question 9. According to the principles of ionization energy, the element of the 2 with the smaller ionization energy would have the more loosely bound electron. If we compare the ionization energy values for element C (Al) and B (Mg) from the above table, we see that element C has the lower value (6.0) as compared to 7.6 for B.

Wrong choices explained:

(1) According to the table above, element C has a smaller covalent atomic than element B.

(2) According to the table above, element C has a larger atomic mass than element B.

(3) According to the table above, element C has a larger electronegativity value compared to element B.

67. Ans. 2 The element with the greatest tendency to gain electrons is most likely element G. The element with the greatest tendency to gain electrons is the element with the higher electronegativity value. Of the four choices listed element G has the highest value according to the table above. Electronegativity is a measure of the tendency an atom has to attract shared

pairs of electrons. Elements A, C and D have lower electronegativity values according to the table above.

68. Ans. **1** The number of grams of an 8-gram sample of ^{131}I that would remain after 24 days is 1. Iodine-131 is a radioactive isotope (radioisotope) of iodine-127. An isotope differs in the number of neutrons in the nucleus. Many isotopes are radioactive. Some elements have a few isotopes and others have as many as 20. Radioactive isotopes such as iodine-131 have half-lives. A half-life of a radioisotope is the time required for half of the atoms of the radioisotope to change into other atoms. The half-life of iodine-131 listed on *Table G* is 8 days. Thus, after 8 days, only 4 grams of iodine-131 would remain unchanged, after 16 days, only 2 grams would remain unchanged and after 24 days, 1 gram would remain unchanged. We can set up a chart to solve this problem as follows:

Time	now	1st half-life	2nd half-life	3rd half-life
		8 days	16 days	24 days
Amount unchanged	8 grams	4 grams	2 grams	1 gram
Amount changed	0 grams	4 grams	6 grams	7 grams

69. Ans. **2** The number of neutrons in the ^3_1H nucleus is 2. ^3_1H, tritium, is an isotope of hydrogen, ^1_1H. As we stated in the answer to question 68, isotopes differ in the number of neutrons in the nucleus of the atom. To determine the number of neutrons in the nucleus, we subtract the atomic number from the atomic mass (mass number). This is shown as follows:

$$\text{Atomic Mass} = 3$$
$$\text{H}$$
$$\text{Atomic Number} = -1$$
$$\text{2 neutrons in the nucleus of tritium.}$$

70. Ans. **3** The sodium ion, Na^+, differs from a Na^0 atom in particle size. The table below explains some of the properties of the Na^0 atom and Na^+ ion for use in this question:

	Atomic Number	Mass Number	Particle Size	Nuclear Charge
				Number of Protons in the Nucleus
Na^+ ion	11	23	0.95 Å IONIC RADIUS	+11
Na^0 atom	11	23	1.86 Å COVALENT RADIUS	+11

When the Na^0 atom becomes the Na^+ ion, it loses one electron as follows:

$$Na^0 - 1 \text{ electron} \rightarrow Na^+$$

As a result the effective nuclear charge of the ion is greater than the atom. This results in a smaller radius for the ion since the nuclear charge ($+11$) has to contend with 10 electrons rather than 11 electrons.

Wrong choices explained:
(1),(2) and (4)   The table above tells us that the atomic number, the mass number and the nuclear charge are the same for each particle.

GROUP 3

The electron-dot diagrams for the following three compounds are shown as follows:

(1) CCl_4

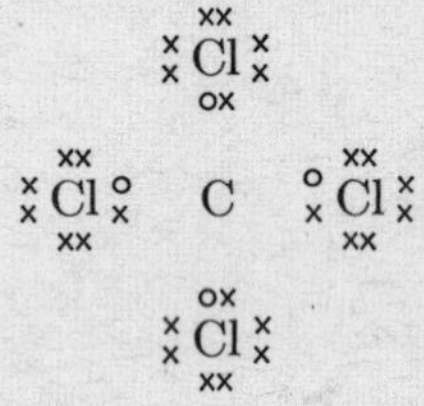

The C—Cl bond is polar covalent. The molecule is non-polar due to its symmetrical distribution of electrons.

(2) $MgCl_2$

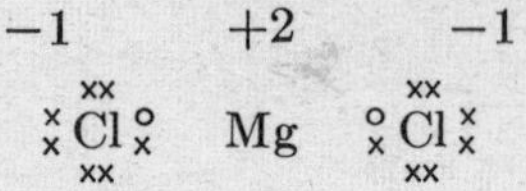

$$-1 \qquad +2 \qquad -1$$

The bonds between the Mg and Cl are ionic. The difference in electronegativity is 1.8. (55% ionic).

(3) H_2O

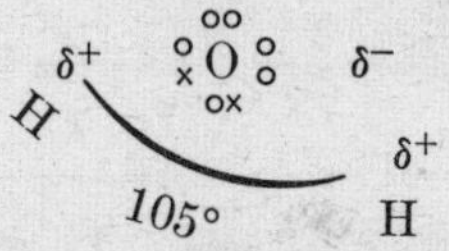

The bond between the hydrogen and oxygen is polar covalent. Since we have an unsymmetrical distribution of electrons, the molecule is polar.

71. Ans. **2** The compound which has the highest degree of ionic bonding is $MgCl_2$. The electron-dot diagram for this ionic compound is shown above. The difference in electronegativity is 1.8 which indicates it is 55% ionic. Active metals such as magnesium and active nonmetals such as chlorine form ionic compounds.

72. Ans. **3** The compound which has polar molecules is H_2O. A compound that has polar covalent molecules is a dipole. Water is a dipole because the bonding electrons are closer to the oxygen atom due to its higher electronegativity. In the polar water molecule, the hydrogen ends are slightly positive and the oxygen end is slightly negative. The electron-dot diagram is shown above. The difference in electronegativity between the hydrogen atom and the oxygen atom is 1.4 which indicates that the bond is polar covalent.

73. Ans. **1** The most probable formula for a compound consisting of element X, $1s^2 2s^1$ and element Y, $1s^2 2s^2 2p^4$ is X_2Y. The electron configuration for element X is $1s^2 2s^1$. Element X is lithium. The electron configuration for element Y is $1s^2 2s^2 2p^4$. Element Y is oxygen. The element lithium has an oxidation number of $+1$ and oxygen has an oxidation number of -2. When lithium combines with oxygen, the compound lithium oxide is formed. Lithium oxide has the formula Li_2O. The formula is shown as follows:

$$Li^{+1} = X \quad | \quad Li_2^{+1}O^{-2} \qquad (+2 - 2 = 0)$$
$$O = Y \quad | \quad X_2Y$$

74. Ans. **1** Hydrogen fluoride (HF) has an unusually high boiling point compared to hydrogen chloride (HCl) because of the hydrogen bonding between the HF molecules. Hydrogen fluoride contains aggregated groups of the type H_2F_2, H_3F_3 etc. up to H_6F_6. These aggregated groups are due to hydrogen bonding. The comparatively high boiling point of HF compared to HCl, HBr, or HI is due to hydrogen bonding. A hydrogen bond is a weak chemical bond between a hydrogen atom in one polar molecule and the more electronegative atom in a second polar molecule of the same substance. For example:

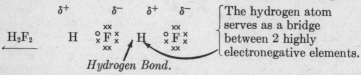

Hydrogen Bond.

The unexpectedly high boiling point (shown in the graph below) of HF in the series HF, HCl, HBr and HI is attributed to hydrogen bonding.

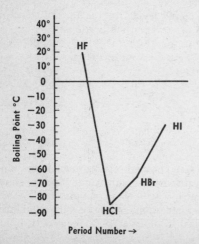

	Boiling Point
HF	19.4°C
HCl	−85°C
HBr	−67°C
HI	−35°C

Wrong choices explained:

(2) *Van der Waal's* forces are weak intermolecular forces between nonpolar molecules.

(3) A coordinate covalent bond is formed when one atom donates the bonding electrons. It occurs in the NH_4^+ ion.

(4) Nonpolar covalent bond is a bond formed where the bonding electrons are equidistant between the two atoms. Examples include diatomic molecules such as H_2, O_2, Cl_2 etc.

75. Ans. **4** All chemical bonds are the result of the simultaneous attraction of electrons to 2 nuclei. A chemical bond results when the forces of attraction between the 2 nuclei and the electrons of the opposite atoms are greater than the repulsions between the electrons of the 2 atoms and the protons in the nuclei of the two atoms. (Recall that like charges repel and unlike charges attract). This can be shown for the H_2 molecule as follows:

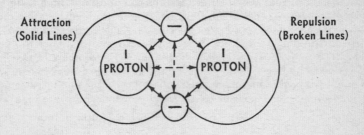

In the hydrogen molecule, we have 4 attractive forces and 2 repulsive forces. Since attractive forces are greater, a bond will form. When the hydrogen atoms combine, we get a more stable system since the energy of the system is lowered.

Wrong choices explained:

(1) Elevation of electrons to higher energy levels creates an excited atom. This can be accomplished by heat, light or electron bombardment.

(2) Transfer of electrons from one atom to another is called ionic bonding. This is just one type of chemical bond. This question deals with all types of chemical bonds, ionic, covalent, metallic etc.

(3) Electrons do not attract each other, they repel one another since they have similar charges.

GROUP 4

76. Ans. **1** Silicon is most similar in chemical activity to carbon. Silicon and carbon are located in the Group 4A family of the *Periodic Table*. The elements in a given Group tend to have some characteristics in common. This property is primarily due to the same number of valence electrons for the elements within the Group. Each element in Group 4 has 4 valence electrons. Group 4 includes carbon, silicon, germanium, tin and lead. Carbon and silicon form oxides, hydrides, halides, acids and salts which are analogous compounds

and have similar properties. Carbon and silicon have nonmetallic properties. Germanium is classified as a metalloid. Tin and lead are classified as metals.

Wrong choices explained:

(2)   Although lead is in Group 4A, it is classified as a metal. Silicon has many properties quite similar to carbon, whereas lead does not. Groups of elements show gradual changes in physical and chemical properties as we go from lower to higher atomic numbers within a Group.

(3)   Sulfur is in the Group 6A family of elements. It has properties similar to oxygen or selenium.

(4)   Nitrogen is in the Group 5A family of elements. It has properties similar to phosphorus.

77.   Ans.   **3**   The element which has a valence electron in the p subshell in the ground state is aluminum. Valence electrons are found in the outermost principal energy level of the atom. The electron configuration for each of the elements listed in this question is shown as follows:

Choice	Element	Electron Configuration	Orbital Configuration	
1	Na	2-8-1	$1s^2 2s^2 2p^6 3s^1$	
2	Mg	2-8-2	$1s^2 2s^2 2p^6 3s^2$	
3	Al	2-8-3	$1s^2 2s^2 2p^6 3s^2 3p^1$	← Correct answer
4	Be	2-2	$1s^2 2s^2$	

The table above tells us that aluminum is the only element with a valence electron in the p subshell. The other choices 1, 2 and 4 do not have valence electrons in the p subshell. They have $3s$ or $2s$ electrons in the valence shells.

78.   Ans.   **2**   The elements that form the strongest bases are the alkali metals. Alkali metals are found in the Group 1A family of elements. They are all active metals. They form bases (hydroxides) which are strongly basic. When the alkali metals react with water, they form strong bases as well as releasing hydrogen gas. An equation for this reaction is shown as follows:

$$\overset{1A}{2K} + 2H_2O \rightarrow \overset{1A}{2KOH} + H_2$$

The oxides of Group 1A metals also react with water. The product is a base. The reaction is shown as follows:

$$\overset{1A}{K_2O} + H_2O \rightarrow \overset{1A}{2KOH}$$

Oxides of active metals which combine with water to form bases are called basic anhydrides.

Wrong choices explained:

(1)   The halogens (Group 7A) do not form strong bases. In reaction with water, they form acids.

(3) Alkaline earth elements (Group 2A) form weak bases when they react with water. The hydroxides of the alkaline earth are only slightly soluble in water. The K_{sp} (solubility product) values for these bases indicate that they are weak hydroxides.

(4) The oxides of the transition elements form compounds that could be classified in one of the following categories:

(1) Weak base
(2) Weak acid
(3) Amphiprotic—(Having both acid and basic properties)

79. Ans. **3** Magnesium has a smaller atomic radius than sodium because the magnesium atom has more protons. The atomic structures for sodium and magnesium are shown as follows:

Sodium
cavalent atomic radius 1.86A
Ionization energy 5.1 ev

Magnesium

The extra electron in the magnesium atom enters the M shell. Notice that sodium and magnesium have 3 principal energy levels. The addition of the extra electron and proton in going from sodium to magnesium does not cause an increase in atomic radius, but rather a decrease. As the nuclear charge increases, the pull on the electrons is increased and the K and L & M shells become smaller. Increased nuclear charge means increased attraction for electrons. Also, notice that the ionization energy of magnesium is greater than that for sodium. This is another indication that the atomic radius for magnesium should be smaller due to the stronger attraction by the nucleus for the electrons. To summarize— As the atomic number increases, from 11 to 12, an electron is added to the M level, but the atomic size decreases. The reason is that, as the positive nuclear charge increases, the force of attraction for these M shell electrons increases, drawing them closer to the nucleus.

Wrong choices explained:
(1) The fact that magnesium has more valence electrons does not account for the smaller atomic radius for magnesium. The reasons for the smaller atomic radius are explained above.
(2) Sodium and magnesium have the same number of energy levels (3).
(4) The number of neutrons in the nucleus of an atom does not affect the atomic radius of the atom.

80. Ans. **4** The element in Period 4 of the *Periodic Table* which is most likely to form a colored compound is nickel. Nickel exhibits oxidation states of $+2$ and $+3$. In aqueous solutions, the Ni^{++} ion gives the solution a green color. Most of the compounds of the transition elements are colored. Transition elements are located in the B Groups and Group 8 of the *Periodic Table*.

The color in these transition compounds is due to the fact that electronic energy levels are close enough together so that electrons can easily absorb light. The Period 4 transition elements have a deficiency of electrons in the $3d$ subshell. The $3d$ level is very close to the $4s$ level. In these elements, the energy needed to raise the $3d$ electrons to a higher level happens to equal the energy found in certain colors of visible light. When white light is shone on transition compounds, some wave lengths of light are absorbed in the movement of the $3d$ electrons.

Wrong choices explained:

(1) Ordinary calcium compounds are white in color. The aqueous Ca^{++} ion is colorless.

(2) Krypton does not ordinarily combine with other elements.

(3) Gallium is a Group 3A element. The chemistry of gallium is much like that of aluminum. Gallium occurs in minute traces in aluminum ores. Ga_2O_3 is white in color. Gallium does not form colored ions in solution.

GROUP 5

81. Ans. **3** The volume occupied by 6.02×10^{23} atoms of argon at S.T.P. is approximately 22.4 liters. The explanation for question 5 explains *Avogadro's Law.* Since argon is a monatomic gas (1 atom per molecule), 6×10^{23} atoms occupy 22.4 liters at S.T.P. 6×10^{23} atoms is equivalent to 1 mole of the gas. 1 mole of a gas occupies 22.4 liters at S.T.P. The following diagram summarizes this question:

6×10^{23} **atoms of argon at S.T.P.**

1 mole   22.4 liters

Wrong choices explained:

(1) 6 liters would contain $6\,l./22.4\,l. \times 6 \times 10^{23}$ atoms.

(2) 11.2 liters would contain 3×10^{23} atoms ($\frac{1}{2}$ mole).

(4) 44.8 liters would contain $2(6 \times 10^{23})$ atoms (2 moles).

82. Ans. **4** If a compound contains carbon and hydrogen in the mole ratio C:H = 2:3, the molecular mass of the compound could be 54. If the mole ratio of C:H is 2:3 then 2 moles of carbon will combine with 3 moles of hydrogen. The simplest formula (empirical formula) for this compound is C_2H_3. The general formula for such a compound is $(C_2H_3)_x$ where x can be 1, 2, 3, 4 etc. The atomic mass of carbon is 12 and the atomic mass of hydrogen is 1. Therefore $(C_2H_3)_x = [(12 \times 2) + 3(1)]_x = (27)x$.

The molecular mass of the compound has to be some multiple of 27. Of the choices given, the only multiple of 27 is 54, choice 4. We can check the answer as follows:

$(C_2H_3)_x = 54$	Molecular formula of compound
$27x = 54$	is $(C_2H_3)_2$ or C_4H_6.
$x = 2$	The molecular mass of C_4H_6
	is 54.

83. **Ans. 3** The number of moles of $AgNO_3$ dissolved in 10 ml. of 1 molar $AgNO_3$ is 0.01. The explanation of molarity is discussed in the answer to question 30. This question is solved as follows:

$$\text{Molarity} = \frac{\text{The number of moles}}{\text{The number of liters of solution}}$$

Molarity = 1 mole/liter

Number of liters = $\dfrac{10 \text{ ml.}}{1000 \text{ ml.}}$

= 0.01 liter

The number of moles
= Molarity × Number of liters of solution

Number of moles = $\dfrac{1 \text{ mole}}{\text{liter}}$ × 0.01 liter

= 0.01 mole

84. **Ans. 4** If NaOH is added to one beaker of distilled water and C_2H_5OH is added to another beaker of distilled water, both of the solutions that are formed will have a lower freezing point than pure water. An analysis of this question is shown as follows:

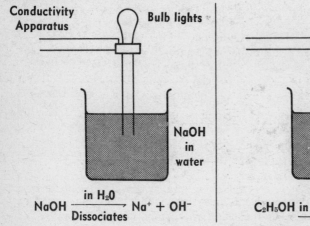

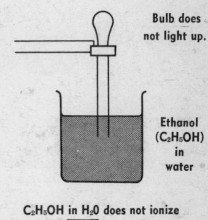

Conductivity Apparatus — **Bulb lights** — NaOH in water

Bulb does not light up. — Ethanol (C_2H_5OH) in water

$NaOH \xrightarrow[\text{Dissociates}]{\text{in } H_2O} Na^+ + OH^-$

C_2H_5OH in H_2O does not ionize

Electrical Conductivity

(1) NaOH is a strong base. It is completely dissociated. It does conduct electricity in solution. NaOH in H_2O is a strong electrolyte.

(1) Ethanol (ethyl alcohol), C_2H_5OH is a non-electrolyte. It does not ionize in water. It is an organic compound. Most all organic compounds are non-electrolytes.

Litmus Paper

(2) Bases such as NaOH turn red litmus paper blue since the OH^- ion is present in solution.

(2) C_2H_5OH will not affect litmus paper since it does not furnish the OH^- ion in solution.

Boiling Point

(3)   The addition of an electrolyte or a non-electrolyte will raise the boiling point of water. It will not lower the boiling point of water as suggested by choice 3. This point is explained in the answer to question 85.

Freezing Point

(4)   The addition of an electrolyte to water will lower the freezing point of water.

(4)   The addition of a non-electrolyte to water will lower the freezing point of water.

These principles are explained in the answer to question 85 below.
Choice 4 is the correct answer.
Choices 1, 2, and 3 explained above are incorrect answers.

85.   Ans.   **3**   A 1 molal solution of $Al(NO_3)_3$ will have the highest boiling point. The presence of dissolved solute particles in a solution affect some properties of the solvent such as freezing point, boiling point and vapor pressure. The molal boiling point elevation of water states that 1 mole of a non electrolyte dissolved in 1,000 grams of water will raise the boiling point by $0.52°$ C. The molal freezing point depression of water states that 1 mole of a non electrolyte dissolved in 1,000 grams of water will lower the freezing point by $-1.86°$ C. If we have an electrolyte, we must multiply the constant in each case by the number of moles of ions formed by the electrolytes. The boiling points for each of the compounds in this question is listed as follows:

Choice	Solution	Dissociation in H_2O	# of Ions	$100° + 0.52$(# of moles of ions)	Boiling Point
1	KNO_3	$KNO_3 \longrightarrow$ $K^+ + NO_3^-$	2 ions	$100° + 0.52(2)$	$101.04°$ C.
2	$Mg(NO_3)_2$	$Mg(NO_3)_2 \rightarrow$ $Mg^{++} + 2NO_3^-$	3 ions	$100° + 0.52(3)$	$101.56°$ C.
3	$Al(NO_3)_3$	$Al(NO_3)_3 \rightarrow$ $Al^{+3} + 3NO_3^-$	4 ions	$100° + 0.52(4)$	$102.08°$ C.
4	NH_4NO_3	$NH_4NO_3 \rightarrow$ $NH_4^+ + NO_3^-$	2 ions	$100° + 0.52(2)$	$101.04°$ C.

Choice 3 has the highest boiling point since it forms the greatest number of moles of ions in solution. All solutions are 1 molal. A 1 molal solution contains 1 mole of solute in 1,000 grams of water. Choices 1, 2 and 4 have lower boiling points than $Al(NO_3)_3$.

GROUP 6

$$A(g) + B(g) \rightleftharpoons AB(g) + \text{heat}$$
Equilibrium constant (K) at $25°$ C. $= 0.50$

86.   Ans.   **3**   If a catalyst is added to a system at equilibrium with the

temperature and pressure remaining constant, the concentration of A would remain the same. The effect of a catalyst is shown as follows:

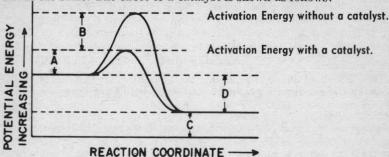

The above diagram tells us that if a catalyst is added to a reaction, the activation energy of the reaction will be lowered. The concentration of the reactants or products will not change. Also, the equilibrium constant will not change. The only factor which affects the equilibrium constant is temperature.

87. Ans. 1 When equilibrium is reached, the concentration of AB compared to the concentration of A times the concentration of B, is less. The equilibrium constant, K_e, was explained in the answer to question 35. Based on the equilibrium reaction shown in question 86, the equilibrium constant equation is shown as follows:

$$K_e = \frac{\text{Concentration of products}}{\text{Concentration of reactants}} = \frac{[AB]}{[A] \times [B]} = 0.50$$

Since the equilibrium constant, K_e, for the reaction is less than 1, the denominator must have a greater value than the numerator. The concentration of $[A] \times [B]$ is greater than the concentration of $[AB]$.

Since the numerator represents the products, the concentration of AB is less than the concentration of A times the concentration of B, the denominator.

88. Ans. 3 As the concentration of B is increased at constant temperature, the value of K_e will remain the same. As we stated above, the only factor which affects the equilibrium constant is temperature. Although changes in concentration shift the equilibrium, they generally do not affect the equilibrium constant. This is illustrated by the following example: $A + B = C$. If B is increased, C is increased and in the process A is consumed so that the concentration of A decreases. For this reason, $\frac{C}{A \times B}$ the equilibrium constant, remains the same.

89. Ans. 1 At 23° C., 100 ml. of a saturated solution of NaCl is in equilibrium with 1 gram of solid NaCl. The concentration of the solution will be changed the most when 80 ml. of water is added to the solution. If we add 80 ml. of water to the saturated solution, the solution will become unsaturated, since the concentration in moles per liter will decrease. *Table B* tells us that at 23° C., we can dissolve 37 grams of NaCl in 100 ml. of water.

If we add another 80 ml. of water, we will have 37 grams per 180 ml. which is a lower concentration of NaCl in H_2O compared to 37 grams in 100 ml.

Wrong choices explained:
(2) If additional solid NaCl is added to the saturated solution, it will not dissolve in the solution. It will fall to the bottom of the beaker.
(3) Pressure has a negligible effect on a solid dissolved in a liquid.
(4) According to *Table B*, if the temperature of the solution is decreased 5 C°, the change in concentration of the solution is negligible.

90. Ans. **2** Carbon dioxide is most soluble in water under conditions of high pressure and low temperature. If, for example, the temperature of the system is increased while the pressure is held constant, gas molecules will escape from the solution at a greater rate than like molecules pass into solution, the rate of escape diminishing until equilibrium is again established, and the resulting solution is saturated. Thus, the solubility of a gas in a liquid diminishes with an increase in temperature. On the other hand, if the liquid is saturated with a gas at given temperature and pressure, and the pressure on the gas above the solution is increased while the temperature of the system is held constant, more molecules of the gas will strike the surface and enter the solution than leaves the solution in the same period of time, thus becoming more concentrated. When equilibrium is again established, the solution will contain a greater concentration of gas per unit volume.

GROUP 7

Relative Concentration of H_3O^+ and OH^-	pH	Solution is
(1) $[H_3O^+]$ is greater than $[OH^-]$.	less than 7	Acid
(2) $[H_3O^+]$ is less than $[OH^-]$.	greater than 7	Basic
(3) $[H_3O^+]$ is equal to $[OH^-]$.	equals 7	Neutral

91. Ans. **2** The H_3O^+ concentration is less than the OH^- concentration in a solution of Na_2CO_3. pH was explained in the answer to question 38. *Table K* tells us that Na_2CO_3 has a pH of 11.6. If the pH is greater than 7, the OH^- ion concentration is greater than the H_3O^+ ion concentration, therefore the solution is basic. When Na_2CO_3 is dissolved in water, it dissociates completely as follows:

$$Na_2CO_3(s) \xrightarrow[\text{Dissociates}]{\text{in } H_2O} 2Na^+(aq) + CO_3^{-2}(aq)$$

$$2H_2O \underset{\text{Slightly ionizes}}{\rightleftharpoons} 2OH^- + 2H^+$$
$$\qquad\qquad\qquad \uparrow \qquad \downarrow$$
$$\qquad\qquad 2NaOH \quad H_2CO_3$$

Since NaOH is completely dissociated, we get a maximum number of OH^- ions in the hydrolysis reaction. Hydrolysis is a reaction in which a salt reacts with water to form a solution which is either acidic or basic. If the solution is basic as in this question, we will have a greater concentration of OH^- ions. The H_2CO_3 is only slightly ionized, therefore we get a smaller number of H^+ ions. As a result the solution is basic.

92. Ans. 1 The H_3O^+ ion concentration is greater than the OH^- concentration when a solution has a H_3O^+ ion concentration of 1×10^{-2}. pH was explained in the answer to question 38. The pH of a solution with a H_3O^+ ion concentration of 1×10^{-2} is 2. H_3O^+ ion concentration = 10^{-pH}. If the concentration is 10^{-2}, we see that the pH is 2. We can also solve the problem as follows:

$$pH = \log \frac{1}{[H_3O^+]} = \log \frac{1}{[1 \times 10^{-2}]} = \log 10^2$$
$$\log 10^2 = 2 \qquad \therefore pH = 2$$

A solution with a pH of 2 is acidic. An acidic solution has a greater concentration of H_3O^+ compared to OH^- ion concentration.

93. Ans. 1 The conjugate base of the H_3O^+ ion is H_2O. Conjugate acid-base theory was explained in the answers to questions 39 and 40. H_3O^+ is a conjugate acid. According to *Table H*, the conjugate base corresponding to the conjugate acid H_3O^+ is H_2O. This question can be summarized as follows:

$$\overset{\text{Conjugate base}}{\underset{\text{Conjugate acid}}{H_3O^+ \quad \rightarrow \quad H_2O \quad + H^+}}$$

A conjugate acid is a proton donor. A conjugate base is a proton acceptor. H_2O is a conjugate base in this question.

94. Ans. 1 If a water solution at $25°$ C. has a H_3O^+ ion concentration of 1×10^{-4} mole/liter, the OH^- concentration is 1×10^{-10}. The expression for the ionization constant of water, K_w, is given as: $K_w = [H^+] \cdot [OH^-] = 1 \times 10^{-14}$ at $25°$ C. This expression tells us that the product of the molar concentrations of H^+ and OH^- must equal 1×10^{-14}. If we substitute the H^+ ion concentration, 1×10^{-4} mole/liter in the expression, we can determine the OH^- ion concentration. The problem is solved as follows:

$$[H^+] = [H_3O^+] = 1 \times 10^{-4} \text{ mole/liter} \qquad [H^+] \cdot [OH^-] = 1 \times 10^{-14}$$
$$[OH^-] = x \qquad\qquad\qquad 1 \times 10^{-4}x = 1 \times 10^{-14}$$
$$OH^- = x = \frac{1 \times 10^{-14}}{1 \times 10^{-4}} = 1 \times 10^{-10}$$

Therefore, the hydroxide ion concentration (OH^-) is 1×10^{-10}.

95. Ans. 4 According to *Table M*, a solution of 0.1 M H_2CO_3 contains the lowest concentration of H^+ ions. The ionization constants for the ionization of acids is a convenient method for comparing the relative strength of acids. Ionization constants can be calculated for all acids that are not completely

ionized. The larger the ionization constant, the stronger the acid. Also, the smaller the ionization constant, the weaker the acid. Since sulfuric acid (H_2SO_4) is completely ionized in water solution it contains a very high concentration of H^+ ions in solution. This information is listed on *Table M*. The ionization constants for H_3PO_4, $HC_2H_3O_2$ and H_2CO_3 are listed as follows:

Formula	Name	Ionization Constant
H_3PO_4	Phosphoric acid	7.5×10^{-3}
$HC_2H_3O_2$	Acetic acid	1.8×10^{-5}
H_2CO_3	Carbonic acid	4.3×10^{-7}

Since H_2CO_3 has the lowest ionization constant, it has the lowest concentration of hydrogen ions. Remember that H_2SO_4 has the greatest concentration of hydrogen ions in this question.

GROUP 8

96. Ans. 4 The half-cell which contains a metal electrode that is the strongest reducing agent is magnesium. A reducing agent loses electrons. Active metals such as magnesium have a strong tendency to lose electrons. Strong reducing agents are located near the top of *Table L*. As we go down *Table L*, the reducing ability of the elements decrease. In other words their role as reducing agents diminishes. Since Mg is higher than Zn^{+2}, Cu^{+2}, and Ag^+ on *Table L*, it is a stronger reducing agent.

97. Ans. 4 When half-cell 2 is connected to half-cell 3 by means of a wire and salt bridge, the voltage at equilibrium will be 0.00. A diagram for this question is shown as follows:

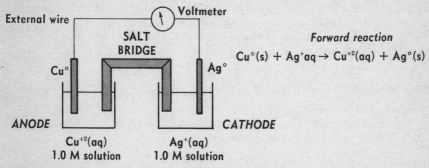

When the reaction reaches chemical equilibrium, the cell voltage will be 0.00 volts. When the cell reaches equilibrium, the reverse reaction, $Cu^{++}(aq) + Ag^0(s) \rightarrow Cu^0(s) + Ag^+(aq)$ proceeds at a rate equal to that of the forward reaction. The E^0 value for the reverse reaction is -0.46 volt and that for the forward reaction is $+0.46$ volt. When the opposing reactions become equal, the total cell potential is zero. This occurs at equilibrium.

98. Ans. **2**   When half-cell 3 is connected to half-cell 4 by means of a wire and salt bridge, the electronic equation which represents the oxidation reaction that occurs is $Mg^0 - 2e^- \rightarrow Mg^{+2}$. When an element is oxidized, it loses electrons. Table L tells us that magnesium, Mg, has a greater tendency to lose electrons compared to silver, Ag. Oxidation occurs at the anode. In this question, Mg is the anode. We can analyze and summarize this question using the following diagram:

Oxidation occurs at the anode. When an element loses electrons, it is oxidized. The oxidation reaction is shown as follows:

$$Mg^0 - 2e^- \rightarrow Mg^{++}$$

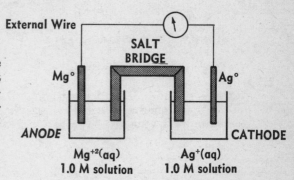

Wrong choices explained:
Choices 1 , 3 and 4 do not take place in this question.

99. Ans. **1**   In the half-reaction $Mn^{+2} + 4H_2O \rightarrow MnO_4^- + 8H^+$ the substance oxidized is Mn^{+2}. Oxygen has an oxidation number of -2 in all compounds except in peroxides such as H_2O_2 when it is -1. Hydrogen has an oxidation number of $+1$ in all its compounds except in metal hydrides such as LiH when it is -1. The manganese has oxidation numbers of $+2, +3, +4$ and $+7$. In this question, manganese is oxidized from Mn^{+2} to Mn^{+7}. When a substance is oxidized it loses electrons. The oxidation numbers of all species are shown as follows:

$$Mn^{+2} + 4H_2^{+1}O^{-2} \rightarrow (Mn^{+7}O_4^{-2})^{-1} + 8H^+$$
(LEO) **Oxidation:** $Mn^{+2} - 5e^- \rightarrow Mn^{+7}$

Wrong choices explained:
(2),(3), and (4)   The above equation tells us that there is no change in the oxidation numbers of hydrogen or oxygen.

100. Ans. **3**   On the basis of *Table L*, the reaction which occurs spontaneously is the one in which the net E^0 value is positive. We can determine the net E^0 values using the E^0 values on *Table L* for each half-reaction. Remember that all half-reactions are shown as oxidation reactions on *Table L*. For the reduction reaction, we must reverse the sign of the E^0 value. The E^0 value does not depend on the number of atoms or ions involved in the redox reaction. The only reaction which gives us a positive E^0 value is the following:

Oxidation half-reaction:
$$Zn^0(s) \rightarrow Zn^{++}(aq) + 2e^-$$
$\qquad E^0 = +0.76$ volt

Reduction half-reaction:
$$2H^+(aq) + 2e^- \rightarrow H_2(g)$$
$\qquad E^0 = 0.00$ volt

$$Zn^0(s) + 2H^+(aq) \rightarrow Zn^{++}(aq) + H_2(g)$$
$\qquad$ Net $E^0 = +0.76$ volt

Wrong choices explained:
(1) **Oxidation half-reaction:**
$$Cu^0(s) \rightarrow Cu^{++}(aq) + 2e^-$$
$\qquad E^0 = -0.34$ volt

Reduction half-reaction:
$$2H^+(aq) + 2e^- \rightarrow H_2(g)$$
$\qquad E^0 = 0.00$ volt

$$Cu^0(s) + 2H^+(aq) \rightarrow Cu^{++}(aq) + H_2(g)$$
$\qquad$ Net $E^0 = -0.34$ volt

(2) **Oxidation half-reaction:**
$$Cu^0(s) \rightarrow Cu^{++}(aq) + 2e^-$$
$\qquad E^0 = -0.34$ volt

Reduction half-reaction:
$$Zn^{++}(aq) + 2e^- \rightarrow Zn^0(s)$$
$\qquad E^0 = -0.76$ volt

$$Cu^0(s) + Zn^{++}(aq) \rightarrow Cu^{++}(aq) + Zn^0(s)$$
$\qquad$ Net $E^0 = -1.10$ volts

(4) **Oxidation half-reaction:**
$$2Cl^-(aq) - 2e^- \rightarrow Cl_2^0(g)$$
$\qquad E^0 = -1.36$ volts

Reduction half-reaction:
$$Br_2^0(\ell) + 2e^- \rightarrow 2Br^-(aq)$$
$\qquad E^0 = +1.07$ volts

$$2Cl^-(aq) + Br_2^0(\ell) \rightarrow Cl_2^0(g) + 2Br^-(aq)$$
$\qquad$ Net $E^0 = -0.29$ volt

Notice that the wrong choices are not spontaneous since they have negative Net E^0 values.

GROUP 9

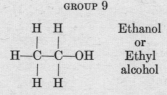

101. Ans. **2** This compound is an alcohol. The general formula for an alcohol is R—OH where is an alkyl group. This alcohol is called ethyl alcohol or ethanol, C_2H_5OH.

Wrong choices explained:
(1) An organic acid has the general formula RCOOH.
(3) An ester has the general formula RCOOR[1].
(4) The general formulas for hydrocarbons are explained in the answers to questions 50 and 51.

102. Ans. **4** When ethyl alcohol is completely burned in oxygen, the products are CO_2 and H_2O. Low molecular weight alcohols are flammable, and burn readily in air. The equation for the complete burning of ethyl alcohol in oxygen is shown as follows:

$$2C_2H_5OH + 6O_2 \rightarrow 4CO_2 + 6H_2O$$

The equation for the *incomplete* burning of C_2H_5OH in oxygen is shown:

$$C_2H_5OH + 2O_2 \rightarrow 2CO + 3H_2O$$

103. Ans. **2** The compound which will react most readily with bromine is ethene. The type of reaction which occurs between C_2H_4 (ethene) and bromine (Br_2) is an addition reaction. An addition reaction is one in which atoms (usually chlorine or bromine) are added to an unsaturated organic molecule. An unsaturated organic molecule contains a double or triple bond. The reaction for the addition of bromine to ethene is shown as follows:

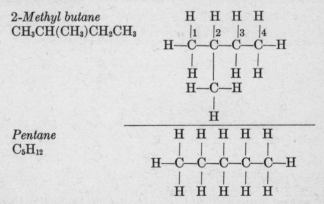

Wrong choices explained:
Wrong choices (1), (3) and (4) are alkanes. They are saturated hydrocarbons. Bromine reacts with alkanes by substitution. Substitution reactions with alkanes are not as reactive as addition reactions with alkenes.

104. Ans. **1** An isomer of 2-methyl butane is pentane. Two or more compounds with the same molecular formula but different structural formulas are called isomers. The rules for naming hydrocarbon chains are listed in the answer to question 52. The structural formulas for the 2 isomers in this question are listed as follows:

2-Methyl butane
$CH_3CH(CH_3)CH_2CH_3$

Pentane
C_5H_{12}

Notice that the isomers have 5 carbon atoms and 12 hydrogen atoms (C_5H_{12}).

Wrong choices explained:
Choices (2), (3) and (4) are not isomers of 2-methyl butane. The structural formulas for the wrong choices are shown as follows:

(2) Propane—C_3H_8

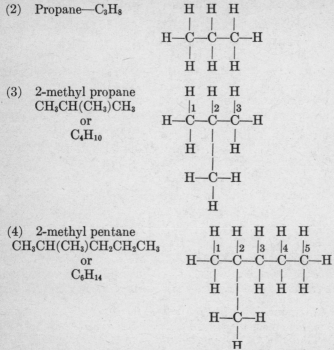

(3) 2-methyl propane
$CH_3CH(CH_3)CH_3$
or
C_4H_{10}

(4) 2-methyl pentane
$CH_3CH(CH_3)CH_2CH_2CH_3$
or
C_6H_{14}

105. Ans. **3** The name of the compound represented by the formula C_4H_8 is butene. Butene (Geneva Name) is also called butylene (common name). Butene is an alkene. Alkenes contain 1 double bond and have the general formula C_nH_{2n}. Alkenes were also explained in the answer to question 57. The structural formula for butene is shown as follows:

(Butene has 2 isomers 1-butene and 2-butene.)

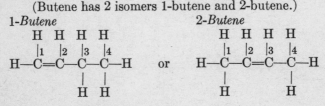

Wrong choices explained:
(1) Butanol (Geneva) is also called butyl alcohol (common name). 1-Butanol has the formula C_4H_9OH. The general formula for primary alcohols is ROH. The structural formula for 1-Butanol is:

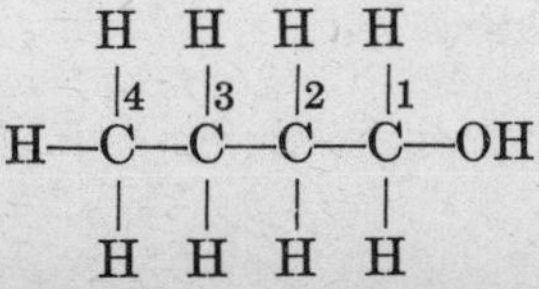

(2)   Butyne is an alkyne. It is a hydrocarbon with one triple bond. The structural formula for 1-butyne is shown as follows:

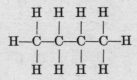

(Butyne has the formula C_4H_6.)

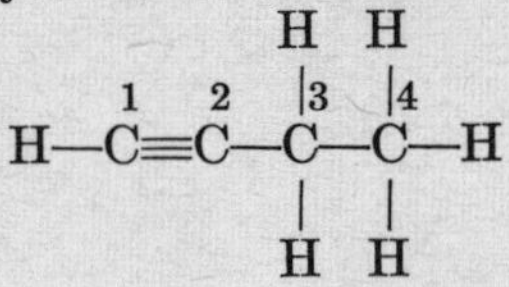

(4)   Butane is an alkane. It is a hydrocarbon with all single bonds. It has the molecular formula, C_4H_{10}. The structural formula for butane is shown as follows:

$$
\begin{array}{ccccccc}
 & H & H & H & H & \\
 & | & | & | & | & \\
H- & C- & C- & C- & C- & H \\
 & | & | & | & | & \\
 & H & H & H & H &
\end{array}
$$

Chemistry

INDEX

This index is organized according to subject areas. These subject area headings appear in bold face. The topics are the subdivisions of the major areas.

References to listings are prepared as follows: the month and year of the examination, followed by the question number. The letter E indicates a special experimental examination: June 1966 E—*34*.

Mathematics in Chemistry

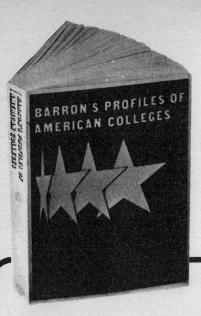

Which good colleges will accept you with SAT scores below 500? ...And which won't?

$4.95 paper   912 pp.

Barron's How to Prepare for College Board Achievement Tests Series

This series can be used to supplement textbooks, clear up difficult areas, highlight significant facts, diagnose students' weak spots, and test their progress. The model College Board Achievement and Placement tests, fully answered, prepare the student on subject matter and test-taking techniques.

Biology
Maurice Bleifeld
288 pp. $6.00 cloth $2.75 paper
Comprehensive review beginning with classification and ending with chapters on the biological effects of atomic energy and on space biology.

Chemistry
Joseph A. Mascetta
240 pp. $6.00 cloth $2.75 paper
Complete subject review, starting with the basic concepts of the structure of matter and including problems and answers in balancing equations.

English
Jerome Shostak
192 pp. $6.00 cloth $1.95 paper
Systematic use of this book in 11th and 12th grades assures maximum improvement and skill in English expression. Includes drills for correct usage, organization, and effective writing.

European History and World Cultures
Leonard James
320 pp. $6.00 cloth $2.95 paper
Complete subject review of world history. Each chapter has a glossary of terms, places to locate, significant names.

French
Louis Cabat, Jacob D. Godin
128 pp. $6.00 cloth $2.95 paper
Covers difficult and tricky grammar areas; vocabulary and idioms; verb charts; reading comprehension passages; practice exercises.

German
Maxim Newmark, Philip Scherer
144 pp. $6.00 cloth $2.25 paper
Concentrated review of all subject matter covered on the German CBAT. Contains grammatical pitfalls, idiom lists, verb charts, reading comprehension.

Latin
Anna M. Gerwig
160 pp. $6.00 cloth $2.25 paper
Stresses vocabulary, idioms and word lists from Caesar, Cicero, Vergil, verb forms, and reading comprehension.

Mathematics Level I
James Rizzuto
208 pp. $3.95 paper
Modern diagnostic review through advanced algebra and trigonometry. 1000 drill items, 400 illustrations, 5 sample tests with 250 questions and answers.

Physics
Herman Gewirtz
160 pp. $6.00 cloth $2.25 paper
A multi-purpose review book for diagnostic class work and self-testing. 198 review questions with explanatory answers; 169 diagrams; comprehensive subject matter review.

Social Studies/American History
David Midgley
384 pp. $6.00 cloth $2.25 paper
Review of early American history, events and accomplishments of each presidential term to present day, analyses of the Constitution and of governmental structure.

Spanish
Louis Cabat, Jacob D. Godin
128 pp. $6.00 cloth $1.95 paper
Covers difficult and tricky grammar areas; vocabulary and idioms; verb charts and reading comprehension.

Barron's Educational Series, Inc.   113 Crossways Park Drive Woodbury, New York 11797

Barron's Efficient Study Guides

You always get what it's all about from Barron's Study Guides. With less brow-mopping, much greater assurance of success you can depend on help from Barron's.

Don't bother to copy your friend's notes . . . read Barron's. Barron's essential study guides offer you the opportunity to learn faster, be better prepared for exams, and get higher marks. You may also find you're enjoying your classes more, too.

All the information you will ever need for a particular subject is right at your fingertips. In fact, some of the problems presented and answered might be what you will be asked in your next exam.

Published by Barron's Educational Series, Inc.

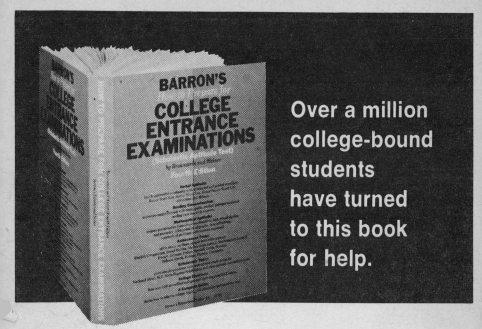